Philosophy by Other Means

Philosophy by Other Means

The Arts in Philosophy and Philosophy in the Arts

ROBERT B. PIPPIN

The University of Chicago Press
Chicago and London

The University of Chicago Press, Chicago 60637
The University of Chicago Press, Ltd., London

Published 2021
Printed in the United States of America

30 29 28 27 26 25 24 23 22 21 1 2 3 4 5

ISBN-13: 978-0-226-77077-2 (cloth)
ISBN-13: 978-0-226-77080-2 (paper)
ISBN-13: 978-0-226-77094-9 (e-book)
DOI: https://doi.org/10.7208/chicago/9780226770949.001.0001

Library of Congress Cataloging-in-Publication Data

Names: Pippin, Robert B., 1948– author.
Title: Philosophy by other means : the arts in philosophy and philosophy in the arts / Robert B. Pippin.
Other titles: Arts in philosophy and philosophy in the arts
Description: Chicago ; London : The University of Chicago Press, 2021. | Includes bibliographical references and index.
Identifiers: LCCN 2020040729 | ISBN 9780226770772 (cloth) | ISBN 9780226770802 (paperback) | ISBN 9780226770949 (ebook)
Subjects: LCSH: Aesthetics. | Arts—Philosophy. | Literature—Philosophy.
Classification: LCC BH21 .P57 2021 | DDC 111/.85—dc23
LC record available at https://lccn.loc.gov/2020040729

♾ This paper meets the requirements of ANSI/NISO Z39.48-1992 (Permanence of Paper).

Contents

PART 1

The Arts in Philosophy

1

Philosophical Criticism

A Continuation

What follows is an attempt to develop an approach to understanding aesthetic objects. The approach is a form of criticism that I want to call philosophical, a contribution to philosophy, even if not in the analytic and discursive form traditionally characteristic of academic philosophy. The claim is twofold: that criticism properly understood often requires a form of philosophic reflection, and that philosophy is impoverished if it is not informed by critical attention to aesthetic objects. Misunderstandings are inevitable in this context. A philosophical illumination of artworks and a philosophy illuminated by attention to artworks are not offered as a delimitation of the only or main value of the arts. The arts are valuable for all sorts of reasons: enjoyment, play, beauty, or simply as an enrichment of the human experience of the human. Different works have different ambitions, some closer to the ambition of craftsmanship, some closer to the ambitions of mythology. This notion of philosophical illumination applies where it does and doesn't apply where it doesn't.[1] I'll begin by trying to contextualize the project.

This volume is a continuation of attempts made in other work, in four books on film—*Hollywood Westerns and American Myth* (2010), *Fatalism in American Film Noir* (2012), *The Philosophical Hitchcock* (2017), and *Filmed Thought* (2019)—in an earlier work on literature, *Henry James and Modern*

1. It is useful here to recall the (former) view that Michael Wood reports as at one time his: "Literature is a form of play, and it plays at knowing as it plays at all kinds of other activities. It is infinitely valuable but valuable as play, not as disguised or sweetened work." I take his point that this is unnecessarily restrictive in the "other" direction, that there is some sort of literary knowledge. But it is good to bear in mind that whatever that is, it should not be a form of "disguised or sweetened work" (Wood 2005, 4).

Moral Life (2000), and in a volume on the philosophical dimensions of visual modernism, *After the Beautiful* (2013). In the discussion of various aesthetic objects in these books, whether of filmed or fictional narratives, or visual objects suffused with intelligence and purpose, the claim was that we could not fully understand the works, or understand them at all, without somehow dealing with the fact that integral to their meaning was some clearly philosophical issue, raised in a way that invites and guides reflection.

In the case of Henry James, the attempt was to show what moral experience in later modernity had become: an emerging form of life in which conventional reliance on an assumed hierarchy of values, role-defined obligations, religion, or a shared sense of moral rules had collapsed, but in which some sense of the inappropriateness of mere self-seeking had survived. The value of James's phenomenology of this new moral experience is that he does not suggest through his characters' reflections and actions that some new moral consensus and general principle has emerged. It is the absence of any such consensus that allows James to portray contingent forms of social interaction and dependence that force characters with some good faith to find their way to what we can now be said to owe each other in various cases difficult to compare with each other and so difficult to generalize from. I can imagine that economic or social research and analysis could also help with this sort of exploration, but I find it hard to imagine how either empirical research or a philosophic insistence on some new principle or law could illuminate such an unprecedented situation, our situation. That situation seems to me much more accessible to philosophically minded literary critics like Lionel Trilling: "Now and then it is possible to observe the moral life in process of revising itself, perhaps by reducing the emphasis it formerly placed upon one or another of its elements, perhaps by inventing and adding to itself a new element, some mode of conduct or of feeling which hitherto it had not regarded as essential to virtue. This ready recognition of change in the moral life is implicit in our modern way of thinking about literature" (Trilling 1982, 1).

In the case of Hollywood westerns, in following the stories of the transition from a prelegal to a bourgeois rule of law, no intelligent viewer could avoid reflecting on the nature of the political allegiance necessary for that transition, on how there could arise the bond that unites subjects to one another in a collective submission to political order and the rule of law. It is highly unlikely that this acceptance has much to do with an appreciation of the quality of the argument strategies for exiting the state of nature or counterfactual state of original contracting. Some appreciation of the psychological dynamics of political life is necessary, especially American political life in the aftermath of the Civil War (the shadow of which still looms over our political life today). This political psychology is not well captured by the unavoidable abstractions and conceptual distinctions in traditional philosophical terms and is not accessible by any empirical research program.

In the case of the best film noir, the problem was whether we adequately understand common assumptions about intentional action, an issue that requires an exploration of the nature of self-knowledge and its relation to knowledge of others. Those assumptions are that *ex ante* reflection leads to the formation of intentions to act, which intentions explain and possibly justify the action (in some accounts, cause the action). If some narrative could show credible cases where characters have no idea what they are doing or why, and where their ability to understand the possible implications of what they do is undermined by an ever more corrupt and chaotic social and political world, the sources of whose corruption are maddeningly hidden and unaccountable, then a number of these common assumptions cannot hold. Not only do these films pose as problems issues like "what it is like" to live in a world like this, and how that illumination might bear on any reflection about agency, responsibility, and individuality, as if such issues were just provocations for reflection, but the narrative itself offers us a distinct form of reflection. (The "results" of such reflection are not comforting.)

With Hitchcock, the interpretive question is why his films, especially the most ambitious ones, concentrate so often on how bad we are at understanding each other, why the wrong person is often so confidently blamed for something he or she is innocent of. The general default position in Hitchcock is "unknowingness," not complete ignorance as in a thoroughgoing other minds skepticism, but a depiction of our fragile (if also ultimately correctable) grasp of what others mean to do or say and why; who they are, who I am. This all reaches a kind of cinematic and philosophical culmination in *Vertigo*, the subject of a scene-by-scene analysis in *The Philosophical Hitchcock*. The important contribution made by his films about this condition of unknowingness is showing us not merely that it exists, at a far deeper and more frequent and consequential level than we appreciate, but also how we might begin to think about how to live with this condition, honestly, without self-deceit or wishful thinking. It is not that he reaches any "conclusion" about this; it is not as if there *is* any reachable conclusion (as is so often the case and sometimes confidently denied in philosophy). The experiences involved are too variegated, not suitable for any generalization. But any reflection on the issue can certainly be informed, both negatively and positively, by what those films show us.

The collection *Filmed Thought* attempts to show that such an approach does not require the contrast and choice between "immanentist" and "contextualist" approaches to aesthetic objects. Many of the films discussed in the volume can easily be shown to have a bearing on both sorts of questions. One of the main arguments in *After the Beautiful* is not only that there is no tension between these approaches, but that they are complementary and indeed mutually required. The main continuous task in the book is to show *how* the films at issue involve a demand for philosophical reflection as part of the attempt to understand them, that we could not understand the point of showing us what they do, as they do, without such reflection. Films and aesthetic objects generally are said to embody implicitly a self-reflective sense of their own form, and so a conatus toward the realization of that form, the point or purpose of making the object. Often this sense of purpose is minimal and unambitious, but in the cases under consideration, that is not so, and this more ambitious purpose cannot be described as anything other than philosophical. And the attempt was to show that this is true not only of films that might be identified as art films, like those by the Dardenne brothers or Malick or Almodóvar, but also in commercial Hollywood cinema: Hitchcock, Nicholas Ray, Polanski, and Douglas Sirk.

The inspiration for the approach in *Filmed Thought* and throughout this book is Hegelian and is more explicit still in *After the Beautiful*, an attempt to construct a Hegelian approach to post-Hegelian art, modernism in particular. That inspiration in that book, the others, and this one is mostly from Hegel's *Lectures on Fine Arts* ("Works of art are all the more excellent in expressing true beauty, the deeper is the inner truth of their content and thought" [Hegel 1975, 74]). And *After the Beautiful* takes as exemplary his interpretations of Greek tragedy, lyric poetry, modern painting, Shakespeare, and Goethe. More important, in the light of the controversy over whether the arts, literature and film especially, should themselves be considered instances of philosophy or not, Hegel's approach usefully reframes the whole question. In effect, he splits the difference. He claims that the fine arts are not "philosophy," but that they have the same *content* as philosophy, and that they treat these philosophical issues in a different modality than discursive, argument-driven analysis, and yet that this modality is indispensable in any full understanding of what he called the Absolute, which for our purposes we can treat as simply what the final satisfaction of philosophic inquiry would look like. That modality is said to be sensible, but while there is a difference in Hegel between sensible and conceptual apprehension, the two elements are also inseparable, and so there is no restriction of aesthetic experience to "feeling" alone: "Of course, the work of art presents itself to sensuous apprehension. It is there for sensuous feeling, external or internal, for sensuous intuition and ideas, just as nature is, whether the external nature that surrounds us, or our own sensitive nature within. . . . But nevertheless the work of art, as a sensuous object, is not merely for sensuous apprehension; its standing is of such a kind that, though sensuous, it is essentially at the same time for spiritual apprehension; the spirit is meant to be affected by it and to find some satisfaction in it" (Hegel 1975, 35).

I don't mean to suggest that everything about Hegel's *Encyclopedia* approach, from his metaphysics to his political philosophy, must be taken on board for the approach sketched here to make sense. I consider this passage from Northrop Frye (as does he, apparently) to reflect what it means to consider criticism as "Hegelian" even if not Hegel's.

> As soon as Adam falls, he enters his own created life, which is also the order of nature as we know it. The tragedy of Adam, therefore, resolves, like all other tragedies, in the manifestation of natural law. He enters a world in which existence is itself tragic, not existence modified by an act, deliberate or unconscious. Merely to exist is to disturb the balance of nature. Every natural man is a Hegelian thesis, and implies a reaction: every new birth provokes the return of an avenging death. This fact, in itself ironic and now called Angst, becomes tragic when a sense of a lost and originally higher destiny is added to it. Aristotle's hamartia, then, is a condition of being, not a cause of becoming. (Frye 1957, 213)

But the notion of *philosophical* criticism requires saying some more here about this notion of *criticism*, before an overview of the chapters that follow.[2]

Philosophy and Interpretation

What we now call criticism in the arts descended from so-called high or source criticism of the Bible. In the modern age, roughly from the end of the eighteenth and beginning of the nineteenth century, the tasks of aesthetic criticism—literary, art, and music—came to be primarily interpretive and evaluative. Critics, both academic and journalistic, are supposed to help us understand a work and appreciate its quality and value. The object of attempts at understanding is said to be "meaning": why the work has the appearance and texture it has, how the parts fit into a whole, what the purpose of the work is, how some otherwise obscure element in the work makes the sense it does, how the symbolic and allegorical dimensions should be

2. Cf. Cavell's (2015) notion of the term: "If philosophy can be thought of as the world of a particular culture brought to consciousness of itself, then one mode of criticism (call it philosophical criticism) can be thought of as the world of a particular work brought to consciousness of itself" (313).

understood, as well as biographical and contextual details about its place in the author's oeuvre, its relation to her personal history, the work's historical period and audience, and so forth, all on the assumption that this should help us in that task of understanding the art. This list is only the beginning of several more characterizations of "meaning," and that already indicates that the term is so polysemous that it might not get us very far in any general account of criticism. But we can say that criticism, understood in this general way, should not be taken to be the exclusive domain of specialists, trained in a distinct "science." In this very general sense criticism is simply an extension and deepening of any intelligent encounter between a work and a reader, viewer, or listener, an extension and deepening because some readers and viewers are presumed to have had more experience in these attempts and a broader range of objects to call to mind in pursuing a critical understanding. But any responder to a work has to "follow" the plot, say, its events and characters, understand the intentions and reactions of characters, how the past might bear on a present, whether a claim is self-deceived or hypocritical, whether a character is lying and if so why, why a line in a poem follows another line with which it seems to have no connection, what relation to the beholder a painting seems to assume, whether a revelation is credible or misleading, and any reader or viewer might also be moved to ask about formal characteristics of the work, the point of a narrative or prose style, or an author's intentions in, say, quoting something from a foreign language in a poem. Each of these interpretive questions implicitly appeals to some philosophical understanding of the questions themselves, and any philosophical position is, or can be with the right attentiveness, distinctively informed by the imagined presentation: What is it to understand another's intentions? Can we? How does a person's past bear on the present? Is there such a thing as self-deceit? Can there be? How is it distinguished from hypocrisy? What is the nature of the wrong done another by lying? What is a poem that its sequence of lines can be difficult to follow, or that allusions can be made to other languages? How can a painting be said to assume or construct a relation to a beholder?[3] Are there different assumptions in different periods? Why? How are they to be discovered? "Interpretation" in this sense is always implicitly philosophical, and many

3. To ascribe what might seem like "agency" to an artwork—its own self-understanding, its aim, its conception of itself—is to use a figurative expression for the work and aims of a creator (the implied author, not necessarily the factual one), but nevertheless such elements are embodied in the work, there to be illuminated by attention to the work. They amount to the work's form in the sense we ascribe to Aristotle, the being-at-work of the thing in its distinct way. I have discussed aspects of this issue in the introduction to Pippin 2019.

philosophical claims always already assume that a case under consideration is a case relevant to, potentially clarifying for, the philosophical problem.

This does not mean that any serious critic must constantly be working out these philosophical problems as she attempts to understand the work, at least not in the language of traditional philosophy. The issues can be engaged with, clarified, misleading directions excluded, all in the language of criticism itself, as the examples of Frye, Girard, Trilling, and Cavell cited in this chapter, and the two chapters on Fried in what follows, demonstrate. Moreover, critics who have written on the issue of whether literature can be a form of knowledge often cite the difference between "understanding" a text and possessing "knowledge." But if this claim about the inevitable role of philosophical reflection (in its own critical modality) is correct, that difference cannot be right. This raises the question of the nature of philosophical knowledge, and that is a weighty topic in itself, but we might do well to remember that long ago when Aristotle distinguished understanding and knowledge, the former was a *superior* form of knowledge, metaphysics.

In this sense, interpretation is simply identical to fully experiencing a work as a work of art; everybody does it, must do it.[4] It has nothing to do with merely "translating" the work into another version of content or finding something hidden. If there is something to understand, something that raises a question, demands something of us beyond what a first experience reveals, it is "right there." It simply needs to be understood. A second or third or fourth reading or viewing is not boring deeper until something hidden is found; it is appreciating better and better what is simply "present."[5] The fact that we feel the need for rereading or re-viewing is interesting in itself. It

4. This stands against a common view eloquently expressed by Frye (1957): "The reading of literature should, like prayer in the Gospels, step out of the talking world of criticism into the private and secret presence of literature. Otherwise the reading will not be a genuine literary experience, but a mere reflection of critical conventions, memories, and prejudices" (27). It is easy enough to see how this can happen with some jargon-laden, abstract approach, but that applies only to bad criticism. This is not to say that there should not be specialized systems of criticism, like archetypal criticism, that would not normally arise in the aesthetic experience directly, but that too does not exhaust the possibilities of criticism. I have already cited a passage from Frye that shows the general compatibility of his approach with Hegel's, the one defended here.

5. This is not to say that paraphrase, rightly understood, is not central to criticism. See Cavell's (2015) fine example in discussing the famous "Juliet is the sun." "Juliet is the sun. Romeo means that Juliet is the warmth of his world; that his day begins with her; that only in her nourishment can he grow. And his declaration suggests that the moon, which other lovers use as emblems of their love, is merely her reflected light, and dead in comparison; and so on. In a word, I paraphrase it. Moreover, if I could not provide an explanation of this form, then that is a very good reason, a perfect reason, for supposing that I do not know what it means. Metaphors are paraphrasable" (8–9).

means that we sense that the novel, say, "knows something," and that by having read the novel, we now know something we did not, but we cannot yet say what it is and we know that another look or viewing or reading is necessary. That deeply felt and often deeply gratifying moment of insight when it becomes clear *what* it is we know but could not say is not something we can offer to another simply by formulating and saying it. We have to help another see it, feel that moment as well in the experience of the work. This insight is not subject to the kind of proof one could marshal for a scientific claim; it is not a philosophical argument so that denying it would be contradictory; but it has its own kind of standing. Denying its possibility would come at the cost of denying an enormous amount in human life, from seeing that someone is lying to realizing that an expression of love is sincere but self-deceived. Such interpretation is the most important task of teaching, although it can also provoke defensiveness and a kind of sullen resistance by some students, resentful that they are being told there was something important they "missed." But the injunction that we should "stop interpreting" a work and just "experience" it is like demanding that we just look at the words on a page and not ask what they mean.[6]

The object of the second task of criticism is the work's quality, an assessment of its aesthetic merits in comparison with other works and in itself. Traditionally, an enterprise like this was thought to rely on a critic's taste, and the assumption was that wide exposure to a variety of works could sharpen sensibilities and produce authoritative arbiters of taste. This notion of assessment has fallen out of favor, subject to understandable skepticism about cultural, class, and gender biases. But a different sort of assessment of a work's significance or importance is still understood as a task of criticism. Nonaesthetic factors are also sometimes invoked: whether the work exposes an injustice or corruption or gives voice to voiceless people. A work's importance could be tied to what it tells us about the audience that appreciates or consumes it, or even whether it is a good thing that the work exists at all, whether its inevitable effects on readers are morally suspect.

In some accounts, a work's value or significance is assessed in a very different way. Value is said to reside in whether the work can be said to reveal a kind of truth, for example, a way for a historical community to come to know itself otherwise inaccessible and perhaps inconsistent with its avowed view of its own values and principles, or whether the work can reveal some aspect of the human psychological, social, or even ontological world. This is the task

6. I mean to align myself here with the views expressed by Wilson 2008 and Nehamas 2010, and against those defended by Sontag 2001 and Bordwell 1989.

of "philosophical criticism," and it has emerged in various ways since Hegel and the German romantic movement introduced its possibility. One prominent school of thought developed out of Hegel's social theory and his approach to works like Sophocles's *Antigone*, Diderot's *Rameau's Nephew*, and his account of the historicity of art in his *Lectures*. This approach—the arts as a form of historical self-knowledge—extended through the Marxist tradition, Lukács, Adorno, Löwenthal, Raymond Williams, and in a different way, Walter Benjamin.[7] The idea was not what is sometimes casually assumed, that the task of criticism is to show how the arts support and perpetuate a class ideology, or to show that the arts were produced to do this, but that the arts could help us understand what was happening to us in a historical period, could reveal the tensions and even "contradictions," in general the irrationality or the unbearable pressures created in the way a society organized and regulated itself. One especially interesting aspect of this approach has been a claim to demonstrate the inseparability of various historically distinctive moral psychological issues in an individual from the social dynamics of a time.[8] And should it not be a function of philosophy to be able to say that some notion or norm is no longer available to us, has gone dead, that only a very different way of thinking is available to us, and all of that because of what we can be taught by the arts? Consider Trilling again, and his account of *Rameau's Nephew* and Hegel's view of the text: "In refusing its obedient service to the state power and to wealth it [Hegelian "spirit"] has lost its wholeness; its selfhood is 'disintegrated'; the self is 'alienated' from itself. But because it has detached itself from imposed conditions, Hegel says that it has made a step in progress. He puts it that the existence of the self on its own account is, strictly speaking, the loss of itself. The statement can also be made the other way round: 'Alienation of self is really self-preservation' " (Trilling 1982, 38).

Or consider the more radical claim put by Hugo von Hofmannsthal in the words of "Lord Chandos" in his famous Letter:

> But all that is ended. The word-mirror is broken, irreparably, it seems . . . The words on the page will no longer stand up and be counted, each proclaiming, "I mean what I mean!" . . . There used to be a time, we believe, when we could say who we were. Now we are just performers speaking our parts. The bottom has dropped out. We could think of this as a tragic turn of events were it

7. See Adorno 1997, 15: what "art demands from its beholder is knowledge. . . . The work wants its truth and untruth to be grasped."

8. Cf. Girard 1965, 222: "To the novelist of triangular desire interior life is already social and social life is always the reflection of individual desire."

> not that it is hard to have respect for whatever was the bottom that dropped out—it looks to us like an illusion now. (Hofmannsthal 2005, 19)

The only philosophers attempting to give this thought philosophical expression at around the same time were Nietzsche and Heidegger. It is the same thought in this literary case, but it is indispensable for philosophy that Chandos is seen "living it out," that we see how he might have come to this thought and what it does to him to think it. Otherwise, we would not have understood the thought.

Another approach, associated with Schelling, Schopenhauer, Nietzsche, and Heidegger, saw the arts as aiming at a "disclosure" of the real, of being as such, not empirical or social reality, but "what there truly is," beyond the appearances, the traditional task of metaphysics in philosophy. (There is an unusual confluence here with Lionel Trilling's quite philosophical *Sincerity and Authenticity*, in which he makes use of literature to show not only that there has been a sea change in the availability of concepts but also that that we now seem to need literature and the arts to be able to have any genuine or even vicarious sense *of our own being*.) All of this involves treating the arts as forms of reflective thought, sometimes historically and socially indexed in various ways, sometimes not, aiming at a kind of truth. This view is of course not the same as various philosophies ("theories") of the arts, or the impossibility of the arts, and in some ways at odds with such approaches, but I don't take up that issue in what follows. (The more radical view here, which is sometimes suggested by the philosophers just cited, is that philosophy is no longer possible except as art and aesthetic criticism, perhaps one art in particular, as in Girard's (1965) claim: "If the novel is the source of the greatest existential and social truth in the nineteenth century, it is because only the novel has turned its attention to the regions of existence where spiritual energy has taken refuge" [111]. Schelling's early lectures on all the arts make this point even more insistently.)

But even if we don't go that far, still, why "indispensable"? An aspect of Hegel's answer emerges in something he says about poetry: "The subject-matter of poetry is not the universal as it is abstracted in philosophy. What it has to represent is reason individualized" (Hegel 1975, 977). This says at once that there is a "universal" dimension to a lyric poet's expression, so that a poem is not merely a psychological record of some reaction or inspiration. It should be regarded as "reason individualized." This is to be contrasted with the level of abstraction necessary for discursive philosophy to do its work, which can certainly be valuable for lots of reasons, but which also can lose touch with the life of the concept as used. The aspiration here for the arts is linked to the claim for an explanatory role for the "ideal types" of Weberians, the "perspicuous representations" of the Wittgensteinians, the "concrete universal" of Hegelians in other contexts, and the unique moments of disclosure in what Heideggerians describe as a "happening" or "event" of truth. Hegel puts it another way in this passage: "In this [beautiful] object the self becomes concrete in itself since it makes explicit the unity of Concept and reality, the unification, in their concreteness, of the aspects hitherto separated, and therefore abstract, in the self and its object" (Hegel 1975, 114). A certain sort of philosophical attentiveness is necessary in interpretation so that both criticism and philosophy avoid "the abstract," and so that any work's "concept" of itself is appreciated in its concreteness, in its "unity" with reality. That must mean: in its distinct mode of truth. But this does not mean that having exercised such attentiveness, one can carry away from the reading some bundle of bits of knowledge, a set of propositions, a "moral." That would be the land of abstraction. For the interpreter not to be able to say what he carries away, even as he carries something substantive away that has something to do with knowledge, is the achievement of the work of the most important art and great criticism together. (There are rough analogies. Someone who asked a man who had been through a war what he had learned from the war, and expected some general moral truth, would have grossly misunderstood what that question could mean about such an experience; likewise, if he were bewildered if the soldier simply recounted an anecdote. The role of parables in the Christian Bible would be another analogy.)

This all must also mean that not only can a reader or a viewer get a text or painting "wrong," can miss ambiguities, ironies, formal patterns, or simply misunderstand the plot, but a text that purports to have some purchase on truth can be "wrong" as well. There were certainly persons who behaved as depicted in Griffith's *The Birth of a Nation*, but something goes wrong, is disturbingly "off," about the way they are represented. More often, the work can have nothing to do with the human world as it actually is; it deals instead with caricatures, stereotypes, adolescent fantasies, and so is simply irrelevant. The films of Quentin Tarantino seem to me like this, or Marvel comic superhero movies.

Organization

The chapters that follow are divided into two parts. Since Hegel's views on the significance of the arts are at issue in much of the work done above and lie behind the essays that follow, there is an opening section on the pre-Hegelian appearance of the problem of the relation between the arts and philosophy, aspects of Hegel's own understanding of the issue, and the three essays on approaches to modernism in the arts that I want to say are downstream from Hegel's influence.

The discussion in chapter 2 of Kant's skepticism about the philosophical importance or even the moral worth of the tragedies, ancient and modern, is a reminder of what sort of shift in sensibilities was necessary in Hegel and romanticism for a response to Kant and reformulation of the issue to be possible. More important, Kant's hostility to the idea that we might learn something from an experience of tragic poetry, or at least anything positive, opens a door to a much larger issue specific to tragedy: whether there is a deep incompatibility between the "tragic point of view" (somewhat paradoxically already a kind of philosophical claim) and philosophy itself, at least any philosophy that understands itself as a rational, sense-making enterprise. It might be that the most famous attempts to account for and integrate into some rational order what is implied about the human condition in tragedy are much more attempts to domesticate the challenge raised by tragic drama, and so constitute a strategy of cooption, rather than genuine understanding. The arts, or some of them, might be said to contribute to philosophy by being a challenge to its ambitions. Just so with tragedy; when we encounter what we badly need to know but cannot, *know* that we cannot, we thereby confront another form of knowledge and must begin exploring another: how, therefore, to live.

The three chapters on Hegel attempt to account for various dimensions of his understanding of the relation between philosophy and the arts, evaluate the status of his use of literature in the philosophical project of the *Phenomenology of Spirit*, show in what way, and why, Hegel transformed philosophical "aesthetics" into a theory of art, and describe his understanding of the relation between painting and a philosophical understanding of "subjectivity."

There then follow two chapters on the art historian and art critic Michael Fried. I include Fried's understanding of painting, photography and video in that Hegelian downstream I mentioned earlier for several reasons. For one, as the chapter on Hegel on painting already indicates, a major issue in Hegel's understanding of painting is the expression of mindedness, modalities of subjectivity that are not simply represented, as if thematically, but are corporeally present, "enlivened" in a way that arrests the beholder. To do this, the expression must be credible; it must not be experienced as merely offered for the beholder's pleasure, or "theatrically," but arrest the beholder and hold his or her attention and thereby demand something of such attentiveness. This involves Fried's account of "absorption" (which has a thematic connection to Kant's and Hegel's notion of "enlivening" [*beleben*] as central to the experience of art), the depiction of subjects immersed in their activities, in effect canceling or preventing any acknowledgment of the presence of the beholder, as a strategy in painting in roughly the seventeenth through two-thirds of the nineteenth century, basically beginning, for Fried, with Caravaggio. Fried's account is so rich because, as he notes, this aesthetic exploration of what it is to have a point of view, of "what it is like to be an individual subject" as a possible object of artistic attention, emerges along with the work of Descartes, Shakespeare, Cervantes, and soon thereafter romantic lyric poetry and the novels of individual consciousness. This involves another deep connection between Fried's narrative and two aspects of Hegel's position: for Fried, what accounts for how masterpieces "work," what defines them as substantive achievements in painting (credible, authentic, arresting) must be essentially historically inflected. So, for example, in the course of the nineteenth century, the absorptive strategies begin to fail and new approaches, most dramatically in Manet, turn out to be necessary. Second, and in a deeply related way, the meaning of the painting, if that term can be helpful at all, cannot be said to simply "reside" in the painting, but must lie in the dynamic relation to the beholder. This intersects with Hegel's account of the fine arts in general as modes of communal self-knowledge over time, inseparable from other such development in the other arts, in religion, philosophy, and political life (this goes beyond Fried's aesthetic concerns, but I think it is essential to note the dimension because it undermines the supposed distinction between immanentist and contextualist, or sociopolitical approaches to such meaning). I think the same Hegelian traces are quite visible in Fried's account of the role of intention in photography and video and connect with Hegel's frequent appeal to his theory of agency to account for the role of intentions in artistic meaning.

Finally, I conclude this section with a well-known and explicit anti-Hegelian approach to the same sort of issues, Adorno's in his *Aesthetic Theory*. The commonality is of course that Adorno also believes that advanced modern art is a major vehicle for understanding late bourgeois social reality, as well as a distinctive and powerful "negation" of that society. I take issue with some aspects of his account, especially that notion of negation and his understanding of idealism, as a way of showing the value of the Hegelian approach that I don't believe Adorno has appreciated.

Then I turn to five case studies of what I am calling philosophical criticism. I am aware that there is a certain built-in appropriateness for the choice of James, Proust, and Coetzee as such instances. Their works are all intensely and quite consciously philosophically reflective. This might seem to restrict the possible application of philosophical criticism to these sorts of novelists alone, or only to artists in the Western canon. That is certainly not the intention, and if any restriction is implied, it is only to works that make certain demands on the reader or viewer, something just as possible in commercial Hollywood cinema (or Japanese novels or Hindu mythology, etc.) as in high art philosophical novels.

James's risky experimental ambition in *What Maisie Knew* is not only to try to express the often bewildered and pained point of view of a child but also to explore how someone might be said to come to have a "mind of her own." Part of what James shows us in his narrative is how someone can come to regard herself as speaking for herself, convinced that she is "in touch with herself" and is speaking authentically, even while from our point of view, we can see she is at the outset avowing what others who have an interest in her making such avowals desire and have brought about. Genuinely to have a mind of one's own means being able to deal with and in effect fight through such possible skepticism, something very difficult for a girl between the ages of six and twelve. The difficulties of self-knowledge in a situation of even more extreme dependence than usual in modern society (that of a child) requires of any interpreter reflection on how there could be self-knowledge at all in such a situation, what such an achievement would look like; and seeing Maisie heroically achieve it is deeply instructive about all this even if it is not formulable in a "philosophical theory," even if it emerges for us only in the act of "criticism."

The magisterial novel of Marcel Proust poses unique challenges to any philosophical criticism. It should be the easiest case of all: there are philosophical reflections all over the place, offered both by Marcel, the subject of the narration, as he thinks about his experiences of society, art, love, and many other things, and by the narrator, who often interrupts the narration for reflections that appear to be his own. And neither of these voices can be identified as the real author's, Proust's. To make matters even more difficult, it would also be simplistic to deny that any of these views, especially the narrator's, could be Proust's. It some cases, particularly in the later novels, many clearly are. This is itself a philosophical conundrum, a "Nietzschean" one we could call it: how to understand the appeal of various philosophical thoughts to various psychological types, and how or whether one might transcend such psychological dependence. (If we cannot, then all philosophy ought also to be considered the "confessions of the author," as if voiced by a character in a novel, and the task would be to understand why the philosopher needs to believe what she does.) And the case is paradigmatic for literature itself, certainly for any instance of what might appear to be authorial reflections, whether voiced by characters or implicit in what happens. Such reflective content can never be said to be the author's. That is what it means for the work to present a fictional world, even if it is also true (as in the case of Proust) that some of the reflections are the author's. Active, close reading has as its task coming to terms with this complexity, everywhere and at all times. (The problem is quite prominent and complicated in the two Coetzee chapters as well.)

The two issues discussed, subjectivity (what it is like for Marcel to be Marcel; what it is like for us to understand what it is like) and jealousy (why it is so often shown and asserted that love is inseparable from jealousy, why they are two sides of the same coin), are both elements central to the events of the novel themselves and frequent subjects of reflection in the novel, subject to the conundrum just noted.

The subjectivity issue has three dimensions for Marcel: a skeptical dimension, or how he can know whether anyone else experiences the world as he does; a connected skeptical dimension, or whether some other's subjective life, what it is like to be him, can ever be known, or whether our view of anyone is always a projection connected to what we need to believe; and a final skeptical dimension, whether his own view of his own subjectivity, apparently the most intimate and even incorrigible sense of what it is like to be him, is that, whether the role a fantasy about himself plays in his actual experience is far greater than he suspects. There is no thematic resolution of doubts like these, no answers. But there is a narrative and reflective presentation of what it is like to live with such unavoidable questions and how one might at least be said to come to terms with them, and all of this while the social world of the characters is coming apart on the eve of and then after the First World War.

Jealousy in Proust's novel has an unusual dimension that offers a clue to what we are shown about its nature. Why does it arise? What is the nature of the anxiety at its heart? Is being possessed by it always a sign of some failure of character? Although it is *the* issue that for Swann and Marcel overwhelmingly dominates their love for, respectively, Odette and Albertine, the experiences narrated seem weirdly epistemological rather than passionate. Lovers are typically enraged by jealousy; they murder because of it. In contrast, in the novel what the characters are obsessed with is the issue of certainty in knowledge. Such certainty is impossible, of course, but that dimension of their anxiety allows Proust to explore not only the reasons for such an obsession and why it has the form it takes in the novel, but also how it is connected to the nature of our knowledge of ourselves and others (such as it is).

In the concluding two chapters on J. M. Coetzee, the philosophic dimension of the imagined characters, scenes, and events, and what those literary elements show us about that dimension, are both quite prominent. The theme identified in his first three novels, *Dusklands*, *In the Heart of the Country*, and *Waiting for the Barbarians*, amounts to an exploration of "the paradoxes of power." This returns us to recognizable Hegelian ideas, especially the notion prominent in the famous staging of the Master-Slave dialectic in his *Phenomenology of Spirit* that the exercise of power by the Master, while materially beneficial, is psychologically futile. Some subject demands recognition from another whom he does not recognize, and so the "recognition," status, standing that a subject might achieve is worthless, as worthless as paying someone to be your friend or to tell you how wonderful you are. Hegel's account is linked to a general theory of the relation between independence and dependence in social life, and the experiential depth of what it means to demand recognition from one whom one does not recognize, and for the victim to require recognition from one who does not even recognize him as a potential recognizer—a formulation that already indicates the abstraction of Hegel's treatment—is all transformed in Coetzee's accounts into a fictional treatment that not merely illustrates the issue but contributes to what should count as the fine-grained content of the concepts themselves.

The eight "lessons" Coetzee collected in *Elizabeth Costello* (which are essentially readings Coetzee began giving instead of lectures) purport to be lectures given by an Australian novelist on a variety of literary and philosophical topics. So the question of the relation between a distinct, individual psychological "voice" and the philosophical commitments of such a person is raised again. There is a kind of back-shadowing orientation at the end of the book for all the lectures that I take as important in understanding the whole project. It is a four-page "Postscript," the last thing we read in the book, a fictional letter from Lord Chandos's wife, he of the famous Hugo von Hofmannsthal fictional letter cited above. Lady Chandos pleads with Bacon to help; she says that her husband is being destroyed by the burden of his insight ("the word-mirror is broken") and that she is being destroyed by his suffering: "Drowning, we write out of our separate fates. Save us." In the world-historical context set by this orientation, these lessons, I suggest, have to do with how, in such a world, someone could be understood to "justify herself," primarily to herself, but also to others. (Let us say, in the "Lutheran" and not in the "force of the better argument" sense of justification.) Why she refuses to eat animals, why she writes fiction, why she defends the inheritance of Western humanism, why she has lived the life she has. In a Kafkaesque closing lesson, a parable, "At the Gate," Elizabeth addresses and responds to such a demand, both questioning whether she needs to respond and offering the kind of justification anyone should expect from a writer. It is something I would hope is a fitting conclusion to an exploration like this one: not a model to be imitated, not a general thesis to be argued for, but the only kind of response she could give to such a question, of serious philosophical value, even if not expressible in the language of traditional or academic philosophy.

2

Kant and the Problem of Tragedy

Tragedy and the Tragic

In the two hundred and seventy-six books in the so-called "Warda" list of Kant's library at his death, there is not a single copy of a Greek or Roman or any other tragedy.[1] Moreover, in the only passage I know of where Kant evaluates the significance of tragic drama, he makes it clear that he finds the art form distasteful and possibly morally corrosive.[2] Here is the passage, from his well-known "Theory-Practice" essay. The reference to tragic drama is hidden in most English translations because *Trauerspiel* is mistranslated as simply "drama."

> It is a sight fit for a god to watch a virtuous man grappling with adversity and evil temptations and yet managing to hold out against them. But it is a sight quite unfit not so much for a god, but even for the most ordinary, though right-thinking man, to see the human race advancing over time towards virtue, and then quickly relapsing the whole way back into vice and misery. It may perhaps be moving and instructive to watch such a drama [*Trauerspiel*] for a while, but the curtain must eventually descend. For in the long run, it becomes a farce. And even if the actors do not tire of it—for they are fools—the spectator does, for any single act will be enough for him if he can reasonably conclude from it that the never-ending play will go on in the same way forever. If it is only a play, the retribution at the end can make up for the unpleasant sensations the spectator has felt. But in my opinion, at least, it

1. Warda 1922.

2. He does link the sublime with "verse tragedy" in §52 of the *Critique of the Power of Judgment*, but says next to nothing about it (Kant 2000, 203).

> cannot be reconciled with the morality of a wise creator and ruler of the world if countless vices, even with intermingled virtues, are in actual fact allowed to go on accumulating.[3]

This is not to say that Kant was ignorant of or simply opposed to or ignored all tragedies. In his anthropology lectures, there are several, mostly favorable references to Shakespeare, and he was familiar with *Hamlet*, *King Lear*, and other plays.[4] Aside from some swipes at Shakespeare's crudeness and lack of refined taste, he certainly calls him a genius. Part of Kant's concern has to do with a complex of aesthetic issues (especially the relation between rational and aesthetic ideas) and his disagreements with Herder over the bearing of Shakespeare and other artists on philosophy and over what the anthropologist might or should not learn from plays and novels. It is the anxiety Kant expresses in the quotation above about the moral and philosophical relevance of tragedies that is so striking and is the subject of the following.

This anxiety is first of all somewhat ironic, because Kant's work, especially his framing the main problem of philosophy as that between freedom and necessity, and his account of the dynamical sublime, inspired the greatest period of serious philosophical attention to tragedy in the Western tradition. Hölderlin, Schiller, the Schlegels, Schelling, and Hegel, all in some way influenced by Kant, weighed in on the bearing of tragedy on philosophy, and this sort of attention continued in Schopenhauer and Nietzsche, and on into such figures as Lukács, Adorno, and Benjamin.[5] The general issue is an old one, of course. It began with the ancient quarrel between poetry and philosophy, Plato's banishing the poets from Kallipolis (if there is a quarrel, especially

3. Kant 1989, 88. I am grateful to Terry Pinkard for drawing my attention to this passage. Kant's moral hesitation about tragedy also needs to be placed in a much larger eighteenth-century context. This is one in which the grip of classical tragedy is already clearly loosening for all sorts of reasons, many of which are described by Hegel. But moral concerns were prominent. Beaumarchais, for example (to some extent following Diderot), considered the representation of tragic necessity and fatalism amoral and encouraged dramas of domestic suffering closer to the ordinary and without transcendent significance. See Beaumarchais 1949, 18–20.

4. See Kant's *Vorlesungen über Anthropologie*, especially Menschenkunde 234, 240–41; Mrongovius 65; Dohna 121; Petersburg 167; Gotthold 292–93. I owe these references to Cutrofello 2008, 81. Moreover, Kant studied Latin and the Latin authors intently at the Collegium Fridericianum and could reportedly still recite long passages from Seneca in his old age. And he studied *koine* and classical Greek in the fourth and fifth years of schooling and would certainly have come across authors like Sophocles. But it all does not seem to have made much of an impression.

5. An indispensable study of these developments, focusing especially on the relation between morality and tragedy, and one to which I am much indebted: Gardner 2003.

one of such seriousness, there must be a rivalry over issues claimed by both) and Aristotle's attention to tragedy in his *Poetics*, his claim that poetry, tragic poetry, is more philosophical than history. (If that is so, in what sense *is* such poetry philosophical? It may present a more general picture of human life than history, but a more general picture of what in human life?)

This is not to say that there is not a noticeable tragic dimension to Kant's philosophy. In his theoretical philosophy, he famously said, "Human reason has the peculiar fate in one species of its cognitions that it is burdened with questions which it cannot dismiss since they are given to it as problems by the nature of reason itself, but which it also cannot answer, since they transcend every capacity of human reason" (Kant 1997, Avii). That species is metaphysics, the field of endless controversies, and this picture of fate and failure is as tragic in its presentation of unavoidability and painfully unovercomeable limits as is his unusually literary characterization of the same issue. We can be sure, he insists, that "we will always return to metaphysics as to a beloved from whom we have been estranged, since reason, because essential ends are at issue here, must work without respite either for sound insight or for the destruction of good insights that are to hand" (Kant 1997, A850/B878). Perhaps the picture of an estranged lover continually returning to a beloved, only to be estranged again, is more pathetic or at least melodramatic than tragic, but it is a remarkable picture of inescapable necessity and unavoidable failure.[6]

In his practical philosophy as well, there is a tone of finitude, futility, failure, and something close to possible despair. The worth of our actions depends on our intentions, but we can never be sure that we know what our intentions are; we suspect that the "covert impulse of self-love"[7] is always our motivation, and we are usually right. To be sure, morally required actions *need* not always conflict with our interest in our own happiness, and not every moral choice *must* involve a struggle with inclination (Kant claims his examples of such struggles are for clarification of the true nature of moral worth, not indications of an omnipresent default situation),[8] but our egoism, our crooked timber from which nothing straight can be made, insures that such conformity with our sensible natures is serendipitous and cannot in any

6. Another rare literary flourish—Kant's invocation of Ovid's *Metamorphoses* to describe the sad and pitiable state of metaphysics now: "There was a time when metaphysics was called the queen of all the sciences, and if the will be taken for the deed, it deserved this title of honor, on account of the preeminent importance of its object. Now, in accordance with the fashion of the age, the queen proves despised on all sides; and the matron, outcast and forsaken, mourns like Hecuba: 'Greatest of all by race and birth, I now am cast out, powerless.'" Kant 1997, Aviii–ix.

7. Kant 1997, 19 (AA 4:407).

8. That it is not such an indication is argued, successfully I think, in Wood 1999.

sense be counted on. We know that everything of significance in our lives and the basis of any self-worth depend on the assumption that we have the capacity to direct our lives, that we are free beings, but we have no secure way of knowing that we are, or knowing how such a capacity could be possible in what we now know to be nature, the subject of Newtonian mechanics.

As to the despair this situation might create, consider this remarkable passage from section 87 of the *Critique of the Power of Judgment*, "On the Moral Proof of the Existence of God." It is the same sentiment that prompts his reflections in the *Critique of Practical Reason* about the indispensability for morality of the "Summum Bonum," and so of the Postulates, especially of a judging God and the immortality of the soul, but it has a distinct poignancy.[9] It is long, but worth quoting at length, especially since it is like a little literary narrative. He makes his point with this picture, not an argument.

> We can thus assume a righteous man (like Spinoza) who takes himself to be firmly convinced that there is no God and (since with regard to the object of morality it has a similar consequence) there is also no future life: how would he judge his own inner purposive determination by the moral law, which he actively honors? He does not demand any advantage for himself from his conformity to this law, whether in this or in another world; rather, he would merely unselfishly establish the good to which that holy law directs all his powers. But his effort is limited; and from nature he can, to be sure, expect some contingent assistance here and there, but never a lawlike agreement in accordance with constant rules (like his internal maxims are and must be) with the ends to act in behalf of which he still feels himself bound and impelled. Deceit, violence, and envy will always surround him, even though he is himself honest, peaceable, and benevolent; and the righteous ones besides himself that he will still encounter will, in spite of all their worthiness to be happy, nevertheless be subject by nature, which pays no attention to that, to all the evils of poverty, illnesses, and untimely death, just like all the other animals on earth, and will always remain thus until one wide grave engulfs them all together (whether

9. His formulation: "Now, since the promotion of the highest good, which contains this connection in its concept, is an a priori necessary object of our will and inseparably bound up with the moral law, the impossibility of the first must also prove the falsity of the second. If therefore the highest good is impossible in accordance with practical rules, then the moral law, which commands us to promote it, must be fantastic and directed to empty imaginary ends and must therefore in itself be false" (Kant 2015, 92 [AA 5:114]). It is significant that for Kant what is so threatening to morality would be the impossibility of the highest good. But since one cannot prove a negative (and the concepts of a just God and an immortal soul are not self-contradictory), it is not clear what the implications would be if there were simply no good reason to believe in such postulates, beyond our need to believe them.

> honest or dishonest, it makes no difference here) and flings them, who were capable of having believed themselves to be the final end of creation, back into the abyss of the purposeless chaos of matter from which they were drawn.— The end, therefore, which this well-intentioned person had and should have had before his eyes in his conformity to the moral law, he would certainly have to give up as impossible. (Kant 2000, 317)

From a conventionally religious point of view, of course, Kant's claim that we need such a postulate is remarkable. The assumption is clearly that there is no manifest presence, none at all, of a benevolent or loving or just God *in* human life. He is absent, and it is just and only because he is absent that he must be postulated. The experience of human life is the experience of complete godlessness. Such a picture is not leading us toward any notion of prayer or grace or divine mercy in this life, and again, were someone *not* able to be convinced by the need to make some "postulated" sense of the indubitable experience of the reality of the moral law, then that would bring Kant's picture close to something like a tragic one.[10] (And, given the unconditional nature of moral obligation, and Kant's insistence on "ought *always* implies can," it is not clear that his attempt to avoid the Sisyphean picture his core moral theory has painted is coherent.)

It is, of course, open to Kant to push these considerations to the margins, despite the existential intensity of some of his language. He could say: there is nothing crushingly tragic about the fact that, as knowers, we are finite, and so there are matters we need to know that we cannot. At least we can know why we cannot, can make comprehensible such incomprehensibility, and we at least know with a priori certainty that there is no way ever to *deny* the possibility of what we need to believe. We are forever ignorant of "things in themselves." And we certainly know that morality is a matter of pure practical reason. Amid all this metaphysical ignorance, we can know in every case what we ought to do (there can be no tragic dilemmas, reason cannot oppose itself),[11] and even if

10. Cf. Lukács 1974, 152: "A drama is a play about man and his fate—a play in which God is the spectator. He is a spectator and no more; his words and gestures never mingle with the words and gestures of the players. His eyes rest upon them: that is all. 'Whoever sees God, dies,' Ibsen wrote once; 'but can he who has been seen by God continue to live?' "

11. Like everything in Kant, this is occasionally controversial, and Kant certainly presents difficult casuistical questions that, somewhat strangely, he does not resolve for us. But the passage most often cited to show that he did deny the existence of such dilemmas (in the "Doctrine of Right" section of *The Metaphysics of Morals*) does seem to be dispositive. "A conflict of duties (*collisio officiorum s. obligationum*) would be a relation between them in which one would cancel the other (wholly or in part). But since duty and obligation are concepts that express the objective practical necessity of certain actions and two rules opposed to each other cannot be necessary

we cannot provide any ultimate sense of such requirements within the whole, it is open to us to hope for what we need, armed with a critical assurance that such aspirations cannot ever be foreclosed. And this is all not even to mention that Kant, however responsible he was for isolating the aesthetic domain as one of distinctive human significance, alongside the normative and cognitive domains, still strictly separates the aesthetic, as the domain of the feeling of pleasure and pain, from the experience of and reflection about the moral law,[12] and from any claim to knowledge (viz., "tragic insight"). But such a reaction to what we will need to explore as a tragic assessment of human life as a whole is extremely abstract, and the passage quoted above reveals that Kant is quite interested in the *experience* of such moral demands, interested in it "aesthetically" (as "painful" in light of our interest in happiness) within the general shape of an extended human life; interested in what it is like to live in the absence of any reason to believe there is a connection in this life between virtue and happiness, and in the question of the bearability of such experiences.

We can only speculate about how a Kantian account of the tragic would keep faith with the various sentiments we have noted. We might imagine that a "cathartic" reaction to a tragedy—perhaps like the one in his little Spinoza narrative above—would be in the spirit of his account of the sublime, especially the dynamical sublime.[13] Pain at the experience of our finitude and weakness in the face of natural power and arbitrariness, represented aesthetically, might inspire the same kind of counterreaction as in the sublime. Whatever sensible suffering is represented, we might be nevertheless inspired by the autonomy and inviolability of our "supersensible" moral vocation, and come to feel that whatever horrors are visited on us, these cannot ever determine, make impossible, the call of duty and our capacity to respond. This would be an experience of something beautiful, and a form of self-affirmation. Interestingly, that is not the reaction prominent in the Moral Proof passage. We instead cry out that such unmerited suffering, Iphigenia's, say, or Desdemona's, be redeemed by divine justice, not by tragic heroism, however beautiful, or

at the same time, if it is a duty to act in accordance with one rule, to act in accordance with the opposite rule is not a duty but even contrary to duty; so a collision of duties and obligations is inconceivable (*obligationes non colliduntur*)" (Kant 1996, 50 [AA 6:224]).

12. Aside from the vaguely comforting thought that the beautiful is the symbol of the morally good in section 59 of the *Critique of the Power of Judgment.*

13. An account that was important for Schiller in the essays written in 1792–73, such as "On the Tragic Art," "On the Sublime," "Concerning the Sublime." Kant makes the thinnest possible connection between the tragic (and other artforms) and the sublime in the *Critique of the Power of Judgment* (Kant 2000, 203).

by the revenge prominent in tragedies (another wrong, from Kant's point of view),[14] and we might take some solace in the possibility that we can hope for such a rebalancing of the scales of justice in an afterlife. Both reactions instrumentalize the tragic experience for the sake of morality and its absolute or unconditioned authority. Perhaps Kant is right about such authority. Perhaps he is right that morality is a matter of pure practical reason, and so there can be no such thing as the unresolvable dilemmas tragic heroes face; there is no "having to do something wrong in order to do what is right"; there is no conflict between right and right, no kind of greatness in an attempt that transcends its moral wrongness. But the two reactions that seem to follow from such supremacy of morality—increased respect for the self-sufficiency of our moral vocation, and a rational hope for ultimate justice—are ways of opposing or even defying where great tragedies leave us. Even if it is no easy matter to say where that is, those reactions seem an appropriation of or denial of tragedy, not a response to it as it is. That evaluative category, "the tragic," as it is, still needs a hearing.

So the wager in the following is that Kant's lack of interest in classical and modern tragedy, and what I am assuming is his resistance to there being anything of general philosophical significance in "the tragic," or his attempt with his Postulates to avoid, to foreclose, any such possible significance, have a broader meaning. Tragedy is a notion deeply foreign to him, not because of some peculiarity of Kant's personality or even all that much as a result of his moral theory and critical philosophy, but because tragedy, understood broadly, deeply, and rightly, is foreign to philosophy as traditionally conceived, at least up until Nietzsche's *Birth of Tragedy*. But before we return to Kant, we will need to say something about tragedy such that it could be a challenge to philosophy.

Theories of Tragedy

This is not easy to do economically. There must be dozens of theories of tragedy, and they deal with everything from the distinctive sort of pleasure the spectator takes in watching human suffering to the moral dimensions of tragedy. But insofar as we want to develop a contrast between a distinctive

14. Actually it is hard, requires a great deal of imagination, to get even this far in a Kantian framework. It is hard to imagine Kant getting beyond in any sense the (for him) unqualified and absolute wrongness of what Agamemnon does to Iphigenia, or what Othello does to Desdemona.

evaluative assessment of human life as a whole as "tragic" and a philosophical point of view like Kant's, we need to begin by assuming that we can speak of the "tragic point of view" as involving something like such an assessment. The assumption involves the one Aristotle makes in the *Poetics*. Tragic dramas are not mere sad stories about particular characters. The form itself, in its repetitions, variations, and deep hold on the Western imaginary, aspires to some sort of universality. The narratives have a point, a reflective purpose, and that purpose is an illumination of some central, shared feature of human life. In the simplest sense, within such a form, some heroic effort fails, had to be undertaken and had to fail, and since the effort often involves matters of great importance, the possibility of justice, of love, of self-knowledge, of trust, the assumption is that a point of view is taken on the meaning of such unavoidable failure. This is obscure, not least because it seems an invitation to extract a lesson, a moral, an explanation, from the whole course of characters and events represented. As we shall discuss in more detail, these always represent efforts to domesticate and blunt the force of tragedy. But the horrors that we feel when we read or see tragedies do seem to mean something weighty, even if any critical attempt to make sense of what they mean can seem like a form of avoidance or repression.

If we take as our paradigms of the genre Sophocles and Shakespeare, then there are some features that set off such a point of view. Tragedy is an aesthetic form, of course, a genre, and it is a weighty, interesting question in itself how it differs from comedy, romance, irony, and melodrama, and what might be the significance of these various forms of aesthetic representation of life. But from a sufficiently high altitude, several features stand out that justify understanding "the tragic" in the way suggested: as a general evaluative assessment of matters of great significance in human life (still reserving the possibility that such an assessment might be that no such evaluative assessment is possible).

Matters of great consequence for an entire community, a polis, a kingdom, an empire, are at stake in what the central figure in the drama, the hero or heroine, does or does not do. For Hegel, this immediately explains why any modern tragedy, with credible modern characters, is no longer possible. Once there is a modern state and so many mediated and interrelated sources of power and a vast network of human dependencies, there is no credible way of depicting modern characters on whom so much could depend.[15]

15. "But when there is still no state the security of life and property depends entirely on the personal strength and valour of each individual who has to provide for his own existence and

To some degree, but not completely, he exempts Shakespeare from this judgment, largely because Shakespeare creates his own imaginary Heroic Age where these conditions still apply. "Not completely," because he realizes that in Shakespeare, the focus is on the inner psychological "collisions" within a modern individual. But he notes,

> Shakespeare, for example, has drawn much material for his tragedies out of chronicles or old romances which tell of a state of affairs not yet unfolded into a completely established organization, but where the life of the individual in his decision and achievement is still predominant and remains the determining factor. Shakespeare's strictly historical dramas, on the other hand, have, as a chief ingredient, purely external historical matter and so they are further away from the ideal mode of representation, although even here the situations and actions are borne and promoted by the harsh independence and self-will of the characters. It is true that their independence remains again only a mostly formal self-reliance, whereas in the independence of the heroic characters what must be an essential keynote is the content too which they have made it their aim to actualize. (Hegel 1975, 190)

And he notes one exception: "I will only refer to Goethe's *Faust*, the one absolutely philosophical tragedy. Here on the one side, dissatisfaction with learning and, on the other, the freshness of life and enjoyment in the world, in general the tragic quest for harmony between the Absolute in its essence and appearance and the individual's knowledge and will, all this provides a breadth of subject-matter which no other dramatist has ventured to compass in one and the same work" (Hegel 1975, 1224). But even in this case, the fact that this quest for harmony is "tragic" does not mean, as it properly should, that it is doomed, even if the quest is inevitable. It is very much the point of a good deal of Hegel (reflecting Schiller's influence) that it is not doomed. And so we still find ourselves without a modern form of life in which a tragic situation could be dramatically represented as credible. Instead, in the modern world, "the tragic denouement is also displayed as purely the effect of unfortunate circumstances and external accidents which might have turned out otherwise and produced a happy ending. In this case the sole spectacle offered to us is that the modern individual with the non-universal nature of his character, his circumstances, and the complications in which he is involved, is necessarily surrendered to the fragility of all that is mundane and must

---

the preservation of what belongs and is due to him. Such a state of affairs is the one we are accustomed to ascribe to the Heroic Age" (Hegel 1975, 1: 184–85).

endure the fate of finitude" (Hegel 1975, 1231). This is probably what we would call melodrama, and it is un-Hegelian (if one may dare to lecture Hegel about himself) to isolate the "modern individual" as having a strictly nonuniversal character. It is quite conceivable that the form of modern bourgeois life in general might impose psychological demands on individuals that produce internal, unreconcilable "collisions."[16]

Moreover, it does not seem right, or it is at least an incomplete picture, to portray a tragic point of view as simply and only past. An imagined picture of such heroic power still plays a deeply significant role in (especially) the American imaginary, as in Hollywood westerns and film noir, contexts in which the rule of law is not yet established or has broken down. These forms isolate such imagined possibilities as imaginary, and either they imagine the embourgeoisement of the heroic situation (make vivid the unavailability of such a space for such heroics, and so as a painful, remembered, and present, lived loss), or they blur the lines completely between the heroic and the criminal, leaving us with mere, arbitrary death, a situation beyond tragedy, beyond even meaning, perhaps like the fate that awaits us.[17] They both bear on the present.

Tragedies are not about ordinary life; matters of great consequence are in play. What is done by that central figure in the drama ends in failure, most often in death, very often a horrific death, of the innocent, the wicked, and the hero or heroine. The failure though is not accidental, contingent. It is not just that Iphigenia, or Medea's children, or Ajax, or Cordelia, or Desdemona dies or that Oedipus or Hamlet or Macbeth or Lear or Othello seems to destroy himself. The deaths and their own destruction are brought about by the central figure. And the most interesting feature of this is always *why* the hero brings about these calamities. He or she cannot but bring them about. Some sort of necessity is involved, and this is put in many ways. The very qualities we admire that make the hero heroic are the very same qualities that ensure something calamitous. What Karl Reinhardt says about Oedipus in his great book on Sophocles does not seem as limited to Attic tragedy or to the play as he suggests: "What is tragic is not annihilation as such, but rather that deliverance turns into annihilation; it is not in the hero's downfall that tragedy takes place, but rather in the ruin with which a human being is met

16. An example would be: the modern demand for genuineness or authenticity is both unavoidable, necessary, and unfulfillable. See my chapter on Douglas Sirk's *All That Heaven Allows*, in Pippin 2020, 117–46.

17. Showing this to be so is my project in my *Hollywood Westerns and American Myth: The Importance of Howard Hawks and John Ford for Political Philosophy* (Pippin 2010) and *Fatalism in American Film Noir: Some Cinematic Philosophy* (Pippin 2012).

on the very path that he or she entered in order to escape from ruin."[18] Or, in a formulation of the issue by Seth Benardete: "Tragedy discloses the inevitability of the morally impossible for which there cannot be any expiation."[19] The necessity involved, that the morally impossible is inevitable, does not just produce guilt without expiation (despite that necessity; the necessity does not expiate, provide an excuse); it produces catastrophic consequences, such as the deaths listed as examples above. (Benardete does not much explain what he means by "the morally impossible." Interestingly, he does not just say the necessity of the morally impermissible. Perhaps he means that the tragic dramas disclose a situation where an action is both required and forbidden; hence the impossible.)

But even with a sketchy picture of the tragic point of view, we are on the verge of deep paradox. In *Oedipus at Colonus* Oedipus himself complains bitterly about what appears to him as well to be such a denial of moral expiation.

> The killing and the marriage and all my misfortunes were things I had to endure, alas, against my will. It was the way the gods wanted it, angry perhaps with my family from times past. So far as I myself am concerned, you could not find any offence to reproach me with that led me to these deeds against my self and my kin. Tell me this: if a divine oracle was given to my father, to the effect that he was to die at his son's hand, how can you properly make that into any fault of mine, seeing that my father had as yet done nothing to give me birth, nor my mother either? At the time I was unborn. And if later my ruin became manifest, as it did, and I fought with and killed my father, not knowing what it was that I was doing, and who I was doing it to—how can you reasonably blame me for this act, which was nothing that I intended?[20]

If this were true, of course, then *Oedipus Tyrannus* would be no tragedy, but the sad story of a horrible mistake, the pitiable story of a well-intentioned man who unknowingly and so blamelessly killed his father and married his mother. This is very like the somewhat tone-deaf view of Hegel, who first contrasted ancient tragedy with modern by claiming that in the former the operative agents were really vast "ethical powers" in "collision," and individuals were mere epiphenomena of such powers, whereas in the latter, in accord

18. Reinhardt 1979, 108. This remark too could apply as much to Lear as to Oedipus: "something which is peculiar to Attic tragedy as a whole, the habit of luxuriating in horror, of investing terror with a kind of voluptuousness, has in this play more than any other extended into the attitude of the tragic hero" (130).

19. Benardete 2000, 105. I am grateful to my colleague David Wellbery for discussions about the character of the "morally impossible" and for many other conversations about the philosophical dimensions of tragedy.

20. Dawe 1982, 3.

with the "moral" point of view, there were genuine individuals, subjects of their intentional deeds and personally responsible only for the intentional, and then suggested that the latter view was superior, and the former belonged to the past, that the heroic assumption of absolute responsibility for everything brought out about by the individual even if not intentionally done by him was, in effect, primitive.[21]

Bernard Williams has the right response to Oedipus's complaint, but it returns us to a paradox that Williams does not much acknowledge. In fact what Williams says borders on both the right account of what is genuinely tragic in this situation and yet also deeply unintelligible.

> Not even Oedipus, as he is represented in his last days, thought that blinding and exile had to be the response. But should there be no response? Is it as though it had never happened? Or rather, to put the right question: Is it as though such things had happened, but not by his agency—that Laius had died, for instance, indeed been killed, but, as Oedipus first believed and then, for a short while, hoped, by someone else? The whole of the *Oedipus Tyrannus*, that dreadful machine, moves to the discovery of just one thing, that *he did it*. Do we understand the terror of that discovery only because we residually share magical beliefs in blood-guilt, or archaic notions of responsibility? Certainly not: we understand it because we know that in the story of one's life there is an authority exercised by what one has done, and not merely by what one has intentionally done.[22]

That seems right, "an authority exercised by what one has done." But what is such an authority? It will not do just to point to the unacceptability of an extreme possible reaction: Oedipus, reasoning as he does, might simply shrug off what he has found out and walk away unbothered by it for the rest of life ("as though it had never happened"), beyond being sad, perhaps bitter, that all this "happened to him." That would be, as Williams suggests, inhuman, not credible. But what is it then that Oedipus must bear? What "response" is appropriate? Should Oedipus just be haunted and horribly pained by the memory of that day on the road and by horrific memories of making love to his mother? It is clear that he is, but that is not a "response." Oedipus says he "suffered those deeds more than he did them," and he has a point.[23] There is

21. Hegel 1975, 188–89. Interestingly, Hegel also indicates a dissatisfaction with the moral point of view, saying that, in antiquity, one "knows nothing of this opposition between subjective intentions and the objective deed and its consequences, while nowadays, owing to the complexity and ramification of action, everyone has recourse to everyone else and shuffles guilt off himself so far as possible" (188).

22. Williams 1993, 69.

23. His remarks also make very clear that Hegel was wrong about the distinction he claims we have but the Heroic Age did not.

no indication that he wants it to be "as if he had not done them," but he is raising the question of his agency and so of the justice of any blame.

Reinhardt is closer to the point when he says,

> And even if one were to imagine that a court composed of gods or men had acquitted Oedipus of all guilt, like Orestes in Aeschylus, it would still not help him in the least; for what meaning would such an acquittal have in the face of the contradiction between what he has imagined he is, and what he is? Nor would the opposite verdict of "guilty" add anything to his state. Orestes can be acquitted, by himself and by others, but Oedipus cannot be released from what he has recognized as the truth about himself. . . . What we have had to consider is illusion and truth as the opposing forces between which man is bound, in which he is entangled, and in whose shackles, as he strives towards the highest he can hope for, he is worn down and destroyed. (Reinhardt 1979, 134)

Reinhardt is implying, and I think he is right to do so, that there is something of powerful general significance in Oedipus's fate and, more to the present point, there is no resolution to or consolation for being caught in this painful collision, no lesson to be drawn from it. And it is a possible, and perhaps inevitable, collision everyone faces, between who one takes oneself to be and who one might discover one is.[24]

To be sure, the value of Williams's take on Oedipus is that he does not deflate or try to domesticate the genuine *painfulness* of the situation, but there is still a kind of rationalization in the point he makes. He thinks we see a philosophical truth in Oedipus, that we must bear the burden of what we have brought about; we cannot escape it, and our not finding what Oedipus suffers simply unfair but tragically necessary is a way for us to make an important distinction, between what we think we think (responsibility only for intentional action) and what we really think (we do bear responsibility for what we have brought about whether intentionally or not). And of course Williams is also using classical tragedies to make a point he makes with great passion and incisiveness in many works, a point against what he calls "that peculiar institution," morality (Williams 1986). This rationale or lesson may be an important philosophical point, but the question it raises is whether "drawing such a lesson" or appealing to the play as evidence in this way fully appreciates the tension or, to use that Hegelian word, the "collision" between the necessity or inevitability of "the morally impossible" and, even given that inevitability, the impossibility of moral expiation.

24. Why it might be inevitable is explored in Pippin 2017.

That is, Williams does not domesticate the tragic as egregiously as do the numerous moralistic accounts of tragedy. Everyone is familiar with these, from high school literature courses on. It was Oedipus's *hybris* that brought about his downfall, his arrogant presumption of his riddle-solving powers and assumption of sole political responsibility. Or Oedipus is a true tyrant, confusing the public with the private. (This is Benardete's view.) Or Agamemnon was not hesitant enough about killing his daughter, not conflicted enough. Or Creon was a tyrant, Antigone a heroine of conscience. Lear's catastrophes were the result of his demand that private affection serve a public, political purpose. Hamlet was a melancholic, damaged soul, and so he was weak, not up to what was required of him.[25] Othello could not abide the uncertainty that comes with all love; he demanded a security that is impossible, and when demanded, ruins everything. And so on with the many moral theories of the tragic. There are also more general rationalizations of the tragic perspective. Lessing's view that tragedy transforms the feelings of pity and fear into virtues; Mendelssohn's that our pleasure in tragedy derives from our awareness of our own engaged moral virtues.[26] Even what Gardner (2003), in quoting the passage below, rightly describes as "the most subtle and sensitive attempt in German idealism to square tragedy with morality" (255), Schelling's, nevertheless does try to do just that, albeit in a highly speculative way that makes little sense without his early system. He is, though, clearly confronting head-on the basic issue. Tragedy, he writes in his *The Philosophy of Art*, is

> necessity genuinely caught in a struggle with freedom, yet such that a balance obtains between the two . . . both, necessity and freedom, emerge from this struggle simultaneously as victorious and vanquished, and accordingly equal in every respect. But precisely this is doubtlessly the highest manifestation of art, namely, that freedom elevate itself to a position of equity with necessity, and that necessity appear as the equal of freedom without the latter losing in significance in the process. . . . The essence of tragedy is thus an actual and objective conflict between freedom in the subject on the one hand, and necessity on the other, a conflict that does not end such that one or the other succumbs, but rather such that both are manifested in perfect indifference as simultaneously victorious and vanquished. (Schelling 1989, 251)

Hegel of course saw that tragedy consisted in a collision of equally binding ethical powers, a so-called right vs. right view, but that view indexes such

25. One of the more obtuse views in the history of commentary on Hamlet. It is Knight's (1989).

26. Again indispensable here, Gardner (2003), both for its summary and analysis of these attempts and for what he shows about all attempts to reconcile morality and tragedy.

collisions to historical forms of ethical life, and he finally does deflate the paradoxical power of tragedy.

> The true development of the action consists solely in the cancellation of conflicts as conflicts, in the reconciliation of the powers animating action which struggled to destroy one another in their mutual conflict. Only in that case does finality lie not in misfortune and suffering but in the satisfaction of the spirit, because only with such a conclusion can the necessity of what happens to the individuals appear as absolute rationality, and only then can our hearts be morally at peace: shattered by the fate of the heroes but reconciled fundamentally. Only by adherence to this view can Greek tragedy be understood. (Hegel 1975, 1275)[27]

For all the fame of Hegel's theory of tragedy, it is hard for me to imagine anyone "reconciled" to the blind Oedipus, or the dead Iphigenia, or the dead Antigone, and so forth.[28]

It is true that, as Peter Szondi (1961) and others have pointed out, Hegel's whole account of human spirit is a kind of tragic narrative, that the great power in that narrative is "the negative," spirit's own self-destruction. No other philosopher takes as much to heart that law laid down by Zeus in Aeschylus's *Agamemnon*, *pathei mathos*, that we "learn by suffering,"[29] transforming it into a principle of world history itself, such that "[w]orld history is this divine tragedy, where spirit rises up above pity, ethical life, and everything that in other spheres is sacred to it" (Hegel 1995, 306–7). But the collisions are essentially historical, *temporary*, and in what has come to be the most controversial and very likely the least defensible aspect of his philosophy, essentially unbearable, that is, we have to say, metaphysically unsustainable. Spirit, that agentive like-mindedness that is the subject of Hegel's historical account, *cannot* abide such great contradictions in its collective commitments and must seek, always seeks, to resolve them, and it always can and does (something that echoes Kant on the rational intelligibility of the moral world). At some level, say the level of what Hegel called "logic," this must certainly be true, but in any full history of Spirit, there is no reason to think it is true; in the fractured cultural world of post-Hegelian Western and now World Spirit, there is plenty of reason to think it is not true; and in the persistence of a tragic

27. Hegel has often been criticized for, in effect, defusing tragedy, creating a unity where there is none. See Bradley 1962, 375 and Gardner 2003, 243.

28. But see Pinkard's (2015) view, according to which it might be possible to say that, for Hegel, the kinds of "collisions" depicted in tragedy do not have to mean the sort of ethical incoherence I am suggesting Hegel cannot accept (137–58).

29. Aeschylus 2013, 176–78.

dimension in much psychological drama and in such forms as tragic melodrama, there remains a challenge to Hegel's sweeping insistence on universal intelligibility. To put it another way: there is surely a tragic dimension to Hegel's characterization of Spirit itself as a self-inflected "wound," but there is also a betrayal of that dimension in his claim, really nothing more than a Kantian hope disguised as metaphysics, that "[t]he wounds of the spirit heal and leave no scars behind; it is not the deed which is imperishable, but rather the deed is repossessed by spirit into itself" (Hegel 2018, 387).[30]

There is one qualification here that should be mentioned. It is possible to argue that these remarks by Hegel concern his interpretation of Greek tragedy and need not necessarily be taken as representative of Hegel's views on the fate of the various collisions well known in modern societies as a whole, as if he were a reconciliationist with regard to both. Terry Pinkard (2012) has argued that in this latter context Hegel means to show us that we can become reconciled to living with the unresolvable political and cultural tensions inevitable in a social world that has achieved the level of collective self-consciousness Hegel thinks we have.[31] These are tensions that arise inevitably from our being both natural and spiritual beings (we always remain, as Hegel says, "amphibian" creatures, the very image of an inherent duality that we nevertheless successfully live out); they can be recontextualized in terms of practical problems to be addressed, even if this all means we must be content with not happy but at least meaningful lives.

But these sorts of tensions and collisions are not "tragic" ones in the sense we have been discussing, and even Pinkard argues that Hegel has given us a way of "taming" such tensions. That may all be true, in other words, but it does not touch the challenge raised by tragedy.

Tragedy's Challenge

Where does this leave us? We can begin to formulate an answer by returning to the origins of much of this discussion, the first attempt to rationalize tragedy from a philosophical point of view, Aristotle's. Recall that besides defining tragedy in terms of the plot, the reversal and recognition decisive for

30. See again Pinkard 2015: "What then of people who do not carry out what is required of them? Or those who openly defy them or even unwittingly violate them? It cannot be the case that they will just get away with it. The very nature of the world has to be such that justice will be restored" (142). This may be Hegel's view but it is ad hoc and unconvincing.

31. See also Pinkard 2017. In the latter, his case against reading Hegel as a simple "organicist" or social "holist," and this by attention to what Pinkard calls "infinite ends," is also important in any such discussion.

the hero (the moment when the *hamartia* is realized, already the start of a moralization), tragedy is also defined by the response of the audience, pity and fear. But according to the *Rhetoric*, pity and fear must work together in a tragic response.[32] We pity those things happening to someone else that we fear could happen to us, and we fear those things that, were they to happen to us, would make us fit subjects of pity. If we experience fear without pity, we have something like a contemporary horror movie. If we experience pity without fear, we have a mere tearjerker or "weepie." Our fear cuts off sentimental and potentially patronizing pity, and our pity reveals that we find the suffering undeserved; it blocks any indignant moralism. We find that we cannot that say that the victim/hero got what he or she deserved, and we find we cannot say that he was a victim of a heartless universe, for he brought about what happened himself. But this also means that if we exclude the idea that there is some flaw or sin or defect (*hamartia*),[33] as we must if we rightly emphasize the unavoidability of what the hero is called on to do, then our judgment is completely stymied. That is, there is something we can't make ethical sense of. And it is *this* that can be put in either a "Kantian" or a much more radical way.

We can say that there is something *we* can't make sense of. There is a possible sense to be made, or at the very least we can't rule that out, but we are finite. It is beyond us to understand not just this event and outcome, but what sort of a human world as a whole it could be if we can't integrate these deeply significant events into any general sense of such a world. (Or, as we saw in Kant, *just* that absence must mean, has to mean—and what could this "requirement" be?—that there is *another* world, a just world of absolute meaning awaiting us.)

Or, more radically and more in keeping with the tragic perspective, we could say: there is no sense to be made. The latter, tragic challenge to philosophy is not in the name of something we desperately need to know but cannot (until we finally do, in the case of Hegel), but in the name of the utter absence of anything to be known. There is no "ground" for the collisions that could account for their inevitable emergence. There is no unity intimated or pointed to that could give us some hope for resolution.

This seems to us impossible to say. Agamemnon, we need badly to say, could have and should have acted otherwise; something must have gone wrong in an avoidable way. It makes no sense to us to say that he "had to kill" Iphigenia,

32. See the useful discussion of *Rhetoric* 2 in Salkever 1986, 294ff.

33. This challenge to intelligibility holds even with less moralizing translations, such as "error," "misjudgment," or "missing the mark."

even if the logic of the play as a genuine tragedy insists on it. Likewise with Medea, with Creon, with Oedipus. Lear and Cordelia, Desdemona, Banquo, all "did not have to die," we insist; all of this was avoidable, and even if not, some sense, a lesson in humility or prudence or self-doubt, or something, should be "learned" from the suffering we see and experience in some way ourselves. Even Nietzsche, after all, tried to say that the very depth of tragic senselessness, the futility of the attempted emergence of Apollonian order out of Dionysian chaos, could provide us with "affirmation," an "aesthetic justification," if only by the magnificence and beauty of the futile but heroic effort itself. What we need in our response to tragedy is not understanding, but strength. And then Nietzsche, perhaps prompted by reflections like these, more committed later to tragedy just as it is, rejected this *Birth of Tragedy* view as "romantic," turning instead to the mysterious "Eternal Return of the Same" as a source of affirmation.

One reason we feel compelled to insist on this denial of the radically tragic, and the reason why it seems right to say that the tragic perspective, understood as radically as suggested above, can be understood as a challenge to philosophy itself, can be traced back to the deepest assumption in Western thought. The best way to understand that assumption, Parmenides' identification of Being and Thinking, is as the assumption that to be is to be intelligible. There cannot be anything in principle unintelligible. This was put in quite a radical form by Parmenides because he turned immediately to one of the most difficult issues, nonbeing. Since nonbeing could not be, since it was *alogos*, anything that assumed it, like change or differentiation, must not be either. But the assumption, no matter the complications of negative ontologies, is still deeply familiar to us. It is not an empirical truth that it is not possible to answer a question about why an event, a rise in temperature, say, occurred by saying, "there was no reason, no cause; it just occurred." That cannot be. This does not mean that much of what humans do we cannot find initially unintelligible. They act irrationally. They do what they fully know they have no good reason to do, and even what they know they have powerful reasons not to do. But we do not accept "that they just acted," that there is no way to account for "what led them to do that." (There is no greater rationalist here than Freud, as another way of making the point.)

However much more there is to say about this, Kant and Hegel certainly share the Greek principle that, as Hegel recalled, "*nous* rules the world."[34] In

34. I am clearly interpreting this aphorism by Anaxagoras in a way that has been traditional from Aristotle to Hegel: that the world has an intelligible structure, that to be is to be intelligible. As Karl Ameriks has pointed out, though, Nietzsche interprets Anaxagoras as saying something like: the world is (or is as if) the product of a distinctive intelligence, a person, an agent. Quoting

the practical domain of human action, what renders the actions intelligible, the reasons for which people undertake them, are, in Kant, either moral or prudential. And moral rationality is absolute; even prudential considerations and the deeds they motivate must be morally permissible, and many powerfully self-interested possibilities or prudentially wise deeds that are not morally permissible are proscribed. And Kant clearly thinks that many considerations that seem innocent enough, harmlessly prudential, nevertheless have moral dimensions that must be taken into account. There is a kind of obsessiveness sometimes in his search for comprehensive moral intelligibility, in his interest in such questions as why opium addiction is more base than drunkenness, how much wine one might drink before it becomes morally problematic, or how many guests it is proper to invite to a dinner. Various traits one might consider just character flaws in a general sense have according to him a moral dimension: arrogance, servility, moral "flabbiness." Why is it a question of "*Recht*" that (male) wig makers should have the vote, but not barbers? He thinks there is a kind of practical intelligibility, a justification, for the nuclear family, gender roles, monarchy, and so forth.

One challenge to Kant's attempt to moralize everything is simply the existence of contingency, and so there are unacknowledged and wholly contingent sociohistorical habits of mind behind such views. But we believe that that is how we render the parochial views (if that is what we think they are) intelligible, and we try to account further for why just those habits are as they are. The tragic challenge is more serious and goes well beyond similar considerations that are often confused with it, like why innocent children die and the wicked prosper. If the morally impossible is unavoidable and necessary, and yet bearing the burden of the deed is equally unavoidable and necessary, and without expiation, then there is a kind of moral incoherence that is a distinctive and disturbing form of unintelligibility. If morality makes sense or ethical life is rational, this moral incoherence should not be. The tragic occurs within that frame of possible intelligibility and fails to be intelligible. (By a failure of intelligibility I mean simply representing virtuous persons whose very virtue necessitates actions that are at the same time base, or representing virtuous obligations that are necessary and unavoidable, but *necessarily* futile, not merely uncertain of realization. The challenge is to a deep principle assumed since the very beginning of reflection on the good: the unity of the virtues.) The challenge certainly doesn't mean that, therefore, there is no such

Nietzsche, "As Anaxagoras would say, '*Nous* has the privilege of free random choice [*Willkür*]; it may start at random, it depends only on itself. . . . Nous has no duty and hence no purpose or goal.'" Ameriks connects this to the early romantic reaction to Kant as well. Ameriks 2012, 317.

thing as morality or ethical life, but the comprehensiveness and absoluteness of such perspectives are challenged. In Kant, this would allow a distinction between morality and moralism that he cannot make.[35] What Agamemnon did or what Othello did is simply and unqualifiedly morally horrific and to be absolutely condemned; end of story. In Hegel, if a conflict between right and right emerges, it cannot be permanent; a resolution can and, given the rationalist assumption just discussed, must be found.

The claim that tragedy challenges any claim for complete ethical coherence is subject to so many conceivable objections, starting with the unavoidable imprecision of the concept of tragedy itself, and extending into how a literary object might be said to challenge philosophy, that it is impossible to formulate the challenge without extensive interpretive work on many individual tragedies with such a question in mind. Or, at least, I find it impossible. This is not even to mention philosophers like Nietzsche and Heidegger who, responding to something like this challenge of comprehensive metaphysical intelligibility, set out to begin philosophy anew, still as philosophy but now as what Nietzsche called "psychology" and what Heidegger called "thinking." I can only suggest one final way of making the main point. In his magisterial essay on *King Lear*, "The Avoidance of Love," Stanley Cavell is trying to explain the unavailability any longer of an aesthetic, especially dramatic tragic point of view, something he thinks we see happening with the ending of *Lear*. (He is trying to make a difficult point that would require an extensive exposition, that "Tragedy has moved into the world, and with it the world has become theatrical" [Cavell 1979, 344].) I suggest instead that we read his words as doing complete justice to the tragic point of view itself, as I have been saying, simply as it is. It has not lost its "effectiveness" in any moral or rational sense. It never had any; never could have had any. That is its point.

> That one has to die in order to become reborn is one tragic fact; that one's wholeness deprives others of their life is another; that one's love becomes incompatible with one's life and kills the thing it loves is another. Lear is reborn, but into his old self. That is no longer just tragic, it suggests that tragedy itself has become ineffective, out-worn, because now even death does not overcome our difference. Here again, Gloucester's life amplifies Lear's. For it is one thing, and tragic, that we can learn only through suffering. It is something else that we have nothing to learn from it. . . . Our tragic fact is that we find ourselves at the cause of tragedy, but without finding ourselves. (Cavell 2015, 340 and 349)

35. Kant can be very clear about what he thinks of any way of representing the human fate that does not portray moral progress. See his remarks in "Concerning the Terroristic Way of Representing Human History" (Kant 1979, 145ff.).

3

The Status of Literature in Hegel's *Phenomenology of Spirit*: On the Lives of Concepts

Beauty's Hatred

My question is a simple one, and, on the face of it, may not seem important. Why does Hegel, in a chapter called "Absolute Knowing," end his most exciting and original work, the Jena *Phenomenology of Spirit*, with a quotation, or rather a significant misquotation, of a poet? The poet is Schiller and the poem is his 1782 "Freundschaft" (Friendship). This immediately turns into two questions: Why are the last words *not* Hegel's own, and why *are* they rather a poet's?

I will turn to the details in a moment, but, as noted, such an inquiry may not be worth the trouble. Authors, even philosophers (who, with only a few exceptions, are not known for their literary style), like to cite poets and other writers as a way of summarizing a point, a way of concluding an argument with a dramatic flourish, a way of demonstrating their erudition, or simply as a way of relieving the pressure of sustained and difficult analysis. The device could be merely rhetorical. And, in Hegel's day, authors were often so well read in and familiar with important writers that they clearly cited from memory, frequently carelessly and inaccurately. After all, Hegel's citation in the section "Pleasure and Necessity" of four lines from Goethe's so-called 1790 "Faust-Fragment" is also a misquotation, although in that case, too, the alterations are philosophically significant. But perhaps such carelessness is all there is to it.

But one ought to hesitate before dismissing the issue. For one thing, a mere nine years later, in the *Heidelberger Niederschrift* of the "Introduction" to the *Lectures on the History of Philosophy*, Hegel makes it quite clear that he can quote this particular passage with perfect fidelity when that suits his purposes. For another, this is not the only time a literary work is cited in the *Phenomenology*, and the citations raise a general, not a particular, question. There are many other such instances (Goethe, Sophocles, Diderot, and Jacobi, as well as Schiller, are famous instances), and these invocations do not appear merely illustrative or summary. They enter the text as evidence of a certain kind about Hegel's unusual topic—"spirit's experience of itself." In his discussion of Greek *Sittlichkeit* or "the true Spirit," Sophoclean tragedy is not merely illustrative of some phenomenon of interest to Hegel; it is the phenomenon, and it is hard to imagine Hegel saying what he wants to say about the breakdown in the authority of ethical norms without Attic tragedy at the center of the discussion. (The passages do raise the question, though, of whether there is anything important—as there seems to be—in these being *aesthetic* phenomena, works of the imagination, rather than historical or social events.) For another, this was an extraordinary period in German aesthetics, what with positions by Lessing, Novalis, Schiller, Schlegel, and many others swirling around or about to appear, and it would be unusual if Hegel did not have at least the rudiments of his own theory about the relation between literature (or "die schöne Kunst," fine art in general) and philosophy, and it would be unusual if elements of some view about that relationship were not at work in the treatment of literature in the *Phenomenology*. Of course, much of that account will be made explicit only several years later, in the lectures on aesthetics Hegel gave four times in the 1820s; but some view about the relation is explicit in the *Phenomenology*, and it makes the closing quotation even more mysterious.

I mean, for example, the dramatic remarks made in the preface about the role of beauty in the work. The passage is so striking that I will take the liberty of quoting it at length.

> The activity of separating is the force and labor of the understanding, the most astonishing and the greatest of all the powers, or rather, which is the absolute power. The circle, which, enclosed within itself, is at rest and which, as substance, sustains its moments, is the immediate and is, for that reason, an unsurprising relationship. However, the accidental, separated from its surroundings, attains an isolated freedom and its own proper existence only in its being bound to other actualities and only as existing in their context; as such, it is the tremendous power of the negative; it is the energy of thinking, of the pure I. Death, if that is what we wish to call that non-actuality, is the most fearful thing of all, and to keep and hold fast to what is dead requires only the greatest force. Powerless beauty detests the understanding because the understanding expects of her what she cannot do. However, the life of spirit is not a life that is fearing death and austerely saving itself from ruin; rather, it bears death calmly, and in death, it sustains itself. Spirit only wins its truth by finding itself in its absolute disruption. (Hegel 2018, §32)

This passage would seem consistent with Hegel's deep suspicion and criticism of Schlegel's blurring of the lines between philosophy and poetry, and even with Hegel's dismissal of those who get too caught up in what he called the "mythic" dimensions of Platonic dialogues. But considered in the light of the *Phenomenology* as a whole, this passage must be counted an exaggeration, somewhat one-sided. The "cutting" power of the analytic understanding, of what he elsewhere calls reflection, to dissolve harmonious unity, like the harmonious unity of ethical life, indeed to "tear it apart" (*zerrissen*) and kill it, is so highly praised here that concentrating on such a passage in isolation would make it hard to imagine how Hegel ever acquired the reputation of a *Versöhnungsphilosoph*, a philosopher of reconciliation. He seems like Adorno *avant la lettre*, praising a wholly "negative dialectic." That is, the possibility of reintegration, *Aufhebung*, and affirmation is not as evident in such formulations as it might be. The power of tearing apart the life of *Geist* is ascribed to the understanding (*Verstand*), but we are told nothing here about how *Geist* might also find itself "in" what it has also torn apart. It seems clear that ultimately this sort of opposition between beauty (*Schönheit*) and the understanding (*Verstand*) prepares us for the standpoint of reason (*Vernunft*), a point of view wherein the one-sidedness and division of this contrast can be transcended. Clearly the emphasis has been corrected by the time we reach the end of the work, and some great faith might be expressed in the poet's power by giving him "the last word." And then there is also the fact that this extreme contrast is itself portrayed as if it were a psychological drama (that is, portrayed in a beautiful image, poetically) between *Schönheit* and *Verstand*, and in the personified metaphorical claim that beauty "hates" the understanding for expecting of it what it cannot do.

But *what* is it that beauty cannot do? And why would the understanding, as though it were a bullying character in a play, expect beauty to do something that it could not do? What kind of questions are these?

If we simply adopt the language of the image for a while, then what beauty cannot do is apparently "tarry [*verweilen*] with the negative," look it in the face, endure the self-dissolving character of the human experience of the human. (Novalis's claim that Greek art aestheticized and thereby repressed death and "the negative" comes to mind.) These are odd claims, but in the manner typical of Hegel's idealism, this must be because such disintegration and death cannot, from the aesthetic point of view, be properly understood, and so is experienced as a contingent, irreconcilable event, a surd. This thought suggests something that is not surprising, given the prominence of the aesthetic theories of Kant and Schiller: the proper function of works and things of beauty is *resistance* to disintegration and the *creation* of harmony and unity.

On the other hand, and perhaps more importantly, the passage also rather subtly implies some limitation *on the part of an analytic understanding*. Asking *die Schönheit* to do something it cannot do is, after all, a reasonable ground for the indignation of *die Schönheit*, and it points to the limitations of the point of view of *Verstand* that dominate Hegel's other discussions of this faculty in the rest of his corpus—as in his criticisms of modern philosophies of reflection (Locke, Kant) and in his contrast between *Verstand* and *Vernunft*.

These are mere hints about the link between imaginative, aesthetic phenomena, which Hegel connects to some sort of living unity or resistance to disintegration, and the limitations of the analytic understanding. Since beauty is said to be "lacking strength," it (art) will not be the force that unites what has been pulled asunder, but apparently it is well suited to embody and manifest such new living unities when they arise or are otherwise achieved. But the hints are at least suggestive about the place of *die Schönheit* in a philosophical account like Hegel's, and perhaps even about the much stronger claim concerning the impossibility of doing something like what Hegel is attempting without some reliance on literary phenomena.

The *Phenomenology*

So what *is* Hegel attempting in the *Phenomenology*? Officially, the *Phenomenology* is the "science of the experience of consciousness," as in its alternate title. Experience, however, cannot be described from a sideways-on or third-person point of view. If it is to be made present to us, it must in a sense be reenacted, as if from the point of view of the experiencing subject. This already brings us close to our theme. Such a reenactment must be a kind of dramatic exercise, so it is not for nothing that the *Phenomenology* is often called a *Bildungsroman*.[1] We must be told "what it is like" to be *Geist*, as in one well-known formulation of the subjective viewpoint. But this experience is also said to be developmental. The experience itself counts as the education of a "natural consciousness" burdened with many dualisms (subject and object, self and other, individual and community, inner and outer, human and Divine) up to the standpoint of "absolute knowing," which is absolute precisely by virtue of having reached a way of understanding human experience (and therewith a way of experiencing) that has overcome such dualisms without collapsing them.

1. See Royce 1919, 147–56.

The "engine" driving forward this development is abstractly described as *das Negative*, the negative, and more poetically is said to be a kind of "violence" that consciousness suffers at its own hands, as it struggles with its most basic issue—its attempt at self-knowledge.

There is a more general characterization by Hegel of what he is about that brings us closer to the function of literature. Indeed, it is a passage that follows closely upon the extraordinary evocation of beauty's hatred for the understanding that was quoted above.

> The course of studies of the ancient world is distinct from that of modern times in that the ancient course of studies consisted in a thoroughgoing cultivation of natural consciousness. Experimenting particularly with each part of its existence and philosophizing about everything it came across, the ancient course of studies fashioned itself into an altogether active universality. In contrast, in modern times, the individual finds the abstract form ready-made. The strenuous effort to grasp it and make it his own is more of an unmediated drive to bring the inner to the light of day; it is the truncated creation of the universal rather than the emergence of the universal from out of the concrete, from out of the diversity found in existence. Nowadays the task before us consists not so much in purifying the individual of the sensuously immediate and in making him into a thinking substance which has itself been subjected to thought; it consists instead in doing the very opposite. It consists in actualizing and spiritually animating the universal through the sublation of fixed and determinate thoughts. (Hegel 2018, §33)

This claim about actualizing and especially spiritualizing and enlivening the universal is an extremely valuable hint, and a deep characterization of the *Phenomenology*'s task that has not received the attention it deserves in commentary on the work. The most interesting way to begin to demonstrate this is somewhat risky from a scholarly point of view. It involves reading the early Hegel (the Jena Hegel of the *Phenomenology*) at least partly and in a preliminary way in the light of the Berlin Hegel of the 1820s and the author of the four-lecture series on the fine arts (1820, 1823, 1826, 1828). I have no evidence whatsoever that Hegel had even in a preliminary way worked out during the Jena period the major claims of these lectures, but it is striking that one of the tasks he attributes to philosophy so early on—"enlivening" concepts or norms—plays such a crucial role in those lectures.[2] Perhaps the central conceptual claim throughout about fine art concerns the issue of *Lebendigkeit*

2. I am not claiming that the Berlin lectures can always be used this way. There are also great differences, as in the Antigone interpretation, for example. See Speight 2001, 52.

(life or enlivening). Understanding that role helps us to clarify the appeal to literature in the *Phenomenology*.

The emphasis on *Lebendigkeit* begins already in the early 1820 lectures, continues throughout, and is quite prominent in the Hotho compilation traditionally used (for all its now well-known problems) as the text of Hegel's theory of fine art. Indeed, one might say that even though Hegel pays homage to Kant for recognizing that the core issue to be grasped in understanding the aesthetic domain is a problem of reflection and of judgment (and not simply "the sensuous" or mere feeling), it is the significance of *Lebendigkeit* that is the right focus in any philosophical aesthetics, not *Zweckmäßigkeit ohne Zweck* (purposefulness without purpose) or harmony as such. A characteristic gloss on the concept of beauty, for example, stresses "the look of independent and total life [*Lebendigkeit*] and freedom which lies at the root of the essence of beauty" (Hegel 1975, 149); and it is not uncommon for him, when discussing the particular arts, especially painting and the lyric, to note that "the life [*Lebendigkeit*] and joy of independent existence in general" can be said to be the true subject matter of art (Hegel 1975, 833). Some of his statements go very far and raise controversial issues both about the arts and about the very structure of Hegel's system.

These passages stress the importance of the mediated point of view on human experience occupied by the fine arts.

> Thereby the sensuous aspect of a work of art, in comparison with the immediate existence of things in general, is elevated to a pure appearance, and the work of art stands in the *middle* [*Mitte*] between immediate sensuousness and ideal thought. It is not yet pure thought, but, despite its sensuousness, is no longer a purely material existent either. (Hegel 1975, 38)

And:

> Therefore the world-view of the Greeks is precisely the milieu [*Mitte*] in which beauty begins its true life and builds its serene kingdom; the milieu [*Mitte*] of free vitality which is not only there naturally and immediately but is generated by spiritual vision and transfigured by art; the milieu [*Mitte*] of a development of reflection and at the same time of that absence of reflection that neither isolates the individual nor can bring back to any positive unity and reconciliation his negativity, grief, and misfortune. (Hegel 1975, 437)

Now in the Hegelian universe, the "middle" is not a bad position to occupy (indeed, it seems the natural Hegelian position), and Hegel goes so far in praising this capacity of the arts that he gives one pause about what appears to be his official, systematic *Encyclopedia* architectonic: "Thinking, however, results in thoughts alone; it evaporates the form of reality into the form of the pure Concept, and even if it grasps and apprehends real things in their particular character and real existence, it nevertheless lifts even this particular sphere into the element of the universal and ideal wherein alone thinking is at home with itself. . . . Thinking is only a reconciliation between reality and truth within thinking itself. But poetic creation and formation is a reconciliation in the form of a real phenomenon itself, even if this form be presented only spiritually" (Hegel 1975, 976). Or consider: "In this way the sensuous aspect of art is spiritualized, since the spirit appears in art as made sensuous" (Hegel 1975, 39).

There are even two passages in the discussion of the lyric that go very far indeed in stressing the indispensability of the aesthetic dimension within, not merely as a preparation or propaedeutic for, the proper expression of philosophical science, and they thereby illuminate the corresponding indispensability of the *Phenomenology* itself. That is, the two familiar disputes about the "dispensability" of art in the modern age and the dispensability of the *Phenomenology* for the "system" are deeply linked. In discussing the role of poetry in a prosaic age, burdened with divisions and dualisms (that is, our age, identified as such since the *Differenzschrift*, the Treatise on Difference), Hegel notes the following.

> In these circumstances poetry needs a more deliberate energy in order to work its way out of the abstractions in the ordinary way of putting things into the concrete life [of a new mode of expression]. But if it attains its aim, not only is it liberated from that separation between thinking, which is concentrated on the universal, and feeling and vision, which seize on the individual, but it also at the same time frees these latter forms of consciousness and their content and objects from their servitude to thinking and conducts them victoriously to reconciliation with the universality of thought. (Hegel 1975, 1006)

In the other passage, having differentiated in his usual way "the imagination of heart and vision" from that "form of the spirit" which deals with "free self-consciousness in a more decisively universal way and in more necessary connectedness" (Hegel 1975, 1128), that is, philosophy, he goes on to say the following: "Yet this form, conversely, is burdened with the abstraction of developing solely in the province of thinking, i.e., of purely ideal universality, so that man in the concrete may find himself forced to express the contents and results of his philosophical mind in a concrete way as penetrated by his heart and vision, his imagination and feeling, in order in this way to have and provide a total expression of his whole inner life" (Hegel 1975, 1128). I am sure that I am not alone in being somewhat taken aback by the phrases "burdened with the abstraction" and "solely in the province of thinking," as if the traditional view of the referent of "absolute knowing"—that the phrase refers to "thought's" self-determinations in the *Science of Logic*—is just in itself already one-sided, incomplete without somehow being thought together with the expression of thought in a "concrete way." The passage suggests that many commentators on Hegel might have been misled a bit by Hegel's claims about the "incompleteness" and partiality of religious and aesthetic representation, as if he meant the picture to look thereby like a simple ascent to what was complete and infinite, leaving behind what was not. Even on the face of it, though, this is a nondialectical and implausible picture of the realm of Absolute Spirit.

Moreover, this is a crucial issue in Hegel that goes back at least to *Glauben und Wissen* (*Faith and Knowledge*) and in essence defines the whole Hegelian project. That is, the issue of how we might understand the indispensability of aesthetic representation in the exposition and demonstration of any truth about what Hegel calls *der Begriff*, the concept, is part and parcel of his early insistence that Kant had strayed from his own greatest insight by abstractly separating the contributions of concept and intuition in experience. The passages are familiar and justifiably well known. Hegel contrasts his own "organic idea of productive imagination" with what he attributes to Kant as "the mechanical relation of a unity of self-consciousness which stands in antithesis to the empirical manifold, either determining it or reflecting on it" (Hegel 1977, 92). And he goes on to note that Kant himself (in the second edition deduction) is led to undermine his own official claims about the strictness of the epistemic separability between conceptions and intuitions in experience: "Hence, the original synthetic unity of apperception is recognized also as the principle of the figurative synthesis; i.e. of the forms of intuition; space and time are themselves conceived as synthetic unities, and spontaneity, the absolute synthetic activity of the productive imagination, is conceived as the principle of the very sensibility which was previously characterized only as receptivity" (Hegel 1977, 69–70). Such remarks, when seen in the light of Hegel's characterizations of the indispensability of aesthetic representation in the expression of philosophical truth, and in the light of his insisting in the *Phenomenology* on the need to spiritualize and enliven (*begeistern* and *beleben*) our concepts, suggest that understanding Hegel will require understanding the appeals to art and literature as much more than the invocation of rich, vivid examples, and as much different from mere propaedeutics for the eventual abandonment of just such forms of expression. The inherent conceptuality of sensory experience, one different from both a "thought determination" and any putative sensory immediacy, as well as the way physical, public actions can be said to bear or manifest practical intentions, the "logic" of this relation, all seem at stake. How might the closing words of the *Phenomenology* contribute to this issue?

We need first a few details from the final paragraphs of the last chapter. The main general point to make is that the discussion in these passages continually suggests how misleading it is to understand the *Phenomenology* in terms of the Wittgenstein image that one hears so often invoked in discussions of the book—that it is a ladder to be kicked away once climbed. It is true, of course, that Hegel himself uses this image in §26 of the *Phenomenology*: "science on its part requires that self-consciousness should have raised itself into this Aether in order to be able to live—and [actually] to live. Conversely, the individual has the right to demand that Science should at least provide him with the *ladder* to this standpoint" (Hegel 2018, §26). (We can note here already the problem of being able to live, and of life itself.) The point that is emerging in the passages we have looked at is that it would be precisely the wrong conclusion to draw from this image that such a ladder could be "kicked away." That would result in the standpoint, as it were, of "falling to the ground," of collapsing. Such an error would be the same as thinking that the *Science of Logic* provided something like the conceptual "foundation" or underlying real structure of the world and its appearances.[3] The language in these passages is extremely compressed, but what Hegel is getting at can be sensed even in his most abstract formulations. For example,

> For this reason, it must be said that nothing is known that is not in experience, or, as it can be otherwise expressed, nothing is known that is not available as felt truth, as the eternal which is inwardly revealed, as the holy which is the object of faith, or whatever expressions are otherwise put to use. For experience consists in precisely this, namely, that the content—and the content is spirit—is in itself, is substance and is therefore the object of consciousness. However, this substance, which is spirit, is its coming-to-be what it, the substance, is in itself; and it is as this coming-to-be which is taking a reflective turn into itself that spirit is truly in itself spirit. (Hegel 2018, §802)

A more formulaic expression: "Just as Spirit in its existence is not richer than Science, so too spirit in its content is no poorer" (Hegel 2018, §805). And in a passage stated in almost biblical form: "However, the other aspect of spirit's

3. Again, there is the same error in thinking that because Hegel claimed in the *Aesthetics* lectures that art could no longer on its own convey Spirit's highest truths about itself, either art could manifest no relevant or important truths, or philosophy's putatively "higher" truths could be completely and perfectly expressed in conceptual terms alone, without a concept's *Wirklichkeit*, its reality or effectiveness. But this is clearly a different subject.

coming-to-be, history, is that knowing self-mediating coming-to-be—the spirit relinquished into time."

However, this relinquishing (*Entäusserung*) is likewise the relinquishing of itself; the negative is the negative of itself (Hegel 2018, §808). (I say biblical here because *Entäusserung* is Luther's term in his translation of the Bible for *kenosis*, and Arnold V. Miller, one of the English translators, actually translates here *Entäusserung* with the transliterated word *kenosis*, alongside "externalization.")[4] The religious notion too of God's "emptying of himself" into the world, understood not as a loss (in conceptual terms, say, a loss of determinacy) but as a self-realization, will play a large role in Hegel's poetic ending.

These formulations, together with the remarks on beauty and the understanding, together with the emphasis on enlivening and spiritualizing, together with the role assigned such an enlivening by the aesthetics lectures, prepare us then for the closing passage.

Schiller

Hegel extracts the couplet that ends the *Phenomenology* from Schiller's 1782 poem (in its first version) "Freundschaft." As already noted, and as we shall see in more detail, Hegel misquotes the couplet. He is also quoting out of context, since the poem as a whole concerns friendship between two persons, treated in the poem as an example or image of a possible reconciliation between the *Geisterreich*, or "realm of spirit," and the *Körperweltgewühle*, or the "throng of the corporeal world," as well as between an isolated self and an other. Hegel focuses attention only on the divine side of the issue. One overarching idea in the poem is that friendship is expressive of what we might call a divine logic for the world, one particularly appealing to Hegel, according to which one knows and loves oneself only in one's reflection in another ("Nur in dir bestaun' ich mich" [Only in you do I admire myself] from stanza 5), and that this is true of the divine creator's relation to his creations with the crucial difference that a "world-master" (*Weltenmeister*) cannot find an equal, a true mirror of himself, and confronts instead a "foaming" infinity. Humans in love *can* enjoy a divine "süssen Sympathie," sweet sympathy, with another. (One of the best couplets is: "Todte Gruppen sind wir—wenn wir hassen / Götter—wenn wir liebend uns umfassen" (We are dead groups when we hate / Gods when we lovingly embrace each other). Here is the original last stanza of Schiller's poem:

4. I am grateful to Terry Pinkard for correspondence about this issue.

> Freundlos war der große Weltenmeister,
> Fühlte *Mangel*—darum schuf er Geister,
> Selige Spiegel *seiner* Seligkeit!—
>
> Fand das höchste Wesen schon kein gleiches,
> Aus dem Kelch des ganzen Seelenreiches
> Schäumt *ihm*—die Unendlichkeit. (Schiller 1965, 93)
>
> (Friendless was the great world-master,
> Felt lack—and so created spirits,
> Blessed mirrors of *his own* blessedness!—
>
> The highest essence found no equal,
> From the chalice of the entire realm of souls
> Foams up to *him*—infinity.)

Hegel however cites only two lines:

> Aus dem Kelche dieses Geistesreiches
> Schäumt ihm seine Unendlichkeit.

These brief phrases represent several alterations of the original, all of which have the effect of making Schiller's work seem like a close expression of Hegel's theory: (1) In the closing sentence of the chapter, immediately before the quotation, Hegel refers to the *Weltenmeister* as a way of alluding to "absolute Geist," and he suggests that such a divine being would be "lifeless and alone" (here is the reference to *Lebendigkeit* again) were it not for the "foaming up" of *his own* infinity, interpreted by Hegel as "the inwardizing" (*die Erinnerung*) of its own actual history, its own "actuality." The two lines that Hegel reformulates, in other words, suggest a satisfying self-recognition and apparent self-satisfaction in spirit's products. (2) and (3) "The chalice of the entire realm of souls" ("Kelch des ganzen Seelenreiches") has become "the chalice of *this* realm of *spirits*" ("Kelche dieses Geistes-reiches"). And (4) "infinity" ("die Unendlichkeit") has become "*his own* infinitude" ("seine Unendlichkeit"). Once again, the original suggests that human beings can experience in love and friendship a unity and consolation that any divine being, however divine, also requires. But the Hegelian version shifts the emphasis to the achievement of the perspective of "absolute Spirit" and that subject's experience of *itself* in the infinity of its world. Even though Schiller refers to "Zahlenloser Geister" (countless Spirits) in stanza 8, the substitution in the last lines of *Geist* for *Seele* "Hegelianizes" the passage and has it asking about *Geist*'s experience of itself in *its own creations*, in the historical achievement of forms of nonalienating practices and institutions, *Geistesreiches*, rather than in "the" infinity of the independent or (as in Hegel's *Anthropologie*, natural) "soul" world. And this is not a terminological issue alone. It suggests the answer to the question posed at the beginning of this chapter about the unique appropriateness of works of art for Hegel's purposes in the *Phenomenology*. The *Reich des Geistes* is the *Reich* of *Geist*'s productions, especially reflective attempts at self-knowledge. *Geist* indeed is itself paradoxically said by Hegel to be "the result of itself." It is whatever it understands itself to be, if it can come to understand itself as expressed in its productions.

The citation and Hegel's alterations introduce several issues, but I want to conclude here by mentioning only two. First, the passage introduces us to the language of Hegel's most frequent characterizations of the core issue in his philosophy. That issue is the problem of freedom or *Geist*'s self-determination, and what counts as the true *Verwirklichung*, the "realization" of freedom. In one form, the problem is how to understand how the free activity of making judgments, taking a stand of sorts about how things are (rather than having been caused to be in some doxastic state), could be said to have the required objective purport, the directedness to objects, necessary for such a judging. There is, then, also the question of the normative credentials of such judgments. If they are "freely" made, not mental events that happen to us, how do we hold ourselves and each other to account in the making of such claims? Empirical, nonempirical, aesthetic, and practical judgments are all in play in this issue. Second, the very same issues are involved when Hegel addresses the question of intentional action as well. How should we understand the formation and execution of intentions, which seem matters "internal" to reflective deliberation alone, and their "other," the "outer" movements in public space that seem to issue from such intentions? In both cases we are responsive to reasons about what to believe and do, and being responsive to reasons just is the exercise of rational and so free agency in the post-Kantian tradition. The problem, of course, is that we are not just or exclusively responsive to reasons. We are also subject to the laws of nature in the exercise of our sensory capacities, and we are also so subject in the storms of passions and instincts, and in our movements in space. And in both cases, Hegel suggests frequently, the basic "logical" or conceptual problem is understanding the proper logical or conceptual relation between "inner" and "outer" (what we might call the relation between mind and world in thought and in action), and in both cases he tells us often that the way to understand the issue is not as a duality, but as a kind of speculative identity.

Given these formulations, any summary of Hegel's own position about such a speculative identity sounds just as metaphorical and opaque as this talk of a divine being's experiencing the foaming of its own infinity from a chalice. For he says such things as: concepts and the manifold should not be understood as if either the formation or application of a concept is a matter of such a norm's being restricted or constrained or directly and immediately guided by some exogenous "material." Rather the concept "negates" its own separate or logically distinct status and so "negates" itself,[5] or even should be said to "give itself its own content." And these formulations, since they seem to suggest a weird sort of dependence of the world and embodied action on "thought's self-determination," continue to resist interpretations that could allow Hegel to play much of a role in any contemporary discussion of the issues. Indeed, they are so opaque that they cannot even be referred to as dead historical positions. What "positions"?

However, at the very least the relevance of the poetic claim to Hegel's mature position is not hard to establish. Schiller's poem is about friendship and, at one point (stanza 8), love, and not only is that theme important for the practical philosophy of the young Hegel's writings on Christianity, but it plays a profound role in Hegel's attempt to explain the heart of his theoretical philosophy, his *Science of Logic*. One example can establish that. In his *Begriffslogik*, when he is discussing "the universal Concept" and claims that "the universal is therefore *free power*" (Hegel 2010, 603), he hastens to point out that this should not be understood as something like the exercise of the subject's organizing and abstracting power *over* something separate and resistant. (As one might conceive the rule of a divine *Weltenmeister*.) What is "other" than *der Begriff* can itself play its role as other only as so conceptualized. To explain what he means by that, he makes the following extraordinary remark: "The universal . . . is itself and takes the other within its embrace, but without doing violence to it; on the contrary, the universal is, in its other, in peaceful communion with itself. We have called it free power, but it could also be called *free love* and *boundless blessedness*, for it bears itself toward the other as toward its own self; in it, it has returned to itself" (Hegel 2010, 603). In the poetic sense, this is not legislative power sitting on its self-sufficient throne, legislating to the world, or what John McDowell might call "frictionless spinning." The suggestion that the logic of the mind-world relation is like the "logic of love" remains a strange and forbidding image, but one gets a glimpse of sorts of how Hegel wants to understand the relations of dependence and

5. Here is a typical statement about negation from his *Berlin Phenomenology*, as challenging to an interpreter now as it must have sounded then to his first readers: "The I is now this subjectivity, this infinite relation to itself, but therein, namely in this subjectivity, lies its negative relation to itself, diremption, differentiation, judgment. The I judges, and this constitutes it as consciousness; it repels itself from itself; this is a logical determination" (Hegel 1981, 2).

independence in human experience when finally understood adequately in Absolute Knowing.

Moreover, in the entire last chapter of the *Phenomenology*, Hegel continually reverts to his account of the nature of action in the two most important accounts of action in the book: section Vc, "Individuality which takes itself to be real in and for itself" (where Hegel tries to show that individuality so conceived, in and for itself, cannot be "real"), and section VIc, "spirit that is certain of itself. Morality," all in order to explain the position achieved by absolute knowledge. In both the relevant sections of the *Phenomenology of Spirit*, Hegel tries to exhibit phenomenologically the severe limitations of this position and proposes instead to look not at several distinct, causally initiated phases of an action, but to view actions as evolving and changing expressions of a subject's intentions over an extended time, determinate only in extended confrontation and reaction within what Terry Pinkard has called "social space," and not the causal results of a discrete event. That is, Hegel denies that the right way to fix the determinacy of an action, to determine just what it was that was done, is to look exclusively to a subject's *ex ante* formulated intention. He insists that such putative intentions cannot, if they are to be understood as "actual" intentions, be temporally isolated from their expression in action, that such subjective formulations and reasons change in the course of the deed, and that it is quite possible that persons can be wrong about their actual intentions and motivation, that only as expressed in the deed in this public, social space is it clear what they are committed to and sometimes clear why. This is a counterintuitive position. It means that a subject can often only "learn from the deed," as Hegel says, what it is he did and what his stake in the deed actually was, and it implies a deep dependence on the reception of the deed in society as helping to fix determinately what in fact was done. But in our context, it becomes intuitively clearer why Hegel is referring so frequently to this position as a way of explaining why there is no strict separation between a concept and its "actualization" or "satisfaction," why the comprehension of conceptual content requires attention to the "fluidity" (*Flüssigkeit*) and "living spirituality" (*lebendige Geistigkeit*) of a norm, what I have identified as the core position of the *Phenomenology of Spirit*. In Hegel's view in the relevant sections of the *Phenomenology of Spirit*, actually to have an intention *is* to struggle to express that intention in a public and publicly contestable deed, subject to great temporal fluidity and to appropriations and interpretations by others that can greatly alter one's own sense of what one is about.

It is, to use Hegel's term, to "sacrifice" the purity and certainty (and so security) of one's self-understanding and to subject oneself to the reactions, counterclaims, and challenges of others. Were one to remain in the Inner Citadel of Subjective Certainty or cling only to what can be formally definable, one's self-understanding would have to remain suspended in doubt. The question of whether I am actually committed to what I take myself to be, the question of the *Wirklichkeit* of any self-image or any claim about normative propriety, would be left suspended and because of that could be counted as much a fantasy of resolve or intention or commitment as genuine. Action must be understood as a self-negation in this sense, a negation of the subject's pretension to complete ownership of the nature and import of the deed, and therewith the sharing of such authority with others, or even the sacrifice of philosophy as an ahistorical a priori discipline in the traditional, both Platonic and Kantian, senses. All of this can seem like "the pathway of despair" just in the sense Hegel suggested, "the loss of oneself." But as in many other examples of Hegel's Christian imagery, the experiential *Bildung* can show that by this loss of a false independence and mastery, one has gained true independence, referred to in the *Rechtsphilosophie* as "being oneself in an another" ("in diesem Anderen bei sich selbst") (Hegel 1991, §7).[6] What, then, would it mean *not* to think of absolute *Geist* as *der große Weltenmeister* or a self-sufficient but lonely *Wesenlenker*, a guide for all creatures? I have been trying to suggest that the closing image of the *Phenomenology* does not refer to a pantheistic metaphysics, or a Neoplatonic view about the underlying "divine mind" or "cosmic spirit" of which everything natural and *geistig* is an expression. He is making use of the imagery of such positions to suggest a radically different view on the relation between free agents and the world in which that agency is embodied and expressed; such agents are neither divinely sovereign nor pulled and pushed hither and yon by natural forces. That, I am claiming, is what Hegel's philosophy is simply *about*. The analogy with the logic of action

6. Hegel makes what he would consider a "logical" point about the major events in "both" bibles. The story of creation in the Hebrew Bible represents the insufficiency of a God merely contained within himself, and so the need for him to "empty" (*entäussern*) himself in creating the world. There is little doubt that Hegel accepts the Lutheran take on this word—Luther's translation for kenosis—and goes farther, claiming as a meaning for the image that God had to empty or lose or externalize himself in what appeared other than him in order finally to be God. I follow here Terry Pinkard's (Hegel 2018) translation and reading in his rendering of the *Phenomenology of Spirit*. And in the New Testament the imagery is even more Hegelian. God the Father had to become his own son, externalized in the world and lost to him (to himself), preparing the way for reconciliation, or *der heilige Geist*, the Holy Spirit. The deeper point here is also, I would argue, ultimately politico-ethical: Christ's iconic status as both Master and Servant, his own father and his own son, at the same time.

is the issue he constantly returns to, especially in the last chapter, to make this point, and it is very revealing that he does so.

So from an initial, subjectively self-certain point of view, action looks like a self-negation, a violation of the purity and exclusive ownership of the deed thought to be a condition for seeing myself in the deed and so for freedom. But Hegel tries to illuminate the enormous burden carried by such a self-understanding, tries to render experientially plausible the claim that such stubbornness will eventually "break" under such a burden (as in "das Brechen des harten Herzens" in *Moralität*), and that ultimately such a subject will come to understand such a negation of its own pure subjectivity as the true *realization* of such subjectivity. This "burden" is not solely or even mainly a matter of logically incompatible commitments, and this "breaking" is not merely the conceptual resolution of such incompatibilities. To think of it this way would be to perpetuate the one-sidedness, the hold of which the *Phenomenology of Spirit* is trying to break.

But if this is all true, or at least plausible, what does it mean for the status of literature in the *Phenomenology of Spirit*? The analogy we have been constructing would hold that it is a conceptual confusion to regard an agent's deeds as if they were somehow imperfect expressions of what was purely intended, that the true meaning of the action must reside in the pure intending of the agent, as if all the rest, the actual results, should be seen as the product of intervening contingencies. Instead, as the intention unfolds in the deed over time, it could be said to "acquire" the only determinate shape it could have. This is a hard thought for Hegel to convey. It suggests that it is "in" the complex deed, as that deed is subject to the interpretations and reactions of others, that the intention, or the subject's stake in and sense of the deed, "lives," and we are on the contrary deeply wedded to the notion that a "prior" intention is "responsible" for the deed. Likewise, with any question about the determinate content of thought and action-guiding norms—norms like *Freiheit, Recht, Schönheit, Liebe*, or even *Wahrheit*—we should not say, on this account, that the manifestations of such norms in poetry, drama, sculpture, music, painting, and novels (or politics and religion for that matter) are expressions of independently held commitments and so mere illustrations. It is only *in* such representative attempts at self-knowledge (and Hegel's view that *die schöne Kunst* is best understood as such an attempt at self-knowledge is obviously deeply controversial) that the norm can be said to "live."

Hegel's citation of Schiller (already itself a kind of expression of *Freundschaft*) and his alteration thus serve an appropriately double purpose. The *citation* gives evidence for the indispensability of the living, aesthetic dimension of experience for any philosophical account of norms, all on the theory of conceptual and intentional content alluded to above, and the *alteration*, one might say, likewise gives evidence that the completion and *Aufhebung* of aesthetic representation by philosophic reflection is just as indispensable. The last word, in other words, turns out to be neither Schiller's nor Hegel's alone, making a case by its very presence for the indispensability of a reflective and philosophically informed attention to historical and living *geistige Wirklichkeit* for any genuine philosophy worthy of the name.

4

The Absence of Aesthetics in Hegel's Aesthetics

Hegel's Distinctiveness

A central topic of modern aesthetics after Kant is the problem of aesthetic judgment. The question concerns the proper understanding of the logical form of such judgments (such as "this is beautiful") and their possible objectivity. But Hegel does not offer anywhere in his discussions of fine art a recognizable theory of aesthetic judgment. He does not even work out a well-defined account of aesthetic experience.[1] This divergence from much modern aesthetic theory is largely due to the complexity of the concept of art itself

1. There are really only two loci classici for Hegel's theory of art (besides the theoretical commitments implied by Hegel's use of literature in works such as the *Phenomenology of Spirit* and aside from marginal essays like his "Hamanns Schriften" [Hegel 1956]). There are paragraphs in sections 556–64 in the Absolute Spirit section of the *Encyclopedia* (Hegel 1992), and the four lecture courses on fine art (1821, 1823, 1836, and 1828/1828). In 1835 (and then in a second edition in 1842) one of Hegel's students, H. G. Hotho, working from Hegel's own notes (which are now lost) and student transcriptions, compiled an edition based on (apparently) the last three of these lecture series. This was published in the Moldenhauer-Michel edition and was the basis for Knox's Oxford English translation. Hotho's edition has been vigorously challenged for more than twenty-five years by Annemarie Gethmann-Siefert, the editor of the critical edition of the lectures. She is putting out essentially the student notes for all of the lecture series independently and has long claimed that what people treat as Hegel's aesthetics is actually Hotho's aesthetics. Gethmann-Siefert 1983, 237; 1992a, 26. While there are some indications that the Hotho version may here or there include some of Hotho's enthusiasms for various art objects (See Goehr 2006, 83–86 on Hegel's tastes in music and similar claims by Gethmann-Siefert 1992b, 197ff.) and that he may have edited Hegel as he interpreted Hegel (how could it be otherwise?), I have never seen evidence to the effect that the Hotho version is seriously unreliable or is some kind of fraud, at least with respect to the basic issues treated here. There is one serious issue, but it seems to me unresolvable. See n. 5 below.

as Hegel invokes it. For Hegel's treatment is famously historical; the account of the nature of art is narrative rather than analytic.[2] And he arrives at a most paradoxical conclusion as a result of this narrative: much of what we consider postclassical art (what Hegel calls "romantic" art)[3] is art in the process of "transcending itself as art," somehow "against itself as art," and as much a manifestation of the "limitations" and increasingly dissatisfied "life" of the practice of the production and appreciation of art as it is a part of a continuous tradition. (The even deeper paradox is that romantic art is all of this "*as art*.") In less dramatic terms, Hegel denies the autonomy of the aesthetic, or at least its complete autonomy, and this denial is the basis of the claim that art must be considered as a social institution linked to the development of the norms and values of a society as a whole, and that it is best understood in terms of its similarities with religion and philosophy and not as autonomous.

Hegel's approach remains quite controversial.[4] Someone who denies the autonomy of art seems on the verge of making art a means to something else or the manifestation of a deeper reality: a sign of the contradictions of capitalist society, a formalist refusal of the culture industry, a site of negative resistance to "identity thinking" and so forth. Such approaches often explain away art, rather than render it more intelligible as art. But the fact that Hegel largely ignores the question of the logical peculiarities of aesthetic judgments and their possible validity also highlights two potential advantages of his approach. First it opens up the possibility of addressing the question of the meaning of radical normative change in art making and art appreciating. (If the conceptual content of "the aesthetic" *can* change, and radically so, then there is no obvious way to isolate logically "the" nature of aesthetic judgment and aesthetic experience. All of *that* changes too.) And Hegel's approach might put us in a position to understand the significance of by far the greatest revolution in art history—modernism.

2. Officially, it is both narrative, in the lectures, and systematic, in the *Encyclopedia*. In the latter, though, sections 561 and 562 make it clear that the account there depends on the historical distinction among symbolic, classical, and romantic. For the systematic meaning of those divisions, see Pinkard 2007, 3–28.

3. It should be stressed that Hegel is interested only in a theory of great art and is not terribly interested in the strictly ontological question of art "just as art."

4. One of the main interpretive controversies: does Hegel mean that art is wholly dispensable, in favor of a fully reflective philosophical account ("of the Absolute"), or is it overcome only as the primary mode of human self-knowledge, a position it held basically just once, in fifth-century Athens? My own view is that the evidence is dispositive: he meant the latter. For an account in accord with such a verdict, an account of the "nontranscendent" view of the achievement of absolute spirit, see Nuzzo 2006, 303.

More specifically, what I want to show is that Hegel's account of art has to be understood as relying on two of his most interesting and challenging claims: his understanding of the relation between thought and sensibility and his understanding of what he calls the "inner-outer" relationship in the theory of agency. In both cases a strict duality is rejected, especially in his account of agency, where the model of inner states causing external bodily action is denied. The bearing of these claims on his account of art might help frame the issue of art after Hegel.

Beauty and Its Aftermath

Since Hegel's full position—his claim that art is the sensible experience or "showing" [*Schein*] of "the Idea"[5]—is not as well known as many other positions in the philosophy of art, I want to start with a summary sketch of what I understand to be Hegel's theory of fine art. This will have to be quite breathless, and we will quickly see that no such summary is possible without an interpretation of Hegel's most ambitious general philosophical position, so I will have to say something about that in section 3. Then we can return to the questions posed above. There are four points that we need on the table.

i. One of the things that distinguishes Hegel from many modern philosophers of art is his focus on the centrality of *aesthetic content* in his account of successful and especially great art. Contrary to post-Kantian formalism in philosophical aesthetics and criticism, for Hegel, an inadequate or superficial understanding of content (of the "Idea") is a feature of bad art: "Works of art are all the more excellent in expressing true beauty, the deeper is the inner truth of their content and thought" (Hegel 1975, 74).[6] The great enemy is indeterminacy, mere gestures at the beyond, or worshipful awe at the unsayable; hence Hegel's hostility toward the sublime as regressive.

What does he mean by content? He is given to saying that the reason art should be understood as belonging together with religion and philosophy is that they all "bring to consciousness and express the Divine" (Hegel 1975, 7).[7] But when he first introduces such a claim in the introduction, he follows it with a number of appositives and qualifications that strip it of much

5. This phrase, "das sinnliche Scheinen der Idee," raises the most serious issue about Hotho's reliability, as noted above. It does not appear in the extant student transcripts, only in Hotho's edition. See Gethmann-Siefert 2005, 241ff.

6. Cf. Hegel 1992, §562A.

7. See also: "the Divine is the absolute subject matter of art" (Hegel 1975, 607). Note too that Hegel immediately says that the Divine "*had to objectify itself*, and therefore proceed out of itself into the secular content of subjective personality" (607, my emphasis).

traditional religious association and so must have left his original auditors somewhat confused. He writes of artistic content as the Divine, *das Göttliche* (and not God), and the appositives of the Divine are "the deepest interests of mankind" and "the most comprehensive truths of spirit" (Hegel 1975, 21). Art is said to share with religion and philosophy the attempt to express what is simply called "the highest" (*das Höchste*). This could be taken to mean simply that in all great art issues of the utmost gravity and importance are at stake: justice versus vengeance; the competing claims of city, religion, and family; the gods; human perfection; what it is to live well with blind fate and moral luck; and death—perhaps even the "meaning of Being." But we know from Hegel's other works that for him the highest value or aspiration is freedom, that freedom is a form of rational agency, the actualization of reason,[8] that such responsiveness to reason is constitutive of all intelligibility, and that all other prior expressions of "the highest" are incomplete manifestations of such freedom. This is a considerably more ambitious claim than "important matters are at stake."

He frequently claims in the lectures that the "need" for art springs from a need of human subjects to "externalize themselves" in the public world and so to recognize themselves in the world and in objects and in the other humans who confront any subject. (This need for externalization or relinquishing [*Entäußerung*] in any actual exercise of freedom will play a crucial role in all aspects of the theory, as we will see.)[9] Now Hegel adds that in art (as well as religion and philosophy) this externalization and self-recognition concern "the highest things." Again, he roughly means some sort of self-knowledge about the nature and "actuality" of freedom. Such a highest truth is regularly said to be "the idea," which, in his remarks on Solger, he calls simply and somewhat unhelpfully "infinite absolute negativity," describing the idea's activity as so "negating itself as infinite and universal as to become finitude and particularity." For the moment, it is safe to say that if Hegel is expressing a religious view, then he is a member of a Christian sect with only one member. (All of which is not yet even to mention the flabbergasting claim in §560 of the *Encyclopedia*: "The work of art is just as much the work of free will, and the artist is the master of God [*Meister des Gottes*].")

8. Poetry is, for example, even said to be "reason individualized" (*das individualisierte Vernünftige*) (Hegel 1975, 977). The link between freedom and reason as Hegel understands it is not a Kantian one, and it does not just involve the exercise of an individual faculty. See Pippin 2012.

9. In Hegel's unusual theology, both the account of creation in the Hebrew Bible and the Christian doctrine of Incarnation are "images" of the "logical" necessity of such *Entäußerung*.

ii. The relation between the issue of beauty and the norms relevant to fine art is not one that Hegel states with any clarity. In Hotho's edition, he first announces the subject matter as the "realm of the beautiful" but then immediately says that, more particularly, the subject is art, and then adds that he means *die schöne Kunst*, the phrase regularly translated as "fine" art, as if in testimony to the *kalos k'agathos* issue from antiquity. Officially, Hegel's position is that the beauty of nature is not a proper or significant subject for reflection (nature is "spiritless" [*geistlos*], and by and large natural beauty simply doesn't matter), and that fine or beautiful art reached its culmination in Greek antiquity. Greek architecture, sculpture, and literature amount to the culmination and perfection of what art is qua art, that is, beautiful. Somewhat inconsistently, he will also refer to the task of making the spiritual, inner realm of romantic art *beautiful* ("the spiritual beauty of the absolute inner life as inherently infinite spiritual subjectivity"), although he also refers to such beauty as "something subordinate" and notes that romantic art must aspire to something more "substantial" than this, the realm of the "willing and self-knowing spirit" (which he does not refer to as beautiful) (Hegel 1975, 518). Here is a summary claim of his official position: "Therefore the world-view of the Greeks is precisely the milieu [*Mitte*] in which beauty begins its true life and builds its serene kingdom; the milieu [*Mitte*] of free vitality which is not only there naturally and immediately but is generated by spiritual vision and transfigured by art; the milieu [*Mitte*] of a development of reflection and at the same time of that absence of reflection that neither isolates the individual nor can bring back to any positive unity and reconciliation his negativity, grief, and misfortune" (Hegel 1975, 437). Art after the beautiful (which Hegel calls "romantic" art) is not more beautiful but, Hegel often says, simply "*better*," "more excellent" [*vortrefflicher*] even if not better art.[10] He goes on to remark that what is lacking or defective in classical art is just what is lacking in art itself (Hegel 1975, 79), and he suggests frequently that this defect consists in the very assumption constitutive of art itself: that the "ideal" (the true nature of reality) *can* have an adequate sensible form. Romantic art then must be art in which the limitation of art as a vehicle of self-knowledge is itself expressed and in some way transcended, not present merely as a *failure*, a negative limitation or nostalgic longing or a sublime mystery. His puzzling formula is: "In this way romantic art is the self-transcendence of art within its own sphere and in the form of art itself" (Hegel 1975, 80). Naturally

10. Beauty itself is mostly defined in terms of Hegel's systematic project and does sound "classical," a familiar criticism of Hegel: "the beautiful thing in its existence makes its own Concept appear as realized and displays in itself subjective unity and life" (Hegel 1975, 114).

such a claim raises the question: what *is* art once it has become its own self-transcendence? Hegel has a number of answers, ranging from philosophy to religion to displays of virtuosity to a memorializing art or an art of remembrance alone, but I believe his position itself at least allows us to suggest a possible answer: European modernism.[11]

Actually—in testimony to the fact that any summary of anything in Hegel has to be multiply qualified—for all this philhellenism, Hegel also points out that the limitations of the beautiful as an aesthetic ideal were already dramatically, vividly present in Greek drama, in tragedy.[12] It is already true in tragedy that "art now transcends itself, in that it forsakes the element of a reconciled embodiment of spirit in sensuous form and passes over from the poetry of the imagination to the prose of thought" (Hegel 1975, 89). The impossibility of the sort of reconciliation and harmony necessary for the beautiful to function as an ideal, and the emphasis on the prosaic nature of bourgeois modernity, will play large roles in Hegel's treatment of late romanticism and so in his views of art in modernity. Recall this passage in the preface to the *Phenomenology*, cited before in chapter 3: "Death, if that is what we wish to call that non-actuality, is the most fearful thing of all, and to keep and hold fast to what is dead requires only the greatest force. Powerless beauty detests the understanding because the understanding expects of her what she cannot do. However, the life of spirit is not a life that is fearing death and austerely saving itself from ruin; rather, it bears death calmly, and in death, it sustains itself. Spirit only wins its truth by finding itself in its absolute disruption" (Hegel 2018, §32).[13]

iii. The two key notions in Hegel's account of beauty and fine art are the notions of *Schein* or appearing, showing, or often simply a visual "shining," and variations on liveliness, life, and enliven, *Lebendigkeit*, *beleben*, *Leben*, and so forth. "The beautiful is characterized as the pure appearance of the Idea to sense" (Hegel 1992, 111). In terms of his frequent Ur-image: "the outer must harmonize with an inner which is harmonious in itself, and just on that account, can reveal itself as itself in the outer" (Hegel 1992, 155). The manifestation (or shining) of the Idea in sensuous material, however, is not anything like a cognitive awareness, and Hegel's attempt to explain why is the closest he ever

11. I argue for this much more extensively in Pippin 2014.

12. It is actually Schiller, not Hegel, who simply idealizes the beauty of all Greek art (cf. "Hymnen an die Nacht"), and Hegel seems to accept Novalis's critique of such beauty-worship, both among the Greeks (that they "aestheticized" suffering and death, could make no place for "the negative" in human life) and among the German philhellenists.

13. So Hegel would never go as far as Barnett Newman's "The impulse of modern art was to destroy beauty." See Newman 2007, 13. Nothing needs to be destroyed. The time for the beautiful as the supreme ideal for high art has simply passed.

gets to an account of distinctly aesthetic experience.[14] Rather than cognitive awareness, fine art is said to awaken in us an emotional and spirited responsiveness to everything that has a place in human spirit (Hegel quotes Terence's "Nihil humani . . ." principle). Here is his summary claim.

> [Art's] aim therefore is supposed to consist in awakening [*wecken*] and vivifying [*beleben*] our slumbering feelings, inclinations, and passions of every kind, in filling the heart, in forcing the human being, whether educated or not, to go through the whole gamut of feelings which the human heart in its inmost and secret recesses can bear, experience and produce, through what can move and stir the human breast in its depth and manifold possibilities and aspects, and to deliver to feeling and contemplation for its enjoyment whatever spirit possesses of the essential and lofty in its thinking and in the Idea. (Hegel 1975, 46)

Such claims can sound very much like romantic boilerplate unless we realize that Hegel believes that it is quite possible for the various "highest" norms governing acceptable and authoritative knowledge claims or practical, ethical, and political life actually to "go dead" in a certain way, to function in a matter-of-fact way in constraining claims of authority and kinds of conduct, but to do so, as he says, "positively," merely as an "external" lifeless authority.[15] In such a context, this somewhat Schillerian concern with this enlivening function has its own objective social conditions for successful realization. Indeed this ability, central to art's function, to help sustain (by expressing) the "life" of the highest norms (when they can be so successfully affirmed) is said to be essential to the authority of such norms themselves. We saw this previously in the passage from the *Phenomenology* that contrasted the "course of studies of the ancient world" with what is needed today (Hegel 2018, §33).[16]

It would not be too much of an exaggeration to say that Hegel's philosophy of art is not a theory of representation or expression, not a classical theory

14. It isn't straightforwardly such a theory because what counts as this enlivened responsiveness also changes.

15. In Hegel's development, this concern with the "life" of norms, rules, principles, and ideals, or rather the life and death of such norms, has to count as his most prominent concern, beginning early with his account of love in the Christian community, developing into a general view of "life," and culminating in the mature theory of *Geist* or "spirit." This *Liebe-Leben-Geist* trajectory was first proposed by Dilthey (1990, 105) and reappears in such commentators as Harris (1971) and Henrich (1971).

16. The same language appears in the *Lectures on Fine Art*. Note especially that in the list of modern oppositions he includes the contrast between the "dead, inherently empty concept, and the full concreteness of life" (Hegel 1975, 53–54; cf. also 1006). Since one would presumably want to understand something in its proper life, not dead, or empty, this implies paradoxically a higher, more adequate status for art when compared with philosophy.

of mimesis or a post-Christian theory of creation (genius),[17] but a theory of "enlivening," once we notice too that such enlivening is a crucial condition for the possibility of any norm's grip on those bound to it, and that this grip can loosen and fail, thus requiring something different from art. (That is, such an externalization can be said to help "*bring*" such norms and principles and values "*to* life," not merely to express their life. The sensible showing of the Idea is an attempt not to provide an example or a paradigmatic instance but, as Hegel puts it, to "realize or actualize the universal itself."[18] I will try to make use in a minute of Hegel's account of agency and the realization of an intention to make this clearer.) In sum, we learn something about the "life" of such values when we see them externalized in art objects, and we learn this in a way unique to art.

iv. Aside from these gestures at "quickening" or enlivening, Hegel does not have a particularly rich or detailed theory of aesthetic experience. Most of the time, he speaks rather dryly of a *Kunstbetrachtung*, a way of considering art, and he seems to agree with Schlegel that the critic should now understand himself not as a judge, an avatar of exemplary taste, but as an interpreter. (What "enlivening" inspires is what we now call criticism, not appreciation.) Hegel distances himself from any belief in what he calls the "mere subjectivity" and "affectivity" of the artistic response and speaks instead of the attempt to "plunge the depths of a work" and to go ever "deeper" into it (*das Kunstwerk zu versenken und zu vertiefen*) (Hegel 1975, 54). He also says that the "contemplation [*Betrachtung*] of beauty is of a liberal kind [*liberaler Art*]; it leaves objects alone as being inherently free and infinite" (Hegel 1992, 114). This introduces the problem of the autonomy of the aesthetic dimension and also introduces the relation between these lectures and, let us say, his basic position.[19]

17. Of course, Hegel being Hegel, it is also possible to say that for him art is all of these alternatives, but that they all can be shown to be incomplete manifestations of the full notion of art as enlivening appearing, that such incomplete manifestations are themselves tied to an incomplete (not erroneous) self-understanding of freedom.

18. This highlights a peculiarity in Hegel's treatment of art, made much of by Henrich. The *Ende* or end of art is not treated as a *Vollendung* or completion or fullest realization of possibilities, as is, one could argue, the modern representative state in Hegel's treatment, or Lutheranism, or Hegelian systematic idealism. Art's end is much more, in Henrich's terms, a *Zerfall*, a kind of decay, as if art's possibilities are exhausted, as if "the life had gone out of them," one might put it. Even within the art history lecture, the "ends" of symbolic and classical art are forms of transition; but this is not true for the end of romantic art. See Henrich 2003, 82–83 and 96.

19. See the discussion in Bubner 2003, 216–30. Bubner makes use of what Hegel has to say about symbolic art to work his way toward the "traces" of a theory of aesthetic experience in Hegel. Much of what he says about such an experience is quite suggestive for the category of modernist art.

Art: Spirit Made Sensuous

I have begun by suggesting that the first thing we should understand about Hegel's view is that there is an "absence of aesthetics" in Hegel's treatment of the beautiful and fine art. That is, as is already quite apparent, he is interested in a wide variety of issues that do not have much to do with what became the philosophical issues of aesthetics in the eighteenth century after Alexander Gottlieb Baumgarten's use of that term established a kind of philosophic subdiscipline.[20] I don't mean to suggest that Hegel failed to appreciate that the primary modality in the experience of the beautiful and of fine art is sensible. He makes this point in his own way many times. But primary modality does not for Hegel mean independent modality, and that is the beginning of the Hegelian story that will ultimately associate art with religion and philosophy and that will provide the basis for his claim about the essential historicity of art. His clearest statement occurs in the introduction: "Of course the work of art presents itself to sensuous apprehension. It is there for sensuous feeling, external or internal, for sensuous intuition and ideas, just as nature is. . . . But nevertheless the work of art, as a sensuous object, is not merely for sensuous apprehension; its standing is of such a kind that, though sensuous, it is essentially at the same time for spiritual apprehension; spirit is meant to be affected by it and to find some satisfaction in it" (Hegel 1975, 35). Later Hegel formulates his own version of Kant's disinterestedness claim, insisting that an artwork exists not for the satisfaction of any desire but "for the contemplative side of spirit alone," and that it is "meant to satisfy purely spiritual existence" (Hegel 1975, 36–37).

But again, adding to the complexity, by "for the contemplative side" Hegel does not mean "for contemplation." There *is* supposed to be something distinctively aesthetic about the *Schein* of some ideal, even if such an experience is not autonomous or a realm of experience wholly unto itself. At one point Hegel simply proposes that art be understood as making "every one of its productions into a thousand-eyed Argus," that art makes every human action, event, speech, and tone of voice "into an eye, in which the free soul is revealed in its later infinity" (Hegel 1975, 154). This suggests that the treatment of some action or speech in an artwork, however sensibly apprehended, invites in a unique way interrogation at a more sustained, reflective, and involving—"lively"—level, suggesting that like the eye and the human soul, the artwork becomes both the vehicle of sight, that by which we see, and that in which

20. For a useful, brief summary of the Baumgarten-Hegel history, see Nuzzo 2006, 293–95.

the soul, the human meaning or significance of the action or speech, can be seen.[21]

To be sure, neither Kant's nor Schiller's aesthetics, the greatest influences on Hegel, were sensualist or empiricist, but Kant's claim about the relevance of purposiveness to aesthetic experience and Schiller's interest in the relevance of our moral vocation are not what Hegel has in mind. For in making this point, Hegel is making his usual and most repeated point, familiar since his early Jena writings, the "Difference" essay and *Faith and Knowledge*. This is what is central to Hegel's critique of the putative independence of aesthetic experience, although admittedly, it is a point that is *very* hard to restate properly. It is that the distinguishability of concept and intuition in experience—which Hegel is happy to concede—is not equivalent to and does not entail the separability of concept and intuition as *independent* contributors to experience.[22] Contrary to some criticisms of this position, there is no reason to think that Hegel is collapsing or eliminating the distinction between the sensual or passive and the conceptual or active elements in knowledge. His position is much more complicated than that. There is no reason to think he is collapsing the two, any more than there is any reason to think that someone claiming that "X cannot be representationally significant except as Y'ed" can be assumed to be claiming "There are no X's; there is only Y'ing," or even that to claim that "*X is not playing all by itself a representationally significant role*" means "it plays *no role whatsoever*, has no function within knowledge claims."[23]

21. Cf. "Car je ne le regarde pas comme on regarde une chose, je ne le fixe pas en son lieu, mon regard erre en lui comme dans les nimbes de l'Être, je vois selon ou avec lui plutôt que je ne le vois." Merleau-Ponty 1964, 23. In many respects, *L'oeil et l'esprit* is a powerful restatement of many Hegelian themes. The critique of Cartesian optics is much like Hegel's rejection of a "two-stage" process of perception, as is what Merleau-Ponty calls "un mystère de passivité" in perception, passive but not wholly receptive (52). An important difference: Hegel stresses more the social dimension of artistic meaning.

22. Kant 1998, A51/B75. Kant's claims about the strict distinction between these two "sources," even as he emphasized in his own way Hegel's dialectical point about their necessarily intertwined, even inseparable role in knowledge, were the basis of his critique of the entire prior philosophical tradition, elements of which, he famously claimed, either "sensualized all concepts of the understanding" or "intellectualized" appearances (A271/B327).

23. For Hegel as for the Tractarian Wittgenstein, thought does not "stop short" of the world; a way of thinking about an object [a *Sinn*] is not an intermediary entity between us and the referents of thought; it is a way of seeing the world. There is still plenty of substantive content and empirical guidedness in experience in such a picture. The claim is only, again, that thought's relation to such objects cannot be secured or even intuitionally pinned down by the deliverances of sensibility alone. The broadest way to restate the point is simply that the domain of

More broadly, Hegel's denial of a scheme-content distinction means that for him the question of how discursive thought informs sensibility in our acquiring perceptual knowledge is of the same logical form as the question of how thought or inner intention informs or is manifest *in* bodily action.[24] In neither case is there a "two-stage" process, neither the conceptualization of independently acquired sensory material, nor an inner intention functioning as distinct cause, initiating a subsequent bodily movement as one might kick a ball to start it rolling. It is, in that sense, his Ur-question. Hegel's attempt to state properly the implications of this claim—sensibility is the *primary* aesthetic modality but not an *independent* one, just as concept and intuition are *distinguishable* even if not *separable*, just as intention is not *reducible* to bodily motions, even while not an independent *cause* of such motion—is an attempt that surfaces on nearly every page of his work, early and late.[25] The master image in almost all these discussions is one we have already seen and it is also not easily accessible: that the right way to understand the "inner-outer" relation at work in all such cases is as a speculative inner-outer "identity." This is a frequent enough summary image that we should expect it to inform his treatment of fine art, and that is indeed what we find. (One of his more accessible formulations: "The universal need for art . . . is man's rational need to lift the inner and outer world into his spiritual consciousness as an *object* in which he recognizes *his own self*" [Hegel 1975, 31, my emphasis]). The relation of the artist to her product (inner to outer) and of the art object to human receptivity (outer to inner) is supposed to involve such an "identity," with the latter often expressed as spirit (both producer and appreciator) "finding itself" in the art object. The crucial discussions of the end of symbolic art (in the epigram) and of classical art (in Roman satire) are couched in terms of some unresolved and ultimately unbearable distorted self-understanding of this inner-outer relation. The rather grand and considerably less accessible but canonical formulation from the *Encyclopedia* (the formulation that,

---

the normative—in this case what ought to be claimed—is autonomous. Principles constraining what we ought to believe, what could count as a possible object of experience or what one ought to do, are wholly independent of claims about how the mind works or what people generally do or what the received world determines us to think. Fichte appreciated this point in the deepest way and built his whole philosophy around it.

24. The aesthetic formulation of the point: "art consists precisely in the connection, the affinity and the concrete interpenetration [*dem konkreten Ineinander*] of meaning [*Bedeutung*] and form [*Form*]" (Hegel 1975, 763–64).

25. Cf. the apt formulation in McDowell 1994, 89–90: "similarly intentions without overt activity are idle; movements of limbs without concepts are mere happenings, not expressions of agency."

somewhat unfortunately, guides everything in the Fine Art lectures): "Hence what is only something inner, is also thereby external, and what is only external is also only something inner" (Hegel 1992, §140).

And it is clear often that Hegel makes a great deal of his version of this interdependence in his account of art. "In this way," he claims about art, "the sensuous aspect of art is spiritualized [*vergeistert*], since spirit appears in art as made sensuous [*versinnlicht*]." The artwork is said "to want sensible presence [*sinnliche Gegenwart*]"

> which indeed should remain sensuous, but liberated from the scaffold of its purely material nature. Thus the sensuous aspect of a work of art, in comparison with the immediate existence of things in nature, is elevated to a pure appearance, and the work of art stands in the middle between immediate sensuousness and ideal thought. It is not yet pure thought, but, despite its sensuousness is no longer a purely material existent either . . . the sensuous in the work of art is itself something ideal. (Hegel 1975, 38)

And, "Art by means of its representations, while remaining within the sensuous sphere, liberates man at the same time from the power of sensuousness . . . art lifts [man] with gentle hands out of and above imprisonment in nature" (Hegel 1975, 49).[26]

Again, a conventional view of what Hegel urges as a successor to "aesthetics" is an institutional or social theory of art objects (understood by some Hegel commentators to mean that whatever some community, say the art market, determines to be the norm for art and good art *is* thereby art and good art, that some such norm comes to be an inseparable element in aesthetic experience itself).[27] This is what many understand to be the import of the idealist claim about the mediated, nonindependent status of the

26. It should be noted that Hegel thinks that in his aesthetics Kant came much closer to realizing the nature of the true relation between immediacy and mediation, in general, than anywhere else. He notes that Kant realized that the material element of art—sense, feeling, emotion, and inclination—is not "subsumed under universal categories of the understanding, and dominated by the concept of freedom in its abstract universality, but is so bound up with the universal that it is inwardly and absolutely adequate to it. Therefore thought is *incarnate* in the beauty of art, and the material is not determined by thought externally, but exists freely on its own account—in that the natural, sensuous, the heart, etc., have in themselves proportion, purpose, and harmony; and intuition and feeling are *elevated* to spiritual universality, just as thought not only renounces its hostility to nature but is enlivened thereby" (Hegel 1975, 60, my emphasis). Hegel then goes on to make his usual criticism of Kant for construing this as having only a "subjective" meaning, rather than being about "what is absolutely true and actual" (60).

27. For a survey of the recent (post-1970) history of the institutional theory of art, see Graves 1997, 51–67.

aesthetic dimension. The mediation is supposed by such commentators to be "socially normative," in the "inverted-Hegelian" way that Marx would come to consider the primary mediating or meaning-making function in modern societies, including aesthetic meaning, to be "the commodity form." There is something right about this characterization of Hegel's position, but at the very least Hegel also thinks that the transition to modern, romantic art (and beyond) can be said to make some sort of clear, compelling sense (not at all like a change in fashion or a purely contingent sequence), and at most he undoubtedly wants to understand this transition as progressive in some way, so that such art reflects some truth about norm, meaning, and human activity "better" than earlier art, even if it is not, as he often says, better "as art." (It is at this point that Hegel obviously parts company with the "anything goes" version of the social-institutional theory of art.) At any rate, like the left-Hegelian or Marxist interpretation, Hegel's approach completely alters the sense of the question of "by what right" one would claim that a single work is better or better art or art at all. That question cannot be answered as a question about art alone, certainly when framed about a particular work, and can be approached only if framed in terms of a general theory of a collective attempt at self-knowledge and productive activity. The skeptic's worry that any categorization of or evaluation of art might express idiosyncratic personal preferences already starts off too far downstream for it to have any interest or bite. If such a question arises, it arises "inside" the practice of the production and appreciation of art as a social self-regulating activity, and can be addressed according to the norms of that practice. The "theorist" has no special authority about any such question.

Of course, all such qualifications of the supposed autonomy of the aesthetic cannot be so formulated that such considerations obscure the distinctness of the *aesthetic* manifestation of the idea. This is a dialectical tightrope that appears frequently throughout Hegel's "system." (The fact that moral considerations get a grip only within and as dependent on a distinct and substantive form of ethical life—that they are not matters of pure practical reason—does not mean that Hegel is out to deny the authority or distinctness of moral considerations, any more than his position on the inseparability of concept and intuition means to deny the possibility of empirical knowledge.) Simply put, the Idea's sensible living appearance is a vital but not fully articulated manifestation. The "ethical harmony" of Greek spirit is sensible and, in Hegel's sense, alive, in Greek literature, but not in the way in which it becomes an object of reflection in Greek philosophy, and eventually in Hegel's account in the *Phenomenology*. The painful internal tensions and incompatibilities of that ethical world are directly sensible in Greek tragedy, but not in the more self-conscious (and hence "freer") way such tensions are manifest in Socrates's challenges in the Platonic dialogues.

The second implication is a thoroughly historicized account of such institutional or social settings, given that Hegel treats conceptual norms as necessarily variable in time.[28] His case for the historicity of such norms is complicated, but the basic idea is that the denial of a scheme-content distinction means that traditionally empiricist or transcendental strategies for establishing the normative authority of norms for thought or action are not available. Thought does not exogenously shape the material of thought and is not simply shaped by it; practical reason does not legislate to our material impulses, or merely devise strategies for their efficient satisfaction. Conceptual and normative change, an inevitable result of simple human finitude, must then be accounted for "internally," brought about by the finitude and incompleteness of some attempt to regulate what we allow each other to say and do, again within a general account of how we go about allowing or forbidding each other's claims and actions.[29]

Inner and Outer

So Hegel's philosophy of art is dependent first of all on a theory of spirit, on some account of collective, norm-governed human mindedness and an account of the kind of finitude or lack of it that explains the production of artworks and the legislation of norms for their production and evaluation. We simply need to know how social norms work in order to know how artistic norms work. This theory of such a need and such production is itself double dependent. It is first dependent on what Hegel keeps referring to as the "logic" of the inner-outer relation central to properly understanding spirit and its products. The distinct feature of this logic is its contrary-to-commonsense denial of a strict *separation* or "two-stage" view. So in writing about the

28. This latter is often said to be Hegel's major contribution to not just the philosophical but the academic and scholarly study of art, that, largely thanks to Hegel, the problem of art's intelligibility or meaning should be raised and pursued within "art history" departments. Gombrich famously called Hegel "the father of art history" (although Hegel should not be blamed for anything Gombrich said about art history or art). See Gombrich 1977, 202–19.

29. So for Hegel the question of the status of the beautiful is not simply a matter of dispute for aesthetic theory, as in, say, the dispute between Danto (2003, 58), who regards the "discovery" that art could be great art without being beautiful as an achievement of modern art, and Nehamas (2010), who defends the beautiful. Rather there was a time when an artwork did need to be beautiful to be great, but that time has passed. This is not because one age had a bad theory and another age a good theory.

production of art (Greek art, in this case), Hegel writes about their ideas and doctrines (*Vorstellungen* und *Lehren*), "*And it was not as if these were already there* [vorhanden], *in advance of poetry*, in an abstract mode of consciousness as general religious propositions and categories of thought, and then later were only clothed in imagery by artists and given an external adornment in poetry; on the contrary the mode of artistic production was such that what fermented in these poets they could work out [*herauszuarbeiten*] only in the form of art and poetry" (Hegel 1975, 102; my emphasis). And with respect to the *reception* of the work: "But the self [*das Ich*] in relation to the object likewise ceases to be the abstraction of both noticing, sensuously *perceiving, and observing. . . . In this [beautiful] object the self becomes* [es wird] concrete in itself since it makes explicit the unity of Concept and reality, the unification in their concreteness, of the aspects hitherto separated, and therefore abstract, in the self and its object" (Hegel 1975, 114).[30]

And this way of talking about inner and outer—that the artist's ideas do not exist "before" but that it is only *as* "worked out" in the art production that they become determinate ideas, and that the subject "becomes" concretely the subject it is *in* aesthetic appreciation—is essential to this discussion. The claims go to the heart of the issue of how Hegel is denying the autonomy of the aesthetic, even while he is not thereby rendering art merely illustrative of or sensible instances of "the Idea," a community's most important norms. (There cannot be any conceptual content to such ideals, there is no "actuality" for such ideals, except *as* worked out—*herausgearbeitet* is his term—in artistic production and reception, as well as worked out in other "externalizations" like religion and political life.)

It is also a notion given free and paradoxical rein in Hegel's account of agency, where it does most of its important work, and that introduces the second dependency. As in: "Ethical self-consciousness now learns *from its deed* the developed nature of what it actually did . . ." (Hegel 2018, 235) or "an individual cannot know what he is until he has made himself a reality through action" (401).[31] In the same way, Hegel is trying to say that we do not,

30. Cf. also: "In itself, that is to say, the individual in his essential nature is the totality, not the inner alone, but equally the realization of this inner through and in the outer" (Hegel 1975, 96).

31. "We are accustomed to say of human beings that everything depends on their essence [*Wesen*] and not on their deeds and conduct. Now in this lies the correct thought that what a human being does should be considered not in its immediacy, but only as mediated through his inwardness [*Inneres*] and as a manifestation of that inwardness. But with that thought we must not overlook the point that the essence and also the inward only prove themselves [*sich bewähren*] as such by stepping forth into appearance. On the other hand, the appeal which hu-

cannot, know who we are, what we are up to, until we have found some way to externalize some version of this knowledge or activity, in art among other enterprises, and (to speak highly metaphorically) have found a way to contest *with each other* and settle on some authoritative view.

In this respect (and this is Hegel's most ambitious claim) art making is not an incidental or contingent or merely illustrative *expression* of an already achieved self-knowledge, any more than action is the result of or expression of a distinct inner intention.[32] Art *is* an achieved form of self-knowledge; it is knowledge we would not, could not have, except for this realization, just as antecedent formulations of intention can be mere fantasies of commitment and are realized or "tested" and become what they truly are only "in the deed." For better or worse, this is the claim we have to understand in order to understand Hegel's theory of art.[33]

Moreover, Hegel treats being an agent (a subject to whom deeds can be imputed) in a way that manifests that second dependency in his philosophy of art. This is because being a subject or an agent is treated by Hegel not as an ontological or strictly philosophical category but as an achieved social status such as, let us say, being a citizen or being a professor, a product or result of mutually recognitive attitudes. This means just what it seems to: different historical communities establish this status in different ways, and there is no independent truth-maker or fact of the matter they are getting wrong or more and more right. Likewise, art objects are not manifestations of natural kinds. No one discovered the form of opera, lying around hidden. The status, art object of a kind, is an assigned, historically achieved, socially authoritative status, and to understand the art of an age we have to understand the ethical and

man beings make to inwardness as an essence distinct from the content of their deeds often has the intention of validating their mere subjectivity and in this way of escaping what is valid in and for itself" (Hegel 1992, §112A).

32. As conceded several times, it is difficult to find the right formulation for what Hegel is getting at here, but the interpretive consequences of getting it wrong involve quite a serious departure from Hegel, as in de Man's (1981) misguided insistence on a psychological "interior thought" externalized in some material. I agree with Geuss that de Man also misconstrues what Hegel means by "symbolic" and what he means by saying that "art is for us a thing of the past." See Geuss 1983, 375–82, and de Man's reply (1983, 383–90).

33. This is a sketchy summary, but it should be obvious that many questions could be raised about any of these points. Couldn't it be the case, for example, that some artwork, brought to a suitably "lively" expression/realization of some highest ideal, invited interrogation and appreciation in a way tied to the continuing vitality of that norm and so forth but was still bad art? Hegel's answer is "No," but it would take an independent discussion to defend such a claim.

cultural world within which its reception would make sense, possess some authority,[34] and so could "circulate."[35]

And finally, Hegel wants there to be clear parallels between all these instances of the inner-outer dialectic so prominent in his discussions. That is, the way an action, a bodily movement, can be said to embody a subject's intention and so bear a certain determinate meaning is not a result of prior, determinative subjective cause. The intention unfolds *in* the action over time, responsive as much to what is unfolding over time as "true" to an original formulation; it becomes the intention it is only as the deed unfolds. (In the clearest case of what Hegel is talking about, one can be surprised, given what one was willing to do, by what one's commitments "turn out to be," despite how they were formulated *ex ante*.) But this external dimension of what is only provisionally inner, the actual bodily action, is also dependent on the meaning-making practices in a community at a time; there is no privileged "ownership" of the meaning of the deed by the subject. This publicly authoritative act-description is also not something imposed or arbitrarily stipulated "by others." A large network of such practices must be in place and functioning authoritatively for such an ascription to be possible. (And this process can begin to fall apart, as in Hegel's accounts of tragedy.)

In point of fact, Hegel is suggesting more than parallels. He seems to want us to consider the production of art *as a form of agency*, to understand the "work" as we understand the bodily movements of an action.[36] In this sense, while there might have been a time (a heroic age) when the right ethical and aesthetic norm for an action was the beautiful, it might now be true that the appropriate norm is something like genuineness (more on this in a moment).[37]

Likewise, he wants to say, an artwork bears meaning not as the product or result of the artist's intention. What the artist turned out to have intended is available (even to her) only in the work, as "actualized" or "externalized."

34. "The form of romantic art" is said by Hegel (1975) to require both an account of "a new vision of the world [*Weltanschauung*]" and a "new artistic form" (516).

35. These two dependencies are linked for Hegel, although that is a book-length topic. They are linked because what Hegel understands as the relevant "outer" in the account of *Geist* and its norms is a social, public world, and the dependence of a deed or art product for its sense on that world is a dependence on a mutable, internally "self-negating," restlessly dissatisfied world.

36. In the *Phenomenology of Spirit*, Hegel frequently calls a person's deed her *Werk*. See Hegel 2018, 194.

37. Cf. Cavell (2015) on "the possibility of fraudulence" as "characteristic of the modern" (220), and apropos of the earlier remarks here about whether the question of the point of actions is the same logical kind as the question of the "point" of a painting, cf. his remarks on pp. 225ff.

And such a determinate meaning is itself also dependent on the authoritative social norms at a time, meaning-making practices of criticism, evaluation, categorization, and so forth that, as in the case of action, can begin to break down, or generate incompatible commitments, as at the end of classical or the end romantic art.[38]

Art in Our Time

So what about our age? In the simplest terms, the claim is that the art of modernity, which, for Hegel, in his own time (but *not* for all future time), was late romanticism, primarily lyric poetry, must ultimately also become "an art which transcends itself as art," eschews as nostalgic, not possibly genuine, *both* the beautiful as ideal, as a vehicle for the externalization and recognition of our highest values, and also, in what Hegel calls the "end of romantic art," inwardness, authenticity, purity of heart, and subjectivity in the romantic view of the world. (Persons and buildings and nature can still obviously *be* beautiful; the point is that such manifestations of both natural and artistic beauty have lost their significance. Such beauty doesn't *matter* as it once did.) Such an art will incorporate, in a way necessarily different from beautiful art, the absence of the possibility of reconciliation and harmony and the inspiration typical of classical art (purchased in such art at the price of too weak, incomplete, or repressed an acknowledgment of human subjectivity, understood as self-determining and not merely responsive to or determined by nature), as well as the romantic posture for Hegel prototypical of modernity. Here is how he describes the postclassical or romantic art enterprise we are in the process of "transcending": "spirit is pushed back into itself out of its own

38. Hegel's position on the meaning of actions is not an "expressivist" one, as that would be understood in the context of, say, Herder or Charles Taylor. (He certainly does not believe that art is the "go-cart of spirit," as in Danto 2003, 94.) This is because Hegel believes that this whole process of externalization is also a component of a more inclusive social practice, the giving of and asking for reasons under the pressure of possible social conflict. Such externalizations, in other words, count as a kind of proffer to others made when one's actions or products affect what others would otherwise be able to do (or virtually all actions). This is a very long story, but Hegel conceives of such practical rationality as a "social practice" or he conceives of it "pragmatically" or he has a "historicized" view of what counts as the appeal to reasons. The point is that he understands practical reason as a kind of interchange of attempts at justification among persons each of whose actions affects what others would otherwise be able to do, and all of this for a community at a time, and so in a way that changes. He even considers the production of art as a collective attempt at mutual intelligibility and justification in a way that is a component of such a rationalizing practice. In this context, following that line of thought here would again be a book-length digression, at least.

reconciliation in the corporeal into a reconciliation of itself with itself. The simply solid totality of the Ideal is dissolved, and it falls apart into the double totality of (a) subjective being in itself and (b) the external appearance, in order to enable spirit to reach through this disunity [*Trennung*] a deeper reconciliation with its own element of inwardness" (Hegel 1975, 518).

Hegel is no proponent of such dualism, but he regards this posture (the loss of beauty as an ideal, we might say) as necessary in the self-education of spirit. To use Hegel's narrative metaphors, having discovered that human beings do not have a fixed, purposive "place" in nature, no natural home (that nature is disenchanted), spirit abandons its attempt to "see itself" or "find itself" in nature or in corporeal externality at all, ceases to look "there" for purpose and natural law, and begins the attempt to see itself in its own *products*, to find a way to see its culture, work-world, politics, laws, and religion as "its own," not the contingent concatenation of events that merely happen to it and are arbitrarily produced or are imposed by necessity. Romantic art is then both psychologically sensuous and reflective, expressive of how an experience, another person, a world, seems, or feels, "for the subject" as the most important and privileged dimension of experience, and reflectively trying to make some sense that it *should* feel that way "inwardly."

Hegel understands the aspiration to the beautiful in classical art to be intelligible only as part of a very broad and ambitious human aspiration to understand and properly locate all aspects of human being in a way continuous with the natural or nonhuman world. He also claims that this promise could not be fulfilled, and that the experience of suffering and death in Greek tragedy already started to reveal such a division or alienation from the given natural world.[39] Romantic art is the record of such placelessness and a record of the experience both of the need for the externalization of inner experience, and of the inadequacy of any external corporeal form to bear such a meaning.

But this withdrawn stance inevitably leads to the view of all externality, corporeality, the public social world, as having "the character of being indifferent and vulgar" (Hegel 1992, §562), and such elevation of an inward purity of heart amounts to a kind of pathology in Hegel's many treatments of romantic art and romanticism, what he calls in the *Phenomenology* the "law of the heart," the "frenzy of self-conceit," the "beautiful soul," and so on. It is not possible here to explore why he thinks of these implications as pathologies, or why he thinks that their being pathologies counts toward explaining both why they cannot be sustained and why they ought not to be, why they

39. "We cannot say that the Greeks interpreted death in its essential meaning" (Hegel 1975, 522).

are "irrational" in his sense. But it is at this point that Hegel interprets this limitation of romantic art as a kind of final revelation of the limitation of art itself, as if, very crudely expressed, the alternatives come down to: inscrutable and mysterious "outer" (e.g., Egyptian art); inner fully expressed in and at home in the natural outer (classical sculpture); or the inner struggling to find expression in the outer but never doing so (romantic art). Given this sense of the alternatives, Hegel starts suggesting that a reconciliation of inner and outer can properly occur only in the religious community and finally in philosophical self-knowledge.[40] The only forms of art he allows as "postromantic" are greatly diminished in ambition and importance—a new form of modern comedy, "objective humor,"[41] with a sacralized *Humanus* at its center.

But the broad categories that emerge from Hegel's developmental account seem uniquely suited to a form of art after the beautiful and freed from the romantic polarity of inner purity and the "vulgarity" of merely contingent external barriers to the realization of the inner.[42] In other contexts, such as modern ethical life, or religion, Hegel certainly accepts that highly developed, reflective forms of mindedness can come to be embodied in habits and ongoing daily practice that seem to be counterparts to the sensible, material embodiments required by art. At least, there is nothing in his systematic project to lead one to expect that *alone* among all the projects of human spirit, indeed uniquely among the manifestations of Absolute Spirit, the production of art

40. Cf. Hegel 1992, §563: "Beautiful art, like the religion peculiar to it, has its future in true religion."

41. Hegel was quite fond of Laurence Sterne, and quite peeved about romantic or "subjective" irony. But his model for objective humor is unusual, Goethe's *West-östlicher Divan*. Henrich's (2003) attempt to make some sense out of this choice is important.

42. First, it is thus true that on the surface Hegel seems to take the "inevitability of the collapse of standards of beauty within art" as "evidence that art must be superseded by philosophy" (Guyer 2006, 324). But that is too rapid a leap, not just for a commentator, but so it would seem at least for Hegel. The moments of romantic inwardness generate the same sort of unworldliness in the philosophy of objective spirit, but reconciliation and reintegration occur there in *Sittlichkeit*, not in a leap to religion or philosophy. Second, the existence of romantic art for two thousand years certainly demonstrates that there can be "nonbeautiful" forms of art, so the exclusive disjunction on the basis of which the claim just quoted depends cannot be right. And finally, since what is at stake in all art concerns sensible manifestation and understandings of freedom, and since Hegel's theory is a nonalienation theory of freedom with a subjective and an objective side, a theory in which inner must become outer just in order to be determinately inner, I think we have to say that Hegel's failure to imagine a postromantic form of art (an outer form for a postromantic understanding of freedom) is just that, a failure of imagination, not a systematic or necessary exclusion. See Henrich 2003 on "Zerfall und Zukunft" (100) and §8, "synthesis statt Zerfall" (100–106).

should suffer such a loss of vitality and significance, rather than find a mode of embodiment appropriate to Hegel's theory of the modern world.

Unfortunately, to imagine what Hegel did not seem able to imagine would require a great deal more detail about his theory of Western modernization and—even more difficult—some comprehensive view of visual, musical, and literary modernism. There is little consensus about either issue, but I would hope the trajectory of Hegel's account is at least suggestive. It is possible, for example, to see the modernist novels of James, Proust, Joyce, Woolf, Musil, et al. as presenting a historically distinct representation of human subjectivity, in unprecedented relations of social dependence and independence not capturable by even the greatest "realist" novels and so requiring a distinct aesthetic form, with shifting, unstable and highly provisional points of view and constant experimentation with authorial authority and narrative coherence. Both such an *Idee* in Hegel's sense and its sensible form, its *Schein*, seem to me consistent with and indeed a kind of implication of Hegel's historical account, especially of social subjectivity. Both embody as art what Hegel's modern "ideal," a free life, requires and implies.[43]

It is also possible to imagine a modern form of *Kunstbetrachtung* unconcerned with mere distinctions in taste and committed instead to an always historically inflected interpretation, and so to "depth" of interpretation as a value, and a theory of aesthetic appreciation oriented not from beauty and pleasure[44] but from the question of the concrete meaning of freedom under conditions different from those imagined by Hegel. I am not much of a fan of Adorno on modern music, but I can see and sympathize with what he is trying to do; likewise Dostoyevsky on our historical fate in general, Beckett and Benjamin on Proust, Greenberg on abstraction, Clark on Manet, Fried on Courbet, or Manet on Menzel can all be counted as "Hegelian" interpretations of modernist moments.[45]

What exactly it would be to be moved and gripped by such a compelling postromantic art in conditions of nearly hyperreflexivity and self-consciousness is another question. And it is a very difficult one. Hegel apparently believed something analogous to what Bernard Williams meant when he claimed that "reflection kills ethical knowledge," in this case that a culture of reflection makes the near immediacy of (and so a kind of honesty in) aesthetic encounters hard to imagine. This is not a situation at all improved by

43. For a defense of this claim, see Pippin 2000 and 2014.

44. These are Kantian terms but I do not mean to imply that there is not a great deal of Hegel's theory already in Kant, as with the issue of *Belebung*. See Kant 2000, §49.

45. See Pippin 2014 for a fuller discussion.

the liberation of art from its role in politics or religion. Ironically the autonomy of art in modernity makes this problem worse, not better. Greek architecture and church music can be said to be interwoven into the fabric of daily life in a way that allowed for a more directly sensible, that is, genuinely aesthetic, encounter. Now art is experienced as "*art*," a categorization that creates so many more complex expectations and prohibitions that any direct sensible presence of the work is hard to imagine.[46] It is possible to see such radical moves as Impressionism all the way to Pollock's drip paintings, Caro's abstract steel sculptures, Stella's experiments with eccentric polygons and shaped canvases, and the like as attempts to break through such reflected mediation and reestablish art as sensuous, medium-specific, credible, and "present" under these altered conditions.[47]

In fact, an artwork false to these conditions, one that appears as the simple translation of an idea or plan into an external object, or one that addresses what is clearly assumed to be a fixed social convention, one that denies the provisionality and tenuousness of any claim to authority or even meaning, is an art object that fails in the attempt to be art, is kitsch or a consumer item or propaganda or didactic or—worst of all (and most prevalent)—*an example of a theory*. Worst of all because such objects are *false*, playing the role of art rather than being art (exactly what Hegel was worried about), and so the new aesthetic standard in postromantic art built on such Hegelian grounds is genuineness, the capacity to compel conviction at all under these conditions, to invite interpretation and reflection in the right way. Likewise, one might say that under such conditions an *agent* could be said to act falsely, violating the norms of agency even while relying on them, pretending to a false independence, or subjecting himself to an excessive dependence on social standards.[48] (Failing such a test in art leaves us with mere "objecthood," an exemplary failure when embraced as such and as art, as in literalism, minimalism, and so forth.)[49]

46. This is captured well in Thomas Struth's museum photographs, which render the problem sensible and aesthetic, even while attending to the absence of an aesthetic sensibility in the photograph's beholders.

47. Again, admittedly, all of this means drawing inferences from Hegel's lectures that are different from the ones he apparently drew. But Hegel himself provides the material for such inferences. I have tried to flesh out such a claim with respect to one form of modernism, abstraction, in Pippin 2002.

48. I discuss this issue at greater length in Pippin 2005a.

49. The debt to Michael Fried's "Art and Objecthood" is, I will assume, obvious here, in the discussion throughout this chapter. See Fried 1998a and chapters 6 and 7 in what follows.

It would take a great deal of work to get us from these very vague speculations to the claim that all these compose the postromantic artistic self-understanding and even implied "worldview" of Wagner or Cézanne or Beckett or Proust or Miró, let alone all of them. I have only wanted to suggest why Hegel does not regard the beautiful as a credible aesthetic ideal any longer, why he transforms the problem of aesthetic judgment, and why, in good Hegelian fashion, these absences can suggest something about a positive notion of a reflective and experimental art after both the beautiful and romantic inwardness.

5

Hegel on Painting

Subjectivity and Painting

Hegel's approach to the arts in his various Berlin lectures puts him in a unique position to address two very ambitious questions. First, given some view of the purpose and value of the practice of art making and art appreciating, what does it mean and what sense can we make of the fact that there are different arts: visual, literary, musical? Second, what does it mean and what sense can we make of the fact that the ideals and standards of art making change so dramatically in different societies and in different times? These are the two ways Hegel organizes his account: systematically and historically. Of course, the answer to both questions might well be: we can make no sense out of the variety of the arts. That it is a contingent and wholly accidental fact that raises no interesting philosophical question. And while the second question—what does it mean that aesthetic ideals change?—might be interesting, it too is not a philosophical or "aesthetics" question and is not relevant to any interrogation of the nature and value of art in itself. It is a question for social historians and for them alone.[1]

Both of these issues are in play in Hegel's account of the nature and significance of painting. Structurally, in one of Hegel's beloved hierarchies, painting is to be understood as "between" sculpture and music, doing, in some sense or other, better what painting attempts. And, as is well known, Hegel's historical

1. This is claimed, for example, in the first chapter of Wollheim 1987. For examples of what he is opposing (both of which show, to my mind, that the considerations behind Wollheim's rejection are far too narrow and question-begging), see Gehlen 1960 and Clark 1999. Wollheim's "psychological" theory depends on an isolation of the individual mindedness, that of the artists, which seems arbitrary and poorly motivated.

scheme claims a historical progression from symbolic to classical to romantic art. Painting is the "first" romantic art, the art of a dawning modernity.[2]

At the basis of all such claims is one issue that emerges in Hegel's account of painting. It is quite distinctive, potentially of great significance, and deserves a hearing on its own. That issue is what he means by the role of the inner, or inwardness, or subjectivity, *Innerlichkeit*, uniquely in painting. What dimension of human subjectivity is manifest in, or made more comprehensible by, painting? Only an answer to this question could make it possible to understand what it might mean to "rate" any treatment of such a subject matter as a better or worse realization of the expression of such *Innerlichkeit*. In the following I try to provide a preliminary answer to such a basic question.

First, we need a survey of Hegel's most important claims about painting. Some of them are extraordinarily unusual, and his treatment of European painting is highly selective. For example, the great French painters of the seventeenth and eighteenth centuries play no role whatsoever: no Poussin, Chardin, Greuze, Gros, or even David.[3] Hegel instead concentrates on Italian, German and Northern European, especially Dutch, painting, with an occasional reference to the Spanish.[4] His main thesis is stated directly at the outset. While classical sculpture does allow some manifestation of what he calls "a character's spiritual individuality," so that a Greek statue can be said to be "enlivened," to manifest an inner life (compared with Egyptian statuary, for example), the mode of expression is limited to a material, external form, and the limitations of that external

2. We should pause to note the obvious: that Hegel's approaches—historical, and genre-systematic—do not always line up all that well. Hegel certainly does not believe that the only real art the classical age had was sculpture. It had literature, obviously, but because of a merely preliminary understanding of subjectivity, it could not produce what literature as a genre can best do, something finally realized in modern lyric poetry. I take no position here on the value or implications of such categorical problems and will concentrate on the core of his claim about painting.

3. This is all the more striking since there are plenty of comments about French drama, music, poetry, and even French criticism. Hegel refers several times to Goethe's translation of Diderot's *Essai sur la peinture*. And Hegel did visit Paris in August of 1827. Yet there are still no references to French painting in the 1828/1829 lectures.

4. There is a large issue that I do not have the space to discuss (cf. the chapters in Kottman and Squire (2018) by Rush and Grootenboer): namely, Hegel's treatment of Dutch paintings (at least in Hotho's compilation), although the remarks occur in the 1826 lectures as well, and what appear to be his very positive remarks about the likes of van Eyck, Memling, and Scorel—remarks that seem happily resigned to mere displays of skill and the portrayal of the self-satisfactions ("coziness," "cheerfulness," "comfort") of the rising bourgeoisie. See Hegel 1975, 598. But Rutter 2010 has shown that this would be a very hasty inference. Occasionally an air of "repugnance" creeps into Hegel's account.

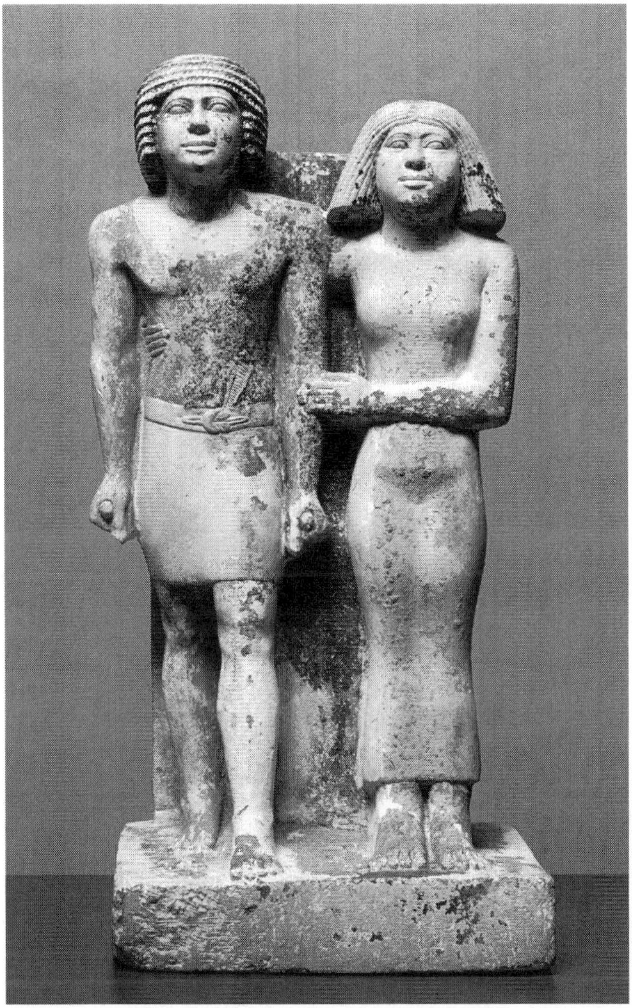

FIGURE 1. Limestone Egyptian statue of Kai-pu-ptah and Ipep from Giza, c. 2400 BC (height 56 cm). Vienna: Kunsthistorisches Museum, inv. 7444. Image from Digital Giza, The Giza Project at Harvard University.

form—marble, stone, clay, bronze—do not truly or fully allow the expression of a "person's own subjective inwardness, the life of his heart,[5] the soul of his most personal feelings" (Hegel 1975, 797) (figs. 1 and 2). Accordingly, we may admire and study classical sculpture, but it ultimately leaves us cold.[6]

5. Knox almost always translates *Gemüt* as "heart." Here the "liveliness of his temperament" could also serve as a translation, even "the liveliness of his mind."

6. For the point, cf. Adolf Heimann's unpublished *Nachschrift* of the *Vorlesung über die*

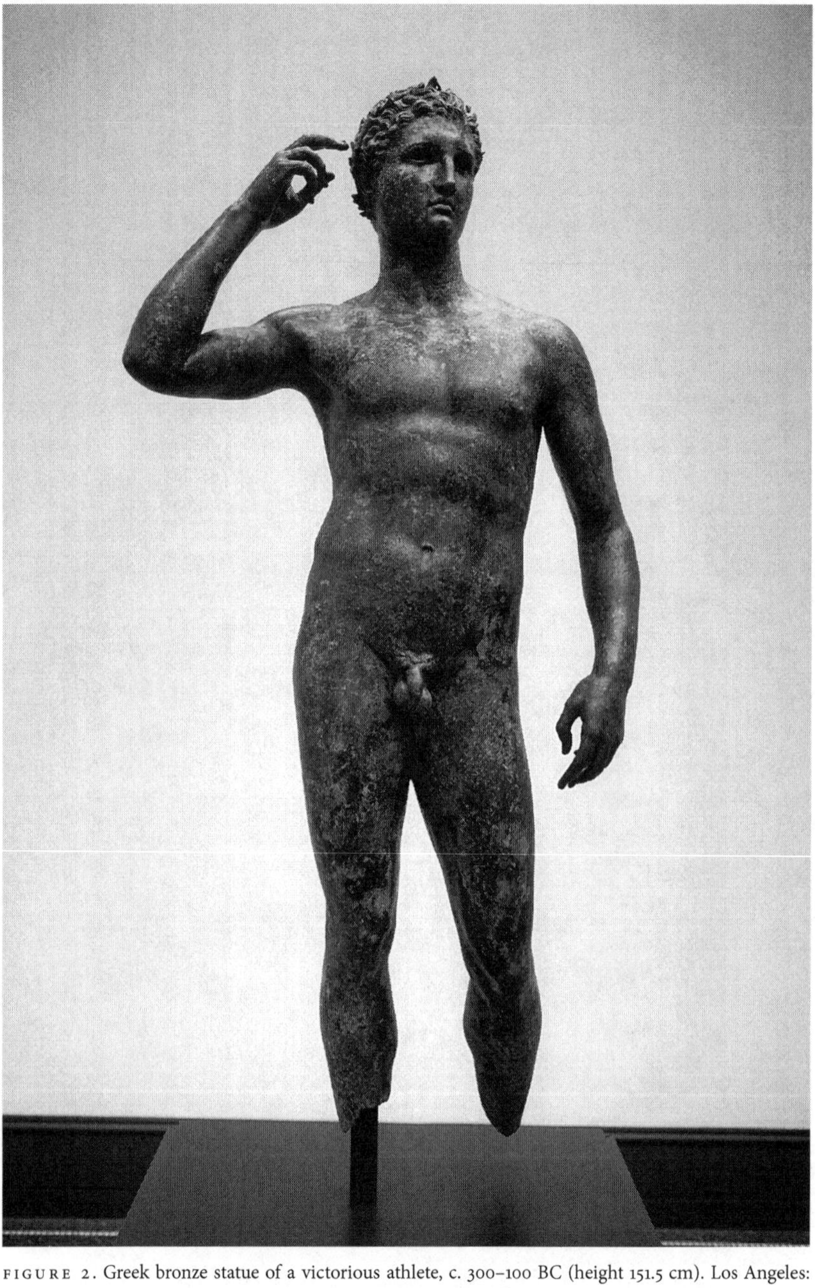

FIGURE 2. Greek bronze statue of a victorious athlete, c. 300–100 BC (height 151.5 cm). Los Angeles: J. Paul Getty Museum, Villa Collection, inv. 77.AB. 30. Image from Wikimedia Commons.

To quote Hegel: "For this reason we are at once more at home in painting. Painting, that is to say, opens the way for the first time to the principle of finite and inherently [*in sich*] infinite subjectivity, the principle of our own life and existence, *and in paintings we see what is effective and active in ourselves* [was in uns selber wirkt und tätig ist]" (Hegel 1975, 797, emphasis mine). This last line sums up in a very compressed way Hegel's main claim and sets the task: *what is it* to see an "in itself infinite subjectivity," and so what is effective and active in us, in a painting, if that painting is a work of art?

Hegel will go on to claim later that it is precisely painting's advantage in these respects, its ability to make *visible* this subjectivity, especially in its affective dimension [*die Seele der eigensten Empfindung*], that is also its limitation. Only some aspects of this self-related subjectivity *can* be made *visible*, and these aspects do not embody the "deeper truth" of such subjectivity, a truth that cannot be fully manifest materially, visibly. (This will have something to do with Hegel's famous claim that art, all art, has become for us a "thing of the past.") This is largely due to the characteristic of self-conscious subjectivity that Hegel calls "infinity." This is his way of insisting that the self's relation to itself in its experience is not a dyadic or subject-object relation. The self to which the self is related *is* the relating self. The relation is not circular, not bipolar, and so Hegel invokes the image of infinity. We shall return to the topic, but his canonical formulation is the following: "The animation [*Beseelung*] and life of spirit alone is free infinity; as such, the spirit in real existence is self-relating as something inner [*für sich selbst als Inneres ist*], because in its manifestation it reverts into itself and remains at home with itself. To spirit alone, therefore, is it given to impress the stamp of its own infinity and free return into itself upon its external manifestation" (Hegel 1975, 154). By contrast, music's mode of sensible embodiment is more adequate to less determinately material or visual dimensions of self-conscious subjectivity, and poetry ultimately relies on a sensible embodiment that is even more "ideal," in Hegel's terms, relying on mere signs, a materiality with no inherent or natural connection to content.[7] The trajectory is toward a greater degree of abstraction or ideality and more purely conceptual complexity, and so, in that sense, greater "success," greater justice to such "in itself infinite subjectivity."[8] And this

Philosophie der Kunst, edited by ed. Niklas Hebing: I refer here to p. 159 of the manuscript. I am grateful to Niklas Hebing, Birgit Sandkaulker, and the Hegel Archiv for making this transcription available to me, and I refer to it as "Hebing MS" in the footnotes that follow. On the ways in which, according to Hegel, classical art must leave us "cold," cf. Squire's chapter in Kottman and Squire 2018, 128.

7. Cf. Hebing MS, 163–65.

8. In one sense more abstract, because it transforms what Hegel calls "real objectivity" into

trajectory parallels, in the various material possibilities of outer expression, and in the changing subject matters appropriate to any such materiality, greater and greater expressive adequacy in doing justice to what he also sometimes called *Innigkeit*, or a self-related inwardness in its proper relation to the outer that has the connotation of "intimacy" or ardor. (One could say: *Innerlichkeit* as "felt" is the proper domain of painting.) As Hegel understands the issues, painting, as the first romantic art, is thus the first appropriate art of modernity, the first aesthetic manifestation of the "truth of such a self-related subjectivity," where "first" means first in both the historical and the systematic series Hegel has proposed.[9]

However, we should also note that Hegel is not completely consistent on the status of painting as a kind of prelude for, or initial version of, music and poetry. That dimension of subjectivity appropriate to painting he calls the "concentration of spirit in itself" (Hegel 1975, 815). We are not in a position to know what this means yet, but we do know from this passage that music's greater abstraction, its near mathematical form, does not allow much of an external, perceptible manifestation of inner life (its materiality is more that of a vehicle), and poetry too can only provide something Hegel calls "incomplete." Painting alone can allow a full expression *in the external* of "complete [affective or felt] inwardness [self-intimacy]" (*volle Innigkeit*). It is even able to make manifest something of the general significance of some "feeling," even while portraying a concrete particular. These—a dialectical unity between inner and outer, and between universal and particular—sound like supreme Hegelian desiderata in general, and they would seem to elevate painting's status, at least above the arts the materiality or externality of which is merely a vehicle or even arbitrary.[10]

"intellectual objectivity," and this largely because it is not bound to three-dimensional representation. It is an "abstract" representation of three-dimensionality (Hegel 1975, 796). But in another sense, spatial form is itself "the most abstract thing in nature" (Hegel 1975, 807), and so painting is in that sense less abstract, because "it is called on to express the inner life particularized in itself and therefore possessed of a wealth of varied specifications." Cf. the contrast with sculpture in this regard (where sculpture's materiality is called abstract and contrasted with the particularity available for representation in painting), in the 1823 lecture notes of Hotho (Hegel 2015, the 1823 and the 1820/21 lectures). See also Hegel 2015, 155: "die Malerie ist eine abstrakte Kunst." For more on the more modern notion of abstraction and its relevance to Hegel, see also Pippin 2002.

9. Another unmanageably large issue: one of the many synonyms for the Hegelian notion of modernity, especially important here, is "Christianity." He is not referring primarily to post-sixteenth-century Europe.

10. In the 1828/29 lectures (*Nachschrift Heimann*), Hegel stresses such a point himself: "Das Schöne ist Allgemeines und besondres, Äußerliches, und nicht getrennt, sondern auf eine Weise, wo beide Bestimmungen sich verbinden" (Hebing MS, 18).

Subject Matter

There is much more to Hegel's account of painting than the central question just summarized: What is the content or subject matter that is uniquely appropriate to painting? (Not to mention: is there one? That is, *one*?) And its subsequent implications: How is that subject matter apparent in religious, landscape, genre, and portrait painting? Of what *significance* is painting's capacity to express such content, or why is it important that painting be able to do this? Hegel has a lot of things to say about many topics, such as two-dimensionality, color, the differences between classical art and modern (understood as essentially Christian) art, and, as we have seen, about which European paintings best fulfill this distinctive purpose of painting, and, ultimately, about the fate of painting.[11] But it is already very clear that he has a unique, radical, and so quite controversial answer to a traditional question in aesthetics: given that not every painting or drawing, perhaps not every painting hung in a museum, is an artwork, when and under what conditions is a painting an artwork? The answer is: when it involves a distinct treatment of a distinct subject matter. Such a claim about subject matter is what makes Hegel's claim so unusual. Painting can make appear ("shine"),[12] can render in visible and "lively" form the "liveliness" of subjectivity or mindedness in its self-relatedness, a more abstract or logical term for human self-consciousness. That distinctive subject matter is described in such a wide variety of ways that it is a daunting task simply to arrive at some overview of these multiple descriptions of what he appears to think amount to variations on the same theme.

In the first place, we can note that Hegel's treatment of the issue of this subject matter sets his account off from many post-Kantian accounts, and this is not merely because he is exclusively interested in fine art, not the beauty of nature. For while he freely uses the language of beauty (as in "the spiritual beauty" [*geistige Schönheit*] in Raphael's Madonnas), he also makes clear that beauty as such, and any putative distinct aesthetic pleasure in the beautiful, at least as these are traditionally understood, are not his topics, not what he regards as significant in artworks. He tells us that "above all it is not the visible beauty [*sinnliche Schönheit*] of the figures but the spiritual animation [*geistige Beseelung*] whereby mastery is displayed, and which leads to the mastery of the presentation" (1975, 801) that is important. In the 1820/1821 lectures, he

11. For a helpful discussion of these elements and more, see Houlgate 2000, 61–82.

12. On the significance of the word, see Grootenboer's chapter in Kottman and Squire 2018.

notes, as if the claim were unproblematic (he declares it well known, *bekannt*) that the beautiful is the representation of the true (Hegel 2015, 23). While Hegel agrees with Kant that what is distinctive to aesthetic appreciation is that all practical or "interested" relations to either the object or the scene depicted or to the art object have been suspended or canceled, he is willing to go much farther than Kant's disinterestedness as such, in characterizing this nonpractical relation, and claim that the artwork requires of us a "wholly theoretical" (*ganz theoretisch*) response (Hegel 1975, 835).[13] For Kant, of course, going anywhere near such an intellectual response in aesthetic appreciation would be to confuse determining and reflective judgment and so reduce the aesthetic response to treating the object as an instance of a concept, missing completely the element of "free play" that makes it distinctive. But as is clear throughout all versions of the lectures, by *theoretisch*, Hegel means not straightforward concept application (much less scientific or empirical inquiry), but (and here a major question for his account, since this claim is hardly self-evident) *a still sensible and affective recognition of lived dimensions of human subjectivity in their "liveliness,"* something apparent already in his reference to spiritual animation, *geistige Beseelung*. Whatever such appreciation is, it involves something very different from the mere application of the "concept of liveliness." For one thing, Hegel's whole architectonic (with regard to "Absolute Spirit") assumes that the aesthetic *manner* of contemplative regard is different from the representational (or religious) manner and the conceptual (philosophical) manner. A typical passage occurs in his discussion of poetry, which he credits, as he does all the arts, for overcoming any "separation [*Trennung*] of feeling and vision from . . . intellectual thinking," and in achieving this "liberation" from "that separation between thinking, which is concentrated on the universal, and feeling and vision which seize on the individual," poetry and the other arts achieve the expression of "concrete liveliness" (*konkrete Lebendigkeit*), and so a "reconciliation [*Versöhnung*] with the universality of thought" (Hegel 1975, 1006).[14] These desiderata of art as such are most adequately realized in one way in Greek art, and in another, quite different way in lyric poetry. Clearly, this assumes that there is a way for our intellectual

13. There is a more detailed discussion of Kant in Hegel's 1820/21 lectures: Hegel 2015, 27–30; cf. also Hebing MS, 16–18.

14. At Hegel 1975, 1128, Hegel is well aware of the Kantian problem. He notes that a philosopher (at least a philosophizing "at peace with itself [*berühigte*]") may "animate" his understanding with his "feeling" and exchange a mere philosophical comprehension with "the free play of particular aspects." Schiller is his example. He also notes that art must "conceal" this "inner" sensible unity lest art "fall into the prosaic tone of expounding them didactically." There is a sense in which this is not all that different from Kant. See Pippin 1996.

or theoretical capacities to be engaged *in* such a sensible and affective appreciation of spiritual liveliness—one can even say here what it feels like to be a self-conscious being, how that dimension is "lived"— a way that denies any strict distinction between determining and reflective judgments, which in turn denies (as he does vigorously and constantly since the first Jena writings) any putative strict logical separation of concept and intuition in any experience, any claim that they are independent contributors to experience. That topic, far and away the most important topic in Hegel's relation to Kant, would take us far afield.[15] What we need now is just to note that for Hegel artworks can compel our attention in a way that involves some sort of epistemic component—a recognitional component in which we "sensibly-affectively" experience important dimensions of our own subjectivity, now concretely expressed, and so engage in a kind of attempt at self-knowledge—the modality of which is tied to the unique embodiment of human subjectivity available in art.

Self-Relatedness

But what is that unique embodiment? It is the embodiment of "self-related subjectivity" (*für sich seiende Subjektivität*) (Hegel 1975, 802). Hegel is here specifying a dimension available to painting as a romantic art that is a specification of the general task he assigned to all art early in the introduction:[16] "Things in nature are only immediate and single, while man as spirit duplicates himself [*verdoppelt sich*], in that (i) he is as things in nature are, but (ii) he is just as much for himself; he sees himself, represents himself to himself, thinks, and only on the strength of this active placing himself before himself is he spirit [*nur durch dies tätige Fürsichsein Geist ist*]" (Hegel 1975, 30). Stated in another summary way: "The universal need for art, that is to say, is man's rational need to lift the inner and outer world into his spiritual consciousness as an object in which he recognizes [*widererkennt*] again his own self" (Hegel 1975, 31). It is important to emphasize here that Hegel is saying that there is

15. See Pippin 1989, 2005a, and 2014.

16. The passage specifies what has to be called a double doubling for *Geist*. First *Geist* distinguished itself from its natural being, and so exists as both a natural and a "spiritual" being (what he will later call an "amphibian"), and second, *Geist* as such is "double," or as conscious, always also self-conscious, in an unusual self-relation. Painting will also have a version of this dual doubleness. It depicts an object but also expresses the artist's "take" on or view of the object. And the beholder as well stands in a relation to the object both visually and reflectively or "theoretically," in the sense of aesthetic intelligibility I think Hegel is struggling to make clear. And any such dimension is also itself potentially self-conscious, as in philosophical aesthetics.

a crucial link between our own duality or self-relatedness and the duality in painting, essentially between whatever is depicted and its *Schein* or appearance, the distinctive way it shows up for the artists and us, the "take" on it by the artist, made available to us. Only a self-conscious or reflective being can see a painted canvas *as a painting*, because only such a being can see both the physical properties of the object and the "mindedness" inherent in its appearance. As he says in the 1820/21 lectures, echoing the "*widererkennt*" above, "the connection between us and the beautiful is that we see the nature of our own essence in the beautiful" (Hegel 2015, 29–30). That essence is our own duality, the way we show up for ourselves in various self-conceptions that are not the result of any self-observation, any immediate presence of the self to itself, but since not immediate, always involve some not yet fulfilled realization.[17] We are not simply what we are, or we need some self-conception to be what we are, in a way analogous to how a painting, or an object depicted in it, is not simply what it is, as it would be in ordinary experience. It is "lifted" out of nature in that sense and "idealized."[18] (One of the core claims in Hegel is that any such self-relatedness remains incomplete apart from its relation to another self-consciousness. This dimension is present in paintings-as-manifestations-of-subjectivity in the address to a beholder implicit in all paintings displayed or shown—i.e., all paintings. But this relation can be proleptic and implicit only in painting. It can be said to address us, but that address cannot be iterated in response to us.) What is so distinctive about painting is that it can make all this not only *visible* but sensible in an *affective* sense as well. This is a difficult point to which we shall be returning frequently.

The self recognized is said most often to be *Gemüt*, the human emotional experience of the human, or "heart," *that* dimension of its status as *Geist* (primarily "feeling," captured best, as noted, by *Innigkeit*, where such a feeling is a kind of self-"intimacy"), but it is often given a uniquely Hegelian gloss. A little later he characterizes painting's subject matter as a "reflection of spirit [*Wiederschein des Geistes*] in which the spirit only reveals its spiritual quality [*seine Geistigkeit*] by canceling [*aufhebt*] the real existent and transforming it into a mere shining [*Scheinen*, or manifesting or seeming] of the spiritual [*im*

17. Cf. Pinkard 2017 and his language about what "shows up" for us: this as something in the world, not the result of subjective projection.

18. As in the passage just quoted and Hegel 1975, 49: "Of course we may often hear favorite phraseology [*beliebte Redensart*] about man's duty to remain in immediate unity with nature; but such unity, in its abstraction, is purely and simply rudeness and ferocity, and by dissolving this unity for man, art lifts him with gentle hands out of and above imprisonment in nature [*hebt ihn mit milden Händen über die Naturbefangenheit hinweg*]."

Geistigen] for the spiritual" (Hegel 1975, 805). This prepares the way for him to explain how such self-related subjectivity is "really" the subject matter of painting even if the painting is a landscape or still life.

One more element: the "*active* for itselfness" (*tätige Fürsichsein*) mentioned earlier is characterized as a process of self-alienation in the external or material (in several dimensions throughout many aspects of Hegel's work), and a return to itself. It has thus *achieved*, through some sort of struggle, which has presumably left some sort of visual and so pictorial traces, a "for itself" determinacy, a self-conception, that is, uniquely for humans (see the contrast above with things of nature), self-constituting (as above), and only thereby *is Geist*. The formula is: "the spiritual inner life . . . can come into appearance in the external only as retiring into itself out of it [*die nur im Äußeren kann zum Vorschein kommen, als aus demselben in sich hineingehend*]" (Hegel 1975, 805).[19]

Examples

This adds yet another layer to that dimension of subjective self-relatedness available in painting. A revealing, if not quite typical, example of such a "return" for Hegel is Correggio's Mary Magdalene in Dresden—lost during the Second World War (fig. 3). The strange-sounding kind of "doubleness" in the subjectivity represented best by painting, that externalization and then return to inner repose, is described in her case as the depiction of a repentant sinner about whom we can say, "now," or postrepentance, that the sin was not a true expression of her, not seriously (*daß es ihr mit der Sünde nicht Ernest ist*), even though only the rejection of sin could have made that clear. His full description of this "return to herself" is: "The artist has left no traces of reflection on one of the circumstances which could hint back [*zurückdeuten*] to sin and

19. The notion of a self-constituting self-relation as human subjectivity helps explain Hegel's highly unusual comments about the chief "physical element" of painting: light. Light is said to be "pure identity with itself and therefore purely self-reposing, the earliest ideality, the original self of nature." Light illuminates the painting; it does not move it or push or change it; it is not in a material relation to the object, but is the element within which, by virtue of which, the object can be what it is, intelligible; the relation is thus "ideal." That is, it is the necessary element whereby the painting can be actually what it is potentially: visible. In different lights, the painting is different. The relation of the self to the self is also not a material but an ideal relation. That is, it is not a subject-object relation (or observational) in a similar sense. Self-understanding allows *Geist* to be what it is as *Geist*, a self-constituting being; it is what it takes itself to be, is what it is only in the "light" of this self-regard, and in that sense is an ideal being. In the 1823 lectures, Hegel (2015) calls light "subjective nature" and "the physical I" (473).

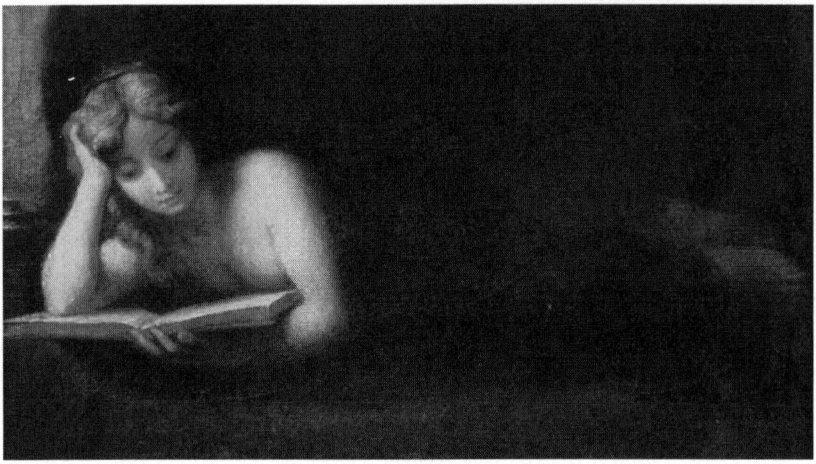

FIGURE 3. Antonio Allegri da Correggio, *Mary Magdalen Reading in a Landscape*, c. 1522 (29 × 39 cm). Oil on canvas. Formerly in Dresden (Staatliche Kunstsammlungen, Gemaeldegalerie Alte Meister, inv. 154), destroyed in the Second World War.

guilt; she is unconscious of those times, absorbed [*vertieft*] only in her present situation, and this faith, this sensitiveness, this absorption [*Versinken*] seems to be her entire and real character" (Hegel 1975, 868). The implication is that nothing about her true nature, her "eigentlicher, ganzer Charakter," *could* have been immediately or simply represented, and so her (or anyone's) real character is apparent not in any representation of purity or innocence, in *sinlessness* or simple passive *oubli de soi*, but only in the results of a struggle with and rejection of (in this case) sin, a rejection that shows that even when sinning, she was no "sinner." Only thereby can the return to herself be marked by a confidence and self-possession so complete as to allow a visible mark of genuineness, deep absorption. To follow Hegel, we have to believe that in the painting itself—in, literally, what we can see—Mary Magdalene is neither innocent, nor a guilty ex-sinner, nor self-deceived about her sinful past; that she has "returned" to her self in a way marked by such self-possession that her complete absorption in the reading is a capacity she has earned or achieved. The genuineness of her self-understanding is reflected by her confident immersion in the book; she is shameless in her half-naked state without a naïve indifference to death or the sufferings of Christ. I think one can see what he means. This is a valuable marker of the double or reflected subjectivity that Hegel singles out as the true object of painting. (That Mary's absorption is not simple self-forgetfulness but an implicitly self-related and achieved genuineness is partly achieved by her nakedness, which manifests not innocence but something like a mature absence of shame, given what she has been through. Not a self-evident point, I concede.)

Another good example is given later, when Hegel discusses Raphael's *Transfiguration* (fig. 4). He notes that the painting has been criticized because it seems to lack unity and be two paintings stuck together, Christ's ascension above, and the chaos surrounding the afflicted, blind child below. But Hegel speaks again of a "double action," a duality that is actually a unity. The end of Christ's visible presence on earth is also the beginning of his (higher, more "ideal") spiritual presence, as he says, "wherever two or three are gathered" in his name. He notes that the two pointing gestures, one up toward Christ and the other toward the child, are indications of how Christ's transcendence is fully compatible with his immanent presence, and so even the love of God for mankind requires the "logical" structure of separation or otherness as well as indwelling unity.[20]

But Hegel does not stay at this level of abstraction. Another step greatly specifies this "subject matter," and it quickly makes his position sound extreme and implausible. In explaining further this notion of a subject "withdrawing" out of its suffering and into itself, and in contrasting the "peaceful repose" (*ein stilles Ausruhen*) of Greek heroes with the "bliss" (*Seligkeit*) visible in painting (a bliss possible only after "conflict and agony" and when a soul has "triumphed over its sufferings"),[21] Hegel says something he repeats several times thereafter: that religious or "passionless" (*leidenschaftslos*) love is the true, ideal subject matter of all painting. So the very best subject matter for painting, wherein it can best be what painting is (that is, in its typical formulation, when painting agrees with itself, when it is what painting essentially is), is the depiction of "the reconciliation of the individual heart with God." Stated with all the flourishes: "The soul wills *itself*, but it wills itself in something other than what it is in its individuality and therefore it gives itself up in the face of God [*sie gibt sich deshalb auf gegen Gott*] in order to find and enjoy itself in him. This is characteristic of *love*, spiritual depth [*Innigkeit*] in its truth, that religious love without desire which gives to the human spirit reconciliation [*Versöhnung*], peace, and bliss [*Seligkeit*]" (Hegel 1975, 816). This contrast between Greek and modern art is interesting in itself. Hegel goes on to explain the inadequate notion of death in the Greek form of

20. The painting could even be read as a Hegelian allegory about the self-transcendence of painting as an art. Christ's physical departure opens the possibility of a higher spiritual presence in the communal life of *Geist*. He is "seen" more truthfully by the blind boy. This at least suggests something about the transcendence of painting in music and poetry.

21. Cf. also Hebing MS, 166.

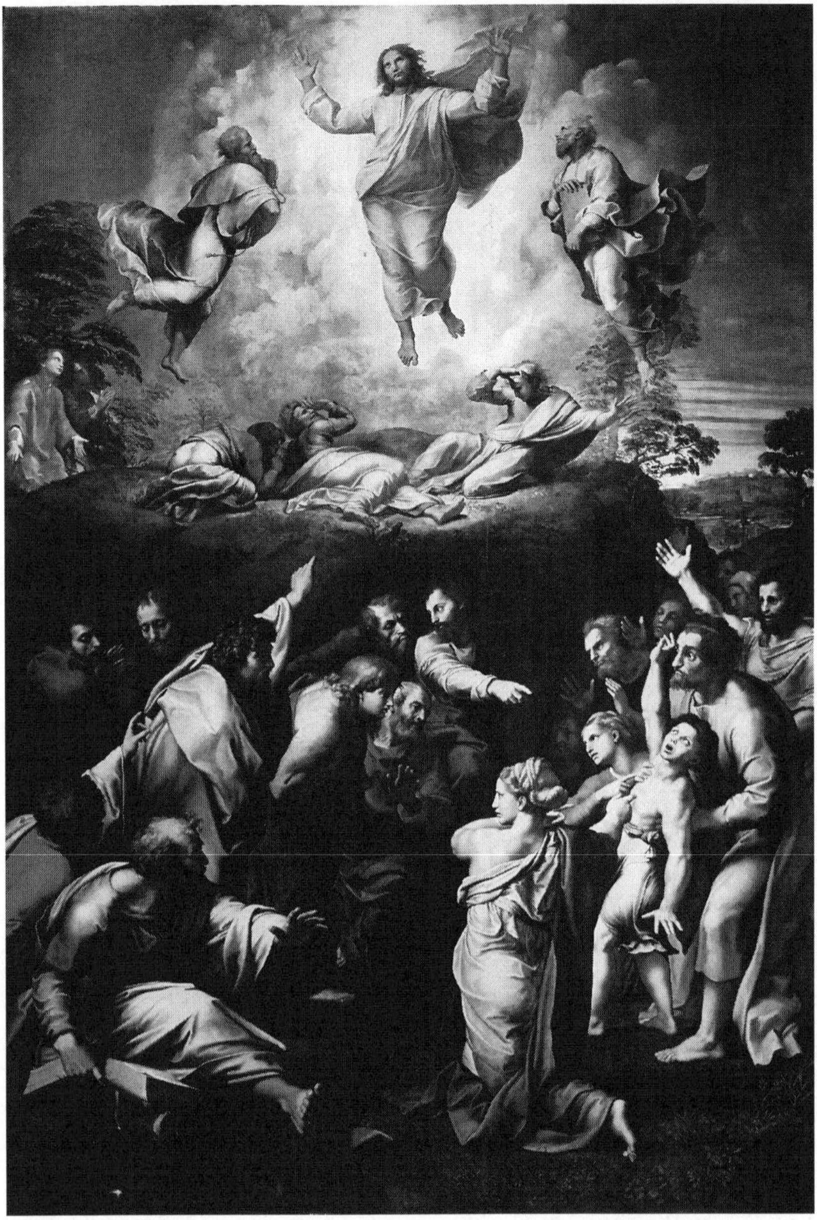

FIGURE 4. Raphael, *Transfiguration*, 1516–1520 (405 × 278 cm). Tempera on wood. Vatican: Pinacoteca Vaticana, Cat. 40333.

life, and the absence of religious love, as a further explanation of why sculpture is the ideal art of the Greeks, and painting is essentially a Christian art. But the subject matter claim is the essential one, and he goes very far with it:[22] "As the most perfect [*vollkommensten*] subject for painting I have already specified inwardly satisfied love, the object of which is not a purely spiritual 'beyond' [*Jenseits*] but is present, so that we can see love itself before us in what is loved. The supreme and unique form of this love is Mary's love for the Christ-child" (Hegel 1975, 824). Where does all this leave us? It first leaves us with a dizzying array of claims, all of which Hegel thinks are related, and point to the same answer. Consider what we have seen: that painting "opens the way for the first time to the principle of finite and inherently infinite subjectivity"; that our relation to painting should be understood as "theoretical," but in a way that presumes no separation between the affective and the intellectual, and that involves a self-recognition on the part of the beholder; that painting concerns itself with "spiritual liveliness" and "spirit's concentration in itself"; that the subject matter of painting is self-related subjectivity, an "active for itself-ness," or it is the human heart, temperament or *Gemüt*; that every painting transforms any "real existent" into the spiritual; that this self-related subjectivity is, must be, the result of a withdrawal from some external suffering into a repose with itself and only thereby is it what it is; and that the paradigm instance of *all* these apparently disparate versions of such achieved self-conscious subjectivity is religious love, primarily of the Madonna for the Christ child.

The first thing to ask is, assuming we can understand how all these accounts come to fruition in the claim about religious love, in what sense should we understand this account to be not an account of *one type* of painting, religious paintings about human-divine love, but an account of what *painting*, with regard to its distinctness as an art, actually is?

Consider first landscapes. How does Hegel include landscapes within what he calls "the absolute spiritual ideal" as "the essential subject matter of painting" (*des absoluten geistigen Ideals als des wesentlichsten Inhaltes der romantischen Malerei*) (Hegel 1975, 831)? When Hegel contrasts an ordinary experience of a landscape with a painted landscape, he emphasizes again that "what" is being painted is not the landscape itself, is not a mere carefully mimetic representation of the world, at least not if the image is a work of fine

22. Cf. also Hegel 1975, 539–40: "The true essence of love consists in giving up the consciousness of oneself, forgetting oneself in another self, yet in this surrender and oblivion having and possessing oneself alone. This reconciliation of the spirit with itself and the completion of itself to a totality is the Absolute."

art.[23] The subject matter is actually, still, some dimension of human subjectivity, or in this case the affective, emotional meaning of the natural world, selected and displayed just this way so as to manifest various experiential states. In this sense the "objects" of a landscape painting are not the mountains, rivers, or forests depicted, but a kind of significance that we can see only when nature is "doubled," transformed into an appearance or "showing" of such spirituality, a *Schein*. That is what a landscape painter does. In that respect his goal is not the conformity of painting with nature but to show the correspondence of the portrayed "object with itself," which is said to be "reality ensouled for itself" (*die für sich beseelte Realität ist*) (Hegel 1975, 843), that is, with what it is in its true (affective) significance. So even natural objects can be said to be both just what they are in their immediate being and reflected as what they truly are in their affective meaning, when treated as objects of painting. That is what we mean by reality "ensouled for itself." It is ensouled because it is affectively intelligible; it means something affectively, and a great landscape can evoke that affective intelligibility *in* the scene and so can avoid the implication of any mere subjective projection. *Its* intelligibility, *its* availability for a form of sensible or affective intelligibility, is its "soul," its "life."[24] Of course, such a notion of affective intelligibility assumes such controversial matters as there being intentional content to affective states, not to mention no separation between thought and feeling, and those assumptions are worthy of several independent discussions.

Moreover, we are natural beings as well, and we experience in landscapes what Hegel calls an "echo of the heart" (*einen Anklang an das Gemüt*) in the "free liveliness [*Lebendigkeit*] of nature," liveliness being another synonym for ensouled or intelligible in this emotionally available way. Moreover, Hegel emphasizes the way a painted landscape can isolate and emphasize what he is willing to call the spiritual dimensions *of nature*, which is experienced by us as a correspondence of *Stimmungen*, states of mind in one sense, but a kind of natural attunement in a broader sense, a fit between an experienced emotion and some objective correlate. This is the affective-sensible version of the "fit" between our demand for intelligibility and the world's being intelligible, the supreme principle of Hegel's idealism, expressed most rigorously in his

23. Stated more formally at Hegel 1975, 155: "Thus the truth of art cannot be mere correctness, to which the so-called imitation of nature is restricted; on the contrary, the outer must harmonize with an inner which is harmonious in itself, and just on that account, can reveal itself as itself in the outer."

24. In the 1823 lectures, Hegel (2015, 474) remarks on how painting, more than any other art, combines the "two extremes": the interests of the object and the interests of subjective art.

Science of Logic and in his confidence that the forms of thought just are the forms of being.

We are clearly dangerously deep into the distinctive vocabulary of Hegel's speculative philosophy, but we can appreciate what he is after by concentrating on the fact that painting turns anything from what it is ordinarily or unreflectively experienced as into a showing of something, a *Schein*. This is what he meant in the passage, some of which was quoted earlier: "So painting does indeed work for our vision, but in a way that the object it presents does not remain an actual total spatial natural existence but becomes a reflection of spirit [*wiederschein des Geistes*] in which the spirit only reveals its spiritual quality [*seine Geistigkeit*] by canceling [*aufhebt*] the real existent and transforming it into a mere shining [*Scheinen*] of the spiritual [*im Geistigen*] for the spiritual" (Hegel 1975, 805). This claim allows us to connect the doubleness of painting (*Wiederschein*)—the fact that at work in an art painting is both the object depicted and the painter's reflection of that object, and thereby what it shows itself *as*, in and by means of painting, its *Schein*—with the double subjectivity theme introduced in the first part here. The claim can be simply formulated as: only in a world of self-conscious subjects could there by objects like painting, because only self-interpreting beings can recognize objects that embody such an attempted self-interpretation; or, only beings who can recognize that such self-interpretations can be false or inauthentic can appreciate the task of a faithful interrogation of the self-relatedness embodied in an artwork. The more general point that connects the two is Hegel's denial that while any form of human subjectivity is a reflected related, a self-relation, no aspect of the self-relation is immediate, the simple presence of the self to itself. In the same sense, a painting (if it is an art) is not a direct mimetic depiction but a *Schein*, an appearing as, or a "minded view." This issue is among the most complicated and possibly the most important in all of Hegel, so it is difficult to deal with economically. It goes to our first indication that painting is "about" a potentially "infinite" subjectivity, one of the several ways he characterizes the true object of painting as a distinct art.[25] The claim is that there is no straightforward subject-*object* relation in this self-relation, even though there is some form of doubleness or separation

25. See Hegel 1992, §163: "When infinity is finally an object for consciousness, and consciousness is aware of it as what it is, then consciousness is self-consciousness." And §178: "self-consciousness exists in and for itself because and by way of its existing in and for itself for an other; i.e., it exists only as recognized. The concept of its unity in its doubling, of infinity realizing itself in self-consciousness, is that of a multi-sided and multi-meaning intertwining, such that, on one hand, the moments within this intertwining must be strictly kept apart from each other, and on the other hand, they must also be taken and cognized at the same time as not distinguished, that is, they must be always taken and cognized in their opposed meanings."

of the self from itself, as well as a distinctive unity. The self-relation is not observational or any form of self-inspection. To say, however, that our self-relation is, on the contrary, self-constitutive, or that we are what we take ourselves to be, is not to say that a self-constitution is uncontrolled and potentially arbitrary. Whatever any subject takes itself to be, any aspect of its practical identity, its self-avowals, expressions of deep commitments and the like, is provisional, realized, Hegel claims, only in deeds that manifest their genuineness, or not (as in the case of exaggerated or self-deceived avowals, however sincerely made). His general formulation for this is that the inner can truly be what it is, what it turns out to be, only in the outer.

Painting as Action

There is more to be said about this inner-outer relation before things can get any clearer,[26] but its relevance to painting is as immediate as its relevance to action. In the former case, any painting (again, if it is an artwork; not all paintings are artworks) is an outer for which we must seek the inner, even though that inner *is* just what is manifested in the outer. In the latter case, attempting to understand outer bodily movements requires that we understand what inner intention rationalized the deed for the agent, although what that intention is is at work and accessible only in the deed itself (and not by asking the agent, or not reliably anyway). The most significant manifestation of the relation, the realization of *Geist* as such in the outer, is the realization of freedom, defined by Hegel as "being-with-self-in-the-other," or paradigmatically, human love (Hegel's chief example of realized human freedom). That already suggests a link back to themes we have already seen.

But consider the bearing of all this metaphysics on painting. One way in which Hegel tries to bring all these themes together is in a discussion of the great importance of two-dimensionality in painting, especially as opposed to sculpture. That requirement means for Hegel that a self-related or "doubled" subjectivity (consciousness as always also self-consciousness) is of a piece with the kind of duality or internal self-relatedness that makes a depiction an artwork and not a mere pictorial record. He says about sculpture that it is relatively "indifferent" to the spectator, independent of her, does not directly address the spectator since she can walk all around the statue from any point of view. Such an artwork is "self-reposing, self-complete, and objective" (*innerlich auf sich Beruhende, Abgeschlossene und Objektive ist*). Here is what he says, by contrast, about painting:

26. See the discussion in Pippin 2014, 139–43.

> Whereas in painting the content is subjectivity, more precisely the inner life inwardly particularized, and for this very reason the separation [*Entzweiung*] in the work of art between its subject and the spectator must emerge [*hervortreten*] and yet must immediately be dissipated [*auflösen*] because, by displaying what is subjective, the work, in its whole mode of presentation, reveals its purpose as existing not independently on its own account but for subjective apprehension, for the spectator. (Hegel 1975, 806)

What he means by saying that there must be both an address to an independent spectator, and the canceling or dissolution of that very separation, is important for everything he says afterward, even if it is typical of Hegel to conjoin what appear to be incompossible requirements. It is yet another example of a duality that is also a unity.[27] His overall point in the paragraph is to emphasize the value of the "idealizing" aspect of two-dimensionality, as if the worked over and so subjectively created depiction/illusion is what makes the "appearing" aspect and so the duality inherent in painting possible. If a painting is a work of art, its unavoidability calls attention to its status as *Schein*, not a simple echo of the thing depicted. This dual aspect is what makes it possible for a painting to manifest the object as reflected or appearing to a subject (and so as separate from the beholder, something shown *to* the beholder) and to be nonetheless *the object's* appearing or *Schein*, and a dissolution of such a separation, an aspect that draws the beholder *into* that shining, requiring of her an articulation of what is appearance and what is "that which appears," requiring, just by virtue of that mark of its subjectivity, an immersion into it in itself.[28]

A realistic or mimetic statue is, on the other hand, like another version of the object or person depicted, and has fewer (although by no means no) technical means either for intimating the artist's subjectivity or for inviting the viewer's involvement in working out the appearance-reality distinction. Hegel goes on to insist on the effects of this two-dimensional and idealizing component. In painting,

> The spectator is as it were in it from the beginning [*von Anfang an mit dabei*], is counted in with it, and the work exists only for this fixed point, i.e. for the individual apprehending it. Yet for this relation to intuition [*Anschauung*]

27. It brings to mind Michael Fried's Diderotian problematic: the painting's fiction that it is indifferent to, closed off to, the beholder, even as it is clearly made to be beheld. See Fried 1998a.

28. This is not to deny that such a "duality" can be missed. Those art historians who think of art history as a science, or as exclusively concerned with authenticating the history of different techniques, technical innovations, the transmission of influence or patronage, miss it. As do those who think of this interpretive requirement as essentially reactive, as going on "in" the interpreter.

> *and its spiritual reflection* [geistigen Reflex] the pure *appearance* of reality is enough, and the actual totality of spatial dimensions is really disturbing [*störend*] because in that case the objects perceived retain an existence of their own and do not simply appear as configured artificially by spirit for its own contemplation [*Anschauung*—probably better translated as intuition or seeing]. (Hegel 1975, 805)

This allows him to conclude as follows: "In painting, however, satisfaction does not lie in the objects as they exist in reality [*im wirklichen Sein*] but in the purely theoretical interest [*in dem bloß theoretischen Interesse*] in the external reflection of the inner life, and consequently painting dispenses with all need and provision for a reality and an organization totally spatial in all dimensions" (Hegel 1975, 805). The idea is that painting is uniquely capable of capturing *in materially embodied, visible form* (a manifestation of an outer with an inner) what we have been calling the duality inherent in human subjectivity, its characteristic ontological uniqueness. That Hegel claims that this is all possible only thanks to Christianity, that it is absent from the Greeks or non-Christian civilizations, is an issue we can leave for another day. Painting is distinctive because the inner-outer dimension of this phenomenon is literally *visible* in painting, in painting's material or outer expression, in a way that is not so for music or poetry. Every art painting embodies a self-conception and can be said to be attempting to realize such a self-conception, a showing or appearing of what it takes itself to be. Its status, what it invites, is thus like a face or a gesture within the painting, intimating its other, *what* is appearing. This is why Hegel calls a painting a "thousand-eyed Argus," like—but infinitely more difficult to interpret than—a human or two-eyed face (Hegel 1975, 153). And in painting, that which appears can both be seen and not be seen *in* the objects depicted. A musical note is not a representation like this (although in a different way, it can be said to have an outer and an inner), and poetic language also bears meaning in such a way that such meaning is not *visible* in the letters and lines and sentences and paragraphs; they are mere vehicles. As noted, this also means for Hegel that painting's ability to express such an inner is limited to what *can* be made visible, and that is only one dimension of this interiority. It has other dimensions that require musical and poetic expression, not to mention religious representation and philosophical conceptuality.

And this dimension of subjectivity is treated by Hegel in a way that presumes a great deal of his full philosophical position. For, as we have seen, "subjectivity" is used here elliptically, such that it ultimately refers not to individual subjectivity alone but to such individuals in relations of dependence, and such that it is also a self-realized true independence, most manifest in relations of human love [*bei sich selbst sein im Anderen*], and supremely manifest when not subject to the contingencies of romantic love. That is figured here as divine or religious ("passionless") love, but could just as well be described as the philosophical love of the truth, and, reciprocally, the availability of truth as the object of such love. (In general, this is what I think Hegel is referring to when he refers to the divine. The god of the philosophers, in other words.) This means that in all such cases, because of its separation from itself, its struggle to be who the subject is, subjectivity must be depicted as in a struggle, leaving visible traces, a successful involvement with, immersion in, the external world and others, and then a return to itself. All painting thus captures a moment in a fundamental narrative that has a certain logic and that must be understood to understand the unique availability of moments in such a narrative in painting. Not all painting is "about" such religious love, but in so far as all painting has as its final object self-related subjectivity, all subject matters are all potentially or *an sich* the *full* realization of such subjectivity, whether they depict the Madonna and child or evoke the human tonality or attunement of a still life or landscape. Such potentialities are intimated in any art painting in its relation to the doubleness of human subjectivity.

This is all an abstract—perhaps insufferably abstract—account of the emotional power of painting. Let me close with a visual indication of its appropriateness. Consider Théodore Géricault's *Head of a White Horse*, 1816–17, now hanging in the Louvre (fig. 5).[29] I want to suggest that painting immediately and vividly brings to life Hegel's dual claims about subjectivity and painting. What is so arresting about the painting is the incontrovertible subjectivity or deep interiority of the horse, *literally visible*, even while mysterious, requiring interpretive work. There is something in the expression of the horse, even given the animal's exoticism and strangeness, with those huge nostrils, and its odd, almost carefully combed mane, all at once accusatory, wise, hesitant, both wary and knowing, uncertain if facing friend or foe, not to mention simply noble, in a pose of great dignity, as if facing and seeking the "other" without which, for Hegel, it cannot be the subject it is, and unsure about finding such a realization. (A common theme I have tried to show elsewhere, in Manet a generation later.)[30] One easily imagines that the horse is looking at a human being, in an expression understandably wary, figuring not only species wariness but an omnipresent human wariness too. Seeing

29. I owe my sense of the immense power of this painting to Michael Fried's essay "Géricault's Romanticism" in Fried 2014.

30. Pippin 2014.

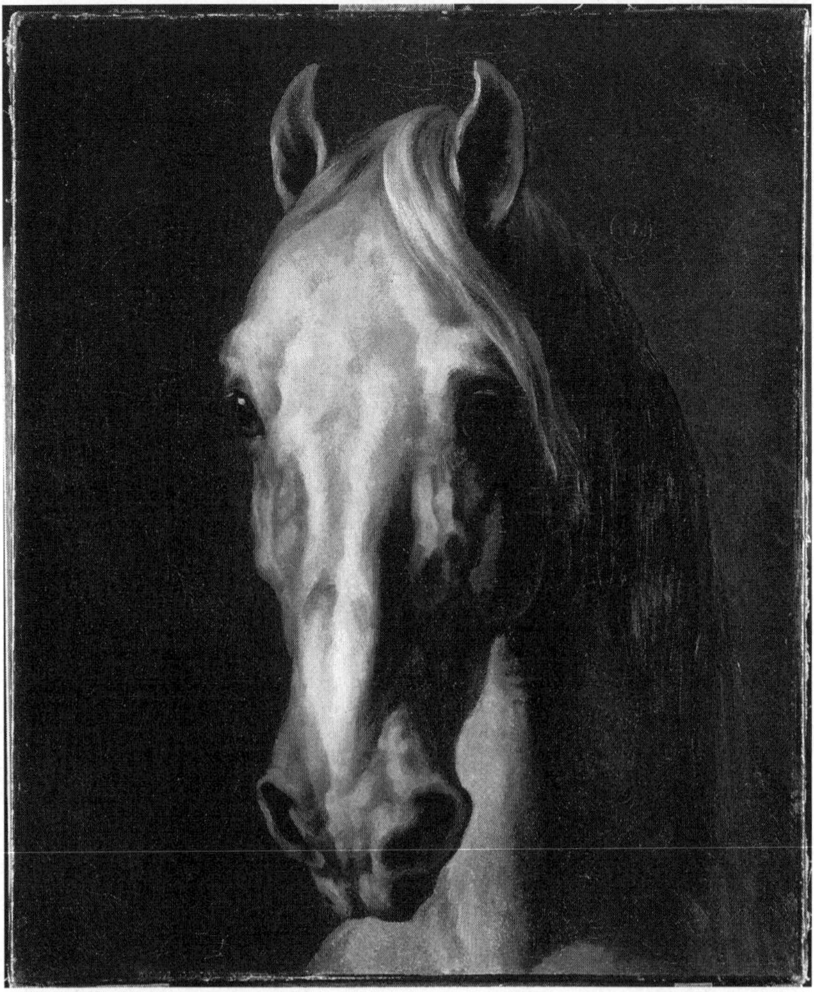

FIGURE 5. Théodore Géricault, *Head of a White Horse,* c. 1815 (65.5 × 54.5 cm). Oil on canvas. Paris: Musée du Louvre, inv. RF544.

it this way (again, a way that can be missed if we take the painting as simply mimetic) is what it would be to understand the "moment" as a moment in the struggle or narrative required by Hegel's account of double subjectivity, here captured by the doubleness of the painting, showing the horse and intimating something not fully shown but still somehow visible. We see expressed, on the two-dimensional surface, the horse's subjectivity; its interiority is visible and, one has to say, "felt," even as it remains to-be-found, present as not present, and given not only that the horse is looking at a fictionalized viewer, but that the painting is directly facing (in Fried's sense)[31] the beholder, it presents the same inner-out dynamic on the surface of the painting as such, the same dynamic, a visible intimation of "inner" meaning—about animality, species relations, wildness, and domesticity, trust, fear, even pride—and all of this not conceptually or discursively, but in a way I have called, I hope following Hegel, affectively intelligible.

31. Fried 1998a.

6

Authenticity in Painting: Remarks on Michael Fried's Art History

My topic is authenticity in or perhaps as painting, not the authenticity *of* paintings; I know next to nothing about the problem of verifying claims of authorship. I am interested in another kind of genuineness and fraudulence, the kind at issue when we say of a person that he or she is false, not genuine, inauthentic, lacks integrity, and especially when we say he or she is playing to the crowd, playing for effect, or is a poseur. These are not quite moral distinctions (no one has a duty to be authentic), but they are robustly normative appraisals, applicable even when such falseness is a case not of straight hypocrisy but of lack of self-knowledge or of self-deceit. (A person can be quite sincere and not realize the extent of her submission to the other's expectations and demands.) This sort of appraisal also has a long history in post-Rousseauist reflections on the dangers of uniquely modern forms of social dependence, and it is a prominent worry in the modern novel.

Why talk about paintings in such terms? The Western art tradition has been in a famous conundrum about the status of artworks—the dissolution of the borders between art and nonart, and the possibility of great art—for some time now, but it has rarely seemed to any discussant in that tradition that the normative issues at stake in a possibly modern art are *like* the questions sketched above about authenticity in a life. But it began to seem that way to Denis Diderot, a dimension of his work rescued, developed, and transformed with great elegance and persuasiveness by Michael Fried. In Diderot's case, he linked his distaste for "mannered" paintings with his distaste for what he saw all around him as an ever more mannered life. He made clear that his art criticism was informed by the same distinction as that between "a man presenting himself in company and a man acting from motivation, between a man who's alone and a man being observed."[1] Likewise in *The Salon of 1767*, Diderot's frequent synonym for the theatrical—the "mannered"—is invoked "in morals, discourse or the arts" as a general "vice of regulated society," and in a particularly telling definition in the same work he associates being so mannered with being "less than fully committed" to one's role or occupation or pretended virtue.[2] It might seem odd to say that paintings can be *true to life* in ways quite different from simple verisimilitude and so can be *false* in a way similar to the ways in which a person can be false. (This would appear to claim that a painting can seem to proclaim a "commitment" to painting itself, to being a painting, but then be "less than fully committed.") But, however odd, that is what Diderot seems to be suggesting. And it is not all *that* strange. New movements or schools in all arts are often oriented from some such claim—that the prior school or tradition was phony, had become mannered or theatrical and in that sense had lost its vitality, its life.[3] At any rate, such corresponding forms of falseness (in painting and in life), and the question of *why* both might seem a growing threat, are the issues I want to raise in what follows.[4]

Now Diderot was very probably not thinking in world-historical or philosophical terms and was likely concerned much more with the contemporary results of a corrupt court culture, by his time already a very old theme in French literature, especially drama. However, by the middle of the nineteenth century, the falseness theme had become much broader, and it also came to seem to some philosophers (especially Kierkegaard and Nietzsche) that there can be a unique way in which a whole mode of being in a world can lose

1. Diderot 1995, 1: 214.

2. Diderot, "On Mannerism," *The Salon of 1767*, in Diderot 1995, 2: 320, 323.

3. A later, better known, similar claim: Nietzsche's in *The Birth of Tragedy* that, to speak with Diderot, ancient tragedy had ceased to be drama and had become theater, that tragedy had died from a kind of suicide, had become untrue to itself by becoming philosophical, by addressing the audience, as if with problems and puzzles. There are many other permutations of the claim of a false or dead life. Theodor Adorno (1951) was willing to go very far: "Our perspective on life has passed into an ideology which conceals the fact that there is life no longer" (13; my trans.) This air of paradox is only intensified by the epigraph for *Minima Moralia*, from the Austrian writer Ferdinand Kürnberger: "Life does not live." Such an evaluation is not unprecedented, although one sees it mostly in modernist literary contexts. T. S. Eliot in *The Waste Land* compared modern office workers crossing London Bridge to the lost souls described in Dante's Inferno ("I had not thought death had undone so many") (Eliot 1952, 39). And the accusation (that we have become the living dead) is prominent in George Orwell, D. H. Lawrence, Nietzsche of course, and many other modernists.

4. On the general issue of responding to pictures, or "physiognomies," or even words, as like responding to another human being, see Cavell 1979, 355.

its vitality and honesty, that the normative constraints and guidance at work within such a world, directions of a sort about how to go on, make sense of things, can lose genuine hold in some way. Many post-Hegelian philosophers seemed to think this was especially true of the modern world as a whole, the product of the European Enlightenment. This proved extremely hard to explain coherently in traditional terms since the most sophisticated of these post-Kantian philosophers did not believe that what was going wrong was infidelity to a moral ideal, a falling away from the true religion, or a failure to realize the truth of human nature as such. Some ahistorical or internal critique seemed necessary to explain how, in effect, living a life could come to be false to life itself, could only *seem* to be living or leading a life. (Or living in a world without appreciating this possibility of failure could come to look comic. Don Quixote cannot be a knight, can only theatrically pose as one, not because he is insincere or phony, but because the world has changed.)[5] If modern paintings could also be said both to reflect such anxiety and to respond to it, to confront it and to try to avoid such falseness, then there might be in the history of modern painting something documented that goes beyond the reverberations of Diderot's criticisms. Said one final way: this sort of falseness (to "life") might be odd and philosophically problematic, but perhaps problematic in the same way that painting in the course of its development might be said to have finally turned against its very status as painting, to have become false to itself or aspired to mere "objecthood."[6] (Fried has, in other words, discovered a distinct way in which paintings can be said to *fail*, and his narrative, on its art-critical side, points to the highly paradoxical situation in which some painters then *embrace* this "failure," much as Lui embraces, is deliriously proud of, his own theatricality in *Le neveu de Rameau*.)[7]

For such an art history and art criticism, noting Diderot's own understanding of what was going wrong in theatricality in general, and both the historical and the philosophical assumptions that might lie behind such a claim, would lead one to tie painterly meaning not so much to problems in perception, mimesis, iconography, formal organization, and the like, but to the problem of genuine and false "modes of being" of the artwork itself, all within a more general understanding of meaning-responsive beings at work in a social world in historical time. Paintings thereby might be said to teach us how to appreciate their "ontological status" and the historical fate of such

5. Some of the anxiety in philosophy about philosophy is clearly like this worry about seeming a Quixote figure, playing the role (the ancient role) of rather than being philosophers.

6. See "Art and Objecthood" in Fried 1998a.

7. See Diderot 1956.

embodied self-understanding. I think that it is the great achievement of Fried to have shown how profoundly important these ontological dimensions are in our appreciation of many modern paintings. As is well known, the heart of Fried's project involves a brilliant interpretation of modern French painting from the early eighteenth century until around the mid-nineteenth century, or from the time of Chardin and Greuze, through David and Géricault and then especially through Courbet to Manet. The normative terms at issue in this interpretation remain the title terms of his first pathbreaking book on the subject, inspired so much by Diderot's art criticism and the influence of drama on those terms: *absorption* and *theatricality*. The former might be called (or at least I want to stress this dimension here) a complete identification of a subject with the role or activity undertaken, so much so that the subject can seem completely absorbed in the activity, self-forgetful, lost in reverie, and so on; the latter is what it would be to act without such identification, to perform an activity controlled and directed by an anticipation of what others expect to occur, as when subjects are posed in a painting in classic poses assumed to connote heroism or fidelity.[8] Even more important is the narrative line developed by Fried, the *ever less successful attempt* within this French tradition to avoid, or to defeat, or otherwise to come to grips with theatricality. Conventionally, of course, paintings *are* in some obvious sense theatrical objects, made in order to be displayed and beheld by others and presumably organized and executed with this attribute always in mind. But around the time of Chardin and Greuze, Fried argues, it began to seem important to painters to avoid the suggestion that the subjects of their paintings were acting self-consciously under the gaze of others and so inevitably acting for others. By virtue of this avoidance they also implied that the proper relation between the beholder of the painting and the painting should also not be a theatrical one, as if the *painting* were posed there primarily for the beholder. Instead the beholder must be ignored, or actively negated, or displaced spatially, or even corporeally drawn into, merged with the painting, all until in historical time there came to be no way to avoid or negate theatricality except by theatrical means, paradigmatically by those stunningly direct, bold looks at the beholder by the idiosyncratically nude females in Manet's *Olympia* and *Déjeuner sur l'herbe*, oddly and decisively reversing the relation of activity and passivity, subject and object.

8. For reasons of space I am going to ignore other important features of Fried's interpretation, especially the importance of absorption in establishing a graspable unity, a closed composition within the frame, and the strategy of the tableau in effecting this. I do not think that will lead to any distortion of Fried's claims.

This problematic has been developed and expanded by Fried in contexts as varied as American realism and literature, sixteenth- and early seventeenth-century Italian painting, German art of the nineteenth century, the work of other art critics like Roger Fry, abstract painting and sculpture, and photography. Now I say here "developed and expanded," but I should note parenthetically that Fried himself distinguishes sharply between his art criticism and art history and says that the use of theatricality in the latter is not as polemical and evaluative as in the former.[9] But all I need for present purposes is Fried's demonstration (which I take to be successful) that, internal to the development of the French tradition he is interested in, theatricality was certainly understood as a *failing* of sorts, that the original intuition about the failure by Diderot (mannered painting reflects the same vice as a mannered life) continued to resonate up to and including Manet and then beyond, and that we will not understand the fate of that notion unless we understand such painters as exploring something like the proper understanding of the mode of being of participant-agent-beholders in a complex, rapidly changing social world.[10]

Taking all these contexts together, his account amounts to as rich and challenging an interpretation of painterly meaning in general and of modernism in the arts as any known to me. I am especially interested here in two general questions. I noted before that according to Fried (1) it came to seem important to painters to *avoid* theatricality. The question I want to pose is: Why? What was at stake in the emergence of such a goal for painters? I assume, with Fried, that any answer like "fatigue with mannerism" or with rococo art is neither an interesting nor a sufficient answer, as inadequate as "Who knows and who cares? The important thing is just that it did."[11] (A different but related question that Fried discusses: how would one distinguish

9. See "An Introduction to My Art Criticism" (Fried 1998b, 51) on the "unbridgeable gulf" between the two Frieds.

10. I mean that these painters are actively exploring such possibilities; they are not footnotes to various philosophical theories; indeed they are often exploring the issues even more fruitfully than philosophy could.

11. In general, we won't know what the "it" was that happened without some sort of adequate genealogy. Melville (1996b) has written that Diderot was glimpsing a possible future for painting—"wallpaper, Muzak for the eyes, panels of vague and pleasant prettiness" (156). But there is no inherent connection between a painting's status as beheld object and the dominance of lowbrow expectations about art. That would be true of only a very specific sort of beholding and seems to have nothing to do with beholding in itself. Likewise, paintings—all art objects—never had such a problem with their status as beheld objects before. We need a historically inflected account of why this anxiety, and eventually the connection or future Melville points to, should have occurred then and there. The reasons Melville gives are more typical of Greenberg (1993) in essays like "Modernist Painting."

an attempt to avoid theatricality from an attempt to avoid sociality altogether, from an indulgence in self-absorption or narcissism? Part of the answer might lie in knowing what antitheatrical painting wanted to avoid and why.) And (2) painters found it more and more *difficult* to reach this goal, until the enterprise reached a kind of crisis with Manet. And so a similar question here: Why? Why should this have been so difficult?[12] (What else need one say, in other words, to account for the increasing historical difficulty of presenting a historically believable or compelling antitheatrical mode of being?)[13]

I think it quite likely that these issues are connected with the question of modern forms of social dependence and therefore the conditions under which the appeal of an authentic life, one not mediated by the normalizing or conforming, expectation-generating gaze of others—and, analogously, the appeal of "authentic" paintings—would rise to such prominence. The overall problem must have something to do with such famous claims as the following one by Rousseau, which I take to be a direct statement about the modern threat of theatricality: "The Savage lives within himself; sociable man, always outside himself, is capable of living only in the opinion of others and, so to speak, derives the sentiment of his own existence solely from their judgment" (Rousseau 1997, 187). For Fried, as already noted, the right context for understanding this threat is ontological; he treats the underlying problem, *the historical provocation for paintings of a certain sort*, not as having to do with the solution of painting problems in a prior generation, or with such things as the political misdistribution of power, an unequal social organization of labor, the status of a failed religion, or with bad aesthetic theories or contingent interventions by creative geniuses (creating threats to be met). In his ontological language, the basic provocation is quite general and often repeated in his account (and rises to special prominence in his book on Adolph Menzel). The frequent references and notes to Kierkegaard, Heidegger, and Merleau-Ponty set his question of inauthenticity, the mannered and the theatrical, in a particular context and appeal to a particular vocabulary: the language of

12. It certainly can't be accounted for just by pointing to the brutally obvious fact that the ideas of physically merging with the painting or literally extending the painting act are incoherent, as if that had to be "discovered."

13. Mulhall (2001) notes the great importance of these narrative terms but does not pursue the question of their full meaning or what justifies them; one can note: "had become so pressing," "were forced to resort to intensified and elaborated versions," "more extreme strategies," "ever-intensifying need," "not any longer," and so on. These terms all suggest some claim about something approaching historical necessity (or at least "impossibility") that requires some account. Something like "increasingly exhausted powers of traditional modes of creating absorption" is an unexplained explainer (10, 11).

being-in-the-world and the priority of a practical engagement with, coping with, the world as prior in any account of everyday intelligibility. If we take that context—what he has called "the ontological basis of modern art"—as central,[14] then it would be fair to assume that this threat arises because of a general ontological condition, brought to a crisis starting in Enlightenment modernity. That is, taking the Heidegger references seriously, the threat arises because human being is the only being for whom being is "*always* at issue," not settled or fixed by nature or natural law or practical reason. This can be an excruciatingly discomforting unsettledness and is something that can be distorted, fled from, lived out falsely or in denial in all sorts of ways. Human history might be the history of such avoidance, if Heidegger is right. One of the most tempting escapes is to let the question be settled by others, and the distinct threat Diderot and Rousseau notice is that in the unique conditions of divided labor, ever larger and eventually mass societies, and social dependence in modernity such a loss could become profound and perhaps even so routinized that we could lose the capacity to notice it.[15] Theatricality in paintings (and the theatricality of paintings) can manifest such a distortion and submission and provoke some sort of counterdiscourse, such as the explicit accounts by Diderot in *Le neveu de Rameau*, Kierkegaard in *The Present Age*, Nietzsche on the last men, Heidegger's account of *das Man*, Sartre on the look of the other, or Foucault on bio-power.[16] (In *Courbet's Realism*, Fried says Géricault "sensed in the theatrical a metaphysical threat not only to his art but also to his humanity."[17] In *Absorption and Theatricality*, absorption is sometimes called an "unofficial morality" (Fried 1980, 51). In Cavell's terms, the dissolution of trust between artist and audience in modernist art has to have something to do with the deterioration of the conditions of unreflective trust in the modern historical world itself.)

14. Fried 1980, 61. These assumptions are not just in Fried's account but, I would argue, necessary for its success, something that becomes especially clear, I think, in the book on Adolph Menzel; see Fried 2002.

15. René Girard's notion of reflected or imitated desire is certainly relevant to these dimensions of the threat; see Girard 1965 and Pippin 1999, chaps. 1–2.

16. Another strategy is the fantasy of separation from and mastery of nature, with other persons considered merely further natural obstacles to be overcome. This requires a Cartesian picture of mindedness as spectatorship (and so the world as simply object, standing over against such spectators) that is also captured by theatrical versions of such mindedness.

17. Fried 1990, 23. The Heideggerian and, later, Kierkegaardian resonances are everywhere in Fried's work, but what is of most importance is the possibility of a distinction between a "good" everyday (absorbed, authentic) and a "bad" everyday (mindless, forgetful) in Thoreau and Kierkegaard as well as Heidegger, which is discussed explicitly in Fried 2002, 159. That is the issue I want to return to as the "Hegelian" difficulty with these categories.

Now an obvious qualification is in order. No one is claiming that the likes of Greuze sat around contemplating Heideggerian ontology *avant la lettre.* The underlying claim is rather that the formation of very different sorts of human societies, together with increasingly authoritative modern assumptions about subjectivity, the subject-world relation (not for nothing is modern epistemology associated with the "theatre of the mind" image), and human mindedness, together with equally common modern assumptions about individuality, agency, and the social bond, can be understood as, in their limitations and distortions, provoking a kind of dissatisfaction and counterconception, all in a way headed for a crisis similar to that apparent in works by writers such as Hegel, Kierkegaard, and Nietzsche. There are, so would go the claim, traces of that alarm bell and countermovement in painting as well as in philosophy.

However, to press these issues further we need a bit more of Fried's project, both the complexity of its terms of analysis and the details of the historical narrative. The question being raised about a subject's intentional relation to its world and other subjects is already quite complicated just at the level of the paintings, for we are dealing with so many levels of attention: subjects in the painting and *their* objects and world, painter and depicted scene, painter and painting, beholder and scene or intentional object of the painting, beholder and painting, and so forth.[18] (Fried has lots to say in many texts about self-portraits and landscape painting, but to save time I will limit this discussion to absorption/theatricality issues as they touch on depictions of human beings at work in the world [or asleep in it] and/or with others.) What Fried has discovered by collecting these paintings and analyzing them together is that these painters were in effect "painting," attempting somehow to capture such *forms of mindedness* as their principal object, that they were trying to demonstrate that forms of engaged, absorbed mindedness (and so a kind of genuineness or authenticity) were still possible.[19] I am suggesting that such an enterprise must be a response of sorts to a growing suspicion that they were *not* possible, that there were ever fewer areas of human life not regulated by socially normalizing expectations, fewer objects that could engage

18. The most concentrated discussion of these issues is in Fried 1996 and the development there of what Fried calls Manet's "facing" strategy, although the issue was already quite prominent in his discussion of Courbet's *A Burial at Ornans* in Fried 1990. For a good summary of the Manet argument, see Mulhall 2001, 15–17.

19. Compare the corresponding remark about the sculptures of Anthony Caro: "It is as though Caro's sculptures essentialize meaningfulness as such—as though the possibility of meaning what we say and do alone makes his sculpture possible" (Fried 1998a, 162). See also his remarks on modernist paintings as "a cognitive enterprise" in Fried 1982, 223n8.

such absorptive attention. (That is exactly how Hegel reads the issue of the nephew's theatricality in his account of Diderot's *Le neveu de Rameau*, as we shall see.) The absorbed characters in such paintings are still acting intentionally and purposively but in a way that does not seem *reflexively* guided by some notion of how one ought to do that, how others expect one to act, in the way Boucher's characters seem to be thinking, "Ah, this is the pose one should strike as the god of light! Don't I look wonderful?"

Finally, we should also note something Fried himself stresses, that such attempts are part of a narrative of decline and loss. The claim is that "the evolution of painting in France between the start of the reaction against the Rococo and Manet's seminal masterpieces of the first half of the 1860s, traditionally discussed in terms of style and subject matter and presented as a sequence of ill-defined and disjunct epochs or movements . . . may be grasped as a single, self-renewing, in important respects dialectical undertaking." This is the movement that is said to be "guided, and in large measure determined, by certain ontological preoccupations" (Fried 1980, 4). It is "dialectical" from the outset because denying or ignoring or displacing or corporeally identifying with the beholder does not in fact mean ignoring or negating or merging with such a spectator. (In the conventional, everyday sense, one is never more aware of another than when one is trying to ignore that person. The irony here is of course of a piece with Diderot's famous paradox of acting, how such sangfroid is required for the genuine [seeming] display of passion.)[20] In painting the absorption strategy is instead a way of addressing such a beholder, a way considered ontologically more fundamental than theatrical appeals to external spectators.[21] This painterly suggestion of a mode of presence by the "supreme fiction" of absence is all obviously a fragile pictorial fiction and sometimes depends on reception conditions and historical sensitivities that the artist has no control over. In the case of Greuze, as Fried (1980) points out compellingly, the very aspect of his paintings that we now tend to find repugnant—as if he were seeking a wide audience among the growing bourgeoisie and soliciting favor with it—depends on characteristics that

20. See the helpful remarks Fried makes about some of this in discussing Melville in "How Modernism Works," Fried 1982, 229–30.

21. These two dimensions—that the beholder is being addressed ("invited") in being ignored or negated and that the terms at issue are so ambitious ("ontological")—are sometimes missed in criticisms of Fried, as if in commenting on ignoring the beholder, he is approving of something like the "suppression of desire" or even has modernist paintings themselves aspiring not to be paintings (beheld objects), the temptation Fried sees and criticizes in literalism. See Mitchell 1996, 79–80, and Fried's comments in "An Introduction to My Art Criticism" (Fried 1998b, 72–73n75).

"had virtually the opposite function—to screen that audience out, to deny its existence, or at least to refuse to allow the fact of its existence to impinge upon the absorbed consciousnesses of his figures" (68).[22] And such an irony is certainly "dialectical."[23]

Some prominent aspects of what Fried (1990) calls "the peculiar instability of historical determinations of what is and is not theatrical" (15) are evident in the language Fried uses to describe the transitions between the four main stages of his dialectical narrative. I mean the prominence given everyday absorption and distraction (Chardin, Greuze); the use of genre-hierarchies and dramatic history scenes to achieve antitheatrical effects (David's history paintings, from the *Bélisaire* through the *Leonidas*); the Courbet strategy, closing the distance with the beholder, suggesting a corporeal merging with it; and finally Manet's even more complexly dialectical theatrical strategy to achieve antitheatrical results. For example, in describing Greuze as inheriting and continuing Chardin's "absorptive" tradition, Fried notes that it did not seem "any longer" possible to make use of everyday activities to suggest such a state of being. There is much more "sentimentalism, emotionalism, moralism, exploitation of sexuality, and invention of narrative-dramatic structures" in Greuze, as if in silent testimony to the fact that in Greuze's world such everyday absorption was less and less possible and so in painting less and less credible. (If represented, it would come closer to the sort of falseness mentioned at the beginning here.) Chardin and Greuze can then be said to inhabit different worlds, as that word is used by Heidegger, and the latter world of Greuze should be understood as "one of the first in a series of losses that together constitute the ontological basis of modern art" (Fried 1980, 61). This loss represents what in a note Fried calls the "deterioration" of the absorbed activities of the everyday (Fried 1980, 200n120), such that what before might have seemed a mark of genuineness and authenticity (a complete identification with, absorption in, nonalienated relation to, some activity) now by implication begins to look like mere thoughtless going-along, a falling into a normalized routine. At the beginning of his Courbet book, in discussing Antoine-Jean Gros, Fried recalls what he describes as "the increasingly desperate struggle against the theatrical that we have followed in David's history

22. Compare also Fried's (1998b, 49–50) remarks on David's *Horatii* about the historical instability of these theatrical/antitheatrical distinctions.

23. There are such dialectical ironies throughout Fried's work, for me a measure of how accurately his reading of the paintings tracks corresponding and fundamental dualisms in the late modern world. Compare the account of the corporeal and yet also ocular "realism" of Henri Fantin-Latour in Fried 1996, 379–80.

paintings" (Fried 1990, 20), and in that discussion of David we already heard how "with the passage of time the fiction of the beholder's nonexistence became ever more difficult to sustain" (Fried 1980, 153).

I want to return to the issue of why that fiction should have proven ever more difficult to sustain, but for the moment I need to expand at least a bit on this conception of narrative and, correspondingly, development. It should be understood, in my view, as Hegelian at its core; indeed Fried's narrative almost explicitly invokes the kind of causality of fate so familiar in Hegelian narratives.[24] I mean that the suggestion in these remarks about transition and especially about ever-increasing loss is that what explains these altered techniques in painting is not itself a matter of painting alone but a manifestation of an issue of the greatest and widest significance—something like the very possibility of intelligibility. (Fried's references are to the "ontological" and "ontological basis of modern art," suggesting an underlying struggle to understand a complicated and initially threatening new everyday world; instead Hegel would have spoken of the attempted realization of freedom and growing self-consciousness in a social world threatened by positivity.) As in Hegelian accounts, let us say, the catalyst for change in such ontological self-understanding is a matter not of conflicting theories but of historical alterations in what a world, a form of life, makes credible and the connection among various antitheatrical episodes is coherent, not merely contingent; it is available for some logos; there is a reason internal to the very attempt why some attempted embodiment of beholder-significance and intelligibility should have proven increasingly inadequate, a reason that could then help explain, determinately, a subsequent attempt. (It is not merely a fact that the avoidance of theatricality became "ever more difficult.") The account is somewhat un-Hegelian in the heavy emphasis on loss, but that is one of the issues that will return later.[25] For now I want to stress that we should not be overly

24. This element of Fried's narration is especially on view in his charge that, in effect, T. J. Clark's criticism of Greenberg commits the Hegelian sin of "indeterminate negation." By contrast, Fried wants to affirm (also against Greenberg on painterly "essentialism") that the conventions at work in an era of painting "will bear a significant relation to conventions operative in the most significant work of the recent past." Fried 1982, 227.

25. I note that at a similar point in Cavell's account of the modern the astonishing scope and reach of the "Hegelian" ambitions are even clearer. Cavell writes in "Music Decomposed" of the "necessities of the problems faced by artists, of the irreversibility of the sequence of art styles, of the difficulties in a contemporary artist's continuing to believe in his work, or mean it" (Cavell 2015, 210). He then goes on to describe Beckett's task—the denial of audience—in terms similar to Fried's, a common interest that they have both commented on and that at various points unites and divides their respective interpretation of modernism in the arts and its philosophical

distracted by the Heideggerian and post-Heideggerian (Derridean, Foucauldian) themes increasingly prominent in Fried's work, as if they manifest some anti-Hegelian stance. The important point is this: a declensionist narrative is still a narrative, still assigns to philosophy—broadly construed (not social history or anthropology)—a diagnostic task, whether that declensionist account is written by Nietzsche, Heidegger, or Derrida.[26]

For the time being we should also note that it is certainly possible to stop well before these very sweeping issues and note, first, that there might be a number of purely aesthetic considerations at play in understanding the inspiration for antitheatrical tendencies, many of them emphasized by Diderot. Theatricality of a certain sort, after all, is another way of saying that a work is a dramatic failure and is so because it merely typifies a type, instantiates a set of expectations, makes things too easy for the appreciator, or simply manifests conventions that by mere repetition have gone stale. Las Vegas lounge singers theatricalize jazz standards, even soul and blues songs, by fitting phrasing and expression into extremely predictable, narrow conventions, all in a way clearly designed to fit the elevator music assumptions and expectations of a middlebrow audience.

This aesthetic dimension is, of course, true but still far too abstract or formal a category to capture what is worrying Fried about the growing historical need to avoid theatricality. The difficulty in avoiding it and the kind of crisis building to Manet must, as we have been seeing, be explained in concrete

---

significance. This (the Hegelian themes without much of a Hegelian reception in America) is all not to mention such extraordinary claims as that by Greenberg when he describes the aftermath of what he calls the "avant-garde's" "break" with imitative realism: "so inexorable was the logic of the development that in the end their work constituted but another step towards abstract art. . . . All roads lead to the same place." Greenberg 1940, 309–10; my emphasis. See my discussion in Pippin 2002.

26. I am disagreeing here with Melville's review of *Courbet's Realism*; see "Compelling Acts, Haunting Convictions" (Melville 1996a, 187–98). The notions of increasing difficulty in avoiding theatricality, a theatrically "deteriorating" everyday, and a growing crisis building toward Manet are hardly abandoned in favor of some celebration of postmodern radical contingency. That Fried notes in *Courbet's Realism* that his work on abstraction has prepared him for an account of nineteenth-century realism does not seem to me a momentous reversal of position, but just a stress on the richness and historical continuity of the antitheatricality theme. There is all the Hegelianism one needs in Melville's own appeals: not "merely a historical accident," "inevitable" (Melville 1996a, 191, 192). (Fried's Manet could serve as a model for Fried himself; attempting to establish at once something with a profound historical inflection [French, eighteenth- and nineteenth-century] and something sweepingly universal [art in the condition of modernity]). The only relevant name for this is the Hegelian one: the concrete universal; see the first two chapters of *Manet's Modernism* (Fried 1996).

historical terms, and the stakes for Fried are not just successful drama in performance (or its analogue in painting) but, as throughout, of the highest order—ontological.

Yet there are also more sophisticated dimensions of aesthetic normativity alone where theatricality might be understood as problematic in a restricted, strictly aesthetic sense. Fried's account resonates in all sorts of interesting ways with these but, again, aims for an account of the significance of these norms that encompasses more than the properly aesthetic. When Kant, for example, tried to insist that aesthetic experience could not be understood as a cognitive classification, an application of a concept to an intuitive manifold (as in perfectionist accounts of the beautiful), or as a pleasant stimulation of sense, that it had to involve the free play of the faculties as if conceptualized but without a determinate purpose, that the basis of the claim of the beautiful on others had to be an unformalizable common sense and not a standard assertion of fact, his enterprise could certainly be understood as having formulated an antitheatrical account of aesthetic absorption. (A free play of the faculties, rather than a fixed, recognitive judgment, manifests that absorptive, meditative appreciation pursued in Diderot's and Fried's projects, and in the absence in aesthetic experience of any reference back, as a recognition, to a prior conceptual order, it is, in this freedom, especially close to Fried's famous invocation of the grace of presentness at the end of "Art and Objecthood.") This is most apparent in Kant's account of genius, which could be described as the continually necessary destruction of prior artforms that have (inevitably) become theatrical.[27] Indeed the flight from theatricality could be seen as an inevitable result of the Kantian and post-Kantian assertion of the radical autonomy of the aesthetic, resisting its colonization by religious and commercial interests (both theatricalizing tendencies), all until this insistence on authentic autonomy forces an attack on *all* determinate aesthetic appreciation that is not purely aesthetic, a point of contact (but only that) between Fried's antitheatricality and Clement Greenberg's modernist formalism.[28]

27. Inevitably, for Kant, because of the impossibility of expecting constant freshness—"authenticity"—in the appreciation of art, the inevitability of the formulation of typologies, classifications, and therewith deadening expectations in any historically situated art world.

28. Greenberg famously considers modernism progressively reductionist; Fried does not. There is a particularly lucid summary by Fried of his relation to and differences from Greenberg in Fried 1982, 226. Their other differences are also quite interesting. Greenberg's basic position on modernism remains Kantian; modernist painting discovers the ultimate conditions of—essence of—painting itself (flatness, and so on), the conditions necessary for the possibility of a painting, whereas I understand Fried's position to be basically Hegelian. Painting is the product of the tradition of trying to make and understand paintings, and modernism is what it

Fried himself, in the closing discussion of the Courbet book, suggests a number of points of contact with the larger philosophical issues brought out by his ontologically inspired art history, and these will lead us naturally back to the questions of provocation and failure raised throughout thus far. He notes explicitly what his notes make clear throughout all his books on art history—that paintings cannot but embody some mode of being in the world, reflect some attempt to do justice to visual, motor, laboring, social, and sexual intelligibility. When paintings exhibit an understanding of such intelligibility in terms of spectatorship, representationalism (the world as an object in the theater of the mind), a Cartesian gulf between bodyless mind and world, or when social, intersubjective relations are conveyed as caught in an unavoidable duality of either active subjects or passive subject-objects, we might expect (at least under the broadly Hegelian assumptions mentioned above) *something* in our experience of such paintings *to fail*, to work against itself, to manifest the flatness, narrowness, or, in general, phoniness of the sort of world-engagement depicted.[29] Fried's general Diderotian term for that failure is theatricality. This would mean by contrast, as it does for Fried, a deep commitment to various aspects of the accounts given by Heidegger and Merleau-Ponty about being-in-the-world and embodied subjectivity and intelligibility. It is by appeal to such claims that we might be able to account for just what is going wrong and why.

Likewise, as in chapter 6 of the Courbet book, on Courbet's femininity, the lived-out unacceptability, perhaps unbearability of the dualities inherent in theatrical worldviews also suggests some form of resistance to the gendered meaning of these dualities, beholder-beheld and thereby lover-beloved especially. The refusal of the mere beholder could be seen in that sense as "feminine" resistance to a kind of masculinism, and to the extent that the Courbet merging strategy cannot succeed, the in-between state, neither mere beholder nor merged-with object, could be considered bi-gendered just as the many figures of the artist Fried finds in so many Courbets possess both active,

---

is by understanding what it is to stand inside this narrated development—modernist painting is a result of what painting had become: "Rather the task of the modernist painter is to discover those conventions that, at a given moment, alone are capable of establishing this work's identity as a painting." Fried 1998a, 169n6. Fried on Manet remains the paradigmatic exemplification of what I am calling this basic Hegelianism. (Basic and not essential because Fried understands the role of contingency in art history differently than does Hegel.)

29. It should be stressed again that this failure-in-theatricality is not a manifestation of philosophically false views. It is false in the way a life can be false, and understanding that such a comportment is false is not a matter of understanding that a person does not really believe what they say they believe. (For one thing, their really believing it may make them even more false.)

traditionally masculine aspects (the painter's brush hand) and also those that are traditionally feminine, receptive, passive (the painter's palette hand).

Two more philosophical dimensions are suggested: the implication throughout that avoiding, ignoring, or negating the stance of the beholder is avoiding an unjustifiably controlling, normalizing, or reifying gaze, a manifestation of unequally functioning and socially managerial power, whereas theatricality is submitting to such conventions, resonates with numerous Foucauldian themes; and there is an important parallel, in Fried's suggestions about the priority in the order of intelligibility of a material, embodied, practically engaged making in the world—prior, that is, to simply seeing—with the famous sort of materiality, the priority of writing to speech, in Derrida's well-known project.

But I want now to return to several aspects of the antitheatrical or absorptive to suggest a reason why the implied, contrasting, absorptive, or even broadly Heideggerian ideal, whatever it is called—acknowledgment, embodied intelligibility, bi-gendered status—itself manifests dialectical tensions that make the appearance of Manet and later, more radical modernism comprehensible in another way, a way that goes somewhat further in answering my two questions. The underlying philosophical problem is the problem of Fried's *realism* (for Fried, Courbet, Eakins, and Menzel are the three great realist painters of the nineteenth century),[30] and this has two dimensions relevant here. As we have been noting, no one should be misled by the "supreme fiction" of absent beholders to think that realism amounts to the fulfillment of the fantasy of the world viewed as it would be without a viewer. The deep, even corporeal inseparability of beholder and world is quite a different sort of realism, one wherein the intelligible world is not built up or constructed out of impressions or any succession of momentary mental states, or just there as separate object-to-be-viewed. What is real is this corporeally inseparable original whole of bodies at work in space and moving in time in a shared natural and cultural world, the intelligibility of which is illuminated in terms of these practices, corporeal positions, empathetic projections, and practical motion. Absent any of the latter, *there is no world*, not some putatively truly real world. (It is as embodied that I am a *real* part of the world, and in representing or working on objects in the world I do not cease to be embodied in this sense.)[31]

30. See Fried 2002, 109.

31. See Fried 2002, 109–24. This embodied presence is sometimes discussed by Fried as the problem of the painters' signatures.

Second, while there is much to explore in Fried's account of this modern picture of mindedness, it is important to remember the original resonances of Diderot's formulations: that mannered painting is objectionable not so much because theatricality insures aesthetic failure (breaking the arresting spell great paintings can create) or because of Cartesian or representationalist distortions of our being-in-the-world but because a painting's theatricality should be counted a failure in the same way that a theatrical mode of social existence should be counted a failure. What is the nature of such a failure? Why is it a failure? These are still our questions. Here is a passage from Cavell's "Music Decomposed" that seems to me relevant: "And yet I've been insisting that we can no longer be sure that any artist is sincere—we haven't convention or technique or appeal to go on any longer: anyone could fake it. And this means that modern art, if and where it exists, forces the issue of sincerity, depriving the artist and his audience of every measure except absolute attention to one's experience and absolute honesty in expressing it" (Cavell 2015, 211).

There is something profoundly right about this claim, along with the claim that this situation has become "the condition of art altogether."[32] But it still leaves unanswered the question of why this has turned out to be the modernist fate, and until we know something more about *that*, relying on our own experience, tied as that very experience is likely to be to whatever is responsible for blurring the lines between genuine and fake in general, we seem likely to repeat the problem. (It is surely another condition of late modernity that the private ring of the genuine is not necessarily trustworthy. To quote the other Marx, Groucho, "Ah nowadays, sincerity's the thing. Once you can fake that, you've got it made.")[33]

I suggested earlier in quoting Diderot's contemporary, Rousseau, that such a failure came to be counted as such because it avoids the realization of a condition necessary for any life to have *any* value for me—that it be *my* life (at least on the controversial, Rousseauist, anti-Platonic assumption that nothing can be a good for me unless it is a good to me, recognized as such

32. Cavell 2015, 211.

33. Lionel Trilling's (1982) distinction between sincerity and authenticity is relevant here. Sincerity can be in some straightforward sense genuine—A truly believes she is feeling C—but still self-deceived, a result of manipulative advertising, or whatever. The horrible thing about, say, Barry Manilow songs is not that people are being conned by a fake but that that register of emotion about love is, sincerely, what they recognize as the real thing. Sincerity won't get us very far on this issue, prompting the fascination with situations in extremis, where we will really find out what we believe, are committed to, and so on.

by me).[34] A life in which even the possible sentiment of my own existence depends on being confirmed by others clearly has not met this condition. This assumption thus suggests as an ideal a kind of genuineness, an ability to recognize in my deeds and practices my own agency or, as it is often said, an ability to *identify with* such deeds and practices or, at the most general level, with the social roles I have taken on: father, husband, professor, citizen, whatever. (The Hegelian word for the theatrical in this sense is *positivity*, wherein in submitting to the authority of various normative constraints I do not experience that authority as my own or freely granted and so in effect play at, imitate the role of husband, religious churchgoer, soldier, and so on.) And this view of things makes it straightforward to say that this genuineness and authenticity is manifested by contrast in a kind of absorption in (identification with) a social role, a nonalienated sense of my deeds as my own. Diderot had suggested that what makes the appearance of theatricality in both art and life a sort of failure is that some essential dimension of human sociality has gone out of scale or proportion, such that one could not be said any longer to be acting from one's own motivations but merely in a way responsive to the anticipated reactions and demands of others (as if always, as Diderot put it, "in a room"). This is the distinctly modern threat, initially inspired by Rousseau's worry about the division of labor and the excessive bourgeois interest in order and peace but exacerbated by dimensions Rousseau could not have dreamed of: absolutely massive consumer cultures, psychologically sophisticated advertising, fantastic connectedness through new media, and so on.

Now there is in the romantic tradition a tendency to see this alienation or positivity or nonidentification wherever one can detect the presence of self-consciousness and reflection alone, as if such reflection, a cardinal aspect of modern mindedness, is inherently doubling and so alienating (as if we have incorporated the *other's* view of ourselves, as if this separation from ourselves is what reflective experience amounts to) and so it will not allow any full absorption, any kind of second innocence, a sentiment visible in that side of Rousseau which emphasizes reverie, solitary dreamers, and active self-forgetfulness. But we should pause here long enough to note that this is not an element of that strand of painterly and lived meaning that Fried is tracking, as is manifest in his treatment of Menzel and the problem of reflection (in that case mediated by Kierkegaard) and compressed in his astonishing interpretation of *The Balcony Room*.[35]

34. I pass over quickly here the vexing issues of the many Rousseaus in Rousseau, including the Spartan, legislator-oriented, not-so-democratic one.

35. See Fried 2002, 84–94.

As I understand Fried's Menzelian (and Kierkegaardian) desideratum here, a reflective embodiment is not one that in some way *thematizes* one's role and thereby distances one from it; rather, reflection is meant in the original Kantian sense of apperception, as *adverbial*. An apperceptive awareness of a room is not a direct awareness of a room *and* a second-order self-consciousness *of* one's perceptual state as a new, dual object. (This misunderstanding is the source of the unavoidable self-alienation worries.)[36] Rather one perceives the room *self-consciously*, aware in perceiving the room that one is in a perceptual state (not an imagined or remembered state) as one perceives but is not aware of two intentional or separate objects.[37] The idea would be to understand a reflective absorption as *an intensification of such absorption*, not a thematizing and ultimately theatricalizing distancing. (Just as in realist self-portraiture, the artist's face does not appear as objectified, distanced, or reified, but the artist seems to have been transferred *into* the painting, as if the artist is looking at the beholder, is not a mere copy of the artist.)[38] That sort of theatricalizing might be said to occur only when something like the normative structure of such mindedness begins to break down, fails to sustain allegiance, becomes a *reflected object of inquiry*, not a *mode of life*.

There are also, of course, other notions of freedom very different from this one. The romantic invocation of irony is a possible countermodel, wherein exactly the opposite capacity is praised: the capacity to detach myself from any assigned or assumed role, take on another at will, act always in view of the reactions of others but only so as to manipulate them—a kind of absolutely ironic independence, of the sort praised by Schlegel. But I think that the figures who serve for Fried as philosophical markers of his art-historical themes—Diderot, Kierkegaard, Thoreau, Heidegger, Cavell—all inherit in one way or other (even if some would reject the explicit terms) some aspect of this notion of freedom as self-identification, authenticity, or embodied life, as well as, with varying degrees of explicitness, some sense of why such a free life would be so valuable—that some such attainment is an ur-condition for anything else to be of value, significance, salience. (Again: nothing can be of

36. See, however, Roger Fry's remarks linking "conscious and deliberate study" of design itself with the "decadence of Italian art" after the High Renaissance in his "Dürer and Company," quoted in Fried 2004, 32.

37. Stated in a very compressed way in the language of the *Balkonzimmer*: The details and furniture of the room and the reflection of the room in the mirror on the right are both in the room. Even the hint of defeasibility in the experience, the possibility that the reflected objects do not correspond to the real objects, is, in effect, an element of what one experiences when one looks at the room.

38. See the comments on self-portraiture in Fried 1990, chap. 2.

significance for me unless it is, to me, a condition not met if my life is not, let us say, intimately my own.) And for all of these thinkers, the violation of this condition not only amounts to much more than an individual's lack of integrity but, as Rousseau first prophesied, can come to characterize a whole form of life as such, such that perhaps unavoidable violations of this kind of integrity amount to an entire form of life.[39]

One way for this failure to be manifest is, of course, in explicit experiences of and depictions of alienation, where virtually all aspects of a life come to be experienced as scripted with rules that have only a positive, external authority and where success at managing such a life amounts to an imitation of life, to recall Douglas Sirk's variation on just that theme. We are all familiar with this sense of falseness in everything from German expressionism to J. D. Salinger. But a much more interesting and elusive, certainly more widespread version of the same sort of problem involves what is a form of absorption in a role or practice, but in a deeply thoughtless, even mindless way, a self-less falling into the routinized expectations of a social world, Thoreau's "quiet desperation," let us say, but often so quiet as to be unnoticed as such. Indeed Heidegger's worry is that such a forgetfulness will become so complete that any possible kind of recovery of such a life as my own, *eigentümlich*, will have been foreclosed, that even the dislocating anticipation of my own death and its attending *Angst* will come to be anaesthetized, as it were.

This would be a kind of living death, in effect, and the difficulty of distinguishing these good and bad forms of absorption (itself a figure for the difficulty of understanding how to fulfill this basic condition of freedom under the conditions of a deracinating modernity) is already apparent from the very beginning of the line of antitheatrical development that interests Fried—in the great attractiveness of images of *sleep*. On the one hand, it is a fine technical accomplishment to be able to paint a sleeping body that is still vibrantly alive, not dead. On the other hand, not only is a sleeping state painted with great tenderness a solipsistic state, but, as with all profoundly absorptive states or depictions of the blind, it does not so much ignore or negate the beholder as oddly expose the subject, in quite a vulnerable way, to the beholder. This

39. Hegel professed himself dissatisfied with, even contemptuous of, Schlegel's version of irony, and especially Jacobi's. But there are other moments. For example, his embrace of the nephew (*lui*) over the bourgeois gentleman (*moi*) in Diderot's *Rameau's Nephew*. Or, if objective historical conditions come to be themselves false, mere performances for profit, then it would be entirely "Hegelian" to conclude that the "self-negation" or self-alienation inherent in irony looks like itself a mode of authenticity.

vulnerability is the key to the power of our reaction to the once mighty Bélisaire in David's painting, is so explicit in Greuze's *L'Aveugle trompé*, and has something to do with the slight embarrassment we feel at being able to gaze unobserved at such deep intimacy in the sleeping nudes of Courbet's *Sleep*. All of which suggests a tension of sorts between such longed-for absorptive states and any stable sociality; the tension, I am suggesting, is responsible for the difficulty in avoiding theatricality.

To be sure, there is a form of sociality in the antitheatrical and "embodied intelligibility" traditions, but in such works as Courbet's *An After Dinner at Ornans*, *The Stonebreakers*, and *The Wheat Sifters*, or even in Menzel's scenes of workers building with bricks or his *Iron Rolling Mill*, or later in Gustave Caillebotte's floor workers that unity is silent and, we might say, Leibnizian, not Hegelian, not the result of the intersubjective work of the participants, the felt result of *having overcome* unavoidable social conflict with each other and having arrived at a common task. I mean each absorbed monad is coordinated with, in tune with, the others, but by virtue of the common task being present *individually* to each, as if a preordained harmony had been set from the outside (by the task, the conditions of labor, nonownership, and so on).[40]

If this is so, it might support the suggestion that the threat of theatricality stems primarily from the deteriorating sociality of the common world inhabited by painter and subject (where one means by such a deterioration something quite specific, as I try to show below). When such sociality is by and large restricted to what could be called I-We relations, with an ever more powerful, supervisory, punitive We, and without much in the way of I-You, the temptation to theatricalize, to compromise with such a new form of power, is nearly inevitable and has to make its way into traditions of painting, just as much as it has to inspire rejections of such compromising, ultimately self-undermining strategies. But, in Hegel's terms, these initial rejections, the search for absorption, are understandable "indeterminate negations," fantasies of self-identification and absorbed peace that represent more counterfantasies of escape than markers of a possible new form of life. And, understood that way, they begin to crumble even as possible fantasies under the press of experience and, historically, the growth of the threat in question.

None of this is, I think, either inconsistent with Fried's account or entailed by it. It is meant mostly as a supplement. But there are two other brief ways of

40. See Fried's (2002, 105) remarks on the isolation of members of the audience from each other (interestingly, effected by technology, binoculars).

making this point, and I will close with them. One is from Fried's extraordinary book on Menzel; the other brings us back to Diderot.

There are several paintings that are reproduced in *Menzel's Realism* that intimate a utopian future beyond silent absorption and concessive, slavish theatricality. One of the most beautiful is the 1875 gouache *Bricklayers on a Building Site.*[41] Six workers are depicted at work on a building that seems to be rising, thanks to their efforts, from a world otherwise confusing and disordered but for their collective efforts (the building material is quite scattered, haphazardly on the floor of the building site), and as if also out of a beautiful but equally disordered and unregulated natural world of brush and trees. What is most interesting is that three of the men are at work in a way any reader of Fried would recognize immediately; they are individually absorbed in their work, and even though that work is coordinated, they seem privately absorbed. But three are looking at and apparently talking to each other. In fact it almost looks as if all three are talking at the same time. This intimates a relation among the subjects such that the norm-governed nature of their work is arising *out of* their face-to-face interaction. The overall scene, that is, has a kind of peace and active absorption in it, but there is no intimation of isolation, indifference to the other or lostness. Indeed the painting seems to stand itself as a good piece of work (as John Ford used to say of movies), like the building being made, neither indifferent to the beholder nor slavishly courting him, just part of a common social world (or at least a possible common social world). This might be what it would be to overcome the tension between *being lost in absorption* and *having lost oneself* in theatricality.[42]

Finally, consider the problem in terms of Diderot's *Le neveu de Rameau.* It is important, first, that it is a dialogue, an argument of a kind, reflecting an unsettledness in any consideration of the two "positions," a suggestion that coming down on one side or the other would be hasty. (It thus can serve as

41. Fried discusses this painting in Fried 2002, 157–59.

42. Because I have noted often (as they both do) the way these themes intersect concerns of Cavell and Fried, I should say that this issue—said pictorially, working out the right human logic of the seeing/being-seen relation—is what gives me pause about the invocation of Thoreau and Emerson, who are close to what Hegel calls the beautiful soul and the knight of virtue in the *Phenomenology of Spirit.* It is right to note that the failure to overcome theatricality is the failure of love, and the avoidance of love, the triumph of theatricality, but such a fate has not simply happened to us, and it does not await the proper sort of acknowledgement of "separateness"; see Cavell 2015, 338, 339, 350, and esp. 352 where, after Cavell says, "The world whistles" over Hegel and Marx, he adds, "We cannot hear them." I am not sure we have learned yet how to listen.

a prequel of sorts to Kierkegaard's *Either/Or* on the contrasting claims of the aesthetic and the ethical, themselves very similar to the respective positions of Lui and Moi. There is likewise no position from which either one side or the other can be adopted that is not itself already a commitment to one side or the other; there is no Kierkegaardian position. There is, though, interestingly, apparently no dialogue possible; the respective commitments are incommensurable and unmediatable, a mark either of the dwindling historical confidence in such a mediation, or of Kierkegaard's position, or both.)[43] The Diderot dialogue takes place in a setting one almost has to call Friedian. Lui and Moi meet in a café where the chief activity is the paradigmatically absorptive and minimally social—chess games—and much of their discussion concerns in effect whether there are, apart from such games, any objects, human practices, enterprises, worthy of such engrossed attention. Lui's position is essentially that there are not, and so he has made reflected social success his goal, has gone theatrical; he can be what anyone wants him to be, imitate anything; he can even, in effect, *fake* absorption, taking full on Diderot's "paradox of acting," and can pretend quite effectively to throw himself into, to become, the role of a singer or personality. There is no *there* there in Lui, and he seems the epitome of a deracinated, mannered, corrupt social world. He is countered by Moi, who presents himself as quite comfortable with who he is: confident, settled, a bourgeois but not Flaubert's Homais, for most of the essay a somewhat bemused, occasionally interrogative foil. We have, then, a kind of dialogue between theatricality and absorption.

In a famous passage in the *Phenomenology of Spirit*, Hegel takes Lui to be representative of a world caught between feudal institutions and a modern spirit—placeless, valueless, lost, seeking reassurance in merely stage-managed recognition (manipulated recognition cannot count as genuine recognition)—and Hegel takes the impossibility of any such settled place to help explain the creation of the *Encyclopédie*, to prompt a kind of near religious faith in the new modern science, ultimately wholly inappropriate to the enterprise science is, an attitude eventually becoming the scientism so familiar in modern

43. See Cavell's (2015, 163–79) remarks on Kierkegaard, modernism, the problem of "fraudulence," and the issue most threatened by fraudulence/theatricality—"authority"—in his "Kierkegaard's On Authority and Revelation." One could regard Cavell as searching for a possibly modern sort of authority for philosophy (its presumption to speak for anything at all) and Fried as searching for a genuinely modern form of authority, a historically distinct claim to seriousness, of painting and sculpture.

life. But what Hegel oddly doesn't notice and what is I hope of final relevance to Fried's art history is that the dialogue is considerably more dialectical than Hegel suggests, so much so as to cast doubt on the fixity of the opposition between absorption and theatricality as terms of analysis or as reflective of underlying, hardening ontological positions. In a profound irony, Lui's proclaimed embrace of Absolute Theatricality is itself false, self-deceived; his pretense at Protean malleability is always undermined, first by the initial question about the possibility of *real* (or inherent, not merely socially constituted) genius and then by what emerge as clear, firm commitments, held no matter their cost socially: to his dignity, for example, the equality of his worth and status. On the other hand, Moi's profession of security and the peace of his soul are undermined by his simple presence. He seeks out Lui at least once a year, gets away from it all, and indulges his wilder side, in itself something that expresses the uncertainty (and potential envy) sleeping away somewhere at the heart of his contentment. (This is what Hegel, convinced that Lui is the one on the side of history, most emphasizes about the limitations of Moi's side.) As with Menzel, there is the promise of another form of sociality, the great dream of the bourgeoisie we might call it, the dream of the great bourgeois philosophers, Hegel especially, and reflected in his love for Dutch paintings of interiors in the sixteenth and seventeenth centuries. I hope it will serve as a fitting conclusion. Moi says,

> Mais je ne vous dissimulerai pas, il m'est infiniment plus doux encore d'avoir secouru le malheureux, d'avoir terminé une affaire épineuse, donné un conseil salutaire, fait une lecture agréable, une promenade avec un homme ou une femme chère à mon cœur, passé quelques heures instructives avec mes enfants, écrit une bonne page, rempli les devoirs de mon état, dit à celle que j'aime quelques choses tendres et douces qui amènent ses bras autour de mon cou. Je connais telle action que je voudrais avoir faite pour tout ce que je possède.
>
> (But I must confess I find it infinitely sweeter to succor the unfortunate, to disentangle a bad business, to give helpful advice, to read some pleasant book, to take a walk with a man or a woman who is dear to me, to spend a few instructive hours with my children, to write a page of good prose, to carry out my duties, or to tell her whom I love something tender and true which brings her arms about my neck. I know of certain deeds which I would give all I possess to have done.)[44]

44. Diderot 1956, 36–37.

A marker of the difficulty, perhaps the impossibility of maintaining such an absorbed life lies in Lui's brief, dismissive reply (echoing what Hegel would want, finally, to say as well) and its many, many modern resonances: "Vous êtes des êtres bien singuliers!"[45]

45. Attempting to place Fried's project in this sort of philosophical and historical context raises two further issues that cannot be treated here. First, and most obviously, the painterly struggle with this question of what I have called authenticity tracks a certain kind of historical, relatively continuous problem in modern painting, one that extends up to and through abstractionism and, as Fried has shown, in much important modern photography. But that is not the only modern tradition in painting, and it would be interesting to try to understand the relation between this strand and the bewildering proliferation of schools and styles in twentieth-century art—to borrow a list made by Arthur Danto (1986): "Fauvism, the Cubisms, Futurism, Vorticism, Synchronism, Abstractionism, Surrealism, Dada, Expressionism, Abstract Expressionism, Pop, Op, Minimalism, Post-Minimalism, Conceptualism, Photorealism, Abstract Realism, Neo-expressionism" (108). Second, a kind of abstractionism can be said to be the culmination of this sort of antitheatrical tradition, but a culmination also implies an ending of sorts such that the deep familiarity of the category of abstraction and its widespread commercialization inevitably retheatricalize any such attempt. And the Hegelian framework suggested here would thus have to ask similar sorts of philosophical and sociohistorical questions about post-1960s art (on the assumption that it is as open to Hegel as to anyone else to invoke categories like phoniness, con jobs, kitsch, fraud, a racket, or a wheel-spinning, uninteresting period in art history, if that is where the analysis would lead such a contemporary Hegel).

7

Photography as Art: Fried and Intention

The Project

The temporal reference in Michael Fried's 2008 book, *Why Photography Matters as Art as Never Before*, will have an immediate double implication for readers of his work on the history of painting and on contemporary art. First, "as Never Before" has an obvious direct reference to today, the present age. Photography may have mattered as art before, but it matters in some way now as *never* before. Such a title suggests an attempt that goes beyond a series of readings of some contemporary art photographers. Something about the work of these artists matters in a shared way art photography has never mattered, has never had to matter, one might say. Clearly, what is involved here is the current fate of art,[1] as reflected in the production and reception of artworks, catalog copy for gallery exhibitions, what contemporary art museums buy and show, and the dominant theories of art in the art and philosophy world (insofar as there is any interest in art in that latter world). This is the world of literalism, minimalism, postmodernism, installation art, conceptual art, performance art, and environmental art, not to mention the world of the vast speculative art market. Second, for Fried, one expects that the present state of the artworld (within which some art photography matters so much) extends and is a moment in the narrative history of modern art he has been developing for nearly fifty years. This involves a crisis, actually a series of different but related crises, first attended to by Diderot in his reaction against the rococo in the eighteenth century, abstractly summarizable as the "crisis of theatricality," and corresponding attempts to "defeat theatricality" by

1. I shall be discussing here pictorial or more broadly visual art. There are parallels with the other arts but I will not be treating them here.

successive generations of painters in many different ways. As we saw in the previous chapter, in his first major work, 1980's *Absorption and Theatricality*, Fried saw that something was at stake in Diderot's criticism that went far beyond localized issues at a moment in French art-critical debates. The fate of pictorial art in modernity was at stake, and this at a level that involved ambitious philosophical issues, especially "ontological" ones. That is, a possible, distinct mode of being of the artwork as such, not as decoration, source of religious inspiration, commodity, or entertainment, was at stake, and this in a way that was as historically inflected as is Fried's approach to contemporary art photography. The question of art's survival as art in modernity was at stake, and that meant as a significant vehicle of human self-understanding in unique and intrinsically valuable experiences available in no other mode.

Contemporary art photography matters, in other words, because of some understanding of the way visual art matters, or should matter. And given the point just made about its self-understanding, it could cease to matter. One can, given the modern sensibility, imagine a successful secular demythologization of art that would be as reductive and deflating as the modern reimagining of religion in the light of psychology and sociology. One cannot only imagine it, one can observe that such things as a resistance to any distinction between high and low art, the studied, labored indeterminacy in much contemporary art, claims about the "death of the author,"[2] a concentration on art as a political category, critical theory as the deconstructive demonstration of the failure of meaning in texts, and the treatment of art as a mere occasion for various individual responses, as in neuroaesthetics and affect theory, have largely accomplished this reduction in the minds of many. For Fried, this question of ontological survival turned on the embodiment in the artwork of its own understanding of its relation to its beholder, and so is itself inseparable from an ever-present, implicit thematization of conceptions of sociality and world-involvement by subjects, itself dependent on historical conceptions of and experiences of "world." This set of issues is "the problem of theatricality" and occasions the general response: the creation of the fictional (or, paradoxically, "staged") "negation of the beholder." Such a level of abstraction does not, though, do any justice to the historical variations in such a project, or to the magnitude of the stakes involved.

2. The paradigmatic case, one explicit about the consequences of this "death" for the issue of meaning, was Roland Barthes's essay "The Death of the Author." See Barthes 1978, 142 and 147–48 (original publication date, 1967).

That magnitude resonates in "as Never Before," already an implicit suggestion, given Fried's oeuvre as a whole, that some art photography successfully resists a contemporary submission to, or even an enthusiastic embrace of, the very theatricality that Fried sees as an existential threat to art itself, and by such resistance is able to raise again the larger issues behind the struggle against theatricality. How some photographers achieve this is the main subject of *Why Photography Matters*.[3]

Terms of Art

Fried notes first that certain technical innovations in photography—the possibility of large *tableau* format images, made to be hung on a wall, available to be contemplated at length and closely, as well as digital manipulation and combination of photographs[4]—allowed photography to invoke all the conventions of gallery painting and many elements of artificial composition, and so to participate in the dialectical narrative that for Fried descends from the first crisis of theatricality in the history of painting. And he began noticing in photographers like Jeff Wall, Jean-Marc Bustamante, and Thomas Ruff (around 1980) a concern with the beholder, a thematization of the relation of the photograph to a beholder, which unmistakably invoked the Diderotian problematic.

To bring out and justify this invocation, Fried puts to work various theoretical notions he developed elsewhere, and he applies new conceptual tools for the range of photographers he studies. "Absorptive strategies," "to-be-seen-ness," the representability (or not) of "mindedness," "presentness" and "instantaneousness," *oubli de soi*, and "exclusion" or "negation" of the beholder all make useful appearances. He also brings up the notions of *world*

3. Fried is very clear on two issues that should be highlighted. He does not mean that these photographers matter so much because they make better photographs, of greater artistic quality, than ever before. He lists many great photographers of the past who are of the highest quality but who do not participate in what Fried is interested in. Second, he does not mean to imply that the group he discusses are the only contemporary photographers worth attending to. He lists several others who are world class but whose projects do not involve the theatricality problematic. The idea that Fried's only interest lies in rating all artists on a scale of theatrical to antitheatrical is irresponsible and inaccurate. See, among many other examples, his books *Realism, Writing, Disfiguration: On Thomas Eakins and Stephen Crane* (1987), and *Menzel's Realism* (2002).

4. For an example of the significance of this possibility in thematic terms, see the discussion of Gursky in Fried 2008, 165ff. This is not to say that before digital techniques, photography was "weak in intentionality." Morgan (2012) makes this point in an especially interesting way, or shows us how Godard makes it, especially in *Histoire(s) du cinéma*. See chap. 4, and especially 163–65.

and *worldhood* and of the *everyday* for Jeff Wall; "good" and "bad" objecthood in Welling, Wall, and the Bechers; some thoughts from Wittgenstein for the contrast between the lived world and the pictorial world portrayed in Struth's museum photographs and closed off from us ("*world-likeness* versus *world-apartness*" [Fried 2008, 125]);[5] conventions of the *tableau* form invoked by the new photography of Ruff, Gursky, and Delahaye, especially the "abstracting and hypostatizing of facingness in Ruff's portraits" (140), an element that fits perfectly within Fried's interpretation of the vast significance of Manet for modernism; distance and photographing figures from behind in Andreas Gursky as "severing" (and so showing a world from which the viewer is "banished" or excluded (162), a major antitheatrical strategy in the Diderotian project); the way Delahaye's photographs seem to deliberately withhold from the viewer any indication of where to look; how Struth manages to create some sense of *self-forgetfulness* on the part of the sitters for his portraits and the uncanny role of the *unintentional* exhibited in their physical resemblances; the "*basic structure of photographic address*" at work in Rineke Dijkstra photographs, "rather than the tragic (or tragicomic) fact about human existence" (211). And there is much more, too much to be summarized.

But there is one notion in particular that I want to concentrate on, a notion that has a complicated and contentious history in both aesthetics and philosophy of mind and action: intention. It arises in chapter 9, in the first section of that chapter, which discusses Thomas Demand's "allegories of intention" (Fried 2008, 272) in his photographs.[6]

Ontological Dimensions

But first I need to develop some conceptual machinery of my own, although I believe everything that follows is either implicit in Fried's approach or explicitly formulated in different terminology.

5. This contrast between what is closed off and what allows some exchange is highlighted by Fried's last remarks in the Struth chapter (2008, chap. 5) about the audience photographed looking at the statue of Michelangelo's *David* in Florence. There persists a myth that Fried's work is "formalist," indifferent to "content." See his closing remarks on the substance of this relation of "world" (142). I also discuss the further possibilities suggested by such remarks, a possible complementarity between "politics" and "ontology," in Pippin 2014, chap. 3.

6. There are two other important discussions by Fried of this theme: his later (2014) discussion of Demand's work, *Pacific Sun*, the last chapter in his collection *Another Light*, and the second chapter of his 2011 *Four Honest Outlaws*, a discussion of the work of sculptor Charles Ray. I cite relevant passages from those discussions in the following notes.

The summary just given already suggests something important about the *ontological* status of the artwork. Art is such as to exist as, and only as, its own self-understanding, a self-understanding shared by artists and the historical world. Its self-understanding is self-constitutive. There is no art for the artworld to understand except what is understood to be art. This does not mean that art is "whatever a community takes it to be." A form of self-understanding could develop in which what has been art, and what has mattered as art, ceases to be continuous with its history, and so ceases to matter as it once did. That is, the fact that practices like art, religion, and even sport are what they are only as understood to be what they are by the participants means that the practices have a history,[7] in fact are essentially historical. Baseball is constituted by the rules the participants take and have taken themselves to be following. There are variations (lowering the pitching mound, allowing a designated hitter for the pitcher) that are not so discontinuous as to mean that, given such a history, people are playing another game, but it is easy to imagine changes that, once widely or officially accepted, *do* mean one is playing another game. (As would be the case with the elimination of strikeouts or doubling the number of fielders.)

This is one way in which one of Fried's most important art-historical claims can be understood, that is, his claim about the role of Manet in the modernist revolution. Art's central *telos* (what became in modernity its central *telos*)—to defeat theatricality by either absorptive depictions, high drama, history scenes, or Courbet's radical suggested merging of beholder and work—came to be exhausted, no longer worked. Manet's new antitheatrical strategy was to acknowledge the inevitable theatricality of painting by confronting the beholder, rather than creating the illusion that he or she does not exist, and to do so by a dramatic facingness in the subject that figures the all-over and immediate facingness of the canvas turned toward the viewer. This *acknowledgment* of theatricality ingeniously avoids simply *being* theatrical.[8]

7. It is a separate question why there should have been art at all, such that it came to have this history. For Hegel, for example, answering that question requires another contextualization of art practices, within *Geist*'s or spirit's attempt at comprehensive self-knowledge. In that context, a different sort of question about discontinuity could be raised.

8. A good formulation of this point by Fried: "That high modernist paintings like Louis Morris's 'Unfurleds' may be said to face the beholder with extraordinary directness makes their structural indifference to his or her presence before them only the more perspicuous" (Fried 2008, 270). A good treatment in another medium: Diderot's depiction of Lui in *Rameau's Nephew*. It is part of Lui's charm, not at all lost on Moi, that he calls attention to his own theatricality and falseness, making it hard to "accuse" him of theatricality. The far subtler point is that this acknowledgment is itself a pretense, false, theatrical in another way. For example, he does not want

However, for Fried, Manet also had to relate this strategy to the great paintings of the past, to refer to those paintings as a way of showing that a continuation of the ambition to make paintings worthy of Raphael, Titian, and Velázquez was still possible in this greatly altered situation. This framework also suggests the possibility that a rejection of the *telos* itself, even a rejection of the idea that paintings could be said to bear meaning, and so to demand some distinctive attentiveness on the part of the beholder ("interpretation"), could be possible within an artworld that still called such objects artworks. But it could be shown that and why this was not the case, that whatever new game was being played, it could not count as art, was radically discontinuous with the great art of the past (and so with "art" itself). I take it that this was part of Fried's point in his 1967 essay "Art and Objecthood."[9]

A second ontological dimension of a work of pictorial art, a formulation of why the thing is an artwork and not something else, is more well known. We want to say: any such work has a distinct form, and it is this form, in the standard Aristotelian sense, that "accounts" for its unity, a unity in this case organic ("living"), not additive or mechanical. (The whole is made of parts or elements, but the whole is also that for the sake of which the parts or elements exist. Parts and whole are mutually interdependent.)[10] But as should be obvious even from the previous hasty summary, Fried wants to attribute a form of work in a philosophically ambitious sense to the artwork, one that can seem to involve ascribing a dimension of reflexive subjectivity to it. In Fried's terms, a work can be said to embody an intention to deny, in something like its address to a beholder, that it is such an address. (So these two points coincide. The self-understanding noted previously as constitutive, now understood to involve an understanding of a relation to the beholder, counts as the object's form, and in this way as formal and final cause.) Its mode of theatrical

to succeed in conning people that he is a good musician. He wants to be regarded as a genuinely good musician. This is the Hegelian moment in the exchange, something not at all lost on the Hegel of the *Phenomenology of Spirit*.

9. Fried writes: "And of course it is true that the desire to distinguish between what is to me the authentic art of our time, and other work which, whatever the dedication, passion, and intelligence of its creators, seems to me to share certain characteristics associated here with the concepts of literalism and theater, has largely motivated what I have written." He even notes a whole "sensibility or mode of being" that he calls "corrupted or perverted by theater" (Fried 1998a, 168).

10. In Thomas Demand's *Pacific Sun* Fried notes that, by means of the stop-action photography used to record the event, Demand was in effect replacing the "causality" of the original event (huge waves that caused the ship to rock to and fro) with his intention (Fried 2014, 259). It is such a transformation that requires the logic of teleological, not efficient causality.

self-presentation is to defeat that very theatricality.[11] This is quite a complicated intentional state to ascribe *to a painting*, one that obviously descends from the intention of the artist, available not through biographical research but in, and only in, the work of some mental state formulated *ex ante* by the artist.)

This is properly described as not only the work's intention or form but, as just noted, its end or goal. That is, a work can be said to embody a conception of itself and a conception of the point of its creation and display or publication, its distinct status as something-to-be-achieved. In works that unfold over time (novels, plays, movies) one can say that a work is realizing such a formal self-understanding over that time. And it is important that such a form, its self-understanding, *is* only its progressive realization, the being-at-work (to employ an Aristotelian term, *energeia*) of such a form. In the same way that an organic being's health and flourishing can be said to be the end for which its systems and organs exist and function, that end is achieved by and consists in nothing but the being-at-work of those parts, so an artwork can be said to have such an organic form, and that form is its self-understanding realized over time, or "having been realized" in the stopped time of a painting. We can then say that to understand a work is to understand this form, this self-realization of its concept of itself in the medium of the work. We don't understand such a form as something distinct, as if a mental representation that exists first in the mind of the artist and then realized in a sensible medium.[12] We understand it only as the emerging self-understanding of itself at work in the object. So we "understand" Manet's work, or understand it much better, if we understand his work as having such an end, a new way to deal with the problem of theatricality, and we understand that by understanding how it can be said to go about doing that. That is, *the work's* self-conception is

11. This dialectical relation between an artwork's theatrical self-presentation, understood as an attempt to defeat theatricality, and a beholder has a deep analogue to Hegel's famous dialectical view of basic human sociality as a "struggle for recognition." The dialectic emerges because, despite the famous phrase, recognition cannot itself be a product of a struggle. Trying to be recognized as such, especially struggling to compel recognition from the other, is futile. Recognition cannot be coerced or "given." One is recognized for what is worthy of recognition, and one achieves recognition most meaningfully when one is indifferent to being recognized and achieves that for which recognition is appropriate.

12. For a fine example of what it would mean to insist on the nonpsychological centrality of intention in the meaning of the work (as opposed to confusing such a meaning with the work's effect), but to "find" such an intention only in the work, see Cronan 2013, especially his introduction, "Modernism Against Representation," 1–22, and chap. 1, "Painting as Affect Machine," 23–64.

realized in different ways in different paintings and does not refer to what Manet thought. This is the dialectical dynamic in the ontology, the mode of being of the artwork, that Fried discovered in the photographs he discussed in *Why Photography Matters*.[13]

But this notion of understanding implies something about the attentive beholder, and that too involves a reflective dimension. Attending to an artwork as an artwork is not something that can be said to happen to us, or happen automatically or passively. If we are to have an experience of art, we must take ourselves to be attending to something that is an artwork. This self-understanding is not thematized or explicit, as if a second-order intending. We do not see the artwork and then observe ourselves so attending. For one thing, that would require an infinite regress. Nor does such an attending involve rule-following or some method, and certainly not some worked-out theory and so concept of art. But our attention to the work is *active* and interrogative as well as contemplative, and that could not happen without our being aware of ourselves as so doing that.

Put another way, not all painted canvases count as *paintings*. Some might be, could be said to be intended to be, decorations for an interior design. And here the reflexive character of an artwork and the reflexive dimension of aesthetic experience intersect. In an active attending, we understand the work to manifest elements that cannot be understood if the work is ascribed an end limited to decoration or amusement or display or technical skill alone. Something calls for such an interpretive attending. In Fried's corpus, such things as Caravaggio's repeated theme of severed heads, Chardin's absorbed subjects, Manet's violations of the rules of perspective and absence of sculptural modeling, all provoke an interrogation that must itself be self-consciously interrogative.[14] And in some cases the form, the end we see at work in the painting or photograph, even aspires to a level of generality, general significance, that suggests an ambition that reaches questions of the nature of art itself, the real, perception—reaches the level of philosophy.

13. I mean the dynamic of theatricality and antitheatricality, as described in the summary remark at Fried 2008, 338. See also the remark about bringing "the entire question of antitheatricality in contemporary art photography into the open as regards both the works themselves, and, wherever relevant, the discourse around them" (344).

14. To say that a work has an aesthetic form is to say that that form, the object of understanding, is accessible only by attention to the whole work ("after" finishing the poem or seeing the film), retrospectively, and must be actively sought. Walter Benn Michaels (2007) writes: "The book, even when it's read the first time, is there to be reread; that's what we mean when we say that it has a form. That's the mark of its insistence that we know and don't know at the same time, a claim that is finally not about our psychological state but about the object of our interest."

Thomas Demand

All this brings us to a claim made about the work of Thomas Demand in chapter 9 of *Why Photography Matters*, a claim that does bear on philosophy. Briefly, Demand takes photographs of paper models that he and his assistants have constructed of scenes, many famous or infamous, some as ordinary as a kitchen sink. So while the models evoke a sculptural intention (Demand's early training as a sculptor), the photographs invoke a pictorial art, primarily by fixing the beholder's point of view. A paradigmatic example would be his 2001 work *Poll* (fig. 6).

This is a treatment of a scene in West Palm Beach where a manual recount was underway, until stopped by the Supreme Court, to examine and determine the "intended" choice of 450,000 Florida voters in the 2000 election contest between Al Gore and George W. Bush. One notes the absence of writing, or of numbers on the phones, or of writing on the post-its, the absence of any referential, identifying detail, and, in the large photograph itself, we can see detectable marks of the paper construction. These are the elements that require the kind of active interrogation I outlined previously.

Fried provides and supplements a useful summary of Demand's project by Deal Sobel:

1. Thomas Demand makes large-scale color photographs.
2. His photographs are of life-size paper models he makes himself.

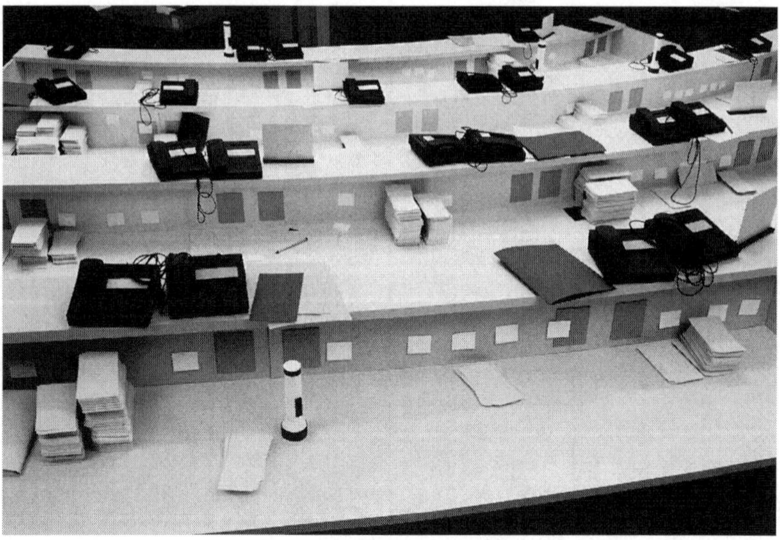

FIGURE 6. Thomas Demand, *Poll*, 2001. Courtesy of VG Bild-Kunst, Bonn/ARS, New York.

3. These models are recreations of actual places.
4. He bases these models on images he obtains from a variety of sources. (Fried 2008, 261)

Fried goes on to complete the summary with a claim from Roxana Marcoci: that because Demand's photographs are laminated behind Plexiglas and displayed without a frame they are triply removed from the scenes or objects they depict. This point calls the Plato of the tenth book of the *Republic* to mind, who criticized artworks in general for their remove from reality. If we count the object itself as the original, then Marcoci is counting the image of the object (the one used by Demand to create his models) as one remove, the model as the second, and the photograph as the third. If we are true Platonists, however, there are really four removes, since the original for Plato is itself a copy or image of the Idea. As we shall see, this removal or distance bars any claim that the photograph's "intentionality" in the other philosophical sense, its "aboutness," is due simply to the imprint of reflected light from the object on photosensitive material. The aboutness is *achieved* and Plato's values are reversed. The distance allows a perspective *on* the real, not a distorted image of it.

Fried then remarks on several aspects of these unusual photographs. As already noted, Demand leaves invisible traces of the imperfection of the models, flaws that he could not have fixed. He takes off any referentially identifying sign, writing, or image. The object-models are blank, creating a dehistoricized endless moment, as if timeless, and an atmosphere of stillness, a kind of dead, lifeless air. The banality and ordinariness of the objects and scene are stressed. This creates, quoting Demand, the subject matter as a "dull, obstinate, mysterious presence . . . a suffocating dullness," one that cannot "elicit any projected desire or presence on our part" (quoted in Fried 2008, 266). It is this unmistakable feature of the works, especially in this last respect, that creates the perfect occasion for Fried to remind us that this indifference to, exclusion of, the beholder (the absence of elicited desire or elicited involvement) is part of an antitheatrical strategy. There is not only an absence of anything that would call to mind any human involvement (except, as we shall see, exactly that unnerving *absence*). Rather, any such involvement seems excluded, negated, and not just absent. (The models seem constructed with that effect in mind.) This helps account for the fact that the objects are contextless, perhaps what it might look like if Heidegger were wrong and objects were not normally encountered "within a world," a "work-world," but were mere mute present-at-hand (*vorhanden*) things. Photographs of *them* are the last thing that could be considered to have been presented "for the beholder." (Again we must always say, even though they are.)

And there is something else of even greater importance for Fried, an element that, I want to say, is connected in a somewhat circuitous way with the largest theme raised by his whole project—the fate of art in modernity. That is, in place of "the original scene of evidentiary traces and marks of human use," Demand wants to show "a counter-image of *sheer artistic intention*." (The work manifesting its being so intended is the ontologically decisive moment of its self-understanding discussed previously.)[15] The bizarre blankness of the objects "throws into conceptual relief the determining force—also the inscrutability, one might say the opacity—of the intentions behind them." Or, "Demand effectively replaces real-world context with a merely depicted one, every detail and aspect of which is exactly what he intended it to be" (Fried 2008, 271). And Fried erects a very important barrier to a possible misunderstanding of these claims: "Demand's aim is not to make a wholly intended object—in this case, a wholly digitized photograph—but rather to make pictures that *represent or indeed allegorize intendedness as such*" (272). Taking these points together, one can say that the felt inscrutability or opacity of identifiable authorial intention is just what allows the author's, Demand's, general intention—to represent or allegorize intendedness as such, not a particular intention—to emerge. To make his point a more general one, Fried then extends his account and shows that there is a similar kind of dialectical structure, in which some sense of absence allows an intentional (aesthetic) presence, in several of Thomas Struth's early street photographs (fig. 7), those "reticent, inexplicit, but meaning-impregnated cityscapes" (281). That is, a sense of meaningfulness *in the art*, in the photo's having been made of this street that way, is opened by the still, mute, eerie *absences in the objects* depicted.

So we can say, in the terms introduced earlier, that Fried has tried to exfoliate (to my mind, convincingly) in each photograph by Demand (and by noting common concerns across many) its concept of itself to-be-realized, its form, the end to be achieved, and he has found a typical modernist concern.

Its form is *form as such*, the principle of unity itself, intendedness. In a way that echoes Kant's famous "purposiveness without a purpose," we have intendedness without a distinct intention other than the fact of intendedness as such. This has a general significance that we will discuss in the last section of this chapter.

This allegorization of intendedness as such in the photograph is then connected to the much-discussed accusation that photography is "weak in intentionality," because the actual production of the detailed image takes place

15. See also the discussion of such a point with respect to sculpture in "Embedment: Charles Ray" (Fried 2014, 102–3).

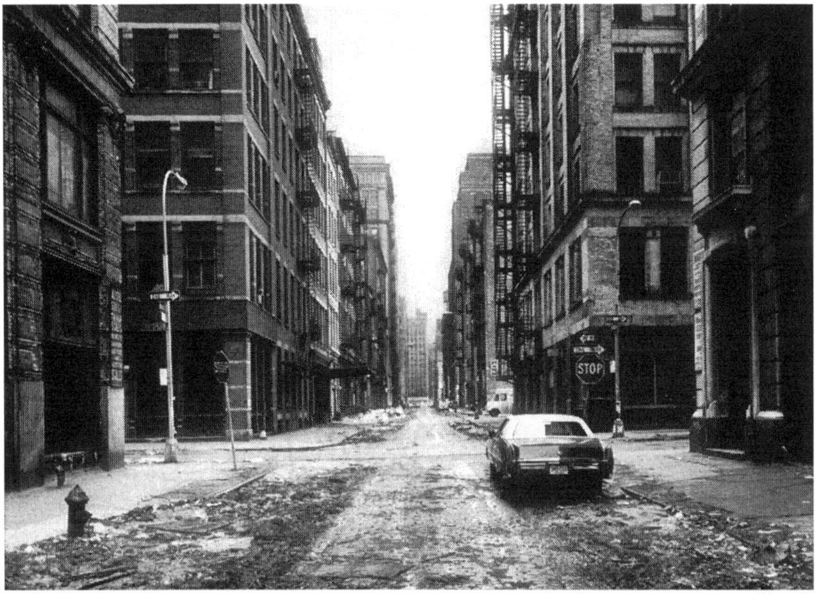

FIGURE 7. Thomas Struth, *Crosby Street, New York, Soho*, 1978. Image courtesy Atelier Thomas Struth, Berlin.

mechanically, automatically. (That is, the image is created by a machine, in a way not subject to a maker's intention.) Given the vast array of new technical possibilities in photographic technology for the assembling and composition of photographs, this whole discussion is somewhat out of date, but Fried, making use of an article by Walter Benn Michaels (2006),[16] notes the general significance of the topic of intentions for art photography. Michaels pointed out that photographs raise a certain problem because it is not clear if, and if so how, they can be said to be pictures of, representations of, objects. The parallel example used to make this point is that of a fossil, say of a trilobite, which we cannot say is either a trilobite or a "picture" of one. (That is, somewhat like a photograph, it is the impression made by a trilobite, a trace or mark of the trilobite form.)[17] But this problem is also a photographic strength in modernity. That is, in a context where the art/nonart distinction has become fraught, or even abandoned (e.g., in Arthur Danto's work),[18] this art's status *as* art object

16. Michaels 2006, 431–50 (discussed in Fried 2008, 335–38).

17. "Every photograph is the result of a physical imprint transferred by light reflections onto a sensitive surface," notes Rosalind Krauss in her "Notes on the Index" (quoted in Fried 2008, 268).

18. I mean such books as *The Transfiguration of the Commonplace* (1981), *The Philosophical Disenfranchisement of Art* (1986), and *After the End of Art: Contemporary Art and the Pale of History* (1977).

cannot directly or straightforwardly borrow from the conventions of painting or from their medium. That does not mean that photographs cannot be art objects, but rather means that their status has to be achieved, intended (even an evocation of the conventions of gallery painting must be achieved and sustained), and in a way distinctive for photography. And Fried is showing how in Demand's photographs, that achievement, that intended-to-be-realized, is itself what is intended and achieved.

Now of course every artifact bears the marks of the intention of the maker. But that intention is manifest by virtue of those marks, the thing's being worked over, designed, for a function. Demand has stripped the objects of most of those marks, or so many that he leaves them more like spectral analogues of the original artifacts, or leaves only their being made to be photographed. It is in being "stripped" in this way that the artifacts address the issue of intentionality rather than merely express another determinate intention. It is in that form of address, I want to say, that several philosophical issues are at stake.

"Intended"

I understand the previous discussion to raise a number of questions. The supervening and most important one is: if Demand's photographs represent or allegorize "intendedness as such," just *what* thereby has been represented? It would not be sufficient to say that the photographs of the paper models represent Demand's intention to make paper models of real places and photograph these models. That would be equivalent to saying something like: Manet's intention in painting the *Olympia* was to depict Victorine Meurent in just this way, posing as a courtesan. (This is as informative as Merle Haggard's answer when asked why he wrote the song "Okie from Muskogee": "Because I was the only one who knew the words.") As we noted in discussing formal unity previously, we take the display (or publishing) of an artwork to be *purposive*. This is part of the dual meaning of intention, covering what we take the work to mean (what we take "the artist" to intend it to mean), where what it is "to mean what it does mean" is also the end or purpose of its production, and so, in that second sense of intentionality, what we want to say the painting or photograph is "about." So we can say that representing intendedness as such represents the idea of the bearing of meaning by a sensible object even as it exhibits that idea by bearing *that* meaning, and that the modality of its so bearing meaning is *aesthetic*, and in a *photographic* register. This latter dimension inevitably arises from the context of photography itself and the question of its possible intentionality, as discussed previously.

That the register is photographic is crucial to the self-referential reflexiveness we have seen in art's self-constitution, in a particular way in this case. That is, photographing the life-size paper models accomplishes something that an exhibition of the models themselves could not do. The photograph presents itself to us as if the mode in which the work's content achieves a form of self-consciousness embodies how the photograph's own "self-understanding" is at work. What would look like oddly inadequate paper copies, when photographed, when seen to be for the photograph as the end result, or staged for the photograph, become about themselves in a much more heightened way. Their reproduction or replication in the photograph is what makes possible the distinctive reflexivity of an artwork, its realization of some concept of itself (in this case that realization being of there being such a concept of itself, or the concept of "intendedness as such").[19]

There are a number of ways to say what this latter specification ("photographically *aesthetic*") amounts to. Fried has argued that the very absence of referential markers, and the attending air of strangeness and vacancy, the exclusion of the beholder or the odd self-sufficient presence and autonomy of the made objects, intimate such an aesthetic inflection. This is because of the association of these aspects of the work with the defeat of theatricality central to establishing the work, any pictorial work in modernity, as an artwork, all of which is accomplished nondiscursively. Alternatively put, the *work itself* bears this intention or meaning. It demands something from the beholder, and so cannot rightly be understood as simply an occasion-to-be-experienced. And this blankness prohibits the invocation of a cognitive conceptual classification, in a way we can identify as having a Kantian point.[20] That is, it can invite much more a "free play" of faculties, an imaginative attending—that distinct modality of aesthetic understanding—than a determinate conceptual classification of its point or purpose. In other words, what is allegorized or represented is pictorial art itself in its distinctive, medium-specific mode of being and being intelligible.

But the fact that aesthetic meaning is embodied in this way has a number of presuppositions and implications. I mean not only that the work embodies an aesthetic intention but also that the work's intention is *sensibly* present,

19. Fried formulates a related, similar point in "Thomas Demand's *Pacific Sun*." Noting another "small turn in the dialectic" (Fried 2014, 255), he contrasts the strict indexicality of the photograph with the sheer artistic intendedness of the models. The other important dimension of Fried's interpretation of this work is the relation between what he has called "presentness" and the "duration" of the events modeled in the video. This, another opposition that is dialectically transcended, would require a separate discussion.

20. Its ungraspability, the way the work actually defeats attempts to comprehend it conceptually, suggests the Kantian sublime.

public, and requires interrogation. We have already seen the last element at work. We are stopped short by the oddness and general "indifference" of the photographed objects. In interrogating this, we take ourselves to be inquiring about the artist's intention, but this has little to do with hunting down evidence of what mental state the artist was entertaining at the onset of creation, *ex ante*. We normally have no access to that intention, and, interestingly, in many contexts, neither does he or she, except in what has been realized. The work is the only guide we have to its own intended realization, and Fried's work in many different contexts is as exemplary as an indication of how such an interrogative attending should go on as any we have.

This is worth stressing. Our ordinary sense of intention is of something mental, an idea of the mind of the artist. And when we say that this intention is embodied in the work, we often mean that there are signs in the work to prompt us to think the same idea. But in this account, at least as I understand it, such a strict distinction between mentality and materiality is not maintained. The artist's intention can actually be said to take shape in the process of composing the material work, and the work demands interpretation, for both the artist and the beholder, an interpretation focused on its material details, for the work to be able to be said to bear meaning at all. Just as in the case of intention and bodily movement, we should speak instead of the intention being realized over time in the bodily, and the determinate content of that intention is that realization of being subject to interpretive interrogation just as much for the agent as for the public community affected by what was done. Read in Fried's terms, Demand can be said to have created a "snapshot" of this process of realization.

The intuitive or ordinary understanding cited previously would have to mean that the work is first perceived as having the sensible properties it does, and then, in a second step, an inference would have to occur to what is represented and then a further inference to meaning or intention. But we do not see colored rectangles and other shapes that we then infer to be minimal representations of telephones and notebooks, and then infer that this means intendedness as such. We see blank telephones and see them *in* their strangeness, immediately detect what isn't present as well, that they are "there" simply as "intended." This is all it is when we understand the look of another. We don't see shifting eyes and then infer our friend is lying. We see the lie in his face; at least we see all this in this way in the Heideggerian and Merleau-Pontyean and Wittgensteinian anti-Cartesian accounts that have influenced so much of Fried's narrative and ontology of painting.[21]

21. That the medium is sensible has implications other than those concerning the object's

To admit the obvious: this aspect of the relation between intention and embodiment is difficult to make credible in a brief summary. The connection just stated will seem to many, intuitively, too tight. We know that, owing to some intervening contingencies, the work can turn out differently from what was intended, and not that the work is what the intention turned out to be.[22] But the idea is not to deny that there are *ex ante* intentions, but to say that any *ex ante* representation by the artist of the work to be achieved is highly provisional, and should be understood to be realized in and expressed in the work over time, as to-be-achieved, often in ways that could not have been foreseen but that become extensions and variations of the original intention. Even accidents are either left in the work or not, displayed or not, marking the work everywhere with intentionality, even without any *ex ante* full formulation. I ascribe this tight imbrication of intention-in-work to Fried because he reads *the intention in the work* by *placing the work in the context of a narrative account of the fate of art in modernity* (the work in that context manifests that intention)—i.e., the theatricality problematic—independent of what evidence there is or is not about the artist's awareness of such a problematic. It is the evidence that he finds in the work that realizes and so embodies the intention, and this within the historical world struggling with theatricality at some point in time. The artworks bear the intentions they do in and only in such a historical world, located within such a tradition. This is so, even though the language of intention would seem to restrict us to the artist's self-understanding. That is misleading. An intention can be attributed to "the artist of the work" even if forever unacknowledged or even rejected by that actual artist. That is, the public character of artworks means that the work has entered a domain of interpretability such that there can be no putative "ownership" of the intention in the work by the individual artist. Fried will make use occasionally of what Demand has said in interviews (and Demand is an especially astute commentator on his own work) but only to support points made by interrogation of the work.

This all only introduces the role of the concept of intention in Michael Fried's book on photography. But I have tried to suggest that the stakes in those first pages of chapter 9 are much greater than they might appear to

---

sensible bearing of meaning. It also means that the mode of intelligibility for us is itself a sensible mode. That is, some works, Menzel's for example, suggest that our bodily relation to the world be an empathetic one, not just an ocular or spectatorial one. This can be affective, orientational, involve our sense of motility. See the discussion in Fried 2002, chaps. 3, 4, and 5.

22. I have tried to present a much fuller account in Pippin 2008, especially in chap. 6, section 7, where I deal with the problem of our counterintuitions (see 170–76).

be. The conditions necessary for considering artworks as fit subjects for interpretation turn on the questions of intention and the distinctive aesthetic modality of such embodied expression. That artworks can mean, that the meaning can be interrogated, and that the mode of meaning is distinctive, "aesthetic," are all in play. One modest conclusion, or at least suggestion, from this discussion is that attacks on the notion of intention and interpretation are often fraught with all sorts of assumptions about the status of such intentions. These range from assuming a kind of Cartesianism or mentalism about a subject's intention (originally private and subsequently transferred into the work) or about a dualism in the work as its material embodiment is a kind of vehicle for some nonmaterial, thinglike, semantic entity. None of these assumptions has anything to do with Fried's enterprise, or with the issue of intention itself, as I hope this brief excursus might have made plausible.

8

Adorno, Aesthetic Negativity, and the Problem of Idealism

Hegel

One of Adorno's most sweeping and frequent characterizations of his project in *Aesthetic Theory* has it that *the* "task that confronts aesthetics today" is an "emancipation from absolute idealism" (Adorno 1997, 165).[1] The context (and the phrase itself) makes explicit he means emancipation from Hegel, but only in so far as Hegel represents the culmination and essence of modern philosophy itself, or what Adorno calls "identity thinking." He means by this that reflection on art should be freed from any aspiration for any reconciliationist relation between art and contemporary society, or any sort of role in the rationalization or justification of any basic aspect of late modernity, or freed even from any aspiration for a conceptual comprehension of that society, as if it had some rational structure available for comprehension. He means of course capitalist, bourgeois society. Hegel and his absolute idealism represent the epitome of what must be rejected. Does it matter, beyond the issue of scholarly accuracy, if Adorno's version of Hegelian idealism (and what it typifies) is incorrect, more in the way of a very broad-stroke textbook summary than a confrontation with the thing itself? In one sense the answer is obviously no. We could just let the name "Hegel" stand for whatever Adorno is after in his attack on identity thinking and move on to the substance of what in his own voice Adorno wants to say about the issue mentioned in my title, the status of "the negative" in modern art. That after all is what is philosophically significant. But it would matter if Adorno's position is framed in terms that are incomplete and unclear from the start, and if that problematic framing derives from how he understands his opposition to Hegel and to idealism. I argued elsewhere that Adorno's ethical position is compromised in

1. All references in the text are to this translation.

something like this way by his reading of Kant. I want here to suggest something less critical, more in the way of trying to show how Hegel's aesthetics could be of help in the completion and clarification of Adorno's chief cluster of terms in his account of art in the present age: the negative, or negativity, or the nonidentical.

First, we obviously need to remind ourselves that Hegel's account of art in his lectures is tremendously important for Adorno. For one thing, Hegel was the decisive figure in shifting modern philosophical attention away from "aesthetics" to the philosophy of art. This meant a shift away from the paramount significance of the beautiful and a pretty thorough dismissal of the significance of the beauty of nature in particular. Adorno would disagree strongly with the latter aspect of Hegel's position, but Hegel's rejection of the empiricist focus on a distinctive sensual pleasure as the essence of aesthetic experience and so of a subjectivist priority given to experience over the artwork as the bearer of artistic meaning (both aspects of which were still prominent in Kant, whose position Adorno calls "castrated hedonism" [11]) represents a shift embraced by Adorno. (The role of Schiller in this story is obviously crucial as well.) It was also Hegel who, according to Adorno, first realized that art's completion or end is internal to its concept, and who realized that something decisive for the possibility of all traditional art had happened, that art as a vehicle of truth had become a "thing of the past." (For Adorno, Hegel was the first to recognize art's "lost naiveté" in the modern world.) This means first of all that both Adorno and Hegel had a historicized conception of art. As Adorno put it, "art is what it has become," and art can be "understood only by its laws of movement, not according to any set of invariants" (3). This already raises a problem that Hegel is in a better position to address. Art is what it has become. For whom? *What* has become? What "laws of movement"? And no "invariants" at all?

That is, Adorno begins by theorizing about the fate of art in its contemporary location, and for Adorno that means modernism in the arts, primarily in literature and music. This means attention to an artistic crisis in which nothing about the purpose, nature, or social role of art could any longer be taken for granted. But this historicized approach raises an immediate problem addressed by Hegel but rarely explicitly attended to by Adorno. If any of the questions just noted about art as such, its purpose, nature, or social function, are *thoroughly* historicized with "*no* invariants," if art is understood only by the "laws of its movement," then we are in danger of a positivist reduction of art to whatever is taken to be art at a time. This would be immediately paradoxical. The laws of "what's" movement? It would also open the door to all sorts of historical possibilities in which art would lose any of the distinctive boundary conditions that Adorno clearly wants to invoke. If anything goes, then fashion, costume jewelry, reality television, crude propaganda, and body piercing and tattooing could all have equal status as art. It seems obvious that Adorno needs not only an account of art that would distinguish it from nonart and especially from pseudoart, but also a distinction between what Hegel called "fine art" (*schöne Kunst*), or art in which the highest ambitions of art as such are manifest, and artworks that qualify as art but are poor or inferior art. Indeed, in the contemporary world, Adorno's defense of high modernist art, what is now called "elite" art, is one of his most prominent and controversial positions. (He speaks easily of the difference between the "lower" arts and "pure art" [16].) All of this means he needs, and I think he implicitly presupposes, something like Hegel's position on the possibility of a conceptual clarification of art as such, but one that admits wide, various historical inflections. In Hegel this amounts to the claim that all art is a sensible-affective modality of understanding the Absolute, and its historical manifestations represent the progressive realization of, and its coming to self-consciousness about, its own concept. Adorno wants no part of this theory of course. His charge is that Hegel's "content aesthetics" (*Inhaltsästhetik*) recognized the negative potential of art, what Adorno calls the "otherness" of art, but Hegel misunderstood this otherness in representational and discursive terms and regressed to a pre-aesthetic level, thereby unwittingly helping to transform art into "the ideology of domination" (7). This is Adorno's way of saying that Hegel understood art as a version, but an inferior version, of philosophy, and thereby subjected it to the domain of affirmative, identity thinking. Yet Adorno also agrees with Hegel that what "art demands from its beholder is knowledge. . . . The work wants its truth and untruth to be grasped" (15). What is obviously at stake is what is meant by "knowledge," and what is at stake in that question is that status of the negative or the nonidentical.

So Adorno's own position also commits him to some sort of parallel Hegelian account of the logic of art as such on the one hand, and its unique historical manifestations in late modernity on the other. In the modern period at any rate, aesthetic negativity functions something like this logic, and art's contemporary self-negation, its embodiment of its own impossibility, is how he wants to understand its contemporary fate, and this story subtends a broader narrative in which the development of aesthetic processes is said to correspond (*korrespondiert*) to social developments (5). This would appear to mean that Adorno accepts some sort of quasi-Hegelian narrative in which art succeeds in freeing itself from subservience to religion and politics, but achieves this autonomy at the moment when, because of "social development," the emergence of the system and ethos of capitalism, art must also "turn against its own concept." This is the moment when aesthetics turns into, as he puts it, "art's necrology," the moment when "the darkening of the world makes the irrationality of art rational: radically darkened art [*die radikale verdunkelte Kunst*]." This is the only appropriate response to "a radically darkened objectivity [*verfintersterte Objektivität*]" (19).

Negativity: Variations

But understanding any of this requires attention to a great deal more detail from *Aesthetic Theory*. We should begin with the many variations on the theme of aesthetic negativity that are at work in that book. The concept is polysemous in Adorno, even though there is an important family resemblance. I want to outline six different, occasionally overlapping, invocations of negation before turning back to the issue of idealism. Supervening many of these variations is a general notion familiar from the logic of predicate or propositional negation, although things will quickly get more complicated. This is the straightforward denial of some positive function or argument: a "not," followed by a value or assertion, or location, whatever. So the first obvious sense of contemporary aesthetic negativity is that modernist art is the negation of traditional art, not what art has been (affirmative "voluptuous," beautiful, harmonious, humanist), even though still "art," to return to the problem of the logic of art as such, on the one hand, and its historicity on the other. As he says, "nothing is more damaging to theoretical knowledge of modern art than its reduction to what it has in common with older periods" (19). (Adorno notes that there *is* such a commonality, but he does not explore what that is and insists that modern art's distinctness overwhelms any such trivial commonality.) All of our efforts must be directed to exfoliating its radical differences from the art of the past, not as a matter of style or content, but as a matter of art itself.

Second, Adorno notes that art, and here he seems to mean all art, stands in a negative relation to empirical reality. That reality generates an objective need for art, a need that should be understood as a gap or lack, an insufficiency or dissatisfaction. "Art is the social antithesis of society, not directly deducible from it" (8). Or, as he puts it, "If thought is in any way to gain a relation to art it must be on the basis that something in reality, something back of the veil spun by the interplay of institutions and false needs, objectively demands art, and that it demands an art that speaks for what the veil hides" (18). By and large here, Adorno means that it is objective "suffering" that demands a rejection by art of the necessity or unavoidability of such suffering, although again in an unprecedented way, not as in the humanism of Balzac or Dickens or the naturalistic depiction of suffering by Hardy or Dreiser. We will see why this is so when we come to the notion of mimesis.

Third, as we reach the more complexly dialectical level, art now stands in a negative relation to itself. This has a weaker meaning—art has lost its "self-evidence"; it can no longer rely on itself, on an inner confidence in what it is. Where that had been, there is now a gap, an absence. But the stronger version is of an active resistance to itself, a fate expressed in several of the paradoxical or dialectical ways Adorno was so fond of: "Art responds to the loss of its self-evidence not simply by concrete transformations of its procedures and comportments but by trying to pull itself free from its own concept as from a shackle: the fact that it is art" (16). And even more paradoxically, "If all art is the secularization of transcendence, it participates in the dialectic of enlightenment. Art has confronted this dialectic with the aesthetic conception of antiart; indeed, without this element art is no longer thinkable. This implies nothing less than that art must go beyond its own concept in order to remain faithful to that concept" (29).

This dimension also has a weaker and stronger formulation. In one sense this self-opposition is perennial. "The perennial [*perennierende*] revolt of art against art has its *fundamentum in re*. If it is essential to artworks that they be things, it is no less essential that they negate their own status as things, and thus art turns against art. The totally objectivated artwork would congeal into a mere thing, whereas if it altogether evaded objectivation it would regress to an impotently powerless subjective impulse and flounder in the empirical world" (175). Such formulations clearly reflect the influence of Kant's account of genius. But Adorno clearly thinks something has happened "today" that makes the struggle of art against objectification, repetitiveness, and staleness much more intense and critical: "The inner consistency through which artworks participate in truth also involves their untruth; in its most unguarded manifestations art has always revolted against this, and today this revolt has become art's own law of movement" (169).

Fourth, as already indicated, such a negative relation to social reality should not be taken to mean that artworks bring to bear some standard of humaneness or justice or human flourishing on a historical reality and, functioning as a social critique, point out social failures and try to inspire a reformist response. This would be a kind of "Uncle Tom's Cabin" conception and it is one Adorno rejects. The reason for this brings us a bit closer to the critique of idealism, for Adorno rejects the idea of applying some concept to an independent reality and, finding a gap between the concept and reality, then demanding or implying a demand that the gap be closed, that reality conform to the exogenously imported concept, that the concept and reality be "identical." That is merely the critical variation of identity thinking, and as we shall begin seeing in more detail, identity thinking is exactly what art must help us free ourselves from. Such a view is said to be subjectivist and so linked with the ideology of domination. By contrast, art's relation to the self-negation of contemporary bourgeois society, its double-bind demands, its inability to sustain and reproduce itself, is mimetic. By mimesis Adorno certainly does not mean anything imitative, copying or representational; he means something closer to embodying or sedimenting or assimilating. This is clearest in his discussions of Beckett: "The more total society becomes, the more completely it contracts to a unanimous system, and all the more do the artworks in which this experience is sedimented become the other of this society. If one applies the concept of abstraction in the vaguest possible sense, it signals the retreat from a world of which nothing remains except its *caput mortuum*. New art is as abstract as social relations have in truth become" (31). And most clearly of all: "Because the spell of external reality over its subjects and their reactions has become absolute, the artwork can only oppose this spell by assimilating itself to it" (31).

It is clear from these and many other passages that mimesis is the most important and most elusive concept in Adorno's aesthetic theory. The idea that there can be such a mimesis, "a mimesis of the hardened and alienated" (21) or what he calls "the nonconceptual affinity of the subjectively produced with its unposited other" (54), and that this "defines art as a form of knowledge and to that extent as 'rational'" would require a book-length study to unpack. But for us the signal word in these formulations, what Adorno is trying most of all to avoid, is "nonconceptual." As in so many philosophical positions, Adorno's, it begins to be clear here, is determined by, somewhat captured by, what he thinks he is avoiding, the "logic of the concept," as it would be put by Hegel. There can be no "subject" dominating or devouring the object in modernist aesthetics, and that is its revolutionary potential, its noncomplicity with the ideology of domination. This is also where the common or commonsensical notion of predicate or propositional negation, the active negation of some positive, is no longer applicable. This "unposited other," what Adorno calls the nonidentical, is not the result of the denial of identity. That would make it derivative, secondary, a result, what it has been since the classical metaphysical response to Parmenides. In modern life, it is the nonidentical that has priority, what is on its own, as it is, that eludes conceptual identification, not what results from the denial of identity. More on this vexed notion soon.

This is all given more aesthetic substance in the fifth variation of the theme of negativity as Adorno variously describes a modernist work's refusal to mean in any traditional sense, and so its reliance on indeterminacy, abstraction, dissonance (which he calls "the seal of everything modern" [15]), and even "the irrational." "Dissonance elicits from within the work that which vulgar sociology calls its social alienation" (15). Or more expansively, "The absurd, the category most refractory to interpretation, inheres in that spirit that is requisite to the interpretation of artworks. At the same time, the need of artworks for interpretation, their need for the production of their truth content, is the stigma of their constitutive insufficiency. Artworks do not achieve what is objectively sought in them. The zone of indeterminacy between the unreachable and what has been realized constitutes their enigma" (128). Adorno certainly doesn't mean to deny the possibility of interpretation, but, as he says enigmatically, "Rather, the darkness of the absurd is the old darkness of the new. This darkness must be interpreted, not replaced by the clarity of meaning" (27). Presumably, this involves some interpretation of this very uninterpretability of "the absurd" and of the unstable self-negations of modernist form, of the sort that Adorno himself provides of Baudelaire, Beckett, Proust, and Schoenberg. This would presumably tie the manifestation of such dissonance and abstraction and indeterminacy to the social realities assimilated mimetically in a modernist work, and such an exfoliation of aesthetic modernist content, continually "outstripping" its own embodied concept of art, suggests that we might be on the verge of a kind of mythic repetition in modernism, forcing us to ask how one indeterminacy or dissonance can be determinately differentiated from another. Adorno certainly is aware of this issue and thinks he can answer it, but that answer depends on the resources left over from his critique of absolute idealism, the presumption of the absolute conceptual intelligibility of everything, Hegel's Absolute.

So we arrive at the sixth and decisive variation on the theme of negativity. Adorno's views here about Hegel as the epitome of the identity thinking inherent in the Enlightenment domination of nature and in capitalism's establishment of manifold relations of domination and oppression in a class-stratified society are among the most well-known aspects of his philosophy, and his view both inherits a "finitist" criticism of Hegelian rationalism begun by Schelling and intensified by Kierkegaard and anticipates a great deal of twentieth-century European thought, most prominently and ironically by Adorno's nemesis, Heidegger. Here are some of his formulations.

> As the negation of the absolute idea, content can no longer be identified with reason as it is postulated by idealism; content has become the critique of the omnipotence of reason, and it can therefore no longer be reasonable according to the norms set by discursive thought. (27)

To restate the obvious, this all depends on what one means by a claim for the "omnipotence of reason." And

> Perhaps nowhere else is the desiccation of everything not totally ruled by the subject more apparent, nowhere else is the dark shadow of idealism more obvious, than in aesthetics. (62)

Finally,

> The new wants nonidentity, yet intention reduces it to identity; modern art constantly works at the Münchhausean trick of carrying out the identification of the nonidentical. (23)

Adorno here is especially but not at all exclusively thinking of the aesthetic availability of sensuous particularity in its particularity, as in the experience of natural beauty. And he is not naively proposing any sort of crude nominalist realism. He makes clear in *Negative Dialectics* that Hegel is at least right that "the particular itself is unthinkable without the moment of the universal" (Adorno 1981, 322, 328). Or in *Aesthetic Theory*, "Art cannot be conceived without this immanently idealistic element, that is, without the objective mediation of all art through spirit; this sets a limit to dull-minded doctrines of aesthetic realism just as those elements encompassed in the name of realism are a constant reminder that art is no twin of idealism" (91). But just as obviously, for Adorno this "identification of the nonidentical," as it is uniquely possible for art, is not what Hegel famously meant by the conceptual comprehension of the nonidentical in his account of the moments of the self-negation and the reintegration of the Concept. But we have enough, if only barely, to begin to appreciate how decisively Adorno's project is shaped by his own negation of what he thinks Hegel's system purported, catastrophically, to be able to do. I want to suggest now that because of this negative dependence, it matters a great deal that Adorno has misidentified the heart and soul of Hegel's Absolute Idealism.

Idealism

This idealism in German Idealism, at least the thread that travels from Kant through Fichte to Hegel (Schelling's "idealism" is another issue), has three components.[2] The first is the claim that a priori knowledge of the world, the ordinary spatiotemporal world, as well as of "objects" and practices in it like art, religion, and the state, is possible; knowledge about that world,

2. I am summarizing here claims made in much more detail in Pippin 2019.

but achieved independently of empirical experience. Idealism in this sense is primarily a critique of empiricism (not of empirical knowledge, although it is sometimes confused with such a critique; empiricism is itself an a priori position, intended to explicate what any possible knowing amounts to). Although it might sound strange to say that Adorno also holds that there is a priori knowledge, we have already seen that his view depends on claims about identity, nonidentity, negativity, and the nature of traditional and modern art that are hardly empirical claims and can only be understood as philosophical, that is, a priori claims. The second component is where all the interpretive controversies begin. It is the claim that this a priori knowledge, while, in some sense to be specified, ultimately about the world that exists independent of thought, consists in thinking's or reason's *knowledge of itself*, thinking's determination of thinking, or, as Hegel designates, a "science of pure thinking." This is where Adorno decisively parts company from Hegel, but we need to explore what this claim might mean. It is understandable, but also quite false, to think that these two components can be jointly claimed only if either (a) objects of knowledge depend for their existence on being thought, or (b) access to objects requires some sort of mind-imposed unification of sensory elements, resulting in a "subject-mediated" product and appearance, not the thing as it is in itself. And Adorno often talks this way about idealism as the philosophy of domination, *Herrschaft*. There are many versions of this existential dependence, or subject-mediated interpretation of German Idealism in the extant literature. This view no doubt stems from the understandable but false inference that if such a conceptual structure is not derived from experience, it must be contributed by, or "imposed by," us. This must be so, if objects depend for their experientiability on such "mind-imposed" unity, or, in a different tack, in what is known as "objective idealism," if what there is is, in some sense or other, "really" a concept. (On this view, the idealism in Hegelian idealism refers to the ideal, nonsensible, or noetic true nature of reality itself.)

But there is clearly a question to be answered, and it amounts to the third dimension of idealism: how the first two components could possibly be true (that objective a priori knowledge is possible, and that what pure reason knows in such knowledge is "itself," thinking itself), if the standard versions of the third component are not true too. The most important watchword for Hegel's *Logic*, once we realize that no form of "object *dependence* on subject" is at stake in that project (an extremely widespread general view of what idealism must be to count as idealism), is exactly the word Adorno baptizes as central, but Hegel means it in a sense diametrically opposed to what Adorno thinks he means. For Hegel, we are talking not about any dependence but about an "*identity*" (a "speculative identity" to be sure) between the forms of pure thinking and the forms of being, an identity compatible with maintaining a difference between anyone thinking and anything thought about. Here is Hegel's summary formulation:

> The older metaphysics had in this respect a higher concept of thinking than now passes as the accepted opinion. For it presupposed as its principle that only what is known of things and in things by thought is really true [*wahrhaft Wahre*] in them, that is, what is known in them not in their immediacy but as first elevated to the form of thinking, as things of thought. This metaphysics thus held that thinking and the determination of thinking are not something alien to the subject matters, but are rather their essence, or that the things and the thinking of them agree in and for themselves (also our language expresses a kinship between them); that thinking in its immanent determinations, and the true nature of things, are one and the same content. (Hegel 2010, 21.29)

It will be important (for Hegel, at any rate) that this account of an "identity" ("one and the same content") is true of philosophical or speculative thinking, thinking that has as its subject matter "true being" or "actuality." Hence the identity within difference of being and thinking, the core principle of Hegel's version of idealism. In other words, there is an "identity" between "pure thinking's moments" (suitably well defined) and "any possible object of pure thinking," or pure thinking's "truth." It is an identity within difference because the speculative claim does not mean that the world, what seems other than thinkings, must nevertheless *be* "*thinkings*." It is not, any more than true thoughts (judgments) are true by virtue of the world's being *thoughts*. Once we understand the necessary dependence of any true thinking about anything on pure thinking, and once we understand what constitutes pure thinking (especially its "spontaneity"), and once we understand the "moments" necessary for pure thinking to be pure thinking, we have established thereby the truth about what there is, what there is in its intelligibility. This all requires as a premise the principle of all Western rationalism since its beginning: to be is to be intelligible. There can be nothing wholly *alogos*, in principle unknowable, any more than there can be substances with contradictory properties. Adorno will reject the principle of Absolute Idealism—the claim that a complete, internally self-determined articulation of any possible intelligibility is possible—but I don't think he rejects this basic principle. Another way to put this: He is not a religious thinker. The existence of *Aesthetic Theory* is itself testimony to his acceptance of it. He wants to insist that there is a form of aesthetic intelligibility (with all its paradoxical modernist dimensions, unintelligibility, untruth, absurdity, self-negation) and to distinguish it from any rationalizing moment, but that is all based on an unnecessarily limited notion of rationality and is not something Hegel would disagree with.

So to sum up: a science of logic is a science of pure thinking. Pure thinking's object is, and is only, itself. But this "object" is not a nature, an object. As noted above, the *Logic* has nothing to do with "the mind" as a substance or thing. As in so many cases, Hegel is following *both* Aristotle here *and* Kant, for whom the claim that the "I think" must be able to accompany all my representations *is a logical point*, expresses the form of thought, and is not a claim about how the mind actually operates. If that were the case, and Hegel were making a claim about the mind's nature, knowledge would be limited by its "instrument," something Hegel had been vigorously denying since the introduction to the *Phenomenology*. In knowing itself, what pure thought knows is the possible intelligibility, the knowability, of anything that is. But the intelligibility of anything is just what it is to be that thing, the answer to the "what is it" (*tode ti*) question definitive of many sciences since Aristotle. So in knowing itself, thought knows of all things *what it is* to be those things. Again, as for Aristotle, the task of metaphysics is not to say of any particular thing what it is. That is the task of the individual sciences. It is to determine what must be *true* of anything at all, such that what it is in particular *can* be determined by the special sciences (what in scholasticism were called the *transcendentalia*). Or: it is to know what is necessarily presupposed in any such specification. Put another way, the task of metaphysics is to understand what it is to say of anything what it is.

This result could easily be misinterpreted. The absolute idea, expressed in Hegel's terms as the identity of logic and metaphysics, could be understood as some sort of direct *inference* from the logical structure of thought. The basic form of rendering intelligible, one might reason, is the categorical judgment, S is P. This simply requires, if to be is to be intelligible, that the world be structured as substances and properties. This is how Adorno seems to understand the basic claim. But that would be dogmatism and would be rejected by Hegel. The characteristic and necessary features of judgment must be derived with a claim to necessity from the simplest, most immediate manifestation of any contentful thought, "Being!," the first moment of the being logic and the book itself. This internal derivation of more complex conceptual moments in order for thought to be rightly onto objects, and the kind of necessity claimed, is what answers in Hegel to Kant's insistence on a transcendental deduction of the objectivity of the categories. While it is always possible to suspect that in any such derivation, we are specifying only "what we must think" or even "must believe," in order to judge rightly that something is the case, such a suspicion is arbitrary if there is no reason to suspect such parochialism, as if thinking were a kind of species-characteristic capacity. The radicality of Hegel's presuppositionless beginning and the necessity of the derivation are supposed to eliminate such a suspicion from the outset, and the self-negating and self-correcting derivation is supposed to preserve such purity. He realizes that the avoidance of any such parochialism, the establishment of pure thinking just as such as the "truth" of being, will disappoint anyone used to a more substantive or "furniture of the universe" version of metaphysics. But that is not Hegel's project.

The Concept

So Adorno has formulated a claim about what is unavailable for conceptual articulation, only mimetically manifest aesthetically. But he has framed his account as a negation of an understanding of conceptual articulation that has missed the actual account of such conceptuality in idealism, one that is not subject to his criticisms. For one thing, Hegel's claims for an identity of thought and being hold only for pure thinking, what is necessary for any thinking at all to bear truth value. These involve nonempirical concepts like finitude, substance and property, essence and appearance, causality and so forth, not mass or velocity or the State or the family. There is no presumed "conceptual identity" between concept and reality for such concepts, just a standard, defeasible claim of truth. Again, the task of identity theory or pure thinking is not to say of anything what it is; it is to say what is necessary for anything at all, such that any "what is it" question could have some purchase. This is completely compatible with empirical discovery, empirical falsehood, or even some mismatch between a concept in the philosophy of spirit, like the bourgeois nuclear family, and what is actually necessary for a historical form of ethical life to be an ethical form, a content that matches its own concept. Hegel is quite clear that the transition from the theory of pure thinking to the *Realphilosophie* is not a deduction and requires attention to the physical and biological sciences of the day as well as to concrete historical actuality. In fact, as Adorno knows well, it was Hegel who first gave to philosophy as a task proper to it the task of a historical diagnosis, one's own time comprehended in thought. That sort of historical thought is not a component of identity theory, the science of pure thinking. And any such normative assessment of any such historical form, such as Adorno's interrogation of the culture industry, must be informed by something more than the internal insufficiencies of that form's own self-articulation if the significance of those insufficiencies are to be understood, a larger framework that can ground any claim about unnecessary and unjustified human suffering.

More important for our present topic, appreciating the proper "place" of art in Hegel's *Encyclopedic* account not only reveals that Hegel has not assimilated art and the experience of art to the discursive norms of philosophical conceptuality but also makes clear how important that difference is, as well as reminding us, by contrast, that Adorno's "abstract negation" of what he regards as conceptual identity theory leaves his position with an appeal to a vague indeterminacy or unassimilability that threatens to turn all modernist art into a single repeated "consciousness of plight [*Nöten*]," of "inarticulable suffering so much more serious than Hegel could have imagined as to be approachable at all only by notions of irrationality and untruth" (19). Again what Adorno wants to say is that it is "conceptualized" suffering (*Leiden*) that is "mute and without consequence" (19), but as we have been seeing throughout, that depends on what "conceptualized" amounts to. For one thing, to say about Mozart and classicism in general, as Adorno does,

> Even for an artist like Mozart, who seems so unpolemical and who according to general agreement moves solely within the pure sphere of spirit, excepting the literary themes that he chose for his greatest operas, the polemical element is central in the power by which the music sets itself at a distance that mutely condemns the impoverishment and falsity of that from which it distances itself. In Mozart form acquires the power of that distancing as determinate negation; the reconciliation that it realizes is painfully sweet because reality to date has refused it. The resoluteness of distance—as presumably that of all classicism that is forceful rather than vacantly playing with itself—concretizes the critique of what has been repulsed. (177)

represents a concession in his own voice that *this* sort of protest must be "mute," and there is no indication why merely "setting itself at a distance" should provide anything like a *determinate* negation of reality (or mimetic embodiment of reality's own self-negation). It seems quintessentially indeterminate, mere "distance."

For another, that there can be a logic, reason, in the irrational is familiar to us now from Freud, and it is dogmatic to insist by definition that this assumption must falsify by "conceptualizing" the content of suffering.

In this context, Adorno's claim against Hegel is that Hegel's aesthetics does not resolve the question of how it is possible to speak of spirit as a determination of the artwork without hypostatizing its objectivity as absolute identity (91). And it is true that Hegel famously says such things as: "Now, in this its freedom alone is fine art truly art, and it only fulfils its supreme task when it has placed itself in the same sphere as religion and philosophy, and when it is simply one way of bringing to our minds and expressing the Divine, the deepest interests of mankind, and the most comprehensive truths of the spirit" (Hegel 1975, 7). But "in the same sphere" only echoes what Adorno himself has said, that what "art demands from its beholder is knowledge. . . . The work wants its truth and untruth to be grasped" (15). Adorno's frontal attack on Hegel, understood as Adorno understands him, fails to make contact with Hegel's position. Here is a full statement of Hegel's understanding of the issue:

> For the beauty of art does in fact appear in a form which is expressly opposed to thought and which thought is compelled to destroy in order to pursue its own characteristic activity. This idea hangs together with the view that the real in general, the life of nature and spirit, is marred and killed by comprehension; that instead of being brought nearer to us by conceptual thinking, it is all the more removed from us, with the result that, by using thinking as a means of grasping what the live phenomenon is, man defeats his own purpose. (12)[3]

That is, Hegel is well aware of an interpretation of his project like Adorno's and takes pains to differentiate himself from it, especially with regard to art.

> And even if works of art are not thought or the Concept, but a development of the Concept out of itself, a shift of the Concept from its own ground to that of sense, still the power of the thinking spirit lies in being able not only to grasp itself in its proper form as thinking, but to know itself again just as much when it has surrendered its proper form to feeling and sense, to comprehend itself in its opposite, because it changes into thoughts what has been estranged and so reverts to itself. And in this preoccupation with its opposite the thinking spirit is not false to itself at all as if it were forgetting and abandoning itself thereby, nor is it so powerless as to be unable to grasp what is different from itself; on the contrary, it comprehends both itself and its opposite. (Hegel 1975, 13)

This sort of claim can seem as densely dialectical and so opaque as anything in Adorno, but Hegel is struggling to say that the presence of conceptual determinacy in an artwork does not transform the work into an instance of a concept, or imply that it is conceptually articulable, as if translatable. Hegel here means to say clearly that art is other than, even the opposite of, conceptual thinking, even while he resists consigning it to indeterminate strangeness. Only in its otherness, its being only a sensible-affective modality of understanding spirit, does it accomplish something essential to the Concept that *the Concept cannot accomplish*, and that is, exactly as Adorno would have

3. Anyone who has struggled with, fought their way through, the conceptual complications of *Aesthetic Theory* might be excused for wondering at the claim that "the real in general, the life of nature and spirit, is marred and killed by comprehension" and so forth. Surely that text is not an instance of "nonidentity thinking," is not art. It is fairly straightforwardly "conceptual," at least in some sense that needs to be addressed.

it, the expression of a sensible dimension of self-knowledge that is not articulable conceptually but is rendered intelligible in some way in art, articulable by criticism as its inner logos. If, say, a critic is able also to draw our attention to the author's or composer's or director's control of the formal organization of the work, then we cannot but appreciate how such a narrative form intimates a purposiveness, a point to such formal features and not others, and so manifests that the aesthetic object bears a conception of itself, a source of unity and ultimately interpretive meaning. It can seem odd to say that artworks are in this sense "self-conscious," embody an awareness of themselves, but this is just an elliptical way of saying that the maker is self-conscious of the point of the determinate form. That point in mass culture art may simply be "to create funny situations," or "to scare the audience in a way they will enjoy," but it can clearly be more aesthetically ambitious, for example, to help us understand something better, like the distinct forms of suffering inflicted on people in late capitalism. This all corresponds to our own implicit awareness in experiencing an aesthetic object that that is what we are doing. "Implicitly aware" also requires a lot of philosophical unpacking, but there is a natural sense that something like such potential attentiveness is becoming explicit when we find ourselves asking why the formal features of the work are as they are. But such aesthetic attending already embodies a norm. The work can be done well, or it can be done lazily, sloppily, indifferently, in a biased way, or self-righteously. None of this detracts from the sensible-affective power of the work, something that relies on but is not reducible to its reflective form. This way of understanding art, and not its reduction to an instance of philosophy, is what Hegel means when he claims, "For since thinking is the essence and Concept of spirit, the spirit in the last resort is only satisfied when it has permeated all products of its activity with thought too and so only then has made them genuinely its own" (Hegel 1975, 13). He means "made them its own" *in* their distinct aesthetic modality. And this modality, despite what Hegel says about the so-called end of art, is indispensable to philosophy. For it is this modality that distinctly embodies spirit's restless dissatisfaction with itself and self-negation over historical time, as Hegel in the *Phenomenology* invokes terms that could have been written by Adorno, had he understood the notion of the "pure I" as a logical term, not a psychological or subjective one, as when Hegel extolls "the tremendous power of the negative . . . the energy of thinking, of the pure I." This invocation of the centrality of the notion of self-negation in Hegel opens onto innumerable and unmanageable questions, but it clearly bears on his understanding of art, which plays an indispensable role, indeed, paradoxically, a central role in Hegel's understanding of the task of reflective thought today. In a passage we have seen before, he says that such a task "consists in actualizing and spiritually animating the universal through the sublation of fixed and determinate thoughts. However, it is much more difficult to set fixed thoughts into fluid motion than it is to bring sensuous existence into such fluidity" (Hegel 2018, §33).

This sort of charge against Adorno, that he is basically throwing the baby of aesthetic determinacy out with the bathwater of a misguided version of hyperconceptualism that is no part of Hegelian idealism, does not absolve Hegel of serious limitations in his theory of art. Hegel did not properly understand, for example, the way in which traditional aesthetic form, like realist narration, or lyrical expressivism, could be both invoked and suspended by irony, the dominant modernist trope in its relation to bourgeois culture. (Hegel's somewhat hysterical reaction to the celebration of irony in figures like Schlegel is the chief case in point.) But, I would want to argue, there are resources in both Hegel's conceptual and his historical-diagnostic approach to build on in formulating such an extension, and this in a way that does not run afoul of the genuine and distinctive aesthetic autonomy that Adorno is rightly worried about in an age of consumption frenzy and the culture industry.

PART 2

Philosophy in the Arts

9

On Maisie's Knowing Her Own Mind

The Self-Knowledge Problem

Throughout Henry James's novel *What Maisie Knew* many people claim to speak for Maisie Farange. Since Maisie is a child, ranging from about six to about twelve in the novel, this is not in itself unusual. Neither, given her age, is it unusual that for most of this time none of the people speaking for Maisie is Maisie herself. This is so because most of the novel is not about what Maisie knew but about what she didn't know, and so what she had to learn. One thing she had to learn of course is the dreary truth that hardly anyone who claims to be speaking for her really is. The five adults nominally in charge of her care are each speaking rather grotesquely only for themselves. (This turns out to be true even of the apparently motherly Mrs. Wix.) All of this is not easy for Maisie to see because each of these five characters is more or less "modern" in their exercise of social authority and power. They do not simply want to coerce or bully Maisie, at least not openly. They want everything that they want Maisie to do or to accept to seem to Maisie something that she, Maisie, wants to do or to accept, and aside from her horrid birth mother, Ida, they are not bad at such a strategy.[1]

But to understand that all this is so, Maisie has to learn something: *how* one might speak for oneself. She has to learn *how* to "know her own mind," even how "to come into possession" of her own mind. Now there is a long contestation in modern philosophy about what in general this sort of knowledge, the sort that I (and only I) can have of myself, or "first-personal" knowledge, consists in. Philosophers have been impressed with the asymmetries between first- and third-personal knowledge. That is, I can know of your attitudes

1. Cf. the narrator's remarks about each having "doubtless the best conscience in the world" (James 1998b, 22).

only by observation and inference, but I don't need to observe or infer anything to know that I am sad, or that I hate reality television. When I avow such things, I am not reporting an observation or drawing a conclusion from evidence. And they have been impressed by the striking difference it makes, enabling me to adopt both a third-person and a first-person attitude toward myself. That is, I can believe what my analyst tells me about my resentment of a sibling without experiencing such resentment "first-personally," without being able to recognize what I am feeling toward the sibling as resentment.[2] All of these issues will come into play in the discussion that follows, but James's novel raises that kind of issue in another register than that of the question of first-person authority itself. For one can sincerely exercise such authority, in all its asymmetricality from third-person knowledge, and still be evincing and avowing what *others* want one to; one can avow something other than what one would, were it not for such manipulative interference.[3] Being minded in a distinct way and knowing, uniquely, first-personally, what that way is, is one thing; having a mind of one's own is another. The latter is a difficult *achievement*, and while it relies on the notion of distinctly first-personal knowledge, it extends that issue into much more difficult territory.[4]

What Maisie Knew presents us with an extremely rich, dense picture of this common and arguably most important form of self-knowledge: "knowing one's own mind," that condition necessary to realize the greatest of modern

2. Cf. Moran (2001, 32) and Finkelstein (2003, 20–27). But see Shoemaker's (2003, 393–95) objections and Moran's (2003, 406ff.) reply, which seems to me compelling.

3. There are obviously benign and helpful forms of influence too. I mean to focus on the issues highlighted by James, that is, such manipulative influences as are evident in the treatments of Maisie.

4. The account that follows is in agreement with many of the most important claims of Moran (2001). These include the asymmetry between first- and third-person knowledge, the denial that because first-person knowledge is not observational or inferential, it must therefore be "immediately" inner-perceptual, the claim that first-personal knowledge is more in the way of an avowal than a report, that such a subject must be understood much more as an agent than as a reflective knower and therefore that, in first-person ascriptions, one's attitude toward oneself is "deliberative," not "theoretical." This last claim especially accords with his claims about the "transparency" of such avowals, that beliefs, in which determining what I believe is determining what ought to be believed, are a model for many cases of first-person avowals, so that "being minded in a way" is "making up one's mind." My claim here and elsewhere (see Pippin 2008) is that the picture of such authority changes a good deal when we also consider proper "ownership" of such subjective attitudes and commitments, when we consider what it is not just to be minded in a way, but for that mindedness to count as one's own. This issue reflects back on the first issue, rendering many first-person avowals merely provisional, subject to a good deal of correction when aspects of our social dependence are taken into account.

values, freedom, living one's own life.[5] As in its ordinary sense, so here in the novel, this means for Maisie in particular coming to know what really matters to her, what philosophers sometimes think of as her motivated desires or deliberated attitudes. These must be motivated and deliberated because, given the seriousness of the consequences, she needs to know what *really* matters to her, not what seems to at a given moment or (especially in this case) what it would please others for her to count as mattering. None of this "backing" relies on long moments of extended calm and quiet reflection; indeed, since she is a child, it cannot depend on any mastery of the concepts of deliberation, warrant, and so forth. But as in ordinary life, her coming to a resolution is a process much more deeply entwined with the ordinary, everyday business of leading a life, reacting to surprises, incorporating new experiences, taking on the weight and direction provided by experiences, and so forth.[6]

As we shall see, at a crucial point in the denouement, she is asked to make a terribly difficult choice, and in order to choose, she needs not merely to be able to express what she feels as inclinations and aversions. It is especially important that we come to see that Maisie's knowing her own mind is essentially finally making up her own mind about both what to believe and what to do. "Having a mind of one's own" that one might know reliably is shown to be inseparable from in effect formulating and resolving to have such a mind of one's own, and in most cases, perhaps ultimately in all, it is thereby inseparable from a kind of thrust outward into the world, affecting and changing what others would otherwise have been able to think or to do.[7] (One must stand behind a resolution for it to count actually as a resolution, for one's mind to count as one's own and as finally made up, and in the social world that James

5. There are a great many different issues in discussions of the self-knowledge problem, ranging from issues of sentience (my awareness of my own sensory and affective states) to complex issues of sapience (in what sense I can be said to know my own beliefs and standing attitudes). See Finkelstein (2003) for an account of the current state of play in these discussions and the importance of this distinction between sentience and sapience.

6. I don't pretend this is an adequate account of what a "practically embedded" form of deliberation is. Moran, I think, needs some such position, lest his conclusions be based on too narrow a notion of responsiveness to reasons.

7. This somewhat Sartrean language is prominent in Moran's (2001) book. At least the notion of consciousness always "transcending" itself in this way is Sartrean. The "opening outward" language is a well-known formulation of Gareth Evans (1982, 225). But it is Sartrean only up to a point. While this sort of language ("making up one's mind") can sound voluntarist, James never treats such resolutions as arbitrary, the product of "absurdly free" choice and so forth. Maisie is learning, in effect learning how to have her own point of view and what that entails for her engagement with others. All of this involves a certain responsiveness to reasons (a way of getting it right), even if not a matter of explicit deliberation and argument.

presents to us again and again, that always involves the resolute willingness to sacrifice other possible courses of action and endure the opposition of others whom one's resolve and actions affect.) The most fascinating thing about *What Maisie Knew* is how James imagines for us the *development* of this capacity, Maisie's ultimate ability to separate her own concerns from what she has been told are her own concerns and in effect to commit to what *she* has resolved for herself, to stand behind them when challenged.

She is shown to develop this self-knowledge without "getting better in touch with herself," an inner self buried beneath the self-serving versions of what ought to matter to her that are provided by so many others. Knowing/having her own mind involves much more the achievement of the following: a kind of navigational ability, an ability to steer her own course in a hostile and complicated environment; a capacity to interpret and resist the characterizations of others, to manage the social conflict James seems to treat as essential to, constitutive of, sociality itself; a position where she can assume some even minimal responsibility for her own commitments; and very much a kind of practical or know-how sort of knowledge, rather than a theoretical sort. (The most frequent image for this capacity is knowledge of how to play a game.)[8] James, in other words, represents "knowing one's own mind" not as a perceptual turn inward, but as involving a number of practical abilities concerned with what we have to be able to understand and especially what we must be willing and able to do in order *to come to occupy* such a genuinely first-personal position. We will see Maisie's dawning self-awareness in this unusual sense, and its various conditions, displayed in a kind of organically growing, developing, somewhat unstable social world, as it "lives," James might say, in a network of densely related, finally inseparable, contesting lives. The result will be a lesson of sorts in what a difference it makes to view ordinary, everyday self-knowledge as embedded in such a web of social contestations, practical tasks, and temporal fluidity, rather than as a cognitive task performed by an isolated, reflective individual.[9]

8. A sampling of the many game references: James 1998b, 65, 82, 90, 114 (where we are reminded that Ida likes billiards, a game where the pieces knock against each other violently), 221, 227.

9. So much philosophy is so unavoidably guided by intuitions, and such intuitions are so formed by examples, and such examples must of necessity present so cropped and abstract a picture of an instance or event or decision, that, left to its traditional methods, philosophy might be ill-equipped on its own to answer a question like one about the true content of a historical ideal like "knowing one's own mind," or authenticity, or "leading a free life." One needs to bring so many factors into play at once that one nontraditional but more promising path might be through reflection on the modern novel (or modern drama, or poetry or even visual art). For a discussion of similar themes, see my account of Marcel's "becoming who he is" in Pippin 2005b.

Understanding all of this will also be important in coming to terms with a conclusion as dramatic and ambiguous as any in James. Maisie learns all of this, in other words, but the final turn of the self-knowledge screw visible in the ending is paradoxical. Once one has gotten over the shock at how subtle, complex, and pointed Maisie's proposed "deal" is, another question inevitably arises. Has she learned all this too well? The past tense in the title could refer to a kind of knowledge and (innocent?) self-knowledge Maisie had, but loses when she takes up her new "experienced" position.

The Plot

This is a lot to ask of a "slip of a girl" (6)[10] and a lot to ask of a novel not generally treated as one of James's greatest. To say anything about any of this, I need to summarize the plot. This is not easy; it is a kind of French farce in its complicated erotic geometry.

Our story begins at the conclusion of a nasty divorce between Beale and Ida Farange, two middle-class, fairly well-off, deeply selfish people. Ida is often described as a garish woman who wears too much makeup, chases men, and plays a lot of billiards. Apparently the only notable thing about Beale Farange is his great beard "burnished like a gold breast-plate" (16). They have a child, Maisie, of whom the father originally gains full custody, something, we are given to believe, he wants only to spite his former wife. Mr. Farange cannot, though, account for twenty-six hundred pounds placed in his keeping by his wife for the care of the child three years before, and so Mrs. Farange gains half custody as part of a "deal." We are given to believe that she is pleased by this only because it thwarts what she believes are her husband's wishes. This does not bode well for the little girl's shared life, and indeed Maisie is treated horribly when she is treated at all and is rightly referred to as a tennis ball or shuttlecock in a game between the two former spouses.

Her governess when she lives with her father is a Miss Overmore, a beautiful and accomplished young woman whom Maisie likes very much. (More than her father actually, although the narrator tells us this while admitting that Maisie "couldn't" or at least didn't "put it to herself this way" (28). These unusual ways of referring to Maisie's views of her own attitudes will recur frequently.)[11] While at Ida's, her governess is the "grey, greasy" Mrs. Wix, a

10. Page references in the text are to James 1998b.

11. In this case, Maisie finds a way of expressing this to herself by allowing herself to affirm only what would in effect be her rejoinder to the accusation that it is not proper for a little girl to like her governess more than her father (a thought that she somehow has but "will not allow

name perhaps calculated to draw our attention to the issue of "candle power," of which the poor Mrs. Wix has precious little. This sad widow has lost a child in a traffic accident and enthusiastically adopts Maisie as a surrogate, devoting herself to the child even though completely unable to play the traditional role of a governess. She cannot teach Maisie anything because she knows so little and instead either tells her romantic stories or gossips with her about her wayward parents. She is indeed "as ignorant as a fish" (53).

It isn't long before three things happen. Ida marries a younger man, Sir Claude. Of all the characters he might be said to be the most sympathetic to Maisie, inclined even to occasional protective and nurturing acts. Maisie is immensely fond of him, a fact that will play a large role in the novel's conclusion. Beale Farange meanwhile has fallen for the governess, Miss Overmore, and they marry. (Miss Overmore is thereafter referred to by everyone as Mrs. Beale.) Their premarriage affair and postmarriage gallivanting about ensure that Maisie receives in effect no education at all in either household. She will learn a great deal, but the narrator goes to some lengths to establish a contrast between the richness of this sort of wisdom and the poverty of Maisie's official "learning."

Second, both birth parents come to realize that by not taking Maisie for their six-month turn, by conniving to *escape* such a responsibility, they could each injure the other much more, a strategy that does not of course leave Maisie feeling wanted and loved.

Third, in the final major complication the two new stepparents, Mrs. Beale and Sir Claude, find that their new marriages are not much to their respective liking and take up with each other. Maisie must try to follow all of this and has understandable difficulty. (At various points she finds it hard to understand the content of a concept like "parent.") So the question between Beale and Ida becomes how best to use Maisie to inconvenience the other; and the question for Mrs. Beale and Sir Claude becomes how they might escape their marriages to Maisie's birth parents ("be free") and preserve at least some modicum of respectability. They see that Maisie might be useful for this purpose, perhaps in the eyes of the world redeem their illicit liaison. For Mrs. Wix, who in effect spends more time with Maisie than anyone (at no point are playmates of either gender or any normal social contact with other children mentioned), the question has become how to convince Sir Claude, who, she rightly sees, is the only person involved who feels any pull from the question of what would it be right by Maisie to do, to set up some sort of

herself to affirm")—the rejoinder that Beale also likes Miss Overmore very much indeed. This all in just the last three sentences of chapter 3. The self-referential complexities will grow.

domestic arrangement for the three of them, free from all of these immoral entanglements.

This all comes to a head when Sir Claude, in an apparently very poorly thought out plan, spirits Maisie away to Folkstone and then to Boulogne in France, in preparation for some sort of escape from his wife. Ida hears of it and travels there herself, concerned about how any aspect of such a plan will affect her. There is a scene, she leaves and conspires to send Mrs. Wix over, on the correct view that Mrs. Wix's narrow, rigid moralism, combined with Maisie's attachment to her, will spoil any plans Claude and Mrs. Beale may have made for a life together in France (that natural home, apparently, for free spirits and escapees from bourgeois rectitude). Mrs. Beale then shows up and the final plans of each player now become apparent. First Mrs. Beale tries to convince Mrs. Wix to agree to Sir Claude and Mrs. Beale as a morally acceptable couple (at least in France), and the four of them will live together. That fails. Mrs. Wix wavers, but finally rejects the idea. Sir Claude then tries to convince Maisie to "give up" Mrs. Wix and join the two of them for a domestic trio. Mrs. Wix wants Maisie simply to leave this den of iniquity and return to England with her. (It is not irrelevant here that Maisie has become for Mrs. Wix a meal ticket.) Maisie must herself decide how all these purported adults are to live their lives.

Then the most amazing and complicated event in the novel occurs. Without prejudging the moral status of her action, we could say that Maisie reveals that she has learned how to play this game very well. She tells Sir Claude that she, Maisie, will give up Mrs. Wix if he, Sir Claude, will give up Mrs. Beale, if just the two of them set up house. By this point the whole weight of meaning in the novel comes heavily down on this proposition, on, that is, what Maisie means by it, how she understands it, what she is trying to do by offering it, what she must have learned to be offering it. She may be trying to say what she already knows: that her love for Sir Claude is greater than his for her, given what each is and is not willing to give up. If this somewhat adult reading is true, she may be trying mainly to get rid of Mrs. Beale as a rival and have Sir Claude for herself. She may have figured out that this is simply the only outcome that will leave something for her. Mrs. Wix seems to have convinced her that there is no real possibility of simply running off with the unmarried pair, and/or Maisie may have figured out what her status would be in such a threesome, given Sir Claude's much-discussed weakness for and fear of women. It may all be a test to see just how much she can or cannot count on Sir Claude. At any rate, it is what is presented to us as Maisie finally knowing her own mind, as "what Maisie knew." That comes down to her staking everything on this complicated conditional, and her living with the outcome, which is, predictably, that she and Mrs. Wix sail back to England together; Sir Claude stays with Mrs. Beale.

The Pleasure of Subjectivity

Let us say, with convention, that at the end Maisie has lost her innocence and become experienced. To understand what that means and how it bears on her assertion of her own view of things, we need to understand three things: Maisie's original state of mind; what she has learned; and the nature of the difference between her original and her altered state of mind.

The Maisie we first come to know, when she is six, in the immediate aftermath of the divorce, is described in ways that seem very deliberately to raise questions about both her own state of mind and her *relation* to her own mind. Her division from herself is first described as her being able "to see much more than she at first understood," even though she was also able "at first to understand much more than any little girl" (18). When her first nurse, Maddie, remarks that Maisie must be feeling the great strain of the divorce, we are told, "Thus from the first Maisie not only felt it [the strain], but knew she felt it" (19). This is an odd way of speaking since it implies the possibility that she could experience something like this strain without knowing it, but the scene and the phrase suggest that it is because of Maddie's remark that she learns to call whatever she was feeling "the strain"[12] and that she notices things in this reflective way.

She raises a striking, unusual question about her father. Her mother has told her frequently that her father "lies and knows that he lies," and Maisie wants especially to know not whether he actually lies but "Does he know he lies?" (a question that seems to reveal a settled view on the first of the mother's claims, even if it also slightly hints at quite sophisticated a hope on Maisie's part, as if Beale might be unknowingly telling her things that weren't true, but not lying "because he didn't know").

Maisie is once said to "feel something" with Mrs. Wix, and later to know what it was, even though, even at that, "she couldn't have made a statement of it" (29).[13] We don't know yet if this inability is like her inability to admit to

12. There is of course much that Maisie, amazingly, does see. Her inference about the way Mrs. Wix must have "sidled and ducked through life," given her "elation" at petty acts of normal consideration, is a striking inference for a young child (65). Not to mention her very brave "Mama doesn't care for me. . . . Not really" (73).

13. The inherent "belatedness" of self-knowledge is a major theme in James in general and in particular in *What Maisie Knew*. Cf. James (1998b, 142) and the discussion in Pippin 2000.

herself that she likes Miss Overmore more than her father (a kind of moral hesitation simply to put it that way, that bluntly) or if she is really being said to have determinate experiences that she cannot name or comprehend (something that would again be philosophically obscure). The experience is determinate enough—that Mrs. Wix has been, and is now acting like, a mother, something her own mother was not—and perhaps that already indicates that the description, in the pain it would cause Maisie to admit it, amounts to the former sort of hesitation.

Maisie is said to *be* fatalistic, but essentially not to *know* this; she has an "unformulated fatalism" (47). And there is Maisie's early and sustained strategy for what is increasingly referred to as the "game" that she must learn how to play. Her first move in it at such a young age is startling. After she realizes (or "senses") what her parents are doing in using her to carry messages like "He lies and knows that he lies," and "you're a nasty, horrid pig": "She had a new feeling, the feeling of danger; on which a new remedy rose to meet it, the idea of an inner self, or in other words of concealment. . . . She would forget everything, she would repeat nothing, and when, as a tribute to the successful application of her system, she began to be called a little idiot, she tasted a pleasure new and keen" (23). This might seem an odd strategy, as if she is pretending to be ignorant of motives and meanings that she really is ignorant of, but Maisie is feigning stupidity, not ignorance.[14] That is, she at least knows there is much that she doesn't know, and she quickly learns that she cannot evince any such sense and must play stupid and slow to avoid the burdens placed on her by her hateful parents. It is in this sense that she sees but does not understand. That is, she *sees*; something is marked in her experience as requiring an interpretation she cannot yet give. She knows this about her own experiences, but she pretends not even to be aware of this gap or lack. (She sees "that everything had something behind it; life was like a long, long corridor with rows of closed doors" [36], all without knowing what is behind the doors.) So the first manifestation of "her own mind" is this act of resistance or refusal. It is not a defense of her private views from inspection and manipulation; it is the creation of such a false front even though there as yet is next to no content in such an inner self. She does not have a worked-out view of what to think about what her parents are using her for or why, but she intuits that whatever it is, it has little to do with her and it is *by* resisting their incursions that she *comes to have* a concealed or inner self. This is not yet a mind of her own, but it is something *not theirs*. Feigning stupidity, creating misreadings

14. She is said to practice "the pacific art of stupidity" (63).

on their part, is what gives her that odd, striking, as yet unnamable "pleasure," the pleasure of subjectivity, one might call it.

Knowing and Avowing

Here and in other novels and stories, James seems to suggest a link between a *resistance to the exercise of power over one* and the *achievement of an inner realm of one's own* as well as a link between a *first-personal avowal* or expression or assertion of such a view of one's own and a *stand taken* in the social world that affects what others would otherwise be able to do, often against what they propose to do, and in a way that can function as a sort of test of the genuineness of the avowal. He treats these two dimensions, private and social, as virtually co-constitutive; it is by resisting the "incursions" of others that such a realm is achieved. Its boundaries are the boundaries of such resistance.[15] This is contrary to views of some *prior* private, inner realm, prior in the sense of being formulable as that which one has and defends against the control of others, or possesses and protects against the refusals of acknowledgment and the contrary interpretations, contesting moves, of others. Maisie's mindedness and her attainment of a position from which she can assert her own mind "come to be over time," before our eyes as it were, and are not merely something "there" that is more and more "manifested." Our intuitions tell us that one comes to be sure of oneself, for oneself, and one then and partly thereby acquires the courage to claim something for oneself, against others. But our narrative does not separate things this way. Maisie becomes "Maisie" only *against* Ida, finally against the originally beloved Mrs. Beale, with, but not really for, Mrs. Wix, for and at the same time against Sir Claude, and so forth. But this will require seeing more of what happens to Maisie.

To anticipate this whole process a bit, consider one last example of the unusual reflexive language of the book. Toward the end, it has become clear to Maisie and Mrs. Wix that their only, if often unreliable, ally has been Sir Claude, and they admit, as if two schoolgirls, that they both have mighty crushes on him. Neither is too enamored at this point of Sir Claude's lover, Mrs. Beale, and Mrs. Wix is therefore prompted to ask an obvious "self-knowledge" question of Maisie: "Has it never occurred to you to be jealous of her?" The narrator then tells us, "It never had in the least [occurred to Maisie to be jealous]; yet the words were scarce in the air before Maisie jumped at them." The passage then goes on: "She held them [the words] well, she looked

15. The evidence for attributing such views to James is presented in Pippin 2000.

at them hard; at last she brought out with an assurance, which there was no one, alas, bur herself to admire: 'Well, yes—since you ask me.' She debated, then continued: 'Lots of times!'" (220). As in other similar instances where Maisie has seen but not understood, this one can suggest that Maisie has had experiences she didn't know that she had, even that she has felt things that she didn't know she felt. But the context and language here suggest otherwise. Mrs. Wix's question is not "Aren't you jealous of Mrs. Beale?," nor is it "Have you ever been jealous?," but "Has it never occurred to you to be jealous of her?" This has the tone much more of a suggestion about what attitude Maisie should have taken up, should take up now, of "Don't you think you should start acting jealously toward Mrs. Beale?" And Maisie's response is telling. We know from the narrator that Maisie has not in the least been jealous, but at this point she accomplishes an extraordinary number of things with that "Lots of times." Primarily she takes up a stance toward Mrs. Beale, a commitment to regarding her as, and so treating her as, a rival, something that will have momentous implications later, when Maisie acts out that commitment at the end of the novel. This in effect is a way of admitting that she sees now that she should have been jealous. (Her answer involves not a report about an inner state but a reflexive stance taken up for reasons in a social world.) We are also told, though, that she did not want to appear "simple" (250) and so gave out as if she had felt that way all along, trying to influence Mrs. Wix's perception of her. (Of course she is also, in admitting jealousy, admitting to a state she only imperfectly understands.) She does *this* because she knows that Mrs. Wix thinks that Maisie's "moral sense" is more feigned than real, and that this is "discouraging" Mrs. Wix. So she tries to influence Mrs. Wix's perception of her honesty and forthrightness, hoping that by admitting to "the most restless of passions," one that persons are reluctant to admit to, she will influence Mrs. Wix's estimation of her "sincerity," something she hopes will carry over to the estimation of the sincerity of her moral sense. (This is all quite different of course from trying *to have* a better moral sense, a goal never really of much interest to Maisie.) This succeeds and they have a conversation of "unprecedented frankness," all based on the otherwise deceptive "report" (that is not really a report and is not true) of Maisie's prior "jealousy."

Achieving a Mind

There are many more passages about self-knowledge like the ones just cited, but they all contribute to a point being made that is sometimes neglected in philosophical discussions of self-knowledge: it is *hard* to know one's own mind, and the task of achieving a "mind of one's own" that one can know is *unavoidable*, even for a little girl, especially for this little girl, the object of the manipulations of so many. The fact that such knowledge seems not to be observational or inferential does not mean it is, in its purported "immediacy," easy, and the difficulty in question seems not to be wholly one of clarity or acuity of perception.[16] Maisie's being able to see much in the world around her that she cannot understand applies reflexively too, and the growth of her sureness afoot about the former seems linked to the latter, again deeply linked. She is inclined toward descriptions, attitudes, avowals, commitments without yet being able actually to make them, to "make up" her mind, and the novel makes it easy to see why. She is caught up in so many different, bewildering agendas that her being a child does not seem explanation enough for her confusion.

The difficulty she has though in making up her mind about the conduct of others around her and therewith coming to know her own mind is not the only difficulty that is stressed. By the end of the first third or so of the novel, by chapter 12, she has made extraordinary progress in settling on her own views about what is going on in the circus she must live in. The narrator speaks of a "high quickening of Maisie's direct perceptions, of her sense of freedom to make things out for herself" (85). In fact, Maisie has learned partly to enjoy her position of "spectatorship" at her own life (90). She has in effect learned to understand the game (football is mentioned) and considers that theatrical display in all its fascinating complexity (much of which she now "gets") is a sort of "compensation" for the fact that she is made to, only allowed to, adopt a third-person perspective about her own fate, a compensation for "the doom of a peculiar passivity" (90). This is put in a very striking way:

> It [this experience of spectatorship] gave her often an odd air of being present at her history *in as separate a manner* as if she could only get at such experience by flattening her nose against a pane of glass. (90–91, my emphasis)

This suggests that she can be said in some sense to know her own mind, but in a truncated, incomplete way, "separate" from the living out of her own history. She has come to have views, reactions, interests, aspirations, and these can be in some sense attributed to her, but too much in the way one would attribute them to others, as if it all (her history) were happening to someone she is observing. Something is still lacking; practical views about what ought

16. The social world within which Maisie comes to maturity makes all this doubly hard. She must, as it is sometimes said, see everything for herself (37). There seems to be very little in the way of a shared form of ethical life in the novel, not much commonality for poor Maisie to get her bearings from. For more on this theme, see Pippin 2000.

to be done, what ought always to be avoided, never accepted, and so forth must be views she can take responsibility for, express in action, and all that is denied to Maisie. She is trapped as if in a glass box, trying to figure out what she thinks, but never sure any possible commitments are "her own" precisely because she is prevented from "acting them out," trapped.[17]

There are by this point, though, intimations of her escape out from behind such a glass barrier. After a particularly complicated conversation with Sir Claude about where they all stand, this new, slightly more advanced state of mindedness is introduced first "by an emotion more mature than she had yet known" (99). Claude has asked her if she feels any "dread" at encountering her father at Mrs. Beale's, and Maisie, rather than merely take mental inventory, as it were, feels a sense of shame lest, by her answer, she seem disloyal to her blood relative. However, remembering that Sir Claude himself once mentioned that no one was *really* afraid of her father, she sees a good, somewhat evasive way to answer: "Oh I dare say I can manage him" (99). She sees in other words that she cannot answer the question about "dread" (a question about her mindedness) without taking into account what such a response would mean to Sir Claude, what her expressing it there then would mean to him, given Claude's current position in the social struggle they are all engaged in, and that it would manifest a disloyalty (commit her to *other* claims) she is not yet prepared to embrace.[18] (Not to mention that such disloyalty would also seem to commit her to future courses of action that she is not yet in a position to assume responsibility for.) She is aware of a certain sort of dread in meeting up with her father, but one tinged with this sense of shame and disloyalty, and a reticence to declare such dread under these circumstances. This is what all the emotional flushes, blushing, and coloring mean, and it is therefore quite apposite for Claude, who senses why Maisie answered as she did, to have a reaction described as: "It was as if he had caught his first glimpse of her sense of responsibility" (99). Once again, Maisie's "interiority" is linked with her capacity to understand the complex possibilities of meaning in any putative report of her inner states, and so

17. I don't mean that first-person avowals, especially of intentions, are like predictions about what one will do that one has a stake in seeing come true, as in Velleman 1989. Such avowals are commitments, and until realized in the world, they all must have a merely provisional status, could always be exaggerations, fantasies. See Pippin 2008.

18. Cf. Wittgenstein (1958, II §i) and Finkelstein's (2003, 104–12) very helpful gloss and expansion. Finkelstein's general position, that "mental life is lived in the logical space of animated life" (145), so that "inner and outer" cannot be understood as distinct in first-person ascriptions (144), has much in common with what is discussed here and what I attribute to Hegel in Pippin 2008, at least with respect to self-ascriptions of our standing attitudes and if we bracket the questions of animal sentience and sapience.

her capacity to "take responsibility" for her views and even for her immediate reactions (even her blushing, one might say), and that capacity is influenced by her position in the social world (what is allowed or denied her) that is independent of her and that she must work out for herself, must make a space for herself in.[19] She needs room for action like this in order fully to embody her sense of herself, to come to occupy a truly first-personal perspective, and in *that* way to have a mind of her own.

Maisie's Growth

But Maisie is still suffering from her "dim apprehension of the unuttered and unknown," however much progress she has made. The narrator must still report her condition in elaborate counterfactuals testifying to both the presence and the absence of other- and self-knowledge: "Maisie could only have a sense of something that in a maturer mind would be called the way history repeats itself" (137). She has at this point only "possibilities of vibration, of response" (143).

A great leap in her "education" occurs in a tense scene with her father. Maisie's real brilliance breaks through, as she intuits rightly, first, that her father is asking her to play a certain game, to "pretend" that Beale knows something about his daughter's life, or cares about it, and then she sees that the game is almost a farce, that her father is asking her "to go away with him to America" *only* so that she will refuse, so that he will be "let off" any guilt for abandoning her by having pretended to want her along. As the scene is set, James is willing to go very far in elaborating Maisie's knowledge, so far as almost to parody his own familiar depictions of sociality, as if to embrace the discomfort his brother William and so many other readers have so often expressed about the fussiness of James's novels: "but if he had an idea at the back of his head she also had one in a recess as deep, and for a time, while they sat together, there was an extraordinary mute passage between her vision of this vision of his, his vision of her vision, and her vision of his vision of her vision. What there was no effective record of indeed was the small strange pathos on the child's part of an innocence so saturated with knowledge and so directed to diplomacy" (145). There is a marvelous example of this dialectical "innocence so saturated with knowledge," as Maisie sees exactly what to say that will both amount to a refusal to let her father off, and yet allow no accusation that she is trying to make him

19. It is significant that when Maisie wants in effect to work things out for herself, she imitates adult conversations and dealings with her "French doll," rather than, like Isabel Archer before the fire, sorting out what she has gotten herself into. See 121, for example.

feel guilty, that she is out for herself, or that she is insincere: "Dear Papa, I'll go with you anywhere" (146). Farange nevertheless tries to accuse her of insincerity, of "humbugging" him, but he is not quick enough to keep up with Maisie. Because she sees what he's after, she can safely continue to report her willingness to go with him (not her desire to, but her willingness in principle) in a way very differently inflected than if she had sensed he meant his offer seriously. He knows this; she knows he knows this, he knows . . . and so forth.

But Beale's insistence that they deal with each other as strategic bargainers does manage to move the conversation to a somewhat cruder, more direct model, and it culminates in a strange, unsettling frankness. For Beale realizes (and calls Maisie a "deep little devil" in realizing it) that Maisie is far beyond thinking of her negotiating options as limited to her birth parents. Beale reacts with a kind of "Aha!" realization:

> "You've settled it with the other pair!"
>
> "Well, what if I have?" She sounded to herself most bold.
>
> Her father, quite as in the old days, broke into a peal. "Why, don't you know they're awful?"
>
> She grew bolder still. "I don't care—not a bit!" (149)

This is quite a new Maisie, and it will take the reader a while to assess what has happened to her. And she is still a beginner at this game. When Ida storms into Folkestone, determined to part from Maisie in a way that will not reflect badly on her publicly, Maisie feels the flush of her "deep diplomacy," but plays her hand too strongly, forgets "that she had never been safe unless she had also been stupid" (173). She remarks that one of Ida's lovers, with whom Maisie has had a long private conversation, remarked that Ida was "good," a report Maisie means to carry to her as a compliment. But it reveals immediately that there is in general and for Maisie some real *question* of her being good, and Maisie's remark clumsily appeals for authority to someone Ida announces is "the biggest cad in London," in effect revealing how low one has to go to find someone who will issue such praise of the makeup-abusing, billiard-playing mama. But even this mistake teaches Maisie a great deal, for she now allows herself to become angry in response to Ida's rage and insults ("the first flare of anger that had ever lighted her face for a foe" [175]), or she knows what she feels about Ida, how to evaluate Ida in a way that can be expressed, in an attitude she can manifest and stand behind. She can resist Ida's fury (Maisie could now "look up quite as hard as anyone could look down" [175]). It is by virtue of this insight, both emotionally embodied as her own and expressed in resistance to Ida, that Maisie can reach a new level of imagination, can see her mother's possible, pitiful fate, can see "madness and desolation . . . ruin." (175).

Maisie's Deal

So Maisie, despite some missteps, has learned a great deal about how to play this game, has had the courage to live out, embody, her self-avowed attitudes and evaluations, and has seen what she must be willing to risk and endure in order thereby to have a mind of her own. But there is a last great test of this new capacity. The fate of Sir Claude and Mrs. Beale and Mrs. Wix have all come to rest on a decision by Maisie, and with resolve, courage, grace, confidence, and, one must say, not a little cunning, she makes one.

The option of all four living together has been taken off the table by Mrs. Wix. In explaining her reasons, she reverts often to the need for Maisie to have a "moral sense," something she discusses as if it were an instrument that could be found and lost rather easily, such that she, Mrs. Wix, is needed to keep it from being permanently misplaced by Maisie. It is remarkable how easily this supposed problem rolls off Maisie, never seems to grab her. She seems to have some intuitive sense of how much it suits Mrs. Wix's interests to give out that she, Mrs. Wix, is still needed to teach Maisie something, when it is obvious to everyone that Maisie is already lightyears ahead of Mrs. Wix's point of view.[20] And what Mrs. Wix means is simply that Sir Claude and Mrs. Beale are adulterers, as if that, and not their irresponsibility with regard to Maisie and their thoughtlessness and narcissism and selfishness, is their great sin. (This kind of moralism, the view of morality as a set of fixed, completely determinate principles about the forbidden and the obligatory that one must obey as if external, divine commands, is always treated ironically by James, as with Henrietta Stackpole in *The Portrait of a Lady* and the Pococks in *The Ambassadors* among many others.) At any rate, Maisie clearly doesn't see it that way (210) and never so much as pauses to give the issue much thought.[21]

But she still must decide whether to live with the two of them without Mrs. Wix, or with Mrs. Wix alone, or, as she chooses, with Sir Claude alone, such that each of them will "give up" someone close to them and live together. Since it is clear that it is not a violation of her moral sense that excludes the first,

20. Cf. Mrs. Wix's own revealing worries about how much Maisie has learned and how little there is left to justify her own presence (216).

21. See James's remarks about his family's common horror of moralism, "the conscious conscience—the very home of the literal, the haunt of so many pedantries" (James 1998a, 215–16, quoted in Johnson 1974, 172 and in Tanner 1965, 291).

we are brought to see that what Maisie *is* doing is refusing to function merely as a cover or beard for Sir Claude and Mrs. Beale, refusing to pretend to Wixian moral indignation, and, in essence for the first time, expressing what *she* wants, what arrangement seems to her the best. "Somehow, now that it was there, the great moment was not so bad. What helped the child was that she knew what she wanted. All her learning and learning had made her at last learn that . . . Bewilderment had simply gone or at any rate was going fast" (270). This moment of resolve manifests many of the elements stressed throughout here: that she had to learn to have her own mind, learn that being minded in such a way is a distinct mode of comportment toward the world, one that is expressed in one's resolution about what is to be done, and learn that such a realization is necessary for such an attitude actually to be the attitude or evaluation one takes it to be, and that some complex negotiation between dependence on others and independence from them is often at stake in such a making up of one's (own) mind.

But it all clearly comes at a certain price. Maisie's play in the game may be, as Sir Claude says, "exquisite" (270), but just to the extent that Maisie has matched them all in resolve and even shrewdness, she has nevertheless begun playing an adult "game" that can be as sordid and depressing as it can be exhilarating and fascinating. She has no choice in the matter; she will remain easy prey if she doesn't, but knowing her own mind has landed her on a boat steaming away from the person she cares most about, Sir Claude. A little more innocence and unknowingness (or perhaps self-deceit) and it could easily have been Mrs. Wix sailing away alone. But Maisie is up to such a choice and seems content with its costs. At any rate, she will not hide from them. As they sit on the boat, Mrs. Wix, typically, in a kind of enactment of her own often willed ignorance, does not look back to see if Sir Claude is still on the balcony. Maisie does look back, and reports that Sir Claude isn't there. Mrs. Wix notes that he has returned to "her," Mrs. Beale, and Maisie says simply, "Oh I know," prompting the book's pregnant last line: "Mrs. Wix gave a sidelong look. She still had room for wonder at what Maisie knew" (275).

Coda

One last philosophical coda. It is not easy to do full justice to the position that Maisie has achieved. Maisie's history has revealed a link between the possibility of one's own mindedness and a capacity for the public expression of such attitudes, a capacity to be responsive to and engage with what one understands to be how others will take up and respond to what one says and does, and a capacity for actions consistent with and flowing from such mindedness, and so for being responsible for such a mindedness and for such actions. This latter is often a possibility created by the play of circumstances beyond one's control, but very often it is a matter of seizing opportunities, and both conditions are relevant to Maisie's case. Knowing one's own mind, in other words, turns out to be "having a mind of one's own," which, in turn, must be wrested from others and protected in ways neither indifferent to nor submissive to the demands and interpretations of others, and it means a form of mindedness that one must be able to express and act out, "realize" in the world. But does this mean, one might ask, that one cannot be said to harbor "one's own" commitments, evaluations, attitudes, and preferences "first-personally" that one has no intention of ever acting on or avowing? Indeed, isn't this also the situation of Maisie when she discovers the value, even the indispensability, of a "secret" inner life, one that can be protected from intrusions and manipulation by others just by never being expressed or acted out?

An adequate answer to such a question would have to be quite complicated and very sensitive to the context of any orienting example. So many factors are at play that no general theoretical account of this link may be possible. But in the case of Maisie's secret life, this sort of enforced secrecy is *just* what keeps her feeling so oddly alienated from her own self. Her being denied permission and opportunity to express and act on any preference or attitude of her own is what accounts for her feeling behind that pane of glass, merely observing her own history. Her posing of the offer to Sir Claude amounts to what it takes to step out from behind it.

Still, one might persist, surely there are examples of hypocrisy, where expressions say one thing and actions signal one thing, but an agent's first-personal or secret attitudes are quite clearly (for herself, in her own mind) different. But the point is that there must be *some* sort of expression, social responsiveness, and action in the world consistent with such attitudes for a description of the agent to be coherent (not that *all* expressions and actions must be). One can express trust in another and perform actions that appear to be based on such trust while profoundly mistrusting someone, but it would be paradoxical to the point of incoherence *actually* to entrust one's fate to another whom one mistrusted, rather than seeming to. Indeed, this fact is what is responsible for situations in which hypocrisy can be detected, and why those who suspect it often try to engineer just such tests.

Finally, none of this denies that one's expressions and actions can come apart from what one genuinely believes to be one's attitudes, evaluations, and the like. But in such cases, all one should note is that something has gone wrong, does not make sense, requires perhaps the assumption of an unconscious for it finally to make sense, and that concession (that something would not make sense in such a case) is all that is needed here.

10

Subjectivity: A Proustian Problem

The Problem

Marcel Proust's *In Search of Lost Time* begins with a famous scene in which the narrator describes "what it was like" for Marcel, some past version of himself, to go to bed early, drift between sleep and waking, experience various memories, and finally settle on memories of going to sleep at his grandparents' country house in Combray.[1] The novel thus introduces us to its most radical experiment: a seven-volume, three-thousand-page novel with over two thousand characters, the events of which span several decades, but which presents the reader throughout with the single, intensely reflective, and endless analytic point of view of a single character. Everything that happens in the novel happens "for Marcel." Even what happens to and for others, like Swann in the extended narrative *Swann in Love* or Charlus whose social world is very different from the narrator's, is what it seems to Marcel it must have been like or how it must have happened, the product of his (never unmotivated) imaginings. Indeed, for vast stretches of the novel, Marcel's inner life is completely self-enclosed. His attempt to describe what is happening to him and his sometimes quite ambitious and general theorizing about the

1. The English text, cited first, is Proust 2003, followed by the French edition, Proust 1990. Abbreviations used:

S: *Du côté de chez Swann* (Swann's Way)
JF: *À l'ombre des jeunes filles en fleur* (Within a Budding Grove)
CG: *Le côté de Guermantes* (The Guermantes Way)
SG: *Sodome et Gomorrhe* (Sodom and Gomorrah)
P: *La prisonnière* (The Captive);
AD: *Albertine disparue* (The Fugitive)
TR: *Le temps retrouvé* (Time Regained).

meaning of what he experienced are basically conversations with himself, indirectly revealed to (very occasionally addressed to) only the reader.[2] He rarely makes known to anyone else the character of his experience, his anxieties, suspicions, or his theories. The life we read about is overwhelmingly the life of a mind, one mind, Marcel's. As readers, we live inside its diachronic development for the very long time it takes to read all the volumes.

A novelist's attempt to find a way to describe "what it is like" for a character to experience his or her singular, distinct experiential path through a life, and how such a character would understand and interpret such experiences, is the first and most general manifestation of "the problem of subjectivity." That problem is simply: what would count as success in such a project? It is a different but related problem *in* the novel itself because Marcel thinks frequently about and worries about the issue, and this in roughly three dimensions. These will be the subject of the following discussion. First, he wonders if anyone else experiences the world—its external objects, architecture, nature—as he does, and he feels anxious whenever experiencing anything novel, anything that intrudes on the familiar subjective inner life he has known. Such novelties can appear to him unintelligible and so even hostile, threatening. Second, he wonders whether another's subjectivity, what it is like for them, or really anything about them, can ever be known, as opposed to the role that some imagined other plays in his inner life. (He convinces himself that the answer is no, that another cannot be known and they play only this inner role, but as we shall see, very little of that and many other theories of his can be taken at face value.) And third, he wonders about his experience of himself, how reliable is "who he seems to himself to be." Most dramatically, he believes that he is an aspiring writer, even though he is a writer who cannot write. He asks himself interminably: What does it mean to him to aspire to be a writer, and why, in his own mind, can't he begin? Or he asks himself: Is his experience of himself in love—his feeling, for example, that the state is inseparable from jealousy—*his* experience of love, or *the* experience of love itself?

This aspiration to some sort of generality in all his reflections, often signaled simply by an unremarked-on slide from his first-person characterization to a general theory, from "I think" to "one thinks," and by a constant hedging and qualification ("perhaps," "it could be that . . . ," "it seemed likely that . . . ," and so forth), signals the problem of the novel's status itself. It

2. I proceed on the assumption, admittedly controversial, that what we are reading is a memoir written by the narrator in anticipation of the novel he will write, that is, that what we are reading is not that novel. See Landy (2004) for the extensive evidence he compiles for this claim. I am much indebted to Landy for several conversations about the issues in this chapter.

takes a long time for Marcel's developing views to evolve into the developed narrator's, and so the views of the young Marcel on society and art are often clearly not those of the older Marcel, the narrator who explains the novel he will write after the events of the last volume of the memoir. And neither point of view can be identified with Proust himself, at least not without extreme caution and attention to any number of possible qualifications. There is obviously no easy solution to this problem, although it would be far too extreme to suggest that none of the analytic reflections represent what Proust himself thinks. But since the problem itself is a problem for Marcel, we can trace his ways of dealing with it, while remaining cautious about its final status.

Self and World

That first internal problem, subjective experience and the external world, emerges immediately. After we are introduced to a complex confusion of sleeping and waking states (while he is asleep, the thought that he must go to sleep awakens him; when awake, he keeps on thinking about what he was thinking while dreaming),[3] we are told that he was thinking about the book he had been reading, with a "peculiar turn." It now seemed to him that the book had been about him, but in a way that is indeed quite peculiar. It seemed to him that he *was* a church, a quartet, an aristocratic rivalry (between the Hapsburgs (Charles) and France (François) over leadership of the Holy Roman Empire).[4] This would certainly solve any skeptical problems that arise from what will later emerge as Marcel's concern, that we experience the external world or the social world not directly but via a subjective perspective that may not be sharable or common, and that means that access to the "world as it is in itself" is unavailable.

There is also a subtle irony in this opening. Marcel's dreamy identification of himself with everything he reads about directs us to the world of a book. And the objects he mentions will resonate with *this* book that we are beginning to read, and so the scene is a strange foreshadowing or prelude. A

3. This image itself is worth an extended discussion on its own. Proust is introducing it to us so early because it will play a large role in a crucial conversation with Elstir, whose views seem quite authoritative throughout. The conversation occurs toward the end of JF and is introduced by Elstir: "'Not at all,' he replied. 'When the mind has a tendency to dream, it is a mistake to keep dreams away from it, to ration its dreams. So long as you distract your mind from its dreams, it will not know them for what they are; you will always be taken in by the appearance of things, because you will not have grasped their true nature'" (JF, 577; 407).

4. Marcel also opines that the immobility of things is a function of the immobility of our conception of them (S, 5; 52) and often expresses other such "subjective idealist" views.

church, the Balbec church, will be the occasion for a major lesson from Elstir about art. (In that scene, he imagines writing his name on the church, another way to make it his, or even him.) A quartet signals the massive importance of music, the Vinteuil sonata and especially later the Vinteuil septet. (It would not be an exaggeration to say that he begins to find himself as an artist in hearing the septet for the first time.) And the rivalry he mentions, essentially between Germany and France, will reappear in the later novels because of the Dreyfus affair, First World War, and in Charlus's divided loyalties. As we have just seen, the novel cannot be said to be directly about these objects and events; it is always about what they are for Marcel, and so in a certain sense, he is those things; in reading about them we are always reading about him. (This, that he imagines the book being about him, is ironic in another way: of course Marcel thinks his book is "about him"; he thinks *everything* is about him.)

However, these fantastical imaginings just state another aspect of the problem, not a solution. Marcel's aspiration in the novel to come will be to escape his subjectivity, but if he did so by *identifying* with what is other than himself, he would also lose himself. There would *be* just the world. If he is a church, he is not Marcel. If he is Marcel-being-a-church, then he is not the church itself; the original aspiration is not fulfilled. (This is actually a version of a not unknown philosophical fantasy: to know the world as it is in itself, I must be present to the world without being there, without being present. My being there is always a distortion I must seek to eliminate. This of course insures there is no possible solution to the problem.)[5] The beginning sentences set what will be Marcel's real major aspiration: to escape subjectivity, *while remaining a subject*. This paradox is given an intensifying exemplification a bit later in these opening explorations when Marcel recounts what it was like to experience the magic lantern show he watched, while his great-aunt recounted the plot of the thirteenth-century crimes of Golo, the majordomo of Siegfried, a high official in the empire. Marcel's first reaction is typical. The show is disturbing. It has intruded on the deep familiarity of his bedroom and its objects, objects that by being so familiar seem not alien or other but suffused with his subjectivity. This familiarity is the comforting result of habit, often invoked in the novel as having this result, but habit turns out not to be a stable solution, since after time, habit deadens experience,

5. This is what Virginia Woolf is having fun with in *To the Lighthouse* when Andrew responds to a question about what his philosopher father's books are about. "'Subject and object and the nature of reality,' Andrew had said. And when she said Heavens, she had no notion what that meant. 'Think of a kitchen table then,' he told her, 'when you're not there.'" Woolf 1992, 38.

makes everything *too* familiar; the otherness of objects disappears, absorbed into Marcel's subjectivity. This habit-induced tranquility is what is disturbed by the moving figures, but what is important for the paradox just noted is how he describes the "presence" of Golo in his room: "The body of Golo himself, being of the same supernatural substance as his steed's, overcame every material obstacle—everything that seemed to bar his way—by taking it as an ossature and absorbing it into himself: even the doorknob—on which, adapting themselves at once, his red cloak or his pale face, still as noble and as melancholy, floated invincibly—would never betray the least concern at this transvertebration[6]" (S, 11; 57–58). Golo has "become" those objects on which he is projected, and the objects remain other than him, but Golo is still Golo. This image, which recurs a couple of times more in the novel, is an image of some sort of solution to that paradox, and the task is to understand how such an ideal could be made manifest in more straightforward philosophical and experiential terms.

The realization of the subjectivity of experience can give rise to further skepticism about any attempt to achieve stable knowledge of the world around us. This is the temporality of subjective experience. The picture the narrator presents is one of an experience of objects, events, and others that, subjectively, is a rapid surging of temporal moments succeeding each other, all of them colored by present concerns that exclude from conscious attention a number of dimensions of such experience that would be essential to any truth about what the world offers up to us, and rushing by far too rapidly for us to avoid this involuntary inattention. This notion of what is unattended to as such, but nevertheless in some way sub- or quasi-experienced, is the basis both for the recovery of what it was "*truly* like" for us in the experience, and for the recovery of a social and ontological truth we were in no position to attend to originally. This is of course the famous redemptive notion of involuntary memory, an experience (and here another paradox) that we cannot will or call up or direct the intellect to, and so is greatly subject to chance, but that can return us in a kind of lightning strike to "how it really was" in an experience we cannot be said to have "fully" experienced.

The paradox is of course how this could be, how it could be that what we experienced *is* "back there" in our memory, even though it was not "what we experienced" consciously at the time, and so not what would be called up by voluntary memory. This paradox is embraced by the narrator at several points. A good example occurs in *Within a Budding Grove*: "But when, even

6. This unusual word appears to mean something like "transmogrification," although, crucially, Golo is transmogrified into the doorknob, while remaining Golo.

without knowing it, I thought of them [*Mais quand, même ne le sachant pas, je pensais à elles*], they, more unconsciously still, were for me the mountainous blue undulations of the sea, the outline of a procession against the sea. It was the sea that I hoped to find, if I went to some town where they had gone. The most exclusive love for a person is always the love, really, of something else [*est toujours l'amour d'autre chose*]" (JF, 563, 397).[7] The possibility of an unattended-to experience, and even the suggestion that those aspects of the experience, because not distorted by the self-interestedness, even the wishful thinking of conscious interpretation, contain the recoverable truth of the experience, are in themselves not wholly implausible. We can think back on a conversation and suddenly (involuntarily) recall the tone with which an ambiguous remark was made by a friend and only now realize that the friend was warning us, and in the context of that moment and given later developments, we can realize in a flash and with certainty that that was unquestionably what happened. And in this account, it is not so much that we reinterpret a past event, although that must be part of it, as that we recover what we must have experienced (otherwise how could we "recall" it?) but what was not attended to as such at the time. Perhaps the impression of a warning flashed by so quickly that it was, as we have been saying, unattended to, not fully registered.

But the philosophical presuppositions required to make sense of this are difficult to understand. Marcel says that he was thinking of the little band without realizing he was thinking of them. And this in two senses. He took himself, apparently, to be thinking of the undulations of the waves, and came to realize that he was actually thereby thinking of the band, but not only thinking of the band—he does not say that he was thinking of the undulations and these reminded him of the band, but he realized he was thinking "more unconsciously still," that they *were* the undulations of the waves. One would assume that it is a necessary condition of thinking about X that one be aware one is thinking about X, and that if one is thinking of X as Y, one is aware that one is thinking that identification. But while Proust is clearly assuming that something like this is true (he must have, in thinking of the undulations, been thinking of the band or he would not be able to recover, bring to light, this fact), he is assuming that there are something like degrees of attentiveness in consciousness, in the way that one can see something at one time

7. There is obviously no "as well" in the French, as there was in the uncorrected Moncrief translation, and without it the passage says something much stronger than Moncrief was, apparently, prepared for: that the love of a person is always a love not of that person but of someone or something else.

(and thus "know" that one saw it) but realize only later that one did see it. This is one way one can be said to escape subjectivity while remaining a subject. One can correct the subjective distortions caused by the transitoriness of experience and the self-interestedness of one's interpretive attentiveness by being able to recover "true" dimensions of the experience that registered in one's consciousness without full attentiveness and thus without the manifold causes of distortion in much conscious attentiveness. This is the premise for involuntary memory (but not only for that, as in this passage) as a solution to the subjectivity problem. If one takes one's bearings from the narrator's stance in the last scenes, the entire novel is an example of this, a recovered memoir.

Indeed, these involuntary memories, or any means of recovering what is unattended to in our experiences but nevertheless experienced, serve as a general figure for literature itself, the ultimate solution to escaping subjectivity while remaining a subject, as in this passage, which is worth quoting at length:

> The greatness, on the other hand, of true art, of the art which M. de Norpois would have called a dilettante's pastime, lay, I had come to see, elsewhere: we have to rediscover, to reapprehend, to make ourselves fully aware of that reality, remote from our daily preoccupations, from which we separate ourselves by an ever greater gulf as the conventional knowledge which we substitute for it grows thicker and more impermeable, that reality which it is very easy for us to die without ever having known and which is, quite simply, our life. Real life, life at last laid bare and illuminated—the only life in consequence which can be said to be really lived—is literature, and life thus defined is in a sense all the time immanent in ordinary men no less than in the artist. But most men do not see it because they do not seek to shed light upon it. And therefore their past is like a photographic darkroom encumbered with innumerable negatives which remain useless because the intellect has not developed them. (TR, 298–99; 202)

This is a description of the paradox in all its glory: real life, *la vraie vie, is* literature.

The description of such recovery can often sound like a simple "flash from the past," as it was in all its interpretive complexity. But Proust suggests otherwise. From the first moment of the madeleine episode in *Swann's Way*, it is clear there is work to be done in such recovery. After the first flush of the experience, which caused him great joy, he says, "It is plain that the truth I am seeking lies not in the cup but in myself. The drink has called it into being, but does not know it, and can only repeat indefinitely, with a progressive diminution of strength, the same message which I cannot interpret, though I hope at least to be able to call it forth again and to find it there presently, intact and at my disposal, for my final enlightenment" (S, 61; 101). And then,

"What an abyss of uncertainty, whenever the mind feels overtaken by itself; when it, the seeker, is at the same time the dark region through which it must go seeking and where all its equipment will avail it nothing. Seek? More than that: create. It is face to face with something which does not yet exist, which it alone can make actual, which it alone can bring into the light of day" (S, 61; 102). This passage is important for the last dimension of the subjectivity problem, the self's experience of itself, but in this moment, Marcel figures out that the memory is of Sunday mornings in Combray with his Aunt Léonie, and then all that Combray has meant to him is available for recovery and interrogation. It is striking that even though the memory is involuntary, we must do far more than *simply* reexperience the sensation. Even "seek," *chercher*, is not adequate to the task; we must "create" something "which does not yet exist." The full importance of this interpretive transformation, which he will also call a "translation" of these messages from the past, is on view in this passage from *Time Regained*. The sensual or "material" dimension of the memory (for Marcel a sign of its genuineness) is as prominent as the interpretive task.

> For the truths which the intellect apprehends directly in the world of full and unimpeded light have something less profound, less necessary than those which life communicates to us against our will in an impression which is material because it enters us through the senses but yet has a spiritual meaning which it is possible for us to extract. In fact, both in the one case and in the other, whether I was concerned with impressions like the one which I had received from the sight of the steeples of Martinville or with reminiscences like that of the unevenness of the two steps or the taste of the madeleine, the task was to interpret the given sensations as signs of so many laws and ideas, by trying to think—that is to say, to draw forth from the shadow—what I had merely felt, by trying to convert it into its spiritual equivalent. And this method, which seemed to me the sole method, what was it but the creation of a work of art? (TR, 273; 185)

In the undulations passage, to add to the complexity, he believes that the realization of what he was really thinking without fully knowing he was thinking shows him a general truth (one of the "laws and ideas" above), that love is always of something else than the person loved. The added complication is that this inference is hardly an obvious one, just given the simple fact that he realized that in his fantasy life he thought of the young girls as undulations of the waves. It is very unlikely that he means that he was really in love with wave undulations, not the girls. He must mean that he loved in them something that resonated as meaningful in him, some set of images that meant something to him, that he loved. And, as in all statements of theory, the inference is not entirely trustworthy. (Marcel often defends himself against the vulnerabilities of being in love by insisting to himself that the beloved herself really doesn't matter; something else, internal to the lover, is what resonates in experiencing another.)

It is not entirely clear in the novel how all this is supposed to work. The very premise that makes it possible, experiential distortions in the present, would seem to bear on the stance of any recollecter *in the present*. The idea seems to be that somehow the experiential memory of Sunday morning tea with Aunt Léonie, prompted by the taste of the madeleine, comes rushing back involuntarily *as it really was*, not the fragmentary appearance Marcel experienced at the time, unaffected by what, say, the *recollecting* Marcel needs or wants to believe about Combray, or by what Combray in general has come to mean to him in the present. Something about the brute involuntariness and the sheer sensual force of the memory is supposed to help us understand the possibility of this directness. He goes so far as to admit that what is preserved of the past experience can be said to be differentially *responsive* to the present: "Our ego is composed of the superimposition of our successive states. But this superimposition is not unalterable like the stratification of a mountain. Incessant upheavals raise to the surface ancient deposits" (AD, 733; 126). But this responsiveness concerns just the timing of the returned experience, not its content. There is some common sensory link between the present experience and a past one that, just by being felt, brings the past back. Interestingly, he had described this unsought-out return in language that recalls the Golo image long ago introduced: "And yet should this day from the past, traversing the translucency of the intervening epochs, rise to the surface and spread itself inside us *until it covers us entirely*, then for a moment names resume their former meaning, people their former aspect, we ourselves our state of mind at the time, and we feel, with a vague suffering which however is endurable and will not last for long, the problems which have long ago become insoluble and which caused us such anguish at the time" (AD, 733; 126, emphasis mine). Even so, however, as with the first episode of involuntary memory described above, the return of the event does not obviate the necessity of interpretive work, and that would have to increase the chance of the influence of a present subjectivity. But Proust is phenomenologically convincing enough that there is sufficient directness and force in such a return that the experience serves as a good, even if not perfect, example of "escaping subjectivity while remaining a subject." It is particularly clear how wedded the narrator (and here we can, I think, safely add, Proust) is to the possibility of this reacquaintance in the multiple revelations at the Guermantes matinée in the final volume: "And what I found myself enjoying was not merely these colours but a whole instant of my life on whose summit they rested, an instant which had been no doubt an aspiration towards them and which some feeling of fatigue or sadness had perhaps prevented me from enjoying at Balbec but which now, freed from what is necessarily imperfect in external perception, pure and disembodied, caused me to swell with happiness" (TR 259; 175).

Self and Others

The claim that in loving another we actually love "something else" is consistent with the way he often speaks of his relation to others, and again the problem is the subjective "absorption" of others into oneself. An oft-repeated maxim of sorts for Marcel appears shortly after the undulations passage: "that when we are in love with a woman we simply project on to her a state of our own soul, that consequently the important thing is not the worth of the woman but the profundity of the state; and that the emotions which a perfectly ordinary girl arouses in us can enable us to bring to the surface of our consciousness some of the most innermost parts of our being" (JF, 563; 397).[8] But this projection theory is inconsistent with the distinctiveness of the narrator's treatment of love. For him it is always as much a cognitive as an emotional issue, a need to know the other as she really is, and this aspiration does not appear undermined by skepticism about others' inner lives. For example, Marcel is often surprised, even shocked by what he finds out to be *true* about another.[9] It is belied by evidence throughout the love affairs, Swann's and Marcel's especially, of the need to be loved by the beloved.[10] Admittedly, the characters often flee such a need in self-deceit (as is perhaps the case with the "autre chose" passage above). The purported skepticism about knowing the other and indifference toward her are just as much an expression of a fear of being known and being vulnerable to an other.[11] The theories propounded by Marcel, especially about love and jealousy, are clearly ironic, reflections of Marcel's (and Swann's) self-deceit, and hardly "Proustian views." Perhaps the clearest case of such defensive self-deceit is Swann's famous remark at the end

8. Cf. also S, 326–27; 332; JF, 597; 421; JF, 647; 456.

9. The predominant and repeated example is the discovery that someone is an "invert," that almost all the women Marcel is interested in, Gilberte, Odette, Albertine, Rachel When from the Lord, Vinteuil's daughter, and her friend, are lesbians. He also discovers a number of things about Saint-Loup, the phoniness of his republican politics, his "inversion," and his extraordinary courage in the war, that certainly "get through" to him, are not "absorbed."

10. JF, 133; 95; P, 129; 94.

11. I discuss this issue and the general "reliability" problem in the next chapter in this volume.

of *Swann in Love*, so transparent as to be pathetic, when he bemoans the fact that he has wasted his life for a woman who was not even his type, who did not even please him. The narrator cannot refrain from cluing us in, noting that this was a product of Swann's occasional "caddishness" (*muflerie*) and a result of his having dropped his "moral standards" for himself (S, 543; 517). We are also shown several times both that Odette "pleased" him enormously (their cattleya moments) and that he was desperately in love with her and desperately wanted to be loved by her.[12]

This is not to say that the problem itself, understanding another as she or he understands themselves, perhaps even understanding them better than they understand themselves, is not a serious one. It is obviously of deepest importance in love affairs, where the complexities quickly multiply.[13] This creates the temptation to believe that there could be a fact of the matter one could discover that would resolve the unavoidable doubts about whether, say, the beloved feels about the lover as she represents herself. No such moment is possible; such knowledge requires nothing like a punctual insight into some fact about another's inner life (for one thing, the other may not know how she feels, her feelings might be ambiguous and unsettled, what she believes may be self-deceived), but it requires an engagement with an other over some time, understanding the relation between what is said and what is done, what happens in moments of crisis in the love, a variety of conversations and so forth. In this case, escaping one's subjectivity while remaining a subject requires mostly a kind of openness to the other, a willingness to be known as a subject by an other, and so to confront, potentially, characterizations of, reactions to, oneself that challenge one's own self-understanding and so what one thinks one has learned about the other.

But the temptation is understandable. In the novel that temptation is often connected with a letter and the hope for documentary, final "proof." Swann is devastated by the contents of the anonymous letter he receives, in which Odette's relations with women are revealed. His reaction is gullible, naïve

12. As at JF, 133; 95.

13. Aside from all the complications involved in understanding another with whom one is in love, complications largely a result of one's needs and the fragility of one's ego, Marcel does not treat the problem of interpreting others all that skeptically. He is frequently given to remarks like this one from JF, and there is no indication that he is anything but correct in what he "sees" in Cottard's eyes. "I could see in Cottard's eyes, as anxious as if he was afraid of missing a train, that he was wondering whether he had not succumbed to his natural gentleness. He was trying to think whether he had remembered to put on his mask of coldness, as one looks for a mirror to see whether one has not forgotten to tie one's tie" (JF, 96; 69).

about the writer's motives, reductive and panicked, but the reaction also testifies to his frustration with trying to understand a woman who is much more a match for him in psychological sophistication than he will admit. Likewise, Charlus's relations with Morel slip into jealousy and panic when he reads a letter to Morel from the actress Léa, suggesting that Morel is "one of us," that is, that Morel's temperament is lesbian. It would be an understatement to say that Charlus cannot handle such a claim, but, again, he treats it as some sort of empirical fact he has learned from the letter, and because he believes that, his relation to Morel is permanently affected. Finally, after the famous passage where Marcel watches Albertine asleep, when he sees a potentially revelatory letter in her kimono, he is tempted to read it and "learn the truth" in some way. In this case, though, however desperately Marcel has been trying to learn about Albertine's secret life with other women, in a moment when, he thinks, he could resolve such doubts, he decides not to read the letter. He prefers to leave the issue in doubt, adding another layer to the complexities involved in trying to understand another (that is, also trying to avoid understanding an other). All of these social dimensions of the subjectivity problem remind one of more wisdom by Elstir, when he explained to Marcel the virtues of error in reaching the truth. Here the error is the far too observational or "inspection" view of what it would be to escape one's need to absorb the other into one's imaginative and fantasy world, and so by contrast highlights the much more difficult and uncertain process of engagement and openness as such an escape.

Once again, as with the first "escape," the model for experiencing another's subjectivity is great art and is presented in the most detail in Marcel's reflections on hearing for the first time a new composition by Vinteuil, a septet at a concert at Mme. Verdurin's in *The Captive*. At first the piece seems to him discordant, difficult to understand, but it begins to dawn on him how important the accomplishment of the septet is. He begins with an image of what it is to begin to experience "who Vinteuil is," what it would be to be him: "Each artist seems thus to be the native of an unknown country, which he himself has forgotten, and which is different from that whence another great artist, setting sail for the earth, will eventually emerge. Certain it was that Vinteuil, in his latest works, seemed to have drawn nearer to that unknown country. . . . Composers do not remember this lost fatherland, but each of them remains all his life unconsciously attuned to it; he is delirious with joy when he sings in harmony with his native land, betrays it at times in his thirst for fame" (P, 342; 246). The closer Vinteuil can come to remembering his lost fatherland, the land of his past, the environment that is distinctly his, who he really is, the more authentic his art becomes, the less it could be a mere reflection of his ambition for renown. The image of remembering links the achievement with involuntary memory, and the image of a native land and fatherland suggests that the object of this remembering cannot be isolated as some singular, private ego's. It includes all that he is and was, including his "native land," and his social world.

The link between access to a subjectivity and access to the objects of that subjectivity, its world, is asserted in one of the novel's most famous passages.

> The only true voyage, the only bath in the Fountain of Youth, would be not to visit strange lands but to possess other eyes, to see the universe through the eyes of another, of a hundred others, to see the hundred universes that each of them sees, that each of them is; and this we can do with an Elstir, with a Vinteuil; with men like these we do really fly from star to star. (P, 343; 246)

In aesthetic experience, we experience the world as seen by Elstir and Vinteuil, and by entering imaginatively into those worlds, we do not lose our own, another dimension of the solution to the paradox. In fact it is the felt contrast with our own subjectivity that is so thrilling, and the force, the power, and the strangeness of their vision make it impossible for us to absorb it into ours. This is so important an experience that Marcel says that "music seemed to me truer than all known books" (P, 504; 360),[14] and truer must mean not only truer to the artists themselves, truly what they see, available to us in art, but as he says, truer to "*the* universe" as well as "their universes." Marcel gets somewhat carried away by the exhilarating possibilities of such an escape: "It seemed to me, when I abandoned myself to this hypothesis that art might be real, that it was something even more than the merely nerve-tingling joy of a fine day or an opiate night that music can give; a more real, more fruitful exhilaration, to judge at least by what I felt. It is inconceivable that a piece of sculpture or a piece of music which gives us an emotion that we feel to be more exalted, more pure, more true, does not correspond to some definite spiritual reality, or life would be meaningless [*ou la vie n'aurait aucun sens*]" (P, 504; 360).

14. This touches on the unusual hierarchy of the arts that Marcel seems to assume: literature (Bergotte), painting (Elstir), and "at the top" music (Vinteuil). He says that music seems "to follow the very movement of our being" (P, 504; 360). Understanding why there should be this hierarchy would require a substantial independent discussion. See section 4 below.

Self as Subject and Object

Marcel's exploration of his own identity, the self-knowledge built on experience and reflection on that experience, involves a number of distinctions. He pointed to the difficulties already in *Swann's Way*, noted above: "What an abyss of uncertainty, whenever the mind feels overtaken by itself; when it, the seeker, is at the same time the dark region through which it must go seeking and where all its equipment will avail it nothing" (S, 61; 102). There is no way to achieve a perspective on oneself from outside oneself. In this case the subject and the object *are* identical. Even in cases where one distinguishes one's past self from a present self—and Marcel is frequently given to claiming that he has been many different selves, even that such selves have died and that new ones have been born[15]—there is also clearly some sort of continuity underlying such discreteness, and so a radical discontinuity claim cannot be the whole story. This suggests both logical and psychological difficulties for any subject that wants to turn on itself as an object of knowledge.

> Just as, throughout the whole course of one's life, one's egoism sees before it all the time the objects that are of concern to the self, but never takes in that "I" itself which is perpetually observing them, so the desire which directs our actions descends towards them, but does not reach back to itself, whether because, being unduly utilitarian, it plunges into the action and disdains all knowledge of it, or because it looks to the future to compensate for the disappointments of the present, or because the inertia of the mind urges it to slide down the easy slope of imagination, rather than to climb the steep slope of introspection. (AD 628; 48–49)

This "just as" (*de même . . . de même*) structure highlights the two difficulties. The logical point is first most clearly raised by Kant.[16] The "I" who experiences some content cannot be an object of experience like any other just because any object of experience will always require such a subject as the subject of *that* experience. There is no way for a subject to *experience* itself as an object of experience as well as the logical subject of experience, without setting off an unacceptable regress. This is not to say such a subject cannot be self-conscious. In fact in all its experiences it is self-conscious, aware of itself experiencing, but only *in* experiencing, not in attending to itself as an object. As Kant was the first to point out, that the "I think" must accompany all my

15. See for example S, 529; 505–6, and especially AD, 805; 175–76: "It is not because other people are dead that our affection for them fades; it is because we ourselves are dying."

16. The claim is that Kant illuminates this problem, not that Proust has Kant in mind, was influenced by Kant, and so forth.

representations, any "take" on how things are, for them to be representations, is a *logical* point, not a psychological one. For temporally extended experiences to be possible, this logical or "transcendental" "I" must be the same, continuous subject across such time, but it cannot matter for any of these points who or what such a subject is. It is just "that which thinks." The same is actually true of what we and Proust have been referring to as the "world" or sometimes "the universe" of a subject. The term refers not to the collection of everything in a world, but to the interrelated sense-making practices, saliences of significance, horizon of meaningfulness, determinate features of such meaningfulness so deeply presupposed that they cannot rightly be called presuppositions or beliefs or attitudes. That world, Hegel's "shapes of spirit" (*Gestalten des Geistes*), Wittgenstein's "form of life" (*Lebensform*), or Heidegger's world (*Welt*), cannot be objects within the world as well. This, the coincidence of these two points, is why Wittgenstein can say such things in his *Tractatus* as "I am my world. (The microcosm)" (5.63). Or "The subject does not belong to the world: rather, it is a limit of the world" (5.632). And, "Here it can be seen that solipsism, when its implications are followed out strictly, coincides with pure realism. The self of solipsism shrinks to a point without extension, and there remains the reality co-ordinated with it" (5.64).[17]

But it is the psychological point that is important to Proust, that we desire the objects we desire and know that we do, but do not desire reflexively; desire does not often reflect back on itself. This notion of the subject of desire, itself to be desired, is not immediately clear. As he indicates, the reason for the lack of self-attentiveness is often laziness ("inertia"), utilitarian interest in mere results, and so he appears to mean something similar to what Nietzsche says at the beginning of his *Genealogy of Morals*: "We are unknown to ourselves, we knowers: and with good reason. We have never looked for ourselves,—so how are we ever supposed to find ourselves?"[18] But aside from the various reasons why we are so often unreflective, *what* is it we have not sought, do not desire? When Marcel says that desire "does not reach back to itself" (*ne remonte pas à soi*), or that desire "disdains all knowledge of it" (*dédaigne la connaissance*), to what do "itself" and "it" refer?

In Socrates's invocation of the Delphic oracle, "know thyself," he took that to mean know what it is to be a human being, what life is the best human life, but in later modernity the imperative is connected with a virtue like authenticity: "know who you really are," in the sense of "face who you are, who you've become, what your limits are," and "avoid self-deceit and wishful thinking about

17. Wittgenstein 2002.

18. Nietzsche 2007, 3.

yourself," and so forth. Since such realizations may be unpleasant and deflating, it would be understandable if many avoided any such inquiry. But understanding the injunction that way assumes that what is most needed to carry it out is courage, a willingness to face potentially unpleasant facts. But these are Nietzschean or perhaps Heideggerian (early Heidegger) virtues and are not prominent in Proust's novel. This is so for an obvious reason: he clearly thinks that under any interpretation of what self-reflectiveness would involve, it is inordinately difficult and elusive, especially since the idea of "turning back around" to "see" something is an inappropriate and misleading model. The massive presence of self-deceit in the novel is evidence enough of a typical difficulty, since one of the paradoxes of self-deceit is that, for it to be successful, subjects must (somehow) keep from themselves that they are deceiving themselves. Once "inside" such a structure, it is hard to imagine how it would even occur to one to escape it, much less why one would want to. Almost everyone in the Faubourg St. Germain and in Mme. Verdurin's little clan is, besides being superficial, also vain, simply incapable of such reflection on themselves.

But the greatest difficulty in specifying the referent for those pronouns is clearer when we consider the intersection of the logical and psychological issues. The reason why some substantive "true self" or one's "real identity" cannot be an object of experience or reflection is different in the psychological case, but the result is the same. That is, the drive to understand oneself is unavoidable in life (however common is resistance to such a call), but the temptation to aspire to a punctual and decisive moment of insight, an apprehension of oneself as an object, is a futile aspiration. In the psychological case the reason is the radical temporality of the self. The fundamental experience of oneself is of the variations across time in one's reactions to others, to experiences, and there is the change in perspective due to simple ageing. There is a continuity in these variations, but it cannot be substantive because this self-transformation is constant, unceasing, and deep. The continuity must be something on the order of the logical continuity of the "I" of the "I think," but in contrast to this merely formal structure, this kind of psychological formality must have some sort of distinctive personal inflection. What sort is the question.

As in so many other cases in the novel, the model here, the best way to think about the problem as Proust does, is music. In the first place, music is an essentially temporal medium, making it quite a natural model. The moments of a musical piece emerge and immediately vanish, held together by memory, so that the comprehension of a piece is necessarily retrospective and interpretive. It is only in such retrospectivity that the musical piece is fully available to one, after it is finished, and the narrator treats self-knowledge in the same way. As we have seen, the premise for all of this is the unusual claim that our conscious experience is too transient, pragmatic, and inattentive to be revelatory of external social and psychological reality. The need for self-understanding may be constant, but it is not in the nature of desire, the engine of life, to be reflective.[19] So the "errors" can be profound, as in Marcel's too-late realization of the depth of his love for Albertine: "So what I had believed to be nothing to me was simply my entire life. How ignorant one is of oneself" (AD, 563; 3). But if a post-facto reflective turn cannot seek an object, what would the activity of self-understanding, assuming this post-facto, retrospective musical model, look like? There is no question that Proust has confidence that a work of art can help us understand the question: "How much more worth living did it appear to me now, now that I seemed to see that this life that we live in half-darkness can be illumined, this life that at every moment we distort can be restored to its true pristine shape, that a life, in short can be realized within the confines of a book" (TR, 507; 337). And he is confident that, having been shown such a life within a book, the readers of that book can profit from such exposure with regard to their own lives.

> But to return to my own case, I thought more modestly about my book and it would be inaccurate even to say that I was thinking of those who would read it as my readers. For, as I have already shown, they would not be my readers, but the readers of themselves, my book being only a sort of magnifying-glass like those offered by the optician of Combray to a purchaser. So that I should ask neither their praise nor their blame but only that they should tell me if it was right or not, whether the words they were reading within themselves were those I wrote (possible divergences in this respect might not always arise from my mistake but sometimes because the reader's eyes would not be those to whom my book was suitable). (TR, 508; 339)

The primary example of how this could be possible is Vinteuil and his septet. Everything in Vinteuil's musical expression of himself reflects who he is, distinctly and unmistakably, even though there is no moment or section of the piece that could be pointed to as a distinct moment of revelation. It is in hearing his music attentively that we meet the real Vinteuil, not "the melancholy, respectable little bourgeois" (P, 347; 249) from Combray.

19. Cf. "Impressions such as those to which I wished to give permanence could not but vanish at the touch of a direct enjoyment which had been powerless to engender them. The only way to savour them more fully was to try to get to know them more completely in the medium in which they existed, that is to say, within myself, to try to make them translucid even to their very depths. I had not known pleasure at Balbec any more than I had known pleasure in living with Albertine except what was perceptible to me in retrospect [*après coup*]" (TR, 271; 184).

Something like the tonality of the piece, together with Marcel's ability to appreciate that distinct tonality, can be said to constitute "who Vinteuil is." He is nothing other than this "unique accent, unmistakable voice" (P, 341; 245).[20] One phrase from the older sonata can reappear "the same and yet something else, *as things recur in life*" (P, 345; 248; my emphasis). Thereby the phenomenon counts as "proof of the irreducibly individual existence of the soul" (P, 345; 248). This is all not to say that anyone's life over time can be said to find expression in this way. It requires something equivalent to musical talent and commitment to that talent, come what may, to be able to live out and understand such expressiveness in the way Vinteuil manifests himself in his work. And it is only a great artist who can be said to be "delirious with joy when he sings in harmony with his native land," something clearly not the case in inferior art or in thoughtless lives (P, 342; 246). At the psychological level, it is in such an achievement that one can be said to achieve a consistent fidelity to oneself, honesty, genuineness in the relation between one's very being and one's deeds, and it is something that is achievable only over time and so never final or complete. Readers of Proust's book, by having heard *his* "unmistakable voice" for so long, can then become "readers of themselves" (a phrase that indicates self-knowledge is like reading and interpreting an extended narrative in a book), not by seeing themselves as "like Proust," but by having come, like the narrator, to distrust the intellect as guide, by a receptiveness to the sensual power of involuntary memories, by appreciating the complexities of the interpretive task needed to "translate" such memories, and by a kind of patience in understanding the provisionality and tentativeness of any such interpretation, given what the future might also reveal. It is this task that is summarized in the last sentence of the book.

> So, if I were given long enough to accomplish my work, I should not fail, even if the effect were to make them resemble monsters, to describe men as occupying so considerable a place, compared with the restricted place which is reserved for them in space, a place on the contrary prolonged past measure, for simultaneously, like giants plunged into the years, they touch the distant epochs through which they have lived, between which so many days have come to range themselves—in Time. (TR, 531–32; 353)

20. I discuss such an "accent" view of the self in further detail in Pippin 2005b.

11

The Shadow of Love: The Role of Jealousy in Proust's *À la recherche du temps perdu*

> But then at once his jealousy, as though it were the shadow of his love, presented him with the complement, with the converse of that new smile with which she had greeted him that very evening—and which now, perversely, mocked Swann and shone with love for another—of that droop of the head, now sinking on to other lips, of all the marks of affection (now given to another) that she had shown to him.
>
> *Swann's Way*

Philosophy and the Novel

In academic philosophy, the subdiscipline "moral psychology" concerns itself with the analysis of concepts involved when a person's motives for actions, presumably what explains for her and for others what she did and why, include considerations of what ought to be done, what one is obliged to do, what would be good to do, what the morally proper thing to do is, and so forth. There have been philosophers who deny that anyone ever really acts on such motives, or at least on them alone, and that debate is a major one in moral psychology. But it is not its exclusive focus. A typical concern in this sort of enterprise might very well be jealousy, whether we understand well what we mean when we say that someone acted "out of jealousy." When we say this about ourselves, it is usually an embarrassing admission, especially when the action interferes with what another would otherwise have done. That is, there does not seem to be any good or admirable action motivated by jealousy. It falls into the same box as acting out of pettiness, or greed, or vanity. When we ask someone close to us, "Are you *jealous*?" it is often lightheartedly mocking, as if being in such a state is foolish or childish. We don't usually mean that we are proud of or even indifferent to having acted with such a motive, and when we say it of another we sometimes imply that acting on such a motive is either pitiable, or sad, or weak, perhaps a sign of a bad character or psychological instability. So the appeal to jealousy has both a matter-of-fact/explanatory role and a morally tinged, judgmental role. The latter is especially true when we feel that another has given us no reason to believe that she has pledged any faithfulness to us, and yet we nevertheless feel that complex of anxiety, disappointment, sadness, and sometimes anger—jealousy—when we learn of her liaisons with someone else.[1] The invocation of jealousy to explain a deed has an even more critical edge when someone who *has* pledged faithfulness, and has given no grounds whatsoever for any suspicion of betrayal, is nevertheless constantly suspected of betrayal. Othello is the paradigm instance here, and there is something both horrific and deeply sad when we see how easily he is led into paranoid jealousy by Iago. Jealousy, then, in itself and as a judgment about someone, is a rich and easily recognized phenomenon in any moral psychology.

It is also a theme that appears and reappears with remarkable frequency in Proust's novel, although the most sustained and often surprising passages occur in *Swann's Way*, *Within a Budding Grove*, and *The Captive*.[2] Not only do we see characters subject to the feeling of jealousy, and some who act on the basis of such a motive, but the topic itself is a frequent theme of the narrator's reflections. It would not be unusual to hear from a devoted reader of the novel that "Proust can teach anyone interested in moral psychology a good deal about jealousy: what it is, why people experience it, how and why it can take over and destroy a relationship." The bearing of the novel on a philosophical issue is particularly important because jealousy does not seem suitable for any definitive Socratic definition. Reaching a high enough level of abstraction to suggest necessary and sufficient conditions for the concept's determinacy must inevitably thin out its various connotations to such an extent that we lose hold of its experiential concreteness and so falsify the concept considerably in order to define it precisely. Imagination of some considerable inventiveness is called for in getting the phenomenon in view, so why not rely on a genius at imagining, one of the greatest novelists ever?

1. I understand jealousy to be the distress and anxiety we feel when someone has something we wish very much we had, whether that something is a material good or some kind of intimacy with another, or simply time spent with another, attention devoted to another, that we wish would be spent with us, lavished on us. This is usually distinguished from envy, which arises simply because another has something and we want them not to have it; we resent the fact that they have it and it would please us if they ceased to have it, whether we benefit from depriving them of it or not. Understood this way, envy comes close to evil itself, and the paradigm case is Iago. There are almost no examples of envy in the novel, a possible exception being the machinations of Mme. Verdurin, especially when she sets out to destroy Charlus's relationship with Morel. (I freely concede that this distinction has largely been degraded in common usage and many would apply the terms confidently in just the opposite way. But it is not so much the words and word usage that interest me as the difference between wanting what someone else has [e.g., that my beloved's lover has her love, something I want, which almost always means, want exclusively] and simply wanting another not to have something, whether that means I have it or can get or not. I will use jealousy for the former, which is how Proust uses the term, and envy for the latter.)

2. References and abbreviations are the same as in the previous chapter.

It would also not be so unusual if that person went on to say that "for Proust," there is *no love without jealousy*, that the image in the epigraph above, of love with its shadow, jealousy, is "for Proust" on the way to demonstrating either through what he shows us or by means of Marcel's extensive reflections on the topic that love is, must be, always accompanied by such a shadow, that what we call love is itself inseparable from jealousy; they are two sides of the same coin. All of this poses the two questions to be discussed below. What is the ubiquitous role of and significance of jealousy in Proust's novel? And could Proust's treatment bear on philosophical issues like "What is jealousy?" and "What does the existence and frequency of the emotion show us about romantic love or even human nature?"

Attempting to answer any such question, especially the latter, immediately runs headlong into a very famous barrier. *À la recherche* is a novel, not a treatise. We learn what Swann feels and thinks (or at least what Marcel believes Swann thinks and feels), what Marcel experiences and his various theories, what concerns Saint-Loup about Rachel, Charlus about Morel, and so forth. While love may be inseparable from jealousy *for these characters*, there is no reason to generalize from their experiences, and there are loving relationships in the novel—Elstir's for his wife, the long-term relationship between Norpois and Mme. de Villeparisis, Vinteuil's daughter and her unnamed "friend,"[3] Marcel's grandmother's for him[4]—that are not tormented by jealousy. If the novel as a whole has in some way adopted a perspective on the relation between love and jealousy, the work necessary to flesh it out, which must also scrupulously respect the uniqueness of the individual characters and the literary form of the perspective itself, will be considerable. And that barrier to any easy translation into philosophical content is significantly higher in this novel than in almost any other. The form Proust created is that of a *fictional* narrator, inspired by a moment of involuntary memory, recollecting his past life as he struggles to become a writer. At one point the narrator suggests that we can call the subject of this narration Marcel (P, 91; 67). This "Marcel" develops into the narrator, and the book we are reading seems to be some sort of memoir by Marcel of the life that led this fictional narrator to his vocation, the future novelist he thinks he has become in the last volume. The young Marcel's views change over the course of the years covered

3. Actually none of the lesbian relations seem shadowed by jealousy. See Ladenson 1999.

4. This is true of the saintly grandmother, but Marcel himself is not completely free of jealousy. When she does something for herself, fuss with herself for a photo by Saint-Loup, and is obviously pleased by the prospect, Marcel cannot hide his irritation with her, his jealous resentment that she is not absolutely devoted to him and him alone (JF 500ff., 352ff).

by the novel, so we cannot even identify "what Marcel thinks" with the settled views of the narrator in the final volume, and we certainly can't identify either voice, the developing Marcel's or the mature narrator's, with Proust himself. Joshua Landy has helpfully suggested that we distinguish three separate texts that all have different functions in the novel: what he calls a *récit*, Marcel's memoirs, his autobiography (probably what we are reading); the oeuvre, Marcel's future novel, a fictionalized autobiography; and Proust's novel itself, a work of fiction with some borrowed autobiographical details.[5] The key and still very controversial point is that in the fictional world of Marcel, his memoir of his development into what we are reading is not the novel he now (at the Princesse de Guermantes's matinée) plans to write, and neither can it be identified with Proust's novel. The common view that what we are reading is an account of how Marcel became Marcel Proust and that the narrator's memoir is Proust's novel does not stand up to scrutiny.[6] So, while it is true that Marcel and the narrator are given to extensive philosophical reflection about time, art, society, love, and jealousy, the status of those reflections is, to say the least, not obvious. (All works that present philosophical reflections in a literary form generate the same set of questions, magnified in Proust's novel by the complexity of the point-of-view issue.)[7]

Proust himself is certainly aware of and irritated by the tendency of readers to identify Marcel's and the narrator's views as his own. In a much-cited 1914 letter to Jacques Rivière, he points out that the views expressed in the early novels are actually the *opposite* of what he himself believes, that ignoring this difference would be like equating Wagner's philosophy with what happens in *Parsifal*, and "I did not want to analyze this evolution of a belief system abstractly, but rather to recreate it, to bring it to life. I am therefore

5. Landy 2004, 43.

6. There are many other such reasons for distinguishing the texts this way, many ably pointed out by Landy. Marcel tells us at the final Guermantes matinée that he has not started writing his novel (in his fictional world, everything we have read is biographically true, not a novel), that literature has played no part in his life thus far. He has, though, written parts of his memoir. (Françoise finds the pages in *The Captive*.) When he looks forward to his future novel, he tells us that his intellect will correct the errors of the sense, many of which we have been reading about. The novel is all in the future; he worries that he will not have time left to finish it. Proust started sketching his novel at thirty-seven; Marcel is now old, possibly dying.

7. This was already an issue when philosophy began, with Parmenides's poem and Plato's dialogues, and is especially prominent in modern fiction, in the work of Diderot, Nietzsche, Musil, Mann, and in such genres as Sartre's novels and plays and Camus's novels and the work of such novelists as Iris Murdoch and J. M. Coetzee. (The great peculiarity of Proust, compared with all of these, is that the narrator's philosophical reflections are addressed exclusively to the reader, not to other characters.)

obliged to depict errors, without feeling compelled to say that I consider them to be errors; too bad for me if the reader believes I take them for the truth" (Proust 1992, 232–33).

Proust even seems to take some perverse pleasure in deliberately confusing these issues even more than they need to be, as in *The Captive*:

> And yet, my dear Charles Swann, whom I used to know when I was still so young and you were nearing your grave, it is because he whom you must have regarded as a young idiot has made you the hero of one of his novels that people are beginning to speak of you again and that your name will perhaps live. If, in Tissot's picture representing the balcony of the Rue Royale club, where you figure with Galliffet, Edmond de Polignac and Saint-Maurice, people are always drawing attention to you, it is because they see that there are some traces of you in the character of Swann. (P, 262–63; 189)

Here the narrator (himself a fiction in Proust's novel) begins by addressing a fictional character, Swann, and so the references of the second-person singular pronoun refer back to Swann, but in the last sentence, Swann is distinguished from someone else, someone the character is based on. Of course in *Proust's* novel, not here in the narrator's reflections, *both* "characters" are fictitious.[8] (All of this is not to mention that the narrator, having himself introduced this *roman à clef* convention, then also tells us, "In this book in which there is not a single event which is not fictitious, in which there is not a single personage 'a clef', where I have invented everything to suit the requirements of my presentation . . .") (TR, 225–26; 152).[9] Proust is playing the same game when he has the narrator explain that he did put one real character in the novel, two actually, the Larivière couple, who selflessly helped out their daughter-in-law. We learn from the memoirs of Proust's housekeeper that she did have such cousins, but the narrator says they are the "real" cousins of a fictional character, Françoise, and none of what the narrator tells us is true of the couple is in fact true.[10]

8. Charles Haas, supposedly the model for Swann, is still nowhere in view, if we take seriously the fictional status of what we are reading. Indeed even if a "Charles Haas" were to show up *in* the novel, there would be no reason to think a real historical person was referenced. Nevertheless, it is impossible to avoid the impression that the only voice who could have expressed this duality between Swann and some other "you" is Proust himself, as if he wants deliberately to confuse the relation between the two. This is Bersani's claim and he offers an interesting exploration of why. Bersani 2013, 180–92.

9. This is not credible either. There are real people everywhere in the novel, Dreyfus, the king of Greece, the Prince of Wales, the Goncourt brothers. Not every event is made up (there is after all the First World War).

10. Albaret 2003.

None of these barriers to any philosophical inference based on the novel, however, are meant by Proust to be insurmountable. As he also put it in that same letter to Rivière, "[if I] had no intellectual beliefs, if I were simply trying to remember the past and to duplicate actual experience with these recollections, ill as I am I wouldn't take the trouble to write" (Proust 1992, 232–33).

At this point, then, we should consider ourselves forewarned about any easy identification of anything expressed in the novel with Proust's views, but, as in the last chapter, we should not be so cautious of irony that we ignore Proust's intention that the novel have something to do with his "intellectual beliefs."[11] With that in mind, consider the problem of jealousy.

Love and Jealousy

The issue of jealousy slips into the novel unobtrusively even for the very young Marcel at Combray (a boy of about six or seven) and not just because he is jealous of the time his mother spends away from him after he has been sent to bed. He relates a favorite pastime, watching the changing slides of a magic lantern show projected on his bedroom walls, as he listens to his great-aunt recount the story of Golo and Geneviève de Brabant, itself an early connection with the magic of the Guermantes name. It is not a story suitable for or even comprehensible by such a small boy, although he understands enough to know that Golo had an "infamous design" and that what he did was "a crime." As we saw in the previous chapter, in this thirteenth-century story, Geneviève, the faithful wife of Siegfried, a high official of the empire, is falsely accused by Siegfried's majordomo, Golo, himself a rejected suitor of

11. For example, there is no good reason to think there is some gap between the narrator's views in *Time Regained* about time, memory, the self, and, especially, art and Proust's own views, and plenty of reason, given what Proust wrote in his own name, to take the views "straight," without irony. Even in this case, though, we should be cautious. In the midst of an episode of extensive theorizing by Marcel, in a novel some great percentage of which is the articulation of theories, laws, ideas, ideals, and "spiritual essences," he notes that "A work in which there are theories is like an object which still has its price-tag on it" (TR 278). This can only mean either that what he produces, what we are reading, is not a work of art, or that it is an inferior one, with price tags, neither of which is credible; or there are no theories stated with direct assertoric force by the author anywhere in the novel. There are plenty of theories in the novel, but none are "the novel's." Another warning. (A more radical interpretation would be that the way we read and qualify "theories" expressed by literary characters, tying our interpretation to the issue of why that character would say that, for example, is the way any philosophical theory ought to be, first of all, considered. Something like that appears to be Nietzsche's proposal for a new "philosophy of the future" in which psychology is "the queen of the sciences.")

Geneviève, of adultery, an accusation motivated by his jealousy and the rage it engendered. She is saved by the man who is supposed to execute her and must hide out alone with her son (Marcel's fantasy, no doubt)[12] until found by Siegfried and vindicated. So the young boy learns from the story how easily jealous doubt can be aroused, and how treacherous the issue is, how fraught with the possibility of false accusations and paranoia. Moreover, as we saw previously, since the projections of Golo onto the walls in effect "color" everything Marcel sees ("even the doorknob") with this story of jealousy, and since that image recurs a couple of times,[13] it would seem that we are being alerted to the importance of the theme of jealousy for much of what will now be narrated, as if all illuminated "in its lights (or, better, shadow)."

And so it is. There are four major love affairs in the novel:

1. Swann and Odette
2. Marcel and Albertine
3. Robert de Saint-Loup and "Rachel when from the lord" and
4. Charlus and Morel

There are others—Marcel and Gilberte, Marcel and the Duchesse (unrequited), Vinteuil's daughter and her friend, Robert and Morel—but these four absorb far and away the most attention from the narrator. They all share the same peculiarities. They cross class boundaries for one thing; two aristocrats and two commoners; two wealthy "high society" bourgeois and two not wealthy or socially prominent, one a courtesan. The beloveds are all bisexual, for another thing. And the relationships are all characterized by jealousy, although Charlus is the least consumed by it and is even proud of Morel's feminine conquests. (This changes with the letter from Léa, a lesbian who has written to Morel that he is "one of them" [P, 280; 204ff.]. Thereafter Charlus joins the jealousy club.) The jealousy is all a function of a general state of unknowingness about the other, a great anxiety, even anguish, that one can never really know who the other is, whether the other's self-presentation and declarations of affection are trustworthy, what one's status in the eyes of the other really is. This latter similarity, a state of anxious epistemological

12. Marcel tells us that the Golo story made his mother all the dearer to him and prompted him to examine his conscience regarding his mother, as if he had something to be guilty of, has somewhat identified himself with "fake adultery news" Golo. This strange reaction occurs simultaneously with his father's abandoning his oedipal role by permitting the mother to sleep with Marcel, and manifests his own willingness to be manipulative to gain time and attention from his mother.

13. See especially TR, 342; 231.

uncertainty, seems connected to the first two commonalities. In such a state of uncertainty, an unequal position, socially and financially, can serve to make the beloved dependent on the lover and so, the lover might reason, more dependably faithful. This is of course a bad bargain. The attention one receives is even more untrustworthy if "bought," and it decreases the likelihood that one will have and be able to trust what one most wants, love.[14] And so such a relationship can increase, rather than moderate, jealous suspicions. And the fact that the beloveds are bisexual intensifies the unknowingness and so anxiety of the lovers, since the nature of that affection, even what they actually do, is portrayed as unimaginable by men who do not share that form of love.[15] In short, as has often been pointed out by commentators, love is treated in the novel largely as an epistemological problem, as inseparable from the desire to know and (in a less prominent way) to be known, and so, once posed this way, the inevitable uncertainties in such self- and other-knowledge make the anguish of jealousy equally inevitable. Love is in fact so characterized by anguish, pain, and misery that Ortega y Gasset may have been right when he said that "Swann in Love" shows us every kind of human feeling except love.[16]

He may have been prompted to say this because very little of what is commonly accepted as the nature of romantic love is on display in the novel. This category—common understandings of love—includes multitudes, ranging from the reductionist, the view that romance is a strategic idealization of what is basically animal lust, nature's reproductive imperative, to quite idealized accounts. (An even more cynical version of the former: Swann and Marcel are men who simply want to deny the other any status as an equal free subject. They want instead to objectify them and to possess them as if objects of ownership. They are both simply neurotic, sexist men.)[17] In the idealized accounts, the beloved has qualities that inspire affection and desire

14. I realize that Marcel is forever saying that the views and experiences and even the identity of the beloved do not matter, are of no concern to him, but that is, as we shall see, among the more glaring instances of self-deceit in a novel saturated by that phenomenon.

15. As Ladenson (1999) points out, we get no sense (from the accounts we get of Albertine's liaisons or Odette's or Morel's, who is characterized by his friend Léa as a male lesbian) that any of the lesbian relationships are haunted by jealousy, and in fact, Ladenson compellingly argues, they are rare examples in the novel of genuine mutuality.

16. Ortega y Gasset 1927, 293.

17. Such a view seems to me facile and lazy; it ignores Proust's deep, intricate, and nearly omnipresent reliance on irony. Anyone who has read through the thousands of pages of the book and come away with such a "reading" has obviously wasted a great deal of time. I will deal with the most-cited passage in support of that view, Marcel watching Albertine sleep, below.

for intimacy and acknowledgment from such an admired person. The qualities need not be virtues; they can be wit, cleverness, taste, but our admiration of the other for possessing them is the key origin. The beauty that inspires love is as much physical as moral, in the broadest sense. A variation of sorts is what we might call Hegelian. Love is inspired by someone who, you think or hope, truly understands and appreciates you, as you understand and appreciate her (an emotionally intense version of "mutuality of recognition"). To understand and to be understood in that way invites even greater intimacy, and so also sexual intimacy, but also the risk of a vulnerability to being wounded or judged. Hegel called this being oneself in another, such that dependence on and exposure to the other is understood not as a limitation but as a moment of self-realization. This is something like what people mean when they say that they are completed by another; their life would be poorer without the other, or not complete; they couldn't fully be who they are without the other.

Nothing, it would seem, could be farther from the relatively joyless miseries shared by our four lovers. And readers can formulate what might seem to them the Proustian theory of love on the basis of this common distinctiveness. Here is a typical formulation of a key issue.

> Among all the modes by which love is brought into being, among all the agents which disseminate that blessed bane, there are few so efficacious as this gust of feverish agitation that sweeps over us from time to time. For then the die is cast, the person whose company we enjoy at that moment is the person we shall henceforward love. It is not even necessary for that person to have attracted us, up till then, more than or even as much as others. All that was needed was that our predilection should become exclusive. And that condition is fulfilled when—in this moment of deprivation—the quest for the pleasures we enjoyed in his or her company is suddenly replaced by an anxious, torturing need, whose object is the person alone, an absurd, irrational need which the laws of this world make it impossible to satisfy and difficult to assuage—the insensate, agonizing need to possess exclusively. (S, 326–27; 332)

This is indeed typical, and a fuller statement of the supposed "Proustian theory" would have these four elements.

1. All romantic love is based on unavailability or indifference or the active hostility of the beloved (JF, 597; 422). (Obviously we do not fall in love with everyone indifferent or hostile to us, so there must be many other implicit necessary conditions at play: physical desirability, one's type, some mystery that inspires erotic longing, whatever.)

2. This sort of anguish about impossibility is the necessary, indispensable origin of love; no such anguish, no love. Love is even a kind of sickness; one falls in love the way one catches a cold.[18] (A Marcel corollary: The person whom we love is to be recognized only by the intensity of the pain we suffer.)
3. The beloved herself, who she is, her concrete individuality and qualities, matters little in love.[19] She is just a vehicle for the projection of our fantasy, desires, needs. (Another corollary: The other's feeling for us, as we experience it, is just our own feeling reflected back to us. She can be said to be "an inverted projection, a negative of our sensibility" [JF, 647; 456].)[20]
4. Love in its passionate phase is largely fueled by, even indistinguishable from, jealousy.[21] (Another corollary: the goal of love is possession, where this means dominating the attention and affection of the beloved, leaving no room for any other attentiveness or caring for any other, fully occupying her mind and her time.)

Aside from the problem of irony (these are Marcel's views, and not, or at least not necessarily, Proust's) and aside from the fact they reflect different stages in Marcel's life, reflecting his experiences up to that point, he says a great many other things in the novel not consistent with such a "theory." For example, contrary to (1), he once notes, "for if it is sometimes enough to make us love a woman that she looks on us with contempt, as I supposed Mlle. Swann to have done, and that we should think that she can never be ours, sometimes too, it is enough that she looks on us kindly, as Mme. de Guermantes was doing, and that we should think of her as almost ours already" (S, 250–51; 175). Also contrary to (1) is another passage from the same novel: "In his younger days a man dreams of possessing the heart of the woman whom he loves; later, the feeling that he possesses a woman's heart may be enough to make him fall in love with her" (S, 277; 289).

And there are plenty of passages, contrary to (3), that show us how self-deceived and defensive the various pronouncements are about the irrelevance of the beloved's relation to the lover, as if she is a mere external screen for projection: "Jealousy is moreover a demon that cannot be exorcised, but

18. Love is an "incurable malady" ("l'amour est un mal inguérissable") (P, 105; 77).

19. "we never dream how small a place in it [our love] the real woman occupies" (JF 597; 422).

20. "When we are in love with a woman, we project on her a state of our own soul" (JF 563; 397); we want to know the other, but "after a while we no longer distinguish [her] from ourselves" (JF 648; 457).

21. "To a woman who previously excited in us a mere paltry physical desire he instantly adds an immense value, foreign to her but confounded by us with her. If we had no rivals, pleasure would not transform itself into love" (TR 314; 212).

constantly reappears in new incarnations. Even if we could succeed in exterminating them all, in keeping the beloved forever, the Spirit of Evil would then adopt another form, more pathetic still, despair at having obtained fidelity only by force, despair *at not being loved*" (P, 129; 95, my emphasis).

The gist of such passages is the same: jealousy is not just an anxiety about a lack of "possession," about the absence of the beloved, her possible greater intimacy with someone else. It is an anxiety about her relation *to the lover*, an uncertainty about one's standing in her eyes, a need to know, to secure the knowledge, that one is loved, none of which is compatible with the "projection," and the "her mere unattainability is enough to excite love" view. Consider Swann: "To make Swann's jealousy revive it was not essential that this woman should be unfaithful, it sufficed that for some reason or other she should have been away from him, at a party for instance, and should have appeared to enjoy herself. That was enough to reawaken in him the old anguish, that lamentable and inconsistent excrescence of his love, which alienated Swann from what was in fact a sort of need to attain (the real feelings this young woman had for him, the hidden longing that absorbed her days, the secret places of her heart)" (JF, 133; 95).

Not only does this distinctive anxiety about who they are in the minds of these women touch on one of the most general themes of the novel—something like the existential dimension of unknowingness, or what it is like to live with the impossibility of satisfying a deep need to know—it also helps explain two of the more mysterious and famous passages.

> And with the old, intermittent caddishness which reappeared in him when he was no longer unhappy and his moral standards dropped accordingly, he exclaimed to himself: "To think that I've wasted years of my life, that I've longed to die, that I've experienced my greatest love, for a woman who didn't appeal to me, who wasn't even my type!" (S, 543; 517)

The bizarre paradox, that he has "wasted" his life, but for a *great* love (why would that be a waste?), and for a woman who did not appeal (*ne me plaisait pas*) to him (what could love mean if there were no pleasure in it, and what about all those obviously extremely pleasant "cattleya" episodes?), is softened considerably by the narrator's characterization of the moment as "caddishness" (*muflerie*) and a lowered moral standard. This is an indication that Swann's whining here is dishonest, self-deceived, is as defensive and self-protective as is the general theory of love throughout the novel. What Swann is protecting himself from is his desperate dependence on Odette's *view of him*, how vulnerable he is to what is revealed about that by when and why she is willing to lie and deceive. This is already indicated more honestly in the passages quoted above. Bersani is surely right that Swann is here engaging in a weak, defensive imitation of the "indifference" of the beloved, and it is just as transparent and unconvincing in his case as in most.[22]

The other strange event occurs at the beginning of *The Captive*, when Marcel seems to take a deeply perverse pleasure in Albertine's being asleep, "as if a plant," and believes that "her sleep realized to a certain extent the possibility of love: alone" (P, 84; 62). The image we are apparently encouraged to have is one of possession, domination, control, a free play of fantasy, and finally some form of sexual satisfaction while she is still asleep, all as if some corporeal realization of "the theory" that the beloved is a mere screen, a "silhouette." But that image is undercut by what Marcel points to as the factor that actually attracts him to Albertine asleep: "when she was asleep, I no longer had to talk. I knew that I was no longer observed by her, I *no longer needed to live on the surface of myself*" (P, 84; 62, my emphasis) ("je n'avais plus besoin de vivre à la surface de moi même." The fantasy is not that of feasting his eyes on a passive subject. That is only a consequence of the real fantasy: *not being looked at*, which means both not having to be subject to a gaze he cannot penetrate, whose meaning he cannot fathom, and not having to play the role he thinks necessary to obtain her regard and love, not having to live on the surface of himself.[23] He's not so much feasting his eyes as enjoying hers being closed. This all does not mean that if Marcel were able to endure "being looked at" and all that that entails and could penetrate the opaque gaze and find with certainty Albertine's view of him, he would welcome the chance. On the contrary; such a revelation is both what he wants and what he fears, the fear being responsible for his self-protective defensiveness. This is all made dramatically clear in that "kimono episode" in *The Captive*, discussed in the previous chapter, when Marcel has a chance to read a possibly revelatory letter in Albertine's kimono but does not, in full knowledge of his own inconsistency (P, 89; 66).[24]

22. Bersani 2013, 63. This is also true of Swann's aestheticization of Odette, his attempt to convince himself that his love for her is possible because she instantiates a Botticelli painting, and so he can possess her as one possesses an art object to be appreciated. This is transparently a way of protecting himself from the truth, that it is Odette who possesses him, not the other way around.

23. Obviously none of this excuses his behavior, although it does go to the relationship between self-deceit and blame.

24. He is also aware of this paradoxical attitude; he knows that if he achieves what he desperately wants, knowledge of Albertine's liaisons, it would destroy his love for Albertine and "almost kill" him, neither of which, of course, he wants. He knows he "adds sufficient uncertainty" to his search in order to "deaden the pain" (P 105; 77).

Finally, reverting again to that 1914 letter to Rivière, in which Proust also mentions that although the views that Marcel expresses, especially at the end of *Swann's Way* (that time is lost forever), are errors, and that his own views will be clear in the last volume, we have to notice a strange absence in that discussion. What he discusses in that culminating reflection are themes that have appeared throughout: memory, time, the self, and above all art. But two issues that have greatly preoccupied him do not get this "my final view" treatment: society (and the related issues of snobbery, status, and vanity) and the love-jealousy relationship. Jealousy is mentioned only a half a dozen times in *Time Regained*, and the references are trivial, except for one, where he notes that the suffering caused by jealousy can benefit the artist, which folds it into that other discussion.[25] There is no return to that issue, which made up so much of *Swann's Way*, *Within a Budding Grove*, *The Captive*, and *The Fugitive*. I suggest this is an indirect confirmation of the view that those "theories" are Marcel's and to some extent Swann's (implicitly Robert's, and even more implicitly, an explanation of Charlus's anxiety about Morel). Their views are psychologically revelatory and important in the novel, but not because they indicate any generalized theory of love and jealousy.[26] Not only would it be impossible to generalize from the views of such distinct characters, but even their own views are inconsistent and self-deceived. The gap between what they think they believe and what they actually believe is wide and obvious. As we shall see, the fact that that sort of generalization is impossible does not mean that they do not have a general significance.

That is, none of this means that we are just reading case studies of a few men whose egos are too fragile to bear the uncertainty and anxiety that attend any vulnerable exposure to another in intimate love. Their real anxiety in love is other than what they describe, and while that genuine anxiety is still fueled by the pathologies of narcissism, self-serving self-deceit, and manipulative behavior, it also manifests something of general significance about the world in which they suffer this way, the late modern world emerging right before and after the First World War.[27]

25. And this reference just repeats what Marcel has expressed several times: that suffering is good for inspiring self-knowledge and knowledge of others.

26. There are all sorts of reasons that undermine any possible such theory. See Picherit (2007) for the best demonstration of this, and why the illusion of an objective theory of love is so important to what the novel does to a reader. His account of the different descriptions of the nine "first times" Swann fell in love and why is invaluable.

27. It would require a separate and unavoidably lengthy discussion to understand how Proust thinks of the relation between historical time and the distinctiveness within that time of characters' emotional lives. Given how much of the novel is devoted to chronicling not just the decay

Being Jealous of Oneself

There is one great peculiarity in both the depicted experiences of jealousy and the numerous analyses to which it is subject by Marcel. Contrary to a very widespread representation of the experience, it is never described in Proust's work as provoking what we might normally expect: anger, even violent rage at a possible betrayal of one's trust. In a great many literary representations, from *Medea* to *Othello* to *Effi Briest* to endless detective novels, such anger destroys people's lives and provokes murderous reprisals. Yet jealousy remains a deeply epistemological problem in Proust's depiction, a matter of passive suffering, not active revenge. If jealousy were to be understood as motivated by an egotistical demand for omnipotent control of the beloved, for complete subjugation of the beloved's ego to one's own, rage is what we might expect, jealousy being so often tied to a motive of revenge. Jealousy is of course sometimes very much like this or exactly this. Marcel admits several times that there are many varieties of jealousy, many causes that provoke it, many implications that can follow from it (P, 28; 23). The novel, though, is concerned not with those but with this, let us call it, epistemological version. The absence of such a reaction in Proust thus suggests that he has a different understanding of jealousy. What is that understanding?

Here I want to follow a brief suggestion made by Bersani but not pursued by him in the following way,[28] and one also on the surface in Proust's depiction, as we have already noted. Proust's formulaic account occurs at the end of *The Captive*. Marcel is in the midst of a startling revelation that, despite all the time and energy and emotional investment expended in keeping Albertine prisoner, he himself has been having multiple affairs with other women.[29] He

---

and final dissolution of class boundaries (the realization that class is the "royaume du néant") but also the impact of technology on Europe, and the political "jealousies" between France and Germany, and so forth, he must have intended to show why the anxiety of unknowingness should have assumed such a salient form (jealousy) in *this* world. My suggestion would be that it has something to do with distinctive modern forms of dependence and the vulnerabilities they create, the conformism they require, and the effects of expectations about romantic love in such a world.

28. Bersani (2013, 180ff.) makes the interesting link between this self-jealousy and homosexuality.

29. This is one of many such startling revelations that need their own category. There are several such events in Marcel's life that, given the volumes we have read about him, would seem crucial to understanding him. He has fought many duels? He makes frequent trips to brothels? Wait: he picks up little girls, invites them to his room to sit on his lap, and is arrested for it by the police? Charlus actually intended to murder Morel? I think many of these revelations are meant to disabuse us of any sense that we know these characters any better than anyone in the novel knows anyone, that anyone anywhere knows anyone very well.

thus can imagine his jealousy about Albertine's liaisons as *her* potential jealous anxiety about his own infidelities. Since Albertine is so opaque to him, he must imagine Albertine as *his* unfaithful self. As he puts it, "As there is no knowledge, one might almost say that there is no jealousy except of oneself" (P, 519; 371).[30]

But this image of being jealous of oneself, jealous of oneself both as and "in" the other, is significant in itself. For the image, while extraordinarily unusual, once so formulated, is perfectly apt for the novel's treatment. In being jealous, that is, anxious, suffering because of the possibility of unfaithfulness, you are really anxious about the unavailability of the beloved's *image of you*. You are jealous, in effect, of the affair the beloved is having *with you*, with that unknown you who cannot be reached, seen, known. Her view of you might be revealed in what she is willing to do, whom she is willing to see, and so an investigation of these matters is a pursuit as well and more importantly of her "you." What she does and says in confidence to others expresses the seriousness and meaning of her image of you, of whom she takes you to be, what you mean to her. This reflects a deeply familiar general anxiety in love, one usually held in bounds and subject to reassurance: does the other love me as I love her? Does she love me at all? Or does she love a "me" I have pretended to be in order to secure that affection or a "fantasy me" she has invented for her own reasons? In this form of jealousy, you are anxious not that you will lose her to others but that her possible liaisons with others imply a relation to you (or no relation, it could be, to you) that you have no access to. Despite the characterizations Swann and Marcel give of their jealousy, we have already seen what their anxiety is really about. In the "To make Swann's jealousy revive" passage (JF, 133; 95), it was already clear that the object sought was "what this young woman really felt for him, the hidden longing that absorbed her days, the secret places of her heart." And in the "jealousy is a demon" passage, Marcel admits that what is so upsetting in jealousy is "despair at having obtained fidelity only by force, despair *at not being loved*" (P, 129; 95).

There is a moving passage in *Swann's Way* when much of this becomes clear to Swann himself, as he reflects on the fate of his love for Odette.

> And Swann could distinguish, standing motionless before that scene of remembered happiness, a wretched figure who filled him with such pity, because

30. "Comme il n'est de connaissance, on peut presque dire, qu'il n'est de jalousie que de soi-même" (371). (A separate study is needed of the meaning of the unusual modality of qualified assertion that pervades Marcel's reflections. *On peut presque dire*, which is left out of the translation used, is only one of hundreds of such qualifiers as "perhaps," "it might be said," "one might think," and so forth.)

> he did not at first recognize who it was, that he had to lower his eyes lest anyone should observe that they were filled with tears. *It was himself.* When he had realized this, his pity ceased; *he was jealous, now, of that other self whom she had loved,* he was jealous of those men of whom he had so often said, without suffering too much: "Perhaps she loves them," now that he had exchanged the vague idea of loving, in which there is no love, for the petals of the chrysanthemum and the letterhead of the Maison Dorée, which were full of it. And then, his anguish becoming too intense, he drew his hand across his forehead, let the monocle drop from his eye, and wiped its glass. And doubtless, if he had caught sight of himself at that moment, he would have added, to the collection of those which he had already identified, this monocle which he removed like an importunate, worrying thought and from whose misty surface, with his handkerchief, he sought to obliterate his cares. (S, 493; 475, emphasis mine)

This represents a kind of double unknowingness. You are frustrated because you feel shut out from her view of you, and there can always be plenty of possible indications that that view might not be what you think it is or would like it to be. If Marcel and Swann try to pull the beloved into their own fantasies of who she is, how she might satisfy their own needs, her living presence and her secret other life may and, it turns out in these episodes, do constantly undermine and conflict with that drama going on in their own heads, and reveal that her view of what they are doing and her resistance to it in that other life, the one they don't see (unless they can entomb her up in their house) are not controllable by them. However strong your projected fantasy, you are playing a role in the beloved's mental drama that inspires this form of jealousy, jealousy of you playing that role, that partner of hers you most want to control, indeed to be, but on your terms.[31]

This is a double unknowingness because, at least as Marcel sees it, your own self-knowledge depends on such responsiveness from another, one you can distort by projection or make unavailable by inspiring a worry about jealousy that makes its availability to you even more difficult. ("As soon as jealousy is discovered, it is regarded by her who is its object as a challenge which authorizes deception. Moreover, in our endeavor to learn something, it is we who have taken the initiative in lying and deceit" (P, 73; 54). And that deprives

31. To satisfy this deep need to "see through the eyes of another" is precisely one of the main functions of art. It can satisfy this need, or at least suggest what it might be to satisfy it, as in one of the most famous and lyrical passages about art. "The only true voyage would be not to visit strange lands but to possess other eyes, to see the universe through the eyes of another, of a hundred others . . . and this we can do with an Elstir, with a Vinteuil; with men like these we do really fly from star to star" (P, 343; 246).

you of a major vehicle of self-knowledge, this potential conflict between your self-image and these challenges ("it is only with the passions of others that we are ever really familiar, and what we come to discover about our own can only be learned from them" [S, 18; 205]).

This same surface/reality distinction applies as well to the whole issue of "possession." On the surface, the desire seems to be to end uncertainty about the beloved by totally possessing her, controlling not so much where she goes and whom she sees so much as her desires, to occupy her whole "mental space," leaving room for nothing more. So we get pronouncements like "For the possession of what we love is an even greater joy than love itself" (P, 58; 44). But that sort of possession, the surface version, ends up not possessing anything. If it is successful, the other has vanished, has been absorbed into the lover's fantasy. There is an example of that in the novel, and again it is deeply and obviously ironic:

> She [Albertine] had called back into herself everything of her that lay outside, had withdrawn, enclosed, reabsorbed herself in her body. In keeping her in front of my eyes, in my hands, I had an impression of possessing her entirely, which I never had when she was awake. Her life was submitted to me, exhaled towards me its gentle breath. (P, 84–85; 62)

And again, possess what? What "life"? The reality of the fantasy involves the same paradox that what is sought is *the possession of oneself*, the self, that image of yourself in the beloved, who, you worry, is living in her without your control. That is why this passage precedes the one quoted above, where what is so satisfying to him is that *her* eyes are closed, not so much that *his* can look and analyze all they want. This corresponds to that cliché about love: that one is not in possession of oneself; the other is. And this is important in just the same double sense as jealousy is, fueled first by anxiety about whom exactly the beloved loves, if she loves at all, and second, by an even deeper anxiety about who one is, given that Proust has undermined the value of introspection throughout and, by showing us the near omnipresence of self-deceit, proved that no sort of self-reporting is at all reliable. And in both cases the aspiration is just as impossible to fulfill. There is no certainty in these matters, no reassurance.

Even aspects of snobbery are connected with this dynamic, with what is really at stake in jealousy. The fierce loyalty demanded by Mme. Verdurin, and her avowed contempt for the Faubourg St. Germain, clearly betray an anxiety either that they have no view of her at all, that her status with them is "no status," or that she is regarded with amusing condescension, or that members of her clan, if allied with other clans, could represent her in ways she cannot control. Hence, Marcel opines, "Mme. Verdurin's hatred is just a special, social form of jealousy" (P, 370; 266). She wants to engineer a world that reflects back to her only her elevated, idealized versions of herself, as when we cling to our own social group, gossiping about, hostile to, other groups. We seek to avoid, as with possession of the beloved, disconfirmation of our positive views of ourselves and our group, to engineer a reflection back to us of our own, usually self-deceived view of ourselves. Hence also her intense jealousy, especially of the world of Swann and ultimately of Charlus, in which she probably suspects she is considered a vulgar, middlebrow, arriviste social climber. As in all the cases in the novel, snobbish indifference to others is a preemptive defense against their indifference and contempt for you. Indifference is a way of blocking their threat to you and your self-image. Marcel comes to realize the pathetic and futile nature of this social striving.

A Philosophical Dimension?

The characterization of love and jealousy in the novel, however common to a set of different characters, cannot be considered "Proust's theory" of either. But as we have seen, there is an underlying dimension to the epistemological problematic that animates the anxiety or even anguish at the heart of the character's experience, and that dimension does suggest a more general significance that might bear on the moral psychological issue of love: that is, love's value and the proper attentiveness to and appropriate acknowledgment of its value in human life.

That dimension involves what is so highlighted as to be exaggerated, almost to the exclusion of all else, in Proust's narrative—what we have been calling the epistemological dimension. Any love, aside from some *amour fou*, must inspire an attempt by each lover to know the other, and especially to know what one is for that other. What it is to be somewhat confident that "one knows another" as opposed to knowing a fact or something about an object is what is at issue. Of course, that need to know what one is for the other, and an attendant jealousy of that unknown "you," need not overwhelm the experience, to the exclusion even of coming to know the other, genuinely and in no directly self-related way, to understand who it is whom one has come to care so much about. Moreover, in any such attempt one's own self-knowledge is at stake too. In trying to understand what the beloved makes of one, one measures against some conception of who one thinks one is, and finding in that measure some discordance between your view and hers can cause either mere disappointment that one is not understood or some realization that one is not who one took oneself to be, or it can simply cause one to be stuck between such alternatives, with no obvious resolution in sight.[32]

One might accept that all this is true as an account of the focus for this theme in the novel, but note that it seems to leave everything, just as so stated, as an "issue raised," that all we see in the novel are what would have to be called distortions of such a dimension, an anxiety about both sides of the issue, knowing her and understanding who one is for her, as well as a serious (apparent) indifference to another dimension just as crucial. For that latter dimension is possible only if one *lets* oneself be known. If love is inseparable from a desire to know, it is also inseparable from a desire to be loved (as the passages we have cited show both Swann and Marcel realize at some level, despite what they might sometimes say), and that desire must reflect a willingness to be known.[33] But in the Swann-Odette and Marcel-Albertine relationships, despite occasional guarded revelations to the other about how much the beloved mean to the lover, we see little realization of this and a massive amount of self-deceived self-protectiveness. And we have so little sense of the inner lives of the two beloveds that there is little evidence about how all these issues play out for them. Once again, we seem to have issues raised, and no guide about what, with things going wrong, it might be for them to go right.

But we can take our bearings here from an important passage in *Within a Budding Grove*, a conversation between the young Marcel and Elstir. It is a "truth through (perhaps only through) error" passage that bears on this issue. It is something already signaled in *Swann's Way*: "While the kitchen-maid—who, all unawares, made the superior qualities of Françoise shine with added luster, *just as Error, by force of contrast, enhances the triumph of Truth . . .*" (S, 113; 148, emphasis mine). Here is Elstir's fuller account.

> "There is no man," he began, "however wise, who has not at some period of his youth said things, or lived a life, the memory of which is so unpleasant to

32. Jealousy restricts this inquiry even more. Swann and Marcel seem limited in their ambition to knowing whether someone else is more important than or as important as whoever one is for the beloved. Their search seems limited to "how important" (or not) one is for the other, yet another indication of the narcissism of both.

33. I have mentioned that although there is no possible generalization to a Proustian theory of love, there are a number of other generalities at stake in the account of love and jealousy. Another is that Marcel's epistemological version of the problem of love is an inflection of the broadest theme in the novel discussed in the previous chapter: the attempt to escape subjectivity, while remaining a subject. As we saw, Marcel vacillates between a fantasy of merging with the world in a subject-less identity, and a worry that he can never reach any foreign "other," that he is trapped within his own subjectivity.

> him that he would gladly expunge it. And yet he ought not entirely to regret it, because he cannot be certain that he has indeed become a wise man—so far as it is possible for any of us to be wise—unless he has passed through all the fatuous or unwholesome incarnations by which that ultimate stage must be preceded. I know that there are young people, the sons and grandsons of distinguished men, whose masters have instilled into them nobility of mind and moral refinement from their schooldays. They may, perhaps, have nothing to retract from their past lives; they could publish a signed account of everything they have ever said or done; but they are poor creatures, feeble descendants of doctrinaires, and their wisdom is negative and sterile. We do not receive wisdom, we must discover it for ourselves, after a journey through the wilderness which no one else can take for us, which no one can spare us, for our wisdom is the point of view from which we come at last to regard the world." (JF, 605–6; 427)

So while there are few signs that Swann and Marcel have worked their way through error to truth (*per aspera, ad astra*), there are some.[34] Swann seems to have cured himself of his poisonous jealousy, or at least he stops pestering Odette about it, and he settles into a bourgeois daily life that he actually seems to enjoy. This former star of the Faubourg St. Germain set does not at all seem to mind that Odette's salon must start "at the bottom," and he praises his wife's brilliance and the glamour of her guests (like various low-level ministers) as if they were Guermantes, all with no hint of irony or condescension. He continues his endless affairs, but, in a telling scene, he realizes that he could, and used to plan to, wound Odette the way her past and perhaps recent past wounded him, and this by throwing in her face all his recent liaisons. But he does not; he has no wish to wound her and is quite solicitous.[35] And the very absence of any further reflection by Marcel on Albertine and her lesbian life in *Time Regained* indicates that he may have given up the goal of knowing for sure what she did, with whom she was, and so, we have suggested, what role he actually played in her life.

This can only be speculation at this point, but both seem to have realized that the knowledge of the other they sought, while an inevitable need, is not attainable as some momentous insight, the discovery of some truth-maker that resolves the question of who she is and who you are for her. That "discovery" model is a misconceived one, unsuitable in resolving any question

34. The most extensive treatment of this "method," truth through error, is provided in chaps. 12 through 16 in Descombes 1992.

35. "And he who, when he was suffering at the hands of Odette, so longed to let her see one day that he had fallen for another, now that he was in a position to do so took infinite precautions lest his wife should suspect the existence of this new love" (JF 134; 96).

we might have about the beloved.[36] Knowledge of the other is some sort of diachronic and interactive process, and it is interpretive, not matter of fact. Marcel seems to realize that knowing whom Albertine was with will not be satisfying, will not tell him what any episode meant to her, and thereby what he meant to her. Accordingly, there can never be the certainty they both seek in knowledge of the beloved. There just is no certainty in such a matter, no resolution, just continual, often fraught interpretive work, at some point requiring a large measure of trust.

There is a good hint about what knowing another person amounts to, knowing a subject, that is, not an object. Since the issue of knowing the other, knowing who one is for the other, is deeply connected to the problem raised in the preceding chapter, escaping subjectivity while remaining a subject, it is appropriate that we are led back to Marcel's encounter with the late work of Vinteuil, in particular the septet he hears. He thinks the music convinces him, given the distinctiveness of the style, that the "individual did exist," despite the evidence of "the sciences," and could serve as a kind of "proof of the irreducible individual existence of the soul" (P, 34; 245). He knows Vinteuil by knowing this style, or what he calls the "accent" that is Vinteuil, all as others would know him. As the passage makes extensively clear, realizing this is only the first step in trying to understand what the accent or style amounts to, just what it tells him musically. (The temporal dimension of music, being able to "follow it" successfully in time, is also obviously relevant to getting it all right.) And again, such interpretive work is not terminable, just as what it would be to know Albertine or even himself would not be. Perhaps we are called back to the image of Golo projected by the magic lantern over everything, "accenting" everything with that distinct but shifting "color," the self as a form of a world, but never an object in it like all others.

36. So this is not a "skepticism about other minds" issue. That problem is based on the punctuated discovery model, either perceiving the other's inner life, or inferring what it must be. That form of skepticism is an essentially seventeenth-century version, arising when a modern view of the body inspired the anxiety that it was a brute barrier to knowledge of the other's mind, the immaterial mental. In Proust's version, knowledge of the other is interpretive and, given the nature of the object, the self, necessarily diachronic, not punctual. The problem here is not mainly the body but falseness, inauthenticity, self-deceit, as barriers. Proust's version of skepticism is eighteenth-century, in other words, inspired by Diderot and Rousseau, not Descartes. (This places the issue outside the realm Cavell made famous as the modern problem of skepticism. His is a seventeenth-century version too.)

12

The Paradoxes of Power in the Early Novels of J. M. Coetzee

Quiconque est maître ne peut être libre; et régner, c'est obéir.

MONTAIGNE, *Lettres*

The Problem of Power

Any human social world is obviously finite, limited in resources and space, and it comprises agents whose pursuit of individual ends unavoidably must limit what others would otherwise be able to do, often directly conflicting with such other pursuits. This situation forces the issue of power: who will be subject to whose will, who will subject whom. But these individual agents are finite as well, unable to achieve most of their ends without forms of cooperation and dependence. The biology of human development insures a profound familial dependence throughout childhood, and the variety and breadth of the distribution of human talent and the frailty and vulnerability of human life all ensure that various forms of social dependence will be impossible to avoid. So it has long been acknowledged that a human society is deeply conflictual and competitive, as well as necessarily cooperative and communal.[1] Our nature ensures a constant tension between a self-regarding desire for independence and freedom from subjection to the will of other self-regarding agents and a powerful need to achieve some stable form of dependence and relative trust. The major, though not at all exclusive, area where solutions to

1. The thought expressed in this chapter's epigraph is not unique to Montaigne, or to Hegel, for that matter. Compare: "Tel se croit le maître des autres, qui ne laisse pas d'être plus esclave qu'eux" (Rousseau 1964, 353). And J. M. Coetzee: "In a society of masters and slaves, no one is free" ("Jerusalem Prize Acceptance Speech," in Coetzee 1992a, 96).

Abbreviations used:

W: *Waiting for the Barbarians* (Coetzee 1980)
D: *Dusklands* (Coetzee 1974)
H: *In the Heart of the Country* (Coetzee 1976)

this basic problem are proposed and tried out is commonly known as the political.

Even if we presuppose a great deal of agreement at some time within some community about the proper form of the political (already a great idealization), we cannot ever be sure of the trustworthy compliance of everyone with the basic rules and procedures. So all political life involves the use of violence and the coercive threat of violence by one group of people against another. The claim that there *is* such a thing as political life amounts to the claim that, while there is such violence and coercion, its exercise is legitimate, that power may be justifiably exercised over those who may in fact resist such an exercise. Those, like Marx and Nietzsche, who reject the idea that there really is such a thing as politics deny this claim and so argue that what some call political power is just a disguised version of the exercise of violence by one group against another or by one type against another. According to some versions of such a critique, like Alexandre Kojève's, there never are rulers and subjects, representatives and citizens, never even "human beings" as such. Until the final bloody revolution ensures classlessness, there are always and everywhere only masters and slaves, those who subject the will of others to their own, and those whose will is subject to the will of others.[2]

Those who defend the claim to the legitimacy of politics argue in familiar ways. An ancient claim is that no true human excellence may be achieved without hierarchical relations of power, that without such coercive constraint, the baser instincts of human beings would reign and nothing worthwhile could be collectively achieved. Such baser passions, it is claimed, are not subject to persuasion or argument, and there are some human beings in whom such passions are paramount. These people (sometimes said to be most people) must be constrained "from above" just as any one individual's passion must be ruled, rather than allowed to rule. The appeal to this sort of argument in the project of European colonialism (and the long history of male exercise of power over "naturally inferior" or "emotional" or "irrational" women) has understandably made it difficult for any such possible claim to be entertained now without the suspicion that it must be an apology for the brute exercise of self-interested power, masquerading in the form of such an argument. In "postcolonialism," we are much more suspicious that anyone is ever free of such putatively tyrannical passions, so the "natural rulers" always present the same danger as the "naturally ruled," and that what looks base and nearly inhuman to one might look perfectly fine to another.

2. Kojève 1969.

One might argue that everyone would simply be better off under some system of political rule, perhaps better off with respect to necessary common goods that no one could reasonably reject, perhaps better off merely by avoiding a state of such anarchy that no sane person could reasonably prefer it. Those inclined to think this way often think that even if there are a few who are very, very much better off, a coercive use of violence to preserve such an order is acceptable if everyone is at least better off than they would be otherwise. This kind of argument has its colonial echoes too. ("Yes, we got fabulously wealthy, but we 'gave' them the gift of English, or French schools, or developed industrial societies. Think how much better off they are.")[3] Or one might argue that what appears to be coercion really isn't, that *injuria non fit volenti*, no injury can be done to the willing, and everyone can be presumed to have reasonably consented to such an arrangement or would consent if they were rational agents. On an extension of this approach one could argue that the use of force to protect basic human rights is not only permissible but required, that no claim for the existence of such rights would be coherent unless measures, even violent and coercive measures, could be taken to protect and enforce them. There is no loss of freedom when one is constrained from doing what one may not do or is compelled to perform what is a universal and rational obligation.

This is all familiar and proceeds as classical and modern political philosophies always have: by assuming that the question of the legitimacy (or the goodness or value) of some form of rule involves a search for a rationale, a demonstration by force of the better case, an argument in favor of some arrangement of power and against some others, all in the service of resolving the original tension noted at the outset. But I have sketched this set of issues in its abstract form in order to stress that these familiar ways of looking at the issue *are* abstract. In order for philosophy to get a grip on the core problem of dependence and independence, a great abstraction must be made from, let us say, the complex psychological stake that individuals have in achieving and maintaining independence and the ways they come to care about and understand their varieties of mutual dependence. Of course some of this might inevitably have something to do with what can be rationally defended, justified without reliance on particular interest or bias. We can certainly come to care about such a standard a great deal and base a great deal on it. But there is no a priori reason to think that such a consideration always and everywhere

3. Even at the end of his horrific ordeal, the Magistrate in *Waiting for the Barbarians* can still rehearse for himself this sort of justification. See his remarks on "mulberry jam, bread and gooseberry jam" (W 151).

trumps other ways of mattering, other stakes and investments, and there is no reason to think that we could ever agree on what counts as the actualization of such a standard. Its persuasive trumping power might be illusory, might stem simply from abstractness. To add to the problem, these different ways of caring and kinds of investments vary a great deal across different communities and across historical epochs.

And all of this makes philosophical abstraction both understandable and problematic. One wants some view of the resolution of this tension or problem that can be *shared*, and there is no reason to believe that one's particular investment or the way things happen to matter to one (or to one's group) will or can be shared. The assumption of a rational standpoint, entertaining considerations that rely on no particular point of view, would appear the only way to proceed.

But this comes at a high price. Since no one actually occupies such a rational standpoint (it is artificial, a fiction for the sake of argument), it is unclear what it can affect for finite, concrete agents. We cannot simply assume that, no matter their particular attachments and investments (parents, children, group, status, the motherland, God), people care *more* about what reason demands: the greatest good for the greatest number, what form of law is consistent with pure practical reason, the supreme importance of avoiding the state of nature, what they must be assumed to have consented to, and so forth. None of these considerations have any obvious or inherent psychological actuality, and it seems absurd to wave away such a concern with actuality as a matter of mere "irrationality" that cannot concern philosophers. That approach threatens to turn political philosophy into a mere game, operating under initial abstraction conditions so extreme that they allow such philosophical abstractions no actual role in political life other than as "ideals" that we might hope to approach asymptotically, if even that. Indeed, an insistence on the putative purity of such ideal considerations—the claim that the philosophical cogency of an argument form is one, wholly distinct thing, its possible application in a colonial project another—is just what inspires suspicions that the argument form itself is mere "ideology."[4] What can be said about such a situation?

4. Cf. The self-understanding of Eugene Dawn (the representative of American self-understanding about the Vietnam war) in *Dusklands*: "I am the embodiment of the patient struggle of the intellect against blood and anarchy" (D, 27). Or, in the second half, the "explorer" and elephant hunter Jacobus Coetzee: "I am a tool in the hands of history" (D, 106). As Coetzee points out in another context (an interview), it is an important, not a marginal fact that "British liberalism failed to engender equal and reciprocal relations, period—failed to persuade the colonists, British or Dutch, that equal and reciprocal relations were a good enough thing to make

Power Psychology

Hegel is the most prominent philosopher to argue that "philosophy is its own time comprehended in thought," and he argued for this with an elaborate theory about the necessarily historical and experiential content of normative principles and ideals, especially, in his own historical period, the ideal of a free life. His insistence that philosophy must attend to the actuality of the norms it considers is quite controversial, and he is often accused of accommodating the status quo, forming a "might makes right" theory of history, and abandoning philosophy's critical and reflective task. This is no place to begin to consider such a theory. I mention it only to introduce one important aspect of Hegel's attempt to understand and come to terms with what a norm or ideal has come to mean, how it has come to matter as experienced by subjects who avow it, that is, his appeal in his 1807 *Phenomenology of Spirit* to Sophocles, Goethe, Jacobi, and Schiller, each representative of the literature of an age, as necessary moments of human self-knowledge about themselves and what they value.[5] He does treat such literature not as examples of an ideal or moral commitment or general norm but as criterial aspects of just *what it could be* to espouse or avow such a value or, more important in his account, for such a value to lose its grip on its adherents (something that rarely happens because of any dawning realization about the force of any better argument).

Although his novels are more informed by philosophy, especially by the work of Hegel and Nietzsche and Buber, and by a wider array of literary theory and criticism than those of anyone now writing, and although it is not clear whether his texts are novels or allegories or fables or parables or more generally just "fictions," J. M. Coetzee is obviously not a political philosopher, and novels in general do not in any normal sense express or defend claims about modern political life. Characters in novels are aesthetic constructs, and we "get to know them" in a way that is extraordinarily restricted and controlled, all in a context whose main values are aesthetic. And Coetzee's novels are complex modernist objects: verisimilitude is not the point, and the relation between text and psychological person, narrative and event, is complex,

---

sacrifices for" (Coetzee 1992a, 62). Again, one could always insist that the philosophical merits of "British liberalism" as a position have nothing at all to do with the fact that sincere adherents to such a view could espouse it while "contradicting" it in their colonizing practices. That seems to me an implausible position, but I won't try to argue against it here. One could sum up one central aspect of the problem in Magda's lament in *In the Heart of the Country*: "I am gagging on a diet of universals" (H, 131).

5. Hegel 2018.

dense, and often problematic. But almost all his novels,[6] and certainly the first three, take place in a recognizable historical world charged with explicitly political tension, profound dissension, and violent exercises of power justified by transparently self-serving or self-deceived appeals to reason or fact: the prosecution of the Vietnam war and the eighteenth-century "exploration" and colonization of Africa (*Dusklands*); a colonizer's life in the country and the relations of power between whites and blacks, men and women, colonizer and colonized (*In the Heart of the Country*); and a magistrate administering an outpost at the edges of empire and beginning to disintegrate psychologically under the realization of what he represents, with what he is unavoidably complicit, forced into such a realization by his intense relation with a young "barbarian" girl (*Waiting for the Barbarians*). Indeed, his first novels seem deliberately designed as an extended historical series on colonial political power and its psychological meaning, charting something like the experience or, one might say, the psychological truth of the imperial exercise of power in its founding moments: a moment of European moral exhaustion or ending, a *Götterdämmerung*, a land at dusk in *Dusklands*;[7] in the "heart" of the colonial experience of the eighteenth and nineteenth (and perhaps twentieth) centuries (*In the Heart of the Country*);[8] at the moment of empire's disintegration, potential revolution, and loss of faith in itself (*Waiting for the Barbarians*); and in the historical chaos of civil war in some distant future (*The Life and Times of Michael K*). After this series most of the novels have a more determinate historical place and time (the recent Jesus trilogy being an obvious exception), although there are obviously mythological and allegorical connections for the first series of books. (There is London in the eighteenth century for *Foe*, Cape Town in the 1980s for *Age of Iron*, Petersburg in the nineteenth century for *The Master of Petersburg*, Cape Town and its provinces in the late 1990s for *Disgrace*, and contemporary settings all over the world for the Elizabeth Costello stories and those novels that have followed, some set in Australia.)

In the spirit of the above remarks about the importance of finding a way to understand the "actuality"—experiential, psychological, and historical—of

6. I'll call them novels for convenience's sake. He came to prefer the term "fictions."

7. The "New Life" project, a Vietnam report, in the novel's first half is being written by Eugene Dawn, suggesting by contrast with the novel's title (and the standard characterization of the West as an evening land, *Abendland*) a pretense at a new beginning, dawn not dusk, or essentially the promise of technological, capitalist modernity. Cf. Dawn's remark about "poignant regret" (D, 6).

8. The time frame of the narrative in *In the Heart of the Country* is difficult to pin down. It seems, fantastically, to range from an early-modern farming economy to the age of airplanes.

various ideals and norms, especially political ones, especially the tension and so the need to find some equipoise between the desire for some sort of independence and the deep dependencies among human beings, and with the somewhat fanciful suggestion of Hegel as a model, I want to suggest that Coetzee's novels represent unique, brilliant attempts at a kind of political self-knowledge. The subject of the exploration is the psychological actuality of power, especially the exercise of power over another and even over nature and oneself, and the question asked is not directly about the legitimacy or overall defensibility of such an exercise, at least in the standard philosophical sense. For one thing, the issue of power is always tied to a deeper one in the novels. In modern philosophy we typically link the question of the possibility of agency or subjectivity itself with the exercise of power, either a causal power of initiating bodily movements ("spontaneity") or the general power to achieve one's ends in a world constrained by others' pursuits.[9] So this issue is not limited to a question of politics (of power exercised in the name of the common, the public, the state), although the core problem is the one discussed in the first section here: the right way to understand the relation between independence in a political or constrained, finite context (and so some sense that the life I lead is *my own*), and dependence, something like the proper acknowledgment of such dependence, without mere strategic compromises and certainly without subjection and conformism. Coetzee approaches these issues in an unusual and extremely rich way by means of a trope or figure that is common in his work.

The early novels are, to a large degree, concerned with forms of physical and psychological disintegration. This disintegration in physical and mental illness is in turn clearly linked with a Hegelian theme that Coetzee, in several interviews and essays, terms "reciprocity" or, more exactly, the failure of reciprocity—in explicitly Hegelian terms, the failure to achieve any mutuality of recognition and so the perpetuation of relations of master and servitude in some form (including in relations to nature and to oneself). The exercise of power in situations without reciprocity, situations of gross inequality, is clearly understood to be connected with a kind of illness or suffering that burdens the "master" in Coetzee's presentation of various versions of Hegel's famous "Lord and Bondsman" dialectic. The suggestion, or whatever one

9. Attwell's (1993) study focuses helpfully on the question of agency, especially in the South African political context. There is another take on the issue in Coetzee's later novels (*Slow Man* and *Diary of a Bad Year*): how to understand agency or subjectivity when the capacities or powers of agency begin to decline and erode, in late middle age and afterward (or when the balance between independence and dependence tips, but for nonpolitical, biological reasons).

wants to call it—what we are clearly supposed to appreciate—is that such an exercise of unequal power is in some way difficult to sustain psychologically, difficult at least with the smallest dawning of some self-consciousness, the difficulty escapable only with elaborate self-deceit or labored, deliberate ignorance. Eugene Dawn, trying to write a report about psychological warfare in Vietnam, goes mad and even injures his own beloved son. Jacobus Coetzee in the second half of *Dusklands*, even in his ignorance and willful blindness, becomes deathly ill and dependent on "one whom he does not recognize as a recognizer," one could say in Hegelese, his servant, Klawer. Magda in *In the Heart of the Country* begins as the spinster daughter of a brute colonial farmer. She loses that role and must establish a new one with the black servant Hendrik, and, in some way because she cannot establish anything reciprocal (neither can he, for that matter), she disintegrates into delusional madness. And the Magistrate in *Waiting for the Barbarians* loses hold of his own position and role once he is caught between, on the one hand, the dawning realization, provoked by the visiting brutal Colonel Joll, of just what empire he is administering, and, on the other, his being erotically and, one might say, morally captivated by a tortured barbarian girl. And so he begins to suffer a confusion and disorientation that finally place him well on the other side of the representatives of power he was once part of, finally suffering as their tortured victim.

Coetzee is often termed a bleak, uncompromising dystopian novelist who belongs with Beckett, Musil, Kafka, and other modernist, experimental writers, and in a literary sense, this is obviously the case (although it needs to be immediately qualified). Or he is considered a stern moralist, contemptuous and dismissive of the failings of meat eaters and the compromising, bet-hedging bourgeoisie (far too crude a characterization). But these repeated moments of disintegration suggest something about the internally *self*-defeating exercise of unequal power that is not a moralistic critique but an "internal" one, one that does not presuppose at all a settled moral position brought to bear on the characters from an independent or external point of view. And the suggestion that there is a form of suffering, perhaps (eventually) existentially unsustainable, or that there is a form of self-disintegrating suffering, is a much more complicated view than the stereotypical characterizations would suggest.[10] This

10. So, with respect to the moral issue he has lately been most associated with, our treatment of animals, Coetzee's modernist sensibilities require him to attend to the way this treatment is written and thought about, how it is theorized, mediated through language and experience. So Coetzee does not give lectures about animal rights, but tells Elizabeth Costello's stories/fables. (*The Lives of Animals* is, somewhat ironically, all about *our* lives; we are the animals at issue,

is all certainly linked to similar themes in modernist and postmodernist writing, especially in opposition to the pretense of autonomous subjectivity and authorial independence and related assumptions about the transparency and referentiality of language and the possibility of narrative and so the nature of historical time. In Coetzee, however, these issues are driven not by reflections on language itself, by evocations of the power of the unconscious, or by skepticism about referentiality or even meaning but by a link between a kind of political and a kind of psychological breakdown or failure, a failure that has to imply a possible if limited recovery and success. In some way, it is (in that contemporary modernist and postmodernist context) an unusual expression of hope. At any rate, this is what I would like to understand in what follows.

Dawn and Dusk

Dusklands begins with an epigraph, a quotation from Herman Kahn taken from an actual report written in 1968 by the Hudson Institute, a discussion by several authors, including Kahn, called *Can We Win in Vietnam? The American Dilemma*. Kahn noted the understandable revulsion with which European and American audiences had reacted to scenes of American pilots "exhilarated" by their success in napalm bombing runs, but Kahn then coolly pointed out that "it is unreasonable to expect the U.S. government to obtain pilots who are so appalled by the damage they may be doing that they cannot carry out their missions or become excessively depressed or guilt-ridden." The words "unreasonable" and "excessively" stand out in this attempt to adopt some sort of wholly analytic or objective attitude toward the moral issues involved, as if those issues could be discussed from some wholly third-person and exclusively strategic point of view. *Dusklands* itself is a parody of such a stance and related attitudes, a parody of the presumptions of such a scientific analysis, and, in the second half, a parody of the pretensions of documentary history, of the way first-person reportage comes to be incorporated in what pretends to be the objective historical record. (Kahn's "argument" is almost a parody of itself, as if an argument for the need to hire only sociopaths as pilots.) Both pretensions are also clearly intended to be connected with the kind of general stance or attitude that could make possible the project of a modern neocolonial war like Vietnam, or the original British and Dutch subjection and colonization of South Africa. Presenting the two documents together in one

given what we do to other animals.) So, again, the concern is for what such treatment is doing to us, and it would be grossly inaccurate to read his fables about such themes as moral tracts, simply presented in a narrative way. The same holds for the political novels.

book, with no explanation or connection between them, suggests both a kind of mythic, repetitive, or circular time (as opposed to any linear or progressive history) and thereby an underlying, perhaps archetypal psychological pattern implicated in the extreme violence manifest in both accounts.

That stance, to return to the set of issues I have introduced, is the presumption of mastery, self-sufficiency, or autonomy, and the two aspects of this attitude of interest here are the kind of difficulties encountered in sustaining that stance and what the failure to sustain it implies about some redemption or reconciliation, and ultimately a world of genuine reciprocity. Eugene Dawn has been assigned to write an assessment of the psychological aspects of the US propaganda campaign in the war, and it is the writing of the report that seems to drive him mad. We read the first half of Eugene Dawn's report itself in numbered sections in part 2, but the majority of what we read are his scattered, disjointed remarks about the act of writing it, his understanding of what it is to try to provide an account of the mythological meaning of the propaganda war, and eventually what led him to give up on such a project. (Given all the self-thematization of writing itself, one understandably sometimes hears Coetzee's fiction characterized as "metafiction.") Dawn's supervisor is a man named Coetzee, an expert in game theory whom Dawn mistrusts, and with reason.[11] We learn later that Coetzee deleted and destroyed Dawn's reflections on mythology. Dawn argues that the "self" embodied in US propaganda has been too much a "Cartesian" self, divided against itself, skeptical and self-doubting, too rational, too distanced from itself. He proposes an approach more in tune with traditional Vietnamese folk society, a division of labor in which our Vietnamese allies adopt a "fraternal" role, and we a "paternal" or sky-god voice, striking fear into the rebellious band of sons according to the basic script provided by the (not named) Freudian account in *Totem and Taboo*. But Dawn realizes that such a posture is also self-defeating: "For one thing, the myth of rebellion has a no-surrender clause. Punishment for falling into a father's hands is to be

11. This Coetzee is one of four in Dusklands. There is also Jacobus Coetzee, the eighteenth-century elephant hunter whose report of his adventures is the main text of the second half. (Jacobus is in fact a "remote ancestor" of the historical author, I mean, the real J. M. Coetzee. See "Remembering Texas," in Coetzee 1992a, 52.) Then there is Dr. S. J. Coetzee, who is said to have published an edition and introduction of that report in 1951, and his son, named as "J. M. Coetzee," who presents himself as the translator of that edition. I suppose one has to say that there are five Coetzees, if we make the obvious distinction between this character, J. M. Coetzee, and J. M. Coetzee, the actual historical novelist who taught in Cape Town and at the Committee on Social Thought in Chicago and who lives now in Adelaide. The names introduce issues of inheritance, complicity, and the historicity of an author that would require a substantial independent discussion.

eaten alive or penned eternally in a volcano" (D, 25). The myth, that is, hardly encourages surrender or compromise. But, more important, Dawn comes to realize that the whole notion of a mythic approach to propaganda presupposes a stance toward the world and others that "history" has already "outdated": "The myth of rebellion assumes that heaven and earth, father and mother, live in symbiosis. Neither can exist alone. If the father is overthrown, there must be a new father, new rebellion, endless violence, while no matter how deep her treachery toward her mate, the mother may not be annihilated. The scheming of mothers and sons is thus endless" (D, 26).

Dawn goes on to suggest that it is this presumption of symbiosis (or the acknowledgment of any form of deep dependence) that has become outdated, that "we live no longer by tilling the earth but by devouring her and her waste products" (D, 26). Given that this is so, "When the earth conspires incestuously with her sons should our recourse not be to the goddess of techne who springs from our brains?" (D, 26). So Dawn loses any sense that his report and the approach it embodies any longer make any sense; his text in part 2 in effect deconstructs itself. It is a useless "Phase IV." The *next* phase is all that matters and we should get on with it, Phase V, total victory, an open and merciless bombing campaign (perhaps what was famously known at the time as Curtis LeMay's plan—that we bomb the Vietnamese "back into the stone age"), defeating at once both the enemy and the pretense that there is or can be any great question of the "meaning" of what is being done.

The suggestion of a voracious, devouring predatory subject, flattening any question about meaning and value into the questions of human survival, comfort, and the power to effect one's will echoes with Horkheimer and Adorno's *Dialectic of Enlightenment* and its charge that the Enlightenment attempt to reject myth has turned into its own unreflective myth of absolute self-sufficient power and the total negation of nature, with Marcuse's analysis in *One-Dimensional Man*, and, of course, with Heidegger's attempt to show that the late-modern reliance on technology does not just create technical problems and is not the mere application of a tool but has fundamentally altered our sense of ourselves, our sense of Being itself, so that we have come to live comfortably with a thoughtlessness and forgetfulness so complete it may become final and unredeemable. But as noted throughout, the interesting twist on these issues given by Coetzee is what the embodiment of such a stance comes to mean psychologically for Eugene Dawn.

Dawn comes to understand what the war reveals about "who we have become" as that stance is embodied in three horrific photographs of abuse and violence against Vietnamese people that he carries around with him almost as totems. His realization of his part in it all, even as he (like Kurtz in *Heart of Darkness*) begins encouraging a war of complete annihilation ("Kill them all!"), drives him mad. His paranoia grows; he kidnaps his own son, and when tracked down and confronted by the authorities, impulsively stabs his boy and is captured and confined to a mental hospital. There Dawn adopts a kind of therapeutic, almost third-personal attitude about what he has done, and while generally agreeing with his therapists that it wasn't "him" who stabbed his son and rejecting any guilt, he remains baffled by what he has done. He ends by saying, "I have high hopes of finding whose fault I am" (D, 49).

Clearly Coetzee is associating the political, national subjection of others both with classical mythological meaning (even as Dawn is coming to reject the relevance of this association) and with modern strategic calculations of self-interest, but he is also suggesting that there is something qualitatively different and potentially more inhumane and blind to itself in modern assertions of imperial power. For one thing, such a modern exercise seems associated with a much broader assertion of absolute mastery over oneself and over nature, a presumption that is wholly unchecked by any modesty or humility; it is associated with a worldview, or a form of life itself. At this level of meaning, the concern is not beliefs or principles but a broad, pervasive, and much deeper prereflective orientation that is difficult to view as a whole. For Dawn and the people he works for, in a postmetaphysical or scientific age all that is "other" than the self and human will is merely stuff, obstacle, material, chaos, and dangerous contingency to be mastered. There is pure will and obstacles to the realization of will, and that is all. Potential patterns of meaning and perhaps purpose arise only as possibly strategically useful illusions in a propaganda war, and even in that sense are pronounced "outdated!" The allegorical dimension of Dawn's fate at the end, as a kind of culmination of such a way of being-in-the-world, embodies our own fate: self-reflection and self-knowledge severely limited to a kind of inquiry into causes, as if we don't *do* anything but are mere elements in a causal series. And even with such a reduction and flattening, we get no real answers. We are doing all this over historical time to ourselves—destroying or injuring, like Eugene, our own children, in effect, as well as ourselves and the earth—and we have no idea why. Given what we have come to think counts as genuine knowledge—predictability and control—and the unsuitability of such a model for self-knowledge, this is no surprise.[12] So such independence and autonomy are

12. From the agent's point of view, any "prediction" I make about what I will do is either an avowal, a practical pledge that I will do it (in which case it is not a prediction), or it has to count as a paradoxical (and usually cowardly and self-deceived) denial of one's own agency, something one can do only qua agent.

bought at a high price. We end up with the same sort of stupefied wonder as Eugene in the end, wondering if we can ever discover "whose fault we are." One thinks of Nietzsche's "last men," who have invented happiness and merely "blink" in a similar state of stupefaction.

The question of self-knowledge is foregrounded by a number of literary details that have been much discussed. The document itself is supposed to be the product of Eugene's reflections, his attempt at self-knowledge, and its paranoid, chaotic form is in some way connected with the profoundly monologic, controlling, unyielding character of his voice, a stance that itself embodies the insistence on mastery and control typical of the prosecution of the war, the larger "metaphysical" (for want of a better word) theme of human subjectivity itself (as, essentially, effective power). Dawn recounts few dialogues; nothing "gets through" his own projections and fantasies. His musings about his wife, Marilyn, give us no sense at all of her except as an object of his fantasy and paranoia. The question of who is the "real" author of the document, what role his supervisor "Coetzee" might have played in its current form, what it means for Eugene to worry about "getting it past Coetzee," and the relation of all this to the historical author, J. M. Coetzee, further warn us, at the least, not to take any representation of self-knowledge and self-mastery at face value, even the relation between author and his creations.

This ambiguity is extended in the novel's second half in the flurry of "Coetzees" we have to disentangle, given the four documents that make up the texts concerning Jacobus Coetzee's so-called explorations in the eighteenth century.[13] Self-opacity or self-blindness is not the only implication of the modern conception of subjectivity; the second half of *Dusklands* deals with another. The main document is the narrative written by Jacobus Coetzee of his trip deep into the "land of the great Namaqua." This recounts Coetzee's "detention" of sorts (as he sees it)[14] by Namaquas he calls "Hottentots"; the desertion of some of his crew; his illness, delirium, and slow recovery, during

13. To repeat: there is (1) the text presented as written by Jacobus Coetzee. That text is presented as if (2) in an edition by Dr. S. J. Coetzee, published in 1951, with an introduction by him, and now (3) in a translation done by Dr. S. J. Coetzee's son, who is called J. M. Coetzee. And (4) there is a ludicrously sanitized "official" deposition by Jacobus Coetzee written in 1760.

14. Perhaps the ultimate humiliation of Jacobus, in his narcissistic fantasies of mastery, is that the Namaquas do not torment or torture or take much advantage of him. For the most part, to his unacknowledged shame, they ignore him. Or at least they do until Jacobus does something outrageous, almost as if to make his presence felt. He bites off the ear of a child during a tussle, and so they expel him. Jacobus's self-absorption is as extreme as Dawn's, but more physically embodied. He becomes intensely preoccupied with a carbuncle near his anus until he is able to lance it. See the Lacanian discussion by Dovey 1988, 67–148.

which he is taken care of by his oldest servant, Klawer; their journey back, during which Klawer is killed; and then a horrific second journey of revenge when Coetzee returns and massacres his former tormentors. The voice that we hear in this narrative is full of arrogance, racism, self-satisfaction, and phony, self-deceived humanistic concern for his servant, and a nearly mad sense of his own significance and fury at perceived slights. And the unreliability of the narrative is again stressed. Coetzee narrates incidents, the death of Klawer, for example, that are then contradicted by other incidents, such as Klawer's reappearance in the narrative only to die again, all of which makes us wonder what, if anything, really did happen to Klawer. But there is one point at which another implication of this picture of predatory subjectivity is stressed.

Jacobus Coetzee becomes lyrically articulate about just this issue. He imagines himself a modern, separate, spectatorial master subject, and then by an internal poetic logic, imagines what that means: "I become a spherical reflecting eye moving through the wilderness and ingesting it. Destroyer of the wilderness, I move through the land cutting a devouring path from horizon to horizon. There is nothing from which my eye turns, I am all that I see. Such loneliness! Not a stone, not a bush, not a wretched provident ant that is not comprehended in this traveling sphere. What is there that is not me? I am a transparent sac with a black core full of images and a gun" (D, 79). Coetzee eventually calls this the "metaphysics" of the gun: a subject conceived not as an embodied, desiring, vulnerable, and especially dependent being but a supreme eye, a transparent sac, its world locked away inside it as a core of images, a Cartesian subject locked up inside itself and therefore unable to reassure itself about its claims about the world or its position in the world without a violent assault on nature and others to realize its mere ideas. Colonialism is seen as the extension of this idea of the self-sufficient and masterful self, and its assertion (since the acknowledgment of dependence is rejected) can count as successful only by this test of power. But in the human or, as I am using the word, psychological dimension, this project must result, above all, in a position necessarily and irredeemably *lonely*: trapped by being so successful in denying and negating all dependence-making otherness, such a subject has a voice that is not just monological but monomaniacal, the modern voice still echoing with Descartes's original promise to make us "masters and possessors of nature," to create technical power that will "enable us to enjoy without any trouble the fruits of the earth"[15] and so reverse the fate decreed for human beings in Genesis 3:19 that they must forever toil by the sweat of their brow. The burden of

15. Descartes 1965, 119.

such a project is not just the epistemological skepticism and potential subjective idealism of this Cartesian stance but a cost perhaps manifest only in a novel like Coetzee's, a cost realized by Jacobus in a flash: "such loneliness!"

Independence as Loneliness

Extreme loneliness, extreme to the point of being a kind of ontological burden, the burden of a *failed self* (the way we speak now of a failed state), is most prominent in Magda's suffering in *In the Heart of the Country*. That is, in such a state, a human subject can continue to exist in some form but only as failed, not what a self or state truly is. In the former case, this is because a self is not an object in the standard sense and cannot be apprehended by observation or introspection. To be a self, I must take myself to be who I am in some determinate way or other. And *I am* who I take myself to be. A self is thus self-constituting. But this also means, in the most obvious sense, that I can take myself to be some subject in a way that is not acknowledged, affirmed, or perhaps even noticed in my social world, and in that sense would have to be counted a failed self, living a mere fantasy of self-identity. Without such reciprocal gestures as acknowledgment, love, esteem, solidarity, and respect, I cannot distinguish between who I really am and who I merely imagine myself to be. And this is the language of failure and reciprocity that Coetzee himself frequently uses in his essays and some speeches.[16]

So Magda says at one point, "Drowning, I drown into myself" (H, 54). And the result: "For I seem to exist more and more intermittently. Whole hours,

16. This is the language (the failure of selfhood) used by Coetzee in his essay on Achterberg in *Doubling the Point* (1992a). Here is a particularly illuminating passage: "The hide-and-seek I in Sterne has become a serious game, with dangers to the psyche, in Eliot's 'Love Song of J. Alfred Prufrock.' What has intervened has been the rise and decline of the romantic-liberal notion of the self. The self in Eliot is struggling with problems of authentic being. The self in Beckett is struggling with problems of being at all, unable to get from Descartes's cogito to Descartes's sum. I hint so skimpily at an entire history because I intend no more than to point to what lies behind the metamorphosis of fiction from the adventures of the self in nineteenth-century classical realism to the metafictional commentary on the fictionality of self that precipitates such fictions as Nabokov's *Pale Fire* and Barth's *Lost in the Funhouse* and that forms the whole of Beckett's *The Unnamable*. The poetics of these works is a veritable poetics of failure, a program for constructing artifacts out of an endlessly regressive, etiolated self-consciousness lost in the labyrinth of language and endlessly failing to erect itself into autonomy" (86–87). I think *In the Heart of the Country* and the character of Magda represent such a "poetics of failure" in just this sense, with the difference being that such failure is intelligible in terms of what might have been; that is, in terms of what Coetzee refers to as "reciprocity." See also his Jerusalem Prize speech: "At the heart of the unfreedom of the hereditary masters of South Africa is a failure of love" (97).

whole afternoons go missing. I seem to have grown impatient with the sluggish flow of time" (H, 80). The form of the suffering and its meaning are often given a recognizably Hegelian characterization. It is a burden brought on by the lack of reciprocity or any mutuality of recognition. She says, "I was born into a language of hierarchy, of distance and perspective. It was my father tongue. I do not say it is the language my heart wants to speak, I feel too much the pathos of its distances, but it is all we have" (H, 97). The striking phrase "the pathos of its distance" is from Nietzsche's *On the Genealogy of Morals* and suggests in quite a compressed way something that arises only indirectly in Nietzsche's account of and apparent enthusiasm for "master morality."[17] It is the isolation and loneliness, the complete lack of reassurance and acknowledgment, that results from the master's indifference to those whom his willing affects. (Nietzsche's frequent, though not thematized, expressions of his own loneliness certainly have something to do with such a pathos, whether knowingly or not.) Magda, the only child of a coarse colonial farmer at an isolated farm,[18] says at the beginning, "I create myself in the words that create me, I, who living among the downcast have never beheld myself in the equal regard of another's eye, have never held another in the equal regard of mine" (H 8). Elsewhere she says, "It is not speech that makes man man, but the speech of others" (H 126).

The dense dialectical first phrase in the first quotation, "I create myself in the words that create *me*," poses an ontological problem (what is it to be a self, a subject of one's life, an agent?) that is immediately given a quite modern, romantic meaning ("I create myself") and then a social dimension in the rest of the sentence and the book, as if proposing a social ontology. The self fashions itself and is also itself fashioned in a social world.[19] Such a subject is never the pure or absolute subject dreamed of in much of modernity, autonomously decreeing what its word and actions mean. It is dependent not just on the social conventions of language but on the various ways meaning and significance are

17. Nietzsche 2007, 11.

18. On the conventions of the South African farm novel and its relevance to the setting of *In the Heart of the Country*, see Coetzee's essay "Farm Novel and *Plaasroman*," in Coetzee 1997, and the interesting discussion in Head 1997, 59.

19. In *Doubling the Point*, see Coetzee's essay, "Achterberg's 'Ballade van de gasfitter,'" and his remark in the commentary, "All versions of the I are fictions of the I. The primal I is not recoverable" (Coetzee 1992a, 75). One might argue that if these versions are fictions, there must be something, some I, they are false to. But the denial of any "primal I" means that what gives a fictive I a kind of stability, what redeems it from mere fictionality, is its future, not a relation to a past primal I, and that future is its engagement with and acknowledgment by, and so realization by, others. See also the remarks on Buber and the I-Thou relation on the previous page, 74, and the illuminating discussion by Attwell 1993, 35–69.

always already established and inherited, and all this without mere subjection to the regard of others. (In that case we would lose the first half of the phrase, would lose any grip on the notion of "creating myself." As we shall see, in Magda's world, there is no effective social structure within which this balance can be worked out, and the forms of mastery and even, with Hendriks, her attempts [or imagined attempts] at abject subjection that she acts out are therefore deeply unsatisfying.) Such mutuality would allow me to see myself in the regard of another if and only if I regard that other as an equal. And this kind of language reappears several times. In a frequent image (one we already have seen in Jacobus Coetzee's account), a disembodied eye, *seeing but not being seen*, not allowing oneself to be seen, is often tied to Magda's extreme "solitude and vacancy" (H, 47); her relation to their servants is such that they might as well be on "separate planets' (H, 28). The solitude and sense of isolation is so extreme that it counts as itself a form of insanity. She says at one point, "Too much misery, too much solitude, makes of one an animal. I am losing all human perspective" (H, 53). And the social pathology of what she calls "the psychology of masters" (H, 33) is described in terms that sound like a quotation from Hegel's famous discussion of Lord and Bondsman in his *Phenomenology of Spirit*. Magda writes, supposedly of what she hears spoken by the sky gods in aircraft at the end of the book: "*It is the slave's consciousness that constitutes the master's certainty of his own truth. But the slave's consciousness* is *a dependent consciousness.* So *the master* is *not sure of the truth of his autonomy*. His *truth lies in an inessential consciousness and its inessential acts*"[20] (H, 130; italics in the original).

In the Heart of the Country is also the novel with the most elaborate modernist structure and so the most unreliable and often confusing narration. The diary or journal or whatever we are reading is in numbered paragraphs, emphasizing, Coetzee once noted, what is *missing*, discontinuous, in the narration.[21] The suggestion of gaps, that there is no way to make a narrative out of what we are reading, is only the beginning.[22] I noted earlier that it is difficult to pick an actual historical time for the events, since we seem to range from horse-and-buggy days to the airplane, perhaps even the jet age. Or at least Magda cannot locate herself. Her sense of her historical time seems dreamy,

20. Cf. also the Hegelian formulation at the end: "Was my father crucified by the paradox the voices expound: that from people who bent like reeds to his whims he was asking in his way for an affirmation of his truth in and for himself" (H, 130, my emphasis).

21. Coetzee 1992a, 59. Note especially his remarks about film and its relation to the novel with respect to the speed of narration.

22. Magda says that she wants "my story to have a beginning, a middle, and an end," and she fears she will live only in "the yawning middle without end" (H, 43). Later she says, "Lyric is my medium, not chronicle" (H, 71).

often fantastic. And the narrative is most untrustworthy. Her father is described bringing home a bride. But there is no bride. Magda describes how she axe-murders her father. Then he shows up again and she kills him again, this time with a rifle, to some extent accidentally. The father dies a slow, agonizing death. Hendrik either rapes her several times or one time imagined different ways or the whole thing is an archetypal colonial fantasy of Magda's. Suddenly Magda reports, "The voices speak to me out of machines that fly in the sky. They speak to me in Spanish" (H, 126). And Magda arranges stones in messages, trying to communicate in Spanish, a language she does not understand but finds "immediately comprehensible" (H, 126). Finally, at the end of the book, in paragraph 161, her father seems to reappear, infirm, blind, and old, cared for by Magda with some tenderness. The reader has no idea if this is some compensatory fantasy, or if it is true and Magda has only imagined the affair between her father and Hendrik's wife, imagined killing her father and the rape by Hendrik.

Such unreliability has sparked a lot of discussion about Coetzee's postmodernism and the relation between postmodernism and postcolonialism. This involves a number of large distinctions and labels. I need here to point out only that the unreliability of the narration is not tied in any obvious way to the unreliability of narration itself, but to *Magda's* position. It is her voice that is fractured, discontinuous; she is increasingly unsure of her own reality or of the distinction between reality and fantasy in what she narrates. Having lost confidence in any master narration, she has lost hold of all the norms for rendering intelligible what is happening to her. There is no alternative known to her to the language of power and domination, although she is suffering from the isolation and loneliness that such a "pathos of distance" creates and knows she is suffering from just that. (She resembles the Magistrate at the end of *Waiting for the Barbarians*, "like a man who lost his way long ago but presses on along a road that may lead nowhere" [W, 152].)

This crisis has occurred because to purport to narrate is to claim some sort of authority for the selection of and emphasis on the details one includes and for the claimed irrelevance of what one slights or ignores. And such implied claims to authority raise the same normative and psychological questions as colonial authority itself and can often be deeply linked with that sort of authority. (Recall Magda's complaint about being born into a *language* of hierarchy and distance.) Authority differs from mere power not simply by virtue of the fact that a philosophical argument can be provided justifying its exercise. It also has to have a psychological legitimacy in the eyes of those who administer and accept it, and the minimum condition for that sort of authority is missing in colonial power: some sort of reciprocity, without which no acknowledgment of genuine authority and so no psychological actuality can be possible. Absent that distinction, the claim to genuine authority is empty (compliance is forced not given, and coerced acknowledgment is not acknowledgment), and the one who exercises power sees himself reflected back to himself as other than what he takes himself to be. One might argue that there has been evidence for a long time in human history that such a situation is hardly "unendurable," that there are plenty who have endured it easily. Dawn's supervisor, Coetzee, Magda's father, and Colonel Joll do not seem racked with doubt about their authority. But one can pay a price without acknowledging it, and the sterility and unacknowledged loneliness of such lives count as a high price indeed.

It would be the start of a broad additional discussion to bring these issues to bear on how the question of putative or claimed authority and its true actualization plays out in the stance of J. M. Coetzee himself, the real historical author of all this, and his audience. But one suggestion would be to see the issue as an extension of this discussion. That is, Coetzee's complex presentation of the problem of his own authorship or even control over the meaning of his creation could be understood outside of what has become a fairly standard "postmodernist" way: as dissolving into mere play, toying with its own impossibility, finally being about only itself, not what it purports to be about, and revealing, if that is the right word, only the impossibility of revelation.[23] That is, the issue could be treated in the same way I have been treating Dawn's and Magda's self-narration. The problem with any form of confident assertions of authorial authority could be viewed much more historically and contextually, as a dilemma forced on us by the fractured and unreciprocal context of the writing itself and not "by writing" itself. (Modernism is a historical fate, not a literary and artistic experiment.) The incompleteness and gaps in the text would then be viewed as merely provisional, and much more like an invitation for completion by the work of the reader, completing what the isolation and loneliness caused by this arrangement of power have left hanging and unresolved. But, as noted, that is a much larger issue.[24]

23. See Coetzee's agreement that it is no part of his intention in *In the Heart of the Country* to "dissolve" the problems of selfhood and relationship "into postmodernist game-playing" (1992a, 60); Cantor (1994) makes a similar point (that the issue is not the "unrepresentability of reality" but "false representations" [103]), but he does not much develop it.

24. See Coetzee 1992a, 65: "There is a true sense in which writing is dialogic: a matter of awakening the countervoices in oneself and embarking upon speech with them." There is much of value in Derek Attridge's discussion on the "modalities of otherness," the relevance of modernist techniques in dealing with such modalities, the performative character of texts, and the "ethical demands" that all this raises. See Attridge 2004, 6.

In this context, Magda has some intimation of what it would be not to rely on such authority, on mere power, but no sense of how to realize that aspiration. (As we shall see in the next section, it is perhaps naive to think that such a recalibration of the struggle for recognition can be affected by individual moral gestures.) She tells Klein-Anna (Hendrik's young wife and the girl Magda's father compels to be his mistress), "I only wanted to talk, I have never learned to talk with another person. It has always been that the word has come down to me and I have passed it on. I have never known words of true exchange, Anna" (H, 101). And the consequence of this:

> I find her head and press my lips against her forehead. For a moment she struggles, then stiffens and endures me. We lie together, at odds, I waiting for her to fall asleep. She waiting for me to go.
>
> I grope my way out of the kitchen to my own bed. I am doing my best in this unfamiliar world of touch. (H, 103)

In spite of this confusion and awkwardness, Magda nevertheless has some fairly clear intuition of what would fill the gap in her life that she has come to experience: "Why will no one speak to me in the true language of the heart? The medium, the median—that is what I wanted to be! Neither master nor slave, neither parent nor child, but the bridge between, so that in me the contraries should be reconciled!" (H, 133).

The Meaning of Humanity

There is one last turn of this screw much in play in *Waiting for the Barbarians*, and I will conclude briefly just by noting the questions it raises.

The presence of the themes I have been considering is announced right away by the visiting Colonel Joll's sunglasses. We meet him immediately as a man who insists on seeing but in effect rejects being seen as a like-minded other. He hides his eyes, whereas the young barbarian girl is almost blind; she can be seen but can barely see, cannot return any gaze, even if the gaze is an invitation, not an attempted subjection. That is, Joll's one-sided stance is voluntary; hers is not. She has been made blind and lame by torture. At the end of the novel, after Joll's expedition results in catastrophic failure and his pretension to pure independent agency has been shattered, the sunglasses are gone, and the Magistrate forces on him the lesson of internal disintegration or self-undermining familiar in the other novels: "The crime that is latent in us we must inflict on ourselves . . . not on others" (W, 43). We also hear again of Nietzsche's "pathos of distance," this time, in ways the Magistrate feels but does not understand, distorting and diminishing his sexual pleasure with women (W, 45). And that disturbance, the consequences of that distance, are at the heart of what goes on between him and the girl.

For the Magistrate is clearly moved, touched by the girl's suffering, and clearly feels guilty at being part of the official apparatus of the empire that did this to her. He takes the girl in, and that is clearly intended to begin some act of expiation and penance. He washes the girl, cleans her feet, anoints her with oil, and sleeps with her, but they do not have sex. All this is not completely straightforward. He claims to want to understand her, to "decipher" what the marks of torture on her body mean, much as he tried to decipher what appear to be texts on slips of paper that he has found from an ancient barbarian culture. But he "reads" her *that* way, as a text. He thinks of himself as loving her (W, 74), but he makes no attempt to learn her language, to converse with her as a fellow subject. So his humanist intervention is a limited and confused one, and accordingly his failure to "reach" her cannot be simply read as an indictment of all liberal, humanist, moral gestures in the face of such oppression. But the frustrating limitations of such gestures (and the danger of self-congratulation in making them) are certainly at issue.

Of course, he does return her to her lands and countrymen, and this has catastrophic results for the Magistrate. He is branded a traitor and mercilessly tortured. But he never seems to understand what he actually intended with the girl and so does not understand why it all ended so unsatisfyingly for him, what his history with her amounted to. He does not seem to realize, except confusingly and in disconnected flashes, that in the world they inhabit, even gestures of pity and benevolence are inseparable from the relevant social positions both occupy and so are inseparably implicated in the relations of power firmly established in that world. A moment of such realization occurs when the girl, puzzled that the older man seems to have no sexual interest in her, offers herself and is rebuffed. The Magistrate writes, "Though my heart goes out to her, *there is nothing I can do*. Yet what humiliation for her! She cannot even leave the apartment without tottering and fumbling while she dresses. *She is as much a prisoner now as ever before*. I pat her hand and sink deeper into gloom" (W, 54, emphasis mine). Later, the Magistrate does not appear surprised when a confidante of the young girl reports to him, "She could not understand you. She did not know what you wanted from her. Sometimes she would cry and cry and cry. You made her very unhappy. Did you know that?" (W, 148).

And as with the other novels, this is not an issue that can be restricted to the question of the proper realization of political and institutionally secured egalitarianism, however relevant it is to that question and however important philosophical argument about that question is. There is a deeper form of dependence at work, and a different way of exploring its meaning, in Coetzee's novels. The issue has to do with how the possibility of individual, independent agency in itself, how *that* social status, can be actualized, made psychologically and socially real in the lives of finite subjects faced with the basic dilemma sketched at the beginning here. In the Magistrate's terms, the very "meaning of humanity" is the issue, and the Magistrate comes to realize in his own limited way how such a status must be socially achieved and sustained and how terribly fragile it is. It is not a status one has merely by showing up, and the complexity of the conditions for its achievement (the dialectical relation between independence and dependence) is everywhere apparent in these novels. Here are his reflections on the issue, and it will serve to indicate in one final way the great scope of this recognitional theme in Coetzee's work. It is a fitting closing comment on the deepest issue in the three early novels, the "meaning of humanity":

> They [his torturers] were interested only in demonstrating to me what it meant to live in a body, as a body, a body which can entertain notions of justice only as long as it is whole and well, which very soon forgets them when its head is gripped and a pipe is pushed down its gullet and pints of saltwater are poured into it till it coughs and retches and flails and voids itself. They did not come to force the story out of me of what I had said to the barbarians and what the barbarians had said to me. So I had no chance to throw the high-sounding words I had ready in their faces. They came to my cell to show me the meaning of humanity, and in the space of an hour they showed me a great deal. (W, 113)

13

Philosophical Fiction? On J. M. Coetzee's *Elizabeth Costello*

Philosophy and Fiction

I want to suggest a way of appreciating the achievement of J. M. Coetzee's book *Elizabeth Costello* and its eight "lessons." Given the nature of these lessons, this will make inevitable an attempt to understand the work in terms of what I have been exploring in this book as "philosophical fiction." In this, I take myself to be following the lead given us by the volume *Elizabeth Costello* itself, in which philosophy obviously plays a large role. The idea here and throughout this book has not been to show that fiction is philosophy. Of course it is not. *Elizabeth Costello* is literary fiction, even if a unique genre, not quite a short story collection, and certainly not a mere device for ventriloquizing philosophical claims. But the idea that fiction can be philosophical requires a defense of the claims at issue throughout these chapters: first, that fiction can be a distinctive form of thought, even a form of knowledge; and second, that such knowledge is relevant to, has a bearing on, the sort of knowledge philosophy, or at least some version of philosophy, tries to achieve. The bearing of fiction on philosophy is not that fiction is a form of philosophy. It has this bearing precisely because it is not. It has this bearing even, and especially, when what fiction achieves throws into some doubt the prospects for philosophy to achieve what it is trying to achieve.[1] The immediately problematic or paradoxical nature of this thought can be put into words by saying: if the idea is that fiction is "philosophy by other means," then the emphasis must first of all be on the phrase "*other* means." And that already threatens the claim that it can be philosophical. (How "other" can such means be, and still be means to philosophy?)

As a strictly theoretical question this leads us immediately to the notion of the form of literary fiction. Knowledge is knowledge by being of some

1. As in the discussion of tragedy in chapter 2.

generality, and generality is formal. It involves extending to many instances. This problem is dual. It concerns the distinctive form of all literary thought, as contrasted, say, with forms like mathematical thought. And it concerns the specific content of any fictional insight. If a drama can be philosophical, then, say, the play *Othello* cannot be about, be a way of understanding, Othello's jealousy without also being about, showing us something about, jealousy in general.

One possibility that we have seen throughout: that the form of literary and indeed all artistic knowledge is a form of self-knowledge. This would not be of much interest if it referred to the writer's own self-knowledge as a psychological individual, the revelation of her motivations or even intentions, for example. The scope of the knowledge would also not be very wide if it covered only the undeniable reflexive knowledge embodied in the artwork as artwork. Any artwork realizes (or attempts to realize) a notion of itself, whether this was explicitly attended to by the artist or not. The more ambitious claim is that the artwork, in this case, fiction, also realizes a form of collective self-knowledge of a community at a historical time, that this knowledge has a bearing on what philosophy attempts, and in a way unavailable to philosophy. This is especially so when the attempt at self-knowledge—in which "what has happened to us?" is everywhere imbricated in "what has happened to me?"—is in the service of some sort of project of justification, in Elizabeth's case the justification of a literary life at this time, in this form of life.

My attempt in the following is more in the way of suggesting the plausibility of such suggestions by attending to a particular work and making use of it to illustrate the themes just introduced.

Backshadows

On October 18, 1902, there appeared, in the Berlin newspaper *Der Tag*, a small piece called simply "A Letter," "Ein Brief." It appeared to be a letter written on August 22, 1603, by a certain twenty-six-year-old Lord Chandos to the famous philosopher and scientist Francis Bacon. In it, Chandos, who apparently had had great early success as a poet ("pastorals," he says), tried to explain to Bacon why a certain spiritual paralysis (a *geistige Starrnis*; many have called it a "crisis of language") had prevented him, and would forever prevent him, from writing anything more. The "letter" was actually written by the twenty-eight-year-old Austrian poet and writer Hugo von Hofmannsthal, who had himself experienced great early success. (His work first became known to the leaders of Viennese literary society when he was seventeen.) The letter, now widely known as "the Chandos letter," is regarded as one of the most influential and telling documents of literary modernism. In other words, it is taken as having general significance, as bearing on the form of modernist art and the unique demands on understanding that it makes. (We should note the date of the fictional letter itself, 1603. It was an epochal, momentous time, not only of Bacon, but of Caravaggio, Shakespeare, Cervantes, just after the time of the great Montaigne, just before the revolutionary Descartes, a quintessentially modern moment. Hofmannsthal seems to be suggesting that even in such a heyday, a coming crisis was already emerging.)

J. M. Coetzee's collection of eight Elizabeth Costello "lessons" concludes with two elements.[2] It is inevitable that these passages will then backshadow what we have just read. Since they do not seem proper *parts* of the book, they can easily be taken as, in some sense or other, *about* the book as a whole. One is a quotation from the Chandos letter itself, a famous passage in which Chandos tries to explain the debilitating, paralyzing experiences that convinced him that "everything means something." The other is a "Postscript," a four-page letter that is the last passage we read in Coetzee's book. The letter, also addressed to Francis Bacon, is purportedly from Lady Chandos, written twenty days after her husband, Lord Phillip Chandos, wrote that letter to Bacon. In it, she does not doubt the genuineness of her husband's crisis, either as a psychological problem or as ontological insight, but she pleads with Bacon to help her convince her husband that we are not ready yet to bear the burden of such insight. For her, the crisis seems to involve these elements: First, it has become impossible for her husband to "enter," as she puts it, the dryads and sirens he sees in mythological paintings, and she cannot serve as such, Second, her words, all words, always mean something other than what is intended. ("Always it is not what I say but something else.") And, especially, third, the experience of the interpenetrating unity of all things, her "rapture," is existentially unbearable: "But how I ask you can I live with rats and dogs and beetles crawling through me day and night, drowning and gasping, scratching at me, tugging me, urging me and urging me deeper and deeper into revelation—how?" (E, 229).

We are not, she says, the giants or angels who can someday, perhaps, bear such a burden, but mere fleas. She concludes with what are the last lines of *Elizabeth Costello*: "Drowning, we write out of our separate fates. Save us." (That both letters are addressed to a founder of modern European scientific rationalism—that is, to a man very unlikely to be in any position to respond

2. Page references in the text are to Coetzee 2003 (E).

to such a plea—is an irony worthy of a large separate discussion. As is the fact that one letter is from a man, another from a woman.)

Now we have been listening to the distinctive voice of Elizabeth Costello for the whole of the book, so the first question is obvious. Why end this collection not with her voice, but with the equally fictional voices of Lord and Lady Chandos, from four hundred years ago, and with this sort of reference to a literary text over one hundred years old? Trying to answer this question will lead us eventually to the topic announced in my title.

I would suggest that while this sort of quotational ending is somewhat perplexing, it is not entirely so, or at least it is not unfamiliar. This inhabitation by Coetzee of another author's characters not only is familiar from his other works (as with Defoe or Dostoevsky) but reminds us that Elizabeth Costello's most important work, *The House on Eccles Street*, involves her entry into the fictional world of James Joyce and her inhabitation of one of his characters, Molly Bloom. And this itself of course already represents Joyce's invocation of the Homeric world, the *Odyssey* in particular, and *his* inhabitation, in the setting of modern Dublin, of those characters. Moreover, given that the most discussed lesson, "The Lives of Animals," raises the philosophical question of inhabiting, imaginatively entering, and thereby understanding, both other human and nonhuman animals, the theme has a resonance greater than literary. (In the lesson "Realism," Elizabeth's son insists that his mother "has also been a dog. She can think her way into other people, into other existences" (E, 22). And Chandos compares himself to Crassus, devastated by the death of his pet eel, a figure who, Chandos knows, looks ridiculous, but who inspires in Chandos "a kind of feverish thinking, but thinking in a medium more direct, fluid, and passionate than words" (E, 127). That feverish, nondiscursive "thinking" again brings us close to our theme and is reflected in all these inhabitings, Coetzee's, Elizabeth's, Joyce's, and Chandos's.)

So my strategy in this brief presentation is simple: section 3 presents what in the two Chandos letters brings Elizabeth Costello, what she does and says, to mind and section 4 leads from this presentation to an initial understanding of the "fictional" treatment of philosophical argument, or at least the ethical and aesthetic arguments that make up the core of each of the "lessons."

"Why Can't You?"

To begin to understand this instance of such literary inhabitation, we need to remember the basic elements of the Chandos letter, noting as we go where aspects call Costello to mind. The following associations, echoes, resonances, all suggest that the book itself, and the writer Elizabeth Costello, still must write in the shadow of a crisis, one that threatens to make the writing of poetry and fiction pointless, or at least in need of some sort of distinctive justification.

The letter has a simple narrative structure in three parts.[3] Chandos describes first the period of his confident literary production and success. He was able to write pastorals, histories, and complex Latin prose, and he was filled with confidence about an underlying spiritual unity in all things, a unity of mental and physical, courtly and bestial, art and barbarism, solitude and society. His most vivid portrayal of the unity of sensibilities he experienced in that time is that he felt no difference between drinking "warm foaming milk" freshly drawn by a farmer and "drinking in sweet and frothy spiritual nourishment from an old book" (E, 120). He was also able, he says, to "enter" the personae of ancient mythologies, inhabiting Narcissus, Proteus, Perseus, and Actaeon, speaking and writing from within their personae.

Just this much already calls Elizabeth Costello to mind, from the lesson "Eros." She is, and apparently always was, suspicious of this way of talking about literary inspiration. She asks, "Inwardness. Can we be one with a god profoundly enough to get a sense of a god's being?" This is a question, she says, "that went out of fashion during her lifetime (she remembers it happening, remembers her surprise), just as it came into fashion just before her lifetime commenced" (E, 122). It may be out of fashion but the image still has work to do. In the lesson "Realism," when John is asked if he is a writer, he responds in an "Elizabethan" way: "You mean am I touched by a god?" She also has her doubts about Hölderlin's view of the world: that the world was inhabited by gods once, but that we have arrived too late and the gods have fled. (The past availability and the current unavailability of the gods is also Chandos's lament.) She doubts there was ever a time when we could have understood the gods like this, and she does not think that the gods can "afford" to depart. How bored they would be without us, creatures who can die.

Second there is his present spiritual paralysis and his inability to write, described as a feeling of *Kleinmut*, timidity or faintheartedness, and *Kraftlosigkeit*, powerlessness. There is no single trauma or occasioning event for any of this. What had always seemed possible and good suddenly came to seem futile and pompous, arrogant. Suddenly, he simply saw everything differently. He describes himself as suffering like Tantalus,[4] convinced that there

3. For a discussion (to which I am much indebted) of the structure of the letter and the significance of that structure, see Wellbery 2006, 196–230.

4. See Wellbery 2006, 191, for more on the Tantalus image and the connection it suggests with Schopenhauer.

is a reality to be grasped, but one that always seems to withdraw and vanish as he approaches it with any sort of language or thought. Words now seem like empty abstractions, everything that had some discursive unity seems to fall into pieces and then into further pieces. In the two best-known images from this account he says, "The abstract words which the tongue must enlist as a matter of course in order to make a judgment disintegrated in my mouth like moldy mushrooms [*modrige Pilze*]," and "I felt like someone locked in a garden full of eyeless statuary, and I rushed to get out again" (E, 121).

There is no such intense existential crisis suffered by Elizabeth Costello, but at the end of "At the Gate," when she is contemplating the "special fidelities" of a writer, she has a "vision" of the other side of the gate, the place denied her. It is of an old dog, lying before an infinite desert of sand and stone, and she thinks, "It is her first vision in a long while, and she does not trust it, does not trust in particular the anagram GOD-DOG. Too literary, she thinks again. A curse on literature" (E, 224–25). Both Chandos's and Elizabeth's fidelities to literature or even to a literary life, we can say, are in very different ways being tested, under examination, and they must respond with some sort of justification. To anticipate our topic, not a justification in the way of argument or evidence but, let us say, a kind of "Lutheran" sense, a way in which a life, in this case a literary life, can be justified. (That way has as little to do with arguments as any potential response to great suffering first requires an argument justifying the response.) And it is one that neither Chandos nor Elizabeth can give, at least not in any form that their "judges," the scientist Bacon and the literal-minded tribunal that Elizabeth faces, would recognize.

There is, in the third part of the Chandos letter, his occasional experiences of what he calls "good instants," *gute Augenblicke*. These rather strongly reflect Nietzsche's notion of the Dionysian in art, and they anticipate some of Heidegger's reflections of the 1930s about the disclosive powers of art, especially their ontologically disclosive properties. (All of which is one way of thinking about literary knowledge.) These experiences fill him with a sense of unity and meaningfulness, even as they cut him off from others and also produce a lassitude and apathy that, he knows, are destroying him. What crushes him with frustration is that these experiences cannot be created, intentionally sought by an artwork, brought to mind when one will, and, especially frustrating, cannot be at all communicated. Any object, even a remembered object, can produce one of those "good instants," all of which sound like the ideal sought in much modern aesthetics, the fusion of subject and object in an impersonal or transpersonal subjectivity, a transcendence of normal time into a kind of eternal *nunc stans*, and the revelation of a kind of truth about all of being that cannot be embodied in any such art. (That appears to be what differentiates them from the earlier experiences of unity and fusion just described, but this distinction still remains an open question in the letter.)[5] So he says about these good instants: "These mute and sometimes inanimate beings rise up before me with such a plenitude. Such a presence of love that my joyful eye finds nothing dead anywhere. Everything seems to mean something, everything that exists, everything that I can remember, everything in the most muddled of my thoughts. . . . Or as if we could enter into a new, momentous relationship with all of existence if we began to think with our hearts" (E, 125). Here again we hear Elizabeth, who in "The Lives of Animals" is asked from the floor for what she takes to be "principles" and says only: "Open your heart and listen to what your heart says" (E, 82). And in "At the Gate," she tells her judges, her inquisitors, that "beliefs are not the only ethical supports we have. We can rely on our hearts as well" (E, 203). (We should note for future reference that the panel responds to this with the same kind of self-satisfied rationalist debater's points that her son's wife, Norma, does in "The Lives of Animals." We get a bit closer to our theme.)

But the deepest connections between Elizabeth and Chandos arise when we consider two passages. One is quoted from Hofmannsthal's letter by Coetzee, the author of *Elizabeth Costello* the book, and it is on the facing page opposite the invented letter from Lady Chandos. It is the passage where Chandos says, describing one of these "good instants": "At such moments, even a negligible creature, a dog, a rat, a beetle, a stunted apple tree, a cart track winding over a hill, a mossy stone, counts for more than a night of bliss with the most beautiful, most devoted mistress. These dumb and in some cases inanimate creatures press toward me with such fullness, such presence of love, that there is nothing in range of my rapturous eye that does not have life. It is as if everything, everything that exists, everything I can recall, everything my confused thinking touches on, means something" (E, 226). Having read the lesson that precedes this quotation, we think immediately, first, of Elizabeth's initial statement of belief, a bit ironic, as if ironicizing the passage from Milosz that she quotes, or inhabits (she says that she is "the secretary to the infinite"; John once refers to her as "mouthpiece for the divine" [E, 31]), and especially of her second justification, her story of the buried frogs of the Dulgannon River of her youth. This is her final statement of belief, her final

5. For more on these characteristics of the "good instants" and their bearing on aesthetics, see again Wellbery 2006. Wellbery suggests that the difference between the earlier and later Chandos involves the difference between overpowering the world aesthetically and the passivity and neutral subjectivity of the "good instants," the fact that the poetic, impersonal "I" suffers these moments rather than masters them (210).

justification in literary form, that she believes in these frogs: "The vivifying flood, the chorus of joyous belling, followed by the subsiding of the waters, and the retreat to the grave, then drought seemingly without end, then fresh rains, and the resurrection of the dead—it is a story I present transparently, without disguise" (E, 217).

The tribunal, again rather like an unimaginative PhD examining committee in philosophy, say they take her to mean that she affirms "the spirit of life," that she "believed in life." She cannot explain to them how "vapid" this is, how she believes in those frogs, not such platitudes, even though she cannot yet explain herself. There is something about these frogs, she says, that "obscurely engages her, something about their mud tombs, and the fingers of their hands, fingers that end in little balls, soft, wet, mucous" (E, 219).

But we remember Elizabeth's frogs even more when we read perhaps the most famous account of one of these "good instants." This one concerns rats in Chandos's milk cellar, for whom he had set out fresh poison:

> It was all there. The cool and musty cellar air, full of the sharp sweetish smell of the poison, and the shrilling of the death cries echoing against mildewed walls. Those convulsed clumps of powerlessness, those desperations colliding with one another in confusion. The frantic search for ways out. The cold glares of fury when two meet at a blocked crevice. . . . A mother was there, whose dying young thrashed about her. But she was not looking at those in their death agonies, or at the unyielding stone walls, but off into space, or through space into the infinite, and gnashing her teeth as she looked. If there was a slave standing near Niobe in helpless fright as she turned to stone, he must have gone through what I went through when the soul of this beast I saw within me bared its teeth to its dreadful fate. (E, 123–24)

This horrific passage, clearly as much a description of the unadorned post-Baconian human world coming into view as of Chandos's experience, stands in some contrast with the one cited on the facing page to Lady Chandos's letter, the one that spoke of the presence of love, the unity of life, and the meaninglessness of everything, and it resonates more with Lady Chandos's horror at "rats and dogs and beetles" coursing through her. But it is an appropriate counter and echo because there is of course no life without suffering and death. To be attuned at such a prediscursive level to such an unsayable meaningfulness of being, of life, must also involve the "beast" in Chandos as well as "the presence of love." (To quote Elizabeth, "For that, finally, is all it means to be alive: to be able to die" [E, 211].)

Lord Chandos is in despair because he must simply suffer these episodes, can make nothing out of them, and cannot communicate them in any form, cannot make art out of them. Something has changed in what could be a fit subject for art. And they also cut him off from loved ones and his fellow man in general. "I live a life of scarcely credible emptiness," he says, and he finds it hard to hide "from my wife how hard my heart has become and from the people working for me how bored I am by the affairs of the estate" (E, 125). It is somewhat paradoxical why all of this, this subject-object unity in life (that is, the closing of this alienating gap), the meaningfulness of everything, and the presence of love should have left his heart "hard" rather than open, but the solitude it creates for him, the fact that it cannot be shared with anyone, cannot be made art, seems one likely reason. All he can share with Lady Chandos is this solitude and its causes. This is what she calls his "contagion," expressed not in words but "flaming swords" penetrating and deadening her soul. (Of course, there is irony here too. That the words can be made swords means that the Chandos state of things has been made art.)

And this all certainly brings to mind something similar in the last episode of "The Lives of Animals," a heartbreaking moment of intimacy with Elizabeth's son, John. Like Chandos, Elizabeth asks herself and him how it is possible that she, virtually alone in the world, sees in so many "normal" human beings "crimes of stupefying proportions." "I must be mad," she worries, yet "every day I see the evidence. The very people I suspect produce the evidence, exhibit it, offer it to me. Corpses. Fragments of corpses that they have bought for money." "Everyone comes to terms with it," she asks herself, "why can't you? Why can't you?" To which her son, trying to comfort her, can only say, "There, there. It will soon be over." He probably means the visit, but it certainly must also mean her life, the only true escape for her and for Chandos; to say the least, not much consolation.

The Crisis

This all raises far more than can be dealt with in the next few pages. Let us at least start with the obvious. The reason that the Chandos letter is so well known is that the crisis Chandos describes is hardly a merely personal, psychological crisis. It is expressive of the sense of crisis in the arts since, roughly, the mid-nineteenth century, more generally known as modernism. That is, it is not merely *Chandos's* language that has grown stale, that in the most important instances badly misses its target; not merely *his* everyday world that has grown intolerably boring, without meaning; not merely *his* view of art that now seems impossible. It is typical of a general modernist sensibility in which the value and the very possibility of art can no longer be taken for granted. And if we think of such an aesthetic category as expressive of not merely the mere exhaustion of a classical or romantic style (styles simply become mannered), but a deeper question tied to an emerging, world-historically distinctive form of life, then the questions being raised about what form of art is appropriate to such an age (or *whether* a form of art could be appropriate to such an age—Hegel's question, Nietzsche's question, Heidegger's question, and as we shall see in a moment, Kafka's question) are inseparable from questions about just what such a form of life is or demands from us if we are to answer them. It also thereby raises the question of whether there is anything distinctive that such a form of life—a highly commercialized, consumerist, bureaucratically and in that sense rationally organized, technology-dependent form of life, the one that produces Elizabeth's massive "factories of death"—demands of us ethically, what demands it might place "on our hearts." The two questions are inseparable, and they are both Elizabeth's questions throughout *Elizabeth Costello*.

As noted earlier, the citation of the Chandos letter itself, and the letter from Lady Chandos (which makes clear that their crisis is such as not only to make art impossible but to make their lives impossible, as well as helping to historicize the Chandos moment), alert us to the fact that the book itself, and Elizabeth's discourse within the book, are written under the shadow of this crisis, Chandos's crisis, Hofmannsthal's crisis, a philosophical crisis. We also see this simply by the fact that the book begins and ends with meditations on Kafka, who would not be very well understood if we did not take him to be addressing these questions, and this not "philosophically" in the traditional sense, but by virtue simply of the unusual form of his works, a form demanded now. We begin in the lesson "Realism," with Red Peter and "Report to an Academy," and we end with a reference, so direct that Elizabeth mentions it herself a few times and finds it amusing, to the story or fable "Before the Law" that the priest tells K. in the "In the Cathedral" section of *The Trial*. ("A Hunger Artist" is also mentioned in the last lesson.) At the very least, the references to Kafka evoke a distinctive aesthetic form required by the world of K.

But it is all much more direct at the beginning of the book and in Elizabeth's prize lecture. One could say that the first lesson instructs us on how to read a book that is unsure that it can even begin. For it opens with two paragraphs ("modernist" paragraphs, we can easily if not very informatively say) about the beginning, rather than *with* the beginning of the stories about Elizabeth Costello. It opens with "There is first of all the problem of the opening, namely, how to get us from where we are which is, as yet, nowhere, to the far bank" (E, 1). We need some sort of bridge from the extrafictional world to the fictional, or, we can say, from life to literature, or from Coetzee to Elizabeth.

We need to know what there is in this form of life that would require, suggest, even demand literature, fiction, and if so how to satisfy this demand. We are told to simply assume that such a bridge has been built. Perhaps this assumption suggests that we cannot be *told* how this bridge is built, what it involves, even though that does not mean such a bridge is impossible.

It is not unusual, of course, for the "gentle reader" to be addressed directly in modern fiction, but this level of reflection and this formal problematizing of the beginning suggest a new problem and an unsettling uncertainty. I should also note that several times in this lesson the drama about Elizabeth is interrupted again as we are told that things that happened have been skipped, that they are not part of the text we are reading but part of the "performance," and, once, that something was skipped that is (should have been?) part of the text we are reading and is not a skip in the "performance."[6] This is especially important because the lessons are performances by Elizabeth, which might be connected to her unusual claim that, in fact, she has no beliefs, at least none in a form her judges would realize, and the problem of the artist as mere performer haunts her. But we have to press on toward our theme.

And this all becomes more problematic in Elizabeth's prize lecture on realism, comments that we have to keep in mind as we read what she says later about literature and ethical truth, and of course as we try to understand the book, or the point of presenting her saying it. When she is talking about all the interpretations possible of *Report to an Academy*, she remarks on a time when language functioned like a "word-mirror": "But all that is ended. The word-mirror is broken, irreparably, it seems. . . . The words on the page will no longer stand up and be counted, each proclaiming, 'I mean what I mean!' . . . There used to be a time, we believe, when we could say who we were. Now we are just performers speaking our parts. The bottom has dropped out. We could think of this as a tragic turn of events were it not that it is hard to have respect for whatever was the bottom that dropped out—it looks to us like an

6. One of the many possible ways to understand this distinction: we can understand Elizabeth (ultimately) as pointing out that a great limitation of most philosophical accounts is a lack of appreciation for the enormous difficulty of simply describing what someone is doing in some complicated, morally relevant context: what the relevant act description is, how much it must include to be even roughly adequate. See Murdoch 1956, 32–58. What we are helped by with literary thinking is not then the "story" about the characters, the "performance," but the "text," the way what happens is described by the novelist. This cannot be but a recommendation in itself for how to think about the issue. It is in this sense that moral thinking must always involve, at its best, aesthetic talent. See chapter 7 in Pippin 2000, 171–80. See also Coetzee's (1992a, 99) appeal to the distinction elsewhere, as, for example, between the story of Alonso Quijano and the book (or text) that Cervantes wrote about him.

illusion now" (E, 19). (The fictional Lady Chandos recounts the same experience: "words give way like rotting boards" [E, 228].)

If this is so then Elizabeth faces Lord Chandos's problem. If we can't make any determinate, sharable sense out of, say, *Report to an Academy*, why write literature at all? What is it for? Dramatically and psychologically, this question plays out silently, without ever being addressed as such, in John's relation to his mother, his memories of being shut out of her morning writing life, whining and humming and singing with his sister outside her closed door, memories of Elizabeth screaming at them that they were ruining her life, destroying her. So, here again, the question of justification: is Elizabeth's life, what she sacrificed in her life in order to write, justified, a question always raised together with questions like: what makes any kind of life—a carnivorous life, for example—justified or not? And others. What justifies writing about horrific evil, showing it to us? But what justifies writing at all if subjects like Paul West's (in the part of the book called "The Problem of Evil"),[7] which make up so much of the twentieth century, are in some way unwritable, unfit for art?

None of these questions are raised abstractly. They have whatever meaning and force that they do in a way that is inseparable from what they mean to the characters in a context, and this must entail something about the appropriate way to address such questions of justification. Our sense is that this existential link is not an additional dimension of meaning but the primary one. We wonder at times if Elizabeth's intense passion about the suffering of animals is connected to her guilt about the suffering she was willing to inflict on her children (an unconscious guilt; there is never a hint of anything apologetic about this from Elizabeth). We sense that her own worries about what is an appropriate public role for a writer are not separable from her three-day youthful affair with Emmanuel Egudu. Her defense of the humanities in Africa is not separable from her complex, tense relation with her sister. Her concern with the depiction of evil is not separable from her own experience of sexual predation.[8]

7. West had written in grotesque detail about the torture of the would-be assassins of Hitler, "leaving nothing out." (E, 158).

8. It would take a separate and lengthy discussion to explore the limitations, possible self-deceit, self-righteousness, self-satisfaction, and so forth of Elizabeth Costello the character. I am concerned here with the book *Elizabeth Costello* and its bearing on philosophy. For example, Elizabeth tells the tribunal in "At the Gate" that she does not believe in beliefs, is not allowed to have them as a novelist. What could be farther from the truth? She has plenty of beliefs and she believes in them (whatever that means) ferociously.

And none of this is reductionist or relativist. The questions are not merely each person's concerns, and that brings us the closest yet to our theme. Any such justification is not just to oneself but to others, especially to others who now cannot do what they would otherwise have been able to do (Elizabeth's children, for example). The "locatedness" of these questions is given expression at one point in the first lesson. "Realism," we are told (apparently by the narrator, not by John or Elizabeth), or the kind of realism that clearly survives Chandos's "mirror" doubts, quoted (she still continues to write after all), "has never been comfortable with ideas." For realism, "ideas have no autonomous existence, can exist only in things" (E, 9).

And, "The notion of embodying turns out to be pivotal. In such debates, ideas do not and indeed cannot float free; they are tied to the speakers by whom they are announced" (E, 9). This suggests understanding ideas in a way akin to what we mean when we refer to genuinely understanding a person, and, as noted previously, it brings to mind Nietzsche on all philosophy as the confession of its author. So we are now at the heart of the matter. Is there a kind of thinking relevant to the inescapable question of justification, that is, a thinking with one's heart, "in a medium more direct, fluid, and passionate than words," as Chandos says, an always embodied thinking, one that can inhabit not just the minds of other beings, but their bodies and finally one that accepts Chandos's crisis as genuine, but that can somehow transcend his despair, can bear the burden Lady Chandos has found unbearable?

It might be, let us say, "literary thinking," and this in a way essential to that "Lutheran" sense of justification that I mentioned before, here not meant religiously (e.g., "does one's justification or salvation depend on good works, or faith alone?"), but that still amounts to a kind of answerability to oneself and to others for what one has done, and that depends on the right understanding of what one, or others, actually have done.[9] I mentioned before that while, for "realism," any such thinking and answering cannot "float free," have the purely universal form demanded by traditional philosophy, neither is it the mere expression of unshareable, personal preferences.[10] There is no chance of appreciating the value of such thinking as philosophy, if we think that the task of moral philosophy is, exclusively, to articulate and defend uni-

9. If we imagine again the Lutheran sense of justification, one prominent form of it concludes with "Here I stand, I can do no other." If we ask: what would we have to understand to understand that this was a justification, it would have to be something like "Understanding Luther himself," something that would require the "inhabitation" we have been discussing. For an illuminating discussion of the modality involved, see Gaita 2004, 108–11.

10. See the discussion by Cora Diamond 1995, 179–204.

versal principles that can be applied to direct our action. Put very simply, if we are interested in whether we should eat animals, we have to first understand something, not only the implications of the fact that we now kill them on the model of massive industrial manufacturing, but what it means that we do so, what it means to organize the death of sentient beings in such a way, a question inseparable from: in what sort of a form of life would such a system so easily and, especially, so *invisibly* fit in? Given that it does, what are the implications for other dimensions of such a form of life? For many, this sort of question will not sound philosophical but sociological or social-psychological, and will be available as a question only about individual mindedness, what it means to someone or to some group or class. It will be more recognizably philosophical if the question asked is about the very possibility of such a meaning, but this is also a question that cannot "float free" of the historically embodied dimensions of such a practice and the values that animate it, often in complex, collectively self-deceived ways. Otherwise, we will have no chance of understanding what is involved in even referring to "such a practice." Only a way of thinking animated at the same time by attentiveness to a question like "what values are expressed by the organization of such a practice," *and* "how might it be possible to raise and address such a question," *and* "just what *is* the practice, both as it is explicitly understood and as it actually is carried out" can approach such an issue. My suggestion is that this is happening in *Elizabeth Costello*, the book.

There is an image for this sort of possibility in the lessons, especially in "Eros," but it is mentioned several other places too. The notion of transcendence, attaining a philosophical register of some generality, while remaining embodied, fits the image: it is the image of a human coupling or merging with or inhabiting a god or goddess, the union of human and divine. (John calls it "the mystery of the divine in the human" [E, 28].) And what that is is the bearing of literature on life, that is, the possibility that there can be something of general significance, even universality, yet expressed in all its living, contingent, concrete, and even invented particularity.

I raise the issue of the gods this way because it is of such importance to Elizabeth in "Eros" (not to mention her self-description as "secretary of the infinite," or John's of her as "mouthpiece of the divine"), because the issue of inhabiting gods is of such importance to Chandos and Lady Chandos, as if that is the paradigmatic image for what Elizabeth is struggling with throughout, and because it is an old topic and one that tradition might help us with. That old question is whether the gods philosophize. According to Diotima in Plato's *Symposium*, they do not (203e–204a). They are self-sufficient and immortal, so the most important philosophical question—what is the best life?—does not arise for them. For a god, it is question that answers itself: their life is the best. (There are passages in the *Theaetetus*, 151d1–2, and the *Sophist*, 216b5–6, where Plato suggests that there are at least some gods who do philosophize, so we may be hearing only one side of the issue from Diotima.) At any rate, what interests Elizabeth is the gods' obvious *lack* of self-sufficiency. Why else would they so often want to couple with human beings? Why are they so fascinated by them?

She has her answers, expressed and then qualified with some uncertainty: "Love and death. The gods, the immortals were the inventors of death and corruption, yet with one or two notable exceptions they have lacked the courage to try their invention out on themselves. That is why they are so curious about us, so endlessly inquisitive. In marking us down for death, the gods gave us an edge over them. Of the two, gods and mortals, it is we who live the more urgently, feel the more intensely" (E, 189). And later, "We think of them as omniscient, these gods, but the truth is, they know very little, and what they know they know only in the most general of ways. No body of learning they can call their own, no philosophy, properly speaking. . . . They specialize in humankind because of what we have and they lack: they study us because they are envious" (E, 189). This, by the way, is so reminiscent of the penultimate paragraph of Nietzsche's *Beyond Good and Evil* (§295) that it seems to me another literary "echo," or another inhabitation. In that paragraph, Nietzsche insists that there *is* a god who philosophizes, Dionysus, that what philosophy amounts to is an attempt to understand human beings, and he concludes with "but you can also see that there are good reasons for supposing that the gods could learn a thing or two from us humans. We humans are more human" (Nietzsche 2002, 176).

But we do not understand ourselves either, and so we remain "endlessly inquisitive" as well. When a line (or her memory of a version of the line) from Keats's late poem "To Autumn" ("*Keeping steady her laden head across a bank*") crosses Elizabeth's mind, it helps to remind her and us that we do not easily understand such things as what distinguishes a life in which knowledge of mortality plays the right or balanced or proper role from one where it does not. (Keats's poem is suffused with what such a proper sentiment might be, and so with images of the beauty of autumn, none of which allows discursive translation.)[11] One could put all this by saying we are our own "gods" to our

11. This is in effect to argue that there is an irreducibly sensible-affective modality of intelligibility available aesthetically ("thinking with our hearts," in Elizabeth's and Chandos's terms), and while it is not all we need to understand in order to understand ourselves, it is indispensable. This is a Hegelian idea. See Pippin 2014.

own humanity, endlessly fascinated by and inquisitive about ourselves as well as endlessly perplexed. We do not just inhabit our lives, do not just exist, but in Heidegger's phrase, our own being is always at issue for us, and this in a way that is at once irreducibly about my being, *Jemeinigkeit, and* about the meaning of being in general, *der Sinn des Seins*. It strains credulity, seems a cheap paradox, to say that what it is to be a human being is not to know what it is to be a human being,[12] but such a paradoxical formulation helps explain why Elizabeth reports, "strange how, as desire relaxes its grip on her body, she sees more clearly a universe ruled by desire" (E, 191). For that paradoxical formulation about human being just is the state of desire, the state of incompleteness, dissatisfaction. (There is, for example, no idea of the soul in the Platonic dialogues.)

Now if philosophy is composed exclusively of assertoric propositions and arguments in defense of them (about which Elizabeth asks, "What sort of philosophy is this? Throw it out, I say. What good do its piddling distinctions do?" [E, 111]), then such fictional inquisitiveness has nothing much to do with philosophy. But if it is true that we still do not, and never will, finally understand such things as what counts as betrayal, as loyalty, what makes for a good parent, what it means to live a free life, and so forth, then we will not gain any illumination from asserting definitions and searching for counterexamples. We need to see such concepts and norms alive, in times and places that can give us some concrete intimation of a possible unity among such diversity. There is no method or theory or rule to tell us when such expressions capture the divine in the human, strike us as recognizably general as well as particular, any more than there is a method or theory that can resolve the question of whether we are living well. Something of this enterprise, though—not avoiding such a task and not too narrowly restricting how we might answer it—is part of a possible "justification." It is certainly a major part of Elizabeth's. (It is also an answer of sorts to the Chandos couple; we have no choice but to bear what Lady Chandos cannot bear, and we must make do with whatever disclosive power art has, however inadequate.)

This is all not to assign to literature a nonaesthetic task. It is precisely by being literature that it fulfills such a philosophical task. Responding to her sister Blanche's withering attack on the humanities (only Hellenism, she claims, had a nonreligious vision of the good life, and Hellenism failed), Elizabeth says about secular literature simply, "For my own part, I would say that it is enough for books to teach us about ourselves." And summing up to Blanche,

12. The most thoughtful exploration of this claim and both its ontological and existential dimensions remains Martin Heidegger, *Sein und Zeit* (1927), see especially §62, 308ff.

"The humanities teach us humanity. After the centuries-long Christian night, the humanities give us back our beauty, our human beauty. That was what you forgot to say. That is what the Greeks teach us, Blanche, the right Greeks. Think about it" (E, 151).

The Greeks may have taught us that, and Elizabeth may have learned the lesson (the ceaseless resurrecting return of the frogs of the Dulgannon River is a response to her judges only in its simple beauty), but Elizabeth's reminder is not a resolution. It is rather inspired by, directed to, in Elizabeth's language, "tied" to, a form of thinking responsive to, the misanthrope, Blanche (whose very name tells us that everything for her is black or white, fallen or divine). We need to note that this is not where we end our journey with Elizabeth. We leave the book and her not with the Dulgannon frogs, but with the words of Lady Chandos, which have not been resolved: "Drowning, we write out of our separate fates. Save us" (E, 230).

Acknowledgments

I owe an immeasurable debt to David Wellbery and to Michael Fried for many conversations over the years about the issues discussed in this book. I am also very grateful to Karl Ameriks, who read the manuscript for Chicago with great care and who offered innumerable helpful comments and suggestions, and to an anonymous reader for the Press, clearly a literary critic, who raised a number of important questions. Josh Landy was an indispensable and generous interlocutor for chapters 10 and 11.

I am grateful to several presses and journals for allowing me to retain copyright to republish these essays in my own collection, and in a few cases for generously permitting me to publish the essays here first. Chapter 2 will appear in a Cambridge University Press collection, *Kant and Literary Studies*, edited by Claudia Brodsky. Chapter 3 first appeared in *Inventions of the Imagination: Interdisciplinary Perspectives on the Imaginary since Romanticism*, ed. Richard T. Gray, Nicholas Halmi, Gary Handwerk, Michael A. Rosenthal, and Klaus Vieweg (Seattle: University of Washington Press, 2011). Chapter 4 first appeared in *The Cambridge Companion to Hegel and Nineteenth-Century Philosophy*, ed. Frederick Beiser (Cambridge: Cambridge University Press, 2008). Chapter 5 first appeared in *The Art of Hegel's Aesthetics*, ed. Paul Kottman and Michael J. Squire (Stuttgart: Fink, 2018). Chapter 6 first appeared in *Critical Inquiry* 31, no. 3 (2005). Chapter 7 first appeared in *Michael Fried and Philosophy*, ed. Matthew Abbott (New York: Routledge, 2018). Chapter 8 first appeared in German in *Eros und Erkenntnis: 50 Jahre "Ästhetische Theorie,"* ed. Martin Endres, Axel Pichler, and Claus Zittel (Berlin: de Gruyter, 2019). Chapter 9 first appeared in the *Blackwell Companion to Henry James*, ed. Greg Zacharias (Oxford: Blackwell, 2008). Chapter 10 will appear in the Routledge *Philosophical Minds* series in *Proust*, edited by Tom Stern. Chapter 11 will appear in the Oxford *Philosophy and Literature* series in *Proust*, edited by Katherine Elkins. Chapter 12 first appeared in *J. M. Coetzee and Ethics*, ed. Anton Leist and Peter Singer (New York: Columbia University Press, 2010). Chapter 13 first appeared in *The Intellectual Landscape of J. M. Coetzee*, ed. Tim Mehigan and Christian Moser (Rochester, NY: Camden House, 2018).

I owe a special debt of gratitude to the John Simon Guggenheim Foundation for a fellowship that made possible the writing of chapters 1 and 10 and extensive final work on the manuscript throughout the 2019–20 academic year.

Works Cited

Adorno, Theodor W. 1951. *Minima Moralia. Reflexionen aus dem beschädigten Leben. Gesammelte Schriften*, vol. 5. Frankfurt: Suhrkamp.

———. 1981. *Negative Dialectics*. New York: Continuum.

———. 1997. *Aesthetic Theory*. Ed. and trans. R. Hullot-Kentor. Minneapolis: University of Minnesota Press.

Aeschylus. 2013. *The Oresteia*. Trans. David Grene et al. Chicago: University of Chicago Press.

Albaret, Céleste. 2003. *Monsieur Proust*. New York: NYRB Books.

Ameriks, Karl. 2012. *Kant's Elliptical Path*. Oxford: Clarendon Press.

Attridge, Derek. 2004. *J. M. Coetzee and the Ethics of Reading*. Chicago: University of Chicago Press.

Attwell, David. 1993. *J. M. Coetzee: South Africa and the Politics of Writing*. Berkeley: University of California Press.

Barthes, Roland. 1978. "The Death of the Author." In *Image-Music-Text*, trans. S. Heath, 142–48. New York: Palgrave Macmillan.

Beaumarchais, Pierre. 1949. *Théâtre complet, Lettres*. Ed. Maurice Allem. Paris: Bibliothèque de la Pléiade.

Benardete, Seth. 2000. "On Greek Tragedy." In *The Argument of the Action: Essays on Greek Poetry and Philosophy*. Chicago: University of Chicago Press.

Bersani, Leo. 2013. *Marcel Proust: The Fictions of Life and Art*. Oxford: Oxford University Press.

Bordwell, David. 1989. *Making Meaning: Inference and Rhetoric in the Interpretation of Cinema*. Cambridge: Harvard University Press.

Bradley, Andrew Cecil. 1962. "Hegel's Theory of Tragedy." In *Hegel on Tragedy*, ed. A. and H. Paolucci. New York: Harper.

Bubner, Rüdiger. 2003. "Is There a Hegelian Theory of Aesthetic Experience?" In *Innovations of Idealism*, trans. Nick Walker. Cambridge: Cambridge University Press.

Cantor, Paul. 1994. "Happy Days in the Veld: Beckett and Coetzee's *In the Heart of the Country*." In *The Writings of J. M. Coetzee*, ed. M. Valdez. Durham, NC: Duke University Press.

Cavell, Stanley. 1979. *The Claim of Reason: Wittgenstein, Skepticism, Morality, and Tragedy*. Oxford: Oxford University Press.

———. 2015. *Must We Mean What We Say?* 2nd ed. Cambridge, MA: Harvard University Press.

Clark, Timothy J. 1999. *The Painting of Modern Life: Paris in the Age of Manet and His Followers*. 2nd ed. Princeton: Princeton University Press.

Coetzee, John. M. 1974. *Dusklands*. New York: Penguin.

———. 1976. *In the Heart of the Country*. New York: Penguin.

———. 1980. *Waiting for the Barbarians*. New York: Penguin.

———. 1992a. *Doubling the Point*. Ed. Derek Attridge. Cambridge, MA: Harvard University Press.

———. 1992b. "Jerusalem Prize Acceptance Speech" (1987). In *Doubling the Point: Essays and Interviews*, ed. David Attwell, 96–99. Cambridge, MA: Harvard University Press.

———. 1997. "Farm Novel and *Plaasroman* in South Africa." In *White Writing: On the Culture of Letters in South Africa*. New Haven: Yale University Press.

———. 2003. *Elizabeth Costello*. London: Secker and Warburg.

Cronan, Todd. 2013. *Against Effective Formalism*. Minneapolis: University of Minnesota Press.

Cutrofello, Andrew. 2008. "Kant's Debate with Herder about the Philosophical Significance of Shakespeare." *Philosophy Compass* 3, no. 1: 66–81.

Danto, Arthur. 1977. *After the End of Art: Contemporary Art and the Pale of History*. Princeton: Princeton University Press.

———. 1981. *The Transfiguration of the Commonplace*. Cambridge, MA: Harvard University Press.

———. 1986. *The Philosophical Disenfranchisement of Art*. New York: Columbia University Press.

———. 2003. *The Abuse of Beauty: Aesthetics and the Concept of Art*. Chicago: Open Court.

Dawe, Roger D. 1982. Introduction. In *Sophocles, Oedipus Rex. Greek and Roman Classics*, ed. Dawe. Cambridge: Cambridge University Press.

de Man, Paul. 1981. "Sign and Symbol in Hegel's Aesthetics." *Critical Inquiry* 8: 761–75.

———. 1983. "Reply to Raymond Geuss." *Critical Inquiry* 10: 383–90.

Descartes, René. 1965. *The Discourse on Method*. In *The Philosophical Works of Descartes*, vol. 1, trans. E. S. Haldane and G. R. T. Ross. Cambridge: Cambridge University Press.

Descombes, Vincent. 1992. *Proust: Philosophy of the Novel*. Trans. C. C. Macksey. Stanford: Stanford University Press.

Diamond, Cora. 1995. "Having a Rough Story about What Moral Philosophy Is." In *The Realistic Spirit: Wittgenstein, Philosophy, and the Mind*, 179–204. Cambridge, MA: MIT Press.

Diderot, Denis. 1956. *Rameau's Nephew*. In *Rameau's Nephew and Other Works*, trans. Jacques Barzun. Indianapolis: Bobbs-Merrill.

———. 1995. "What Everyone Knows about Expression and Something Everyone Doesn't Know." In *Notes on Painting*. In *Diderot on Art*, vol. 1, trans. J. Goodman. New Haven: Yale University Press.

Dilthey, Wilhelm. 1990. *Die Jugendgeschichte Hegels*. In *Gesammelte Schriften*, vol. 4. Göttingen: Vandenhoeck & Ruprecht.

Dovey, Teresa. 1988. *The Novels of J. M. Coetzee: Lacanian Allegories*. Johannesburg: A. D. Denker.

Eliot, T. S. 1952. *The Waste Land*. In *The Complete Poems and Plays, 1909–1950*. New York: Houghton Mifflin Harcourt.

Elkins, James, ed. 2006. "Photographs and Fossils." In *Photography Theory*. New York: Routledge.

Evans, Gareth. 1982. *The Varieties of Reference*. Oxford: Oxford University Press.

Finkelstein, David. 2003. *Expression and the Inner*. Cambridge, MA: Harvard University Press.

Fried. Michael. 1980. *Absorption and Theatricality: Painting and Beholder in the Age of Diderot*. Chicago: University of Chicago Press.

———. 1982. "How Modernism Works: A Response to T. J. Clark." *Critical Inquiry* 9, no. 1: 217–34.

———. 1987. *Realism, Writing, Disfiguration: On Thomas Eakins and Stephen Crane*. Chicago: University of Chicago Press.

———. 1990. *Courbet's Realism*. Chicago: University of Chicago Press.

———. 1996. *Manet's Modernism*. Chicago: University of Chicago Press.

———. 1998a. "Art and Objecthood." In *Art and Objecthood: Essays and Reviews*. Chicago: University of Chicago Press.

———. 1998b. "An Introduction to My Art Criticism." In *Art and Objecthood: Essays and Reviews*. Chicago: University of Chicago Press.

———. 2002. *Menzel's Realism: Art and Embodiment in Nineteenth-Century Berlin*. New Haven: Yale University Press.

———. 2004. "Roger Fry's Formalism." In *The Tanner Lectures on Human Values*, vol. 24, ed. Grethe B. Peterson. Salt Lake City: University of Utah Press.

———. 2008. *Why Photography Matters as Art as Never Before*. New Haven: Yale University Press.

———. 2014. *Another Light: Jacques-Louis David to Thomas Demand*. New Haven: Yale University Press.

Frye, Northrop. 1957. *Anatomy of Criticism*. Princeton: Princeton University Press.

Gaita, Raimond. 2004. *Good and Evil: An Absolute Conception*. New York: Routledge.

Gardner, Sebastian. 2003. "Tragedy, Morality and Metaphysics." In *Art and Morality*, ed. J. Bermúdez and Sebastian Gardner, 218–59. New York: Routledge.

Gehlen, Arnold. 1960. *Zeitbilder: Zur Soziologie und Ästhetik der modernen Malerie*. Frankfurt am Main: Klostermann.

Gethmann-Siefert, Anne-Marie. 1983. "H. G. Hotho." *Hegel-Studien*, no. 22.

———. 1992a. "Ästhetik oder Philosophie der Kunst: Die Nachschriften und Zeugnisse zu Hegels Berliner Vorlesungen." *Hegel-Studien*, no. 26.

———. 1992b. "Das 'moderne' Gesamtkunstwerk: Die Oper." In *Phänomen vs. System: zum Verhältnis von philosophischer Systematik und Kunsturteil in Hegels Berliner Vorlesungen über Ästhetik oder Philosophie der Kunst*, ed. A. Gethmann-Siefert. Bonn: Bouvier.

———. 2005. *Einführung in Hegels Ästhetik*. Munich: Wilhelm Fink.

Geuss, Raymond. 1983. "A Response to Paul de Man." *Critical Inquiry* 10: 375–82.

Girard, René. 1965. *Deceit, Desire, and the Novel: Self and Other in Literary Structure*. Trans. Yvonne Freccero. Baltimore: Johns Hopkins University Press.

Goehr, Lydia. 2006. "The Ode to Joy: Music and Musicality in Tragic Culture." *International Yearbook of German Idealism* 4: 57–90.

Gombrich, Ernst. 1977. "Hegel und die Kunstgeschichte." *Neue Rundschau*, no. 88.

Graves, David. 1997. "The Institutional Theory of Art: A Survey." *Philosophia* 31.

Greenberg, Clement. 1940. "Towards a Newer Laocoon." *Partisan Review* 7: 296–310.

———. 1993. "Modernist Painting." In *The Collected Essays and Criticism*, ed. J. O'Brian, 4: 85–93. 4 vols. Chicago: University of Chicago Press.

Guyer, Paul. 2006. "Freedom of Imagination: From Beauty to Expression." *International Yearbook of German Idealism* 4: 311–34.

Harris, Henry. S. 1971. *Hegel's Development: Toward the Sunlight, 1770–1801*. Oxford: Oxford University Press.

Head, Dominic. 1997. *J. M. Coetzee*. Cambridge: Cambridge University Press.

Hegel, Georg Wilhelm Friedrich. Unpublished MS. In *Vorlesungen über die Philosophie der Kunst. Nachschriften*, ed. N. Hebing.

———. 1956. "Hamanns Schriften." In *Berliner Schriften*, ed. J. Hoffmeister. Berlin: Felix Meiner.

———. 1975. *Aesthetics. Lectures on Fine Art*. Trans. T. M. Knox. Oxford: Clarendon Press.

———. 1977. *Faith and Knowledge*. Trans. Walter Cerf and H. S. Harris. Albany: SUNY Press.

———. 1981. *The Berlin Phenomenology*. Trans. M. Petry. Dordrecht: Riedel.

———. 1991. *Elements of the Philosophy of Right*. Ed. Allen Wood. Trans. H. B. Nisbet. Cambridge: Cambridge University Press.

———. 1992. *Enzykopädie der philosophischen Wissenschaften*. Vol. 6 of *Hauptwerke in sechs Bänden*. Hamburg: Felix Meiner.

———. 1995. *Lectures on Natural Right and Political Science (1817–18)*. Trans. J. Stewart and P. Hodgson. Berkeley: University of California Press.

———. 2010. *The Science of Logic*. Trans. Giovanni Di Giovanni. Cambridge: Cambridge University Press.

———. 2015. *Vorlesungen über die Philosophie der Kunst. Nachschriften zu den Kollegien der Jahre 1820/21 und 1823*. Vol. 28.1 of *Gesammelte Werke*. Berlin: Felix Meiner.

———. 2018. *The Phenomenology of Spirit*. Trans. Terry Pinkard. Cambridge: Cambridge University Press.

Heidegger, Martin. 1927. *Sein und Zeit*. Tübingen: Max Niemeyer.

Henrich, Dieter. 1971. *Hegel im Kontext*. Frankfurt: Suhrkamp.

———. 2003. "Zerfall und Zukunft: Hegels Theoreme über das Ende der Kunst." In *Fixpunkte: Abhandlungen und Essays zur Theorie der Kunst*. Frankfurt: Suhrkamp.

Hofmannsthal, Hugo von. 1979. *Gesammelte Werke: Erzählungen, Erfundene Gespräche, und Briefe, Reisen*. Frankfurt am Main: Fischer.

———. 2005. *The Lord Chandos Letter and Other Writings*. Trans. Joel Rotenberg. New York: New York Review of Books Classics.

Houlgate, Stephen. 2000. "Hegel and the Art of Painting." In *Hegel and Aesthetics*, ed. W. Maker, 61–82. Albany: SUNY Press.

James, Henry 1998a. *A Small Boy and Others*. New York: Scribner's.

———. 1998b. *What Maisie Knew*. Ed. Adrian Poole. Oxford: Oxford University Press.

Johnson, L. A. 1974. "James's Mrs. Wix: The 'dim, crooked reflector.'" *Nineteenth Century Fiction* 29: 164–72.

Kant, Immanuel. 1979. "Concerning the Terroristic Way of Representing Human History." In *The Conflict of the Faculties*, trans. Mary Gregor. New York: Abaris Books.

———. 1989. "On the Common Saying: 'That May Be True in Theory but It Does Not Apply in Practice.'" In *Kant's Political Writings*, trans. H. S. Reiss. Cambridge: Cambridge University Press.

———. 1996. *The Metaphysics of Morals*. Trans. Mary Gregor. Cambridge: Cambridge University Press.

———. 1997. *Groundwork of the Metaphysics of Morals*. Ed. and trans. Mary Gregor. Cambridge: Cambridge University Press.

———. 1998. *Critique of Pure Reason*. Trans. Paul Guyer and Allen Wood. Cambridge: Cambridge University Press.

———. 2000. *Critique of the Power of Judgment*. Ed. and trans. Paul Guyer. Cambridge: Cambridge University Press.

———. 2015. *Critique of Practical Reason*. Ed. and trans. Mary Gregor. Cambridge: Cambridge University Press.

Knight, G. Wilson. 1989. *The Wheel of Fire: Interpretations of Shakespearean Tragedy*. Oxford: Oxford University Press.

Kojève, Alexandre. 1969. *Introduction to the Reading of Hegel*. Ed. Allan Bloom. Trans. J. H. Nichols Jr. New York: Basic Books.

Kottman, Paul A., and M. Squire, eds. 2018. *The Art of Hegel's Aesthetics: Hegelian Philosophy and the Perspectives of Art History*. Munich: Fink Verlag.

Ladenson, Elisabeth. 1999. *Proust's Lesbianism*. Ithaca: Cornell University Press.

Landy, Joshua. 2004. *Philosophy as Fiction. Self, Deception and Knowledge in Proust*. Oxford: Oxford University Press.

Lukács, Georg. 1974. "The Metaphysics of Tragedy." In *Soul and Form*, trans. A. Bostock. Cambridge, MA: MIT Press.

McDowell, John. 1994. *Mind and World*. Cambridge, MA: Harvard University Press.

Melville, Stephen. 1996a. "Compelling Acts, Haunting Convictions" (1991). In *Seams: Art as a Philosophical Context*, ed. J. Gilbert-Rolfe, 187–98. Amsterdam: G+B Arts.

———. 1996b. "Notes on the Reemergence of Allegory, the Forgetting of Modernism, the Necessity of Rhetoric, and the Conditions of Publicity in Art and Criticism." In *Seams: Art as a Philosophical Context*, ed. J. Gilbert-Rolfe. Amsterdam: G+B Arts.

Merleau-Ponty, Maurice. 1964. *L'oeil et l'esprit*. Paris: Gallimard.

Michaels, Walter Benn. 2006. "Photographs and Fossils." In *Photography Theory*, ed. James Elkins. New York: Routledge.

———. 2007. "The Death of a Beautiful Woman: Christopher Nolan's Idea of Form." In *Electronic Book Review*. http://electronicbookreview.com/thread/electropoetics/detective.

Mitchell, William. J. T. 1996. "What Do Pictures Really Want?" *October*, no. 77: 79–80.

Moran, Richard. 2001. *Authority and Estrangement: An Essay on Self-Knowledge*. Princeton: Princeton University Press.

———. 2003. "Responses to O'Brien and Shoemaker." *European Journal of Philosophy* 11: 402–19.

Morgan, Daniel. 2012. *Late Godard and the Possibilities of Cinema*. Berkeley: University of California Press.

Mulhall, Stephen. 2001. "Crimes and Deeds of Glory: Michael Fried's Modernism." *British Journal of Aesthetics* 41: 1–23.

Murdoch, Iris. 1956. "Vision and Choice in Morality." In *Proceedings of the Aristotelian Society* (Supplementary Volume) 30: 32–58.

Nehamas, Alexander. 2010. *Only a Promise of Happiness: The Place of Beauty in a World of Art*. Princeton: Princeton University Press.

Nietzsche, Friedrich. 2002. *Beyond Good and Evil*. Ed. R. P. Horstmann. Trans. J. Norman. Cambridge: Cambridge University Press.

———. 2007. *On the Genealogy of Morality*. Ed. K. Ansell-Pearson. Trans. C. Dieth. Cambridge: Cambridge University Press.

Nuzzo, Angelica. 2006. "Hegel's Aesthetics as a Theory of the Absolute Spirit." *International Yearbook of German Idealism* 4: 291–310.

Ortega y Gasset, José. 1927. "Le temps, la distance et la forme chez Marcel Proust." In *Hommage à Marcel Proust*. Paris: Gallimard.

Picherit, Hervé G. 2007. "The Impossibly Many Loves of Charles Swann: The Myth of Proustian Love and the Reader's 'Impression' in *Un amour de Swann*." *Poetics Today* 28, no. 4: 619–52.

Pinkard, Terry. 2007. "Symbolic, Classical, and Romantic Art." In *Hegel and the Arts*, ed. Stephen Houlgate, 3–28. Evanston, IL: Northwestern University Press.

———. 2012. *Hegel's Naturalism: Mind, Nature, and the Final Ends of Life*. Oxford: Oxford University Press.

———. 2015. "Tragedy with and without Religion: Hegelian Thoughts." In *Tragedy and the Idea of Modernity*, ed. Joshua Billings and Miriam Leonard, 137–58. Oxford: Oxford University Press.

———. 2017. *Does History Make Sense? Hegel on the Historical Shapes of Justice*. Cambridge: Cambridge University Press.

Pippin, Robert. 1989. *Hegel's Idealism: The Satisfactions of Self-Consciousness*. Cambridge: Cambridge University Press.

———. 1996. "Kant on the Significance of Taste." *Journal of the History of Philosophy* 34: 549–69.

———. 1999. *Modernism as a Philosophical Problem: On the Dissatisfactions of European High Culture*. 2nd ed. Oxford: Oxford University Press.

———. 2000. *Henry James and Modern Moral Life*. Cambridge: Cambridge University Press.

———. 2002. "What Was Abstract Art? (From the Point of View of Hegel)." *Critical Inquiry* 29, no. 1.

———. 2004. "Hegels praktischer Realismus: Vernünftiges Handeln als sittliches Leben." In *Hegels Erbe*, ed. B. C. Halbig, M. Quante, and L. Siep. Frankfurt am Main: Suhrkamp.

———. 2005a. "Concept and Intuition: On Distinguishability and Separability." *Hegel-Studien* 40: 25–39.

———. 2005b. "On Becoming Who One Is (and Failing): Proust's Problematic Selves." In *The Persistence of Subjectivity: On the Kantian Aftermath*, 307–38. Cambridge: Cambridge University Press.

———. 2008. *Hegel's Practical Philosophy: Rational Agency as Ethical Life*. Cambridge: Cambridge University Press.

———. 2010. *Hollywood Westerns and American Myth: The Importance of Howard Hawks and John Ford for Political Philosophy*. New Haven: Yale University Press.

———. 2012. *Fatalism in American Film Noir: Some Cinematic Philosophy*. Charlottesville: University of Virginia Press.

———. 2013. "What Is Conceptual Activity?" In *Mind, Reason, and Being-in-the-World: The McDowell-Dreyfus Debate*, ed. Joseph K. Schear, 91–109. New York: Routledge.

———. 2014. *After the Beautiful: Hegel and the Philosophy of Pictorial Modernism*. Chicago: University of Chicago Press.

———. 2017. *The Philosophical Hitchcock: Vertigo and the Anxieties of Unknowingness*. Chicago: University of Chicago Press.

———. 2019. *Hegel's Realm of Shadows: Logic as Metaphysics in "The Science of Logic."* Chicago. University of Chicago Press.

———. 2020. *Filmed Thought: Cinema as Reflective Form*. Chicago: University of Chicago Press.

Proust, Marcel. 1990. *À la recherche du temps perdu*. Paris: Gallimard.

———. 1992. *Selected Letters*, vol. 3: 1910–1917. Ed. P. Kolb. Trans. T. Kilmartin. New York: HarperCollins.

———. 2003. *In Search of Lost Time*. Trans. C. K. S. Moncrief and T. Kilmartin. Rev. D. J. Enright. 6 vols. New York: Random House.

Reinhardt, Karl. 1979. *Sophocles*. Trans. H. Harvey and D. Harvey. New York: Barnes and Noble.

Rousseau, Jean-Jacques. 1964. *Du contrat social*. In *Oeuvres complètes*, vol. 3. Paris: Gallimard.

———. 1997. *Discourse on the Origin and Foundations of Inequality among Men*. In *The "Discourses" and Other Early Political Writings*, ed. and trans. Victor Gourevitch. Cambridge: Cambridge University Press.

Royce, Josiah. 1919. *Lectures on Modern Idealism*. New Haven: Yale University Press.

Rutter, Benjamin. 2010. *Hegel on the Modern Arts*. Cambridge: Cambridge University Press.

Salkever, Stephen. 1986. "Tragedy and the Education of the *Demos*: Aristotle's Response to Plato." In *Greek Tragedy and Political Theory*, ed. P. Eubens. Berkeley: University of California Press.

Schelling, Friedrich. W. J. 1989. *The Philosophy of Art*. Ed. and trans. D. W. Stott. Minneapolis: University of Minneapolis Press.

Schiller, Friedrich. 1965. *Sämtliche Werke*. Ed. Gerhard Fricke and Herbert G. Göpfert. 5 vols. Munich: Hanser.

Shoemaker, Sidney. 2003. "Moran on Self-Knowledge." *European Journal of Philosophy* 11: 391–401.

Speight, Allen. 2001. *Hegel, Literature and the Problem of Agency*. Cambridge: Cambridge University Press.

Sontag, Susan. 2001. *Against Interpretation*. New York: Picador.

Szondi, Peter. 1961. *Versuch über das Tragische*. Frankfurt: Insel-Verlag.

Tanner, Tony. 1965. *The Reign of Wonder: Naivety and Realism in American Literature*. Cambridge: Cambridge University Press.

Trilling, Lionel. 1982. *Sincerity and Authenticity*. Cambridge, MA: Harvard University Press.

Velleman, David. 1989. *Practical Reflection*. Princeton: Princeton University Press.

Warda, Arthur. 1922. *Immanuel Kants Bücher*. Berlin: Martin Breslauer.

Wellbery, David. 2006. "Die Opfer-Vorstellung als Quelle der Faszination: Anmerkungen zum Chandos-Brief und zur frühen Poetik Hofmannsthals." In *Seiltänzer des Paradoxen: Aufsätze zur ästhetischen Wissenschaft*, 196–230. Munich: Carl Hanser.

Williams, Bernard. 1986. *Ethics and the Limits of Philosophy*. Cambridge, MA: Harvard University Press.

———. 1993. *Shame and Necessity*. Berkeley: University of California Press.

Wilson, George. 2008. "Interpretation." In *The Routledge Companion to Philosophy and Film*, ed. Paisley Livingston and Carl Plantiga, 162–72. New York: Routledge.

Wittgenstein, Ludwig. 1958. *Philosophical Investigations*. Trans. G. E. M. Anscombe. New York: Macmillan.

———. 2002. *Tractatus Logico-Philosophicus*. Trans. David F. Pears and Brian F. McGuiness. New York: Routledge.

Wollheim, Richard.1987. *Painting as an Art*. Princeton: Princeton University Press.

Wood, Allen. 1999. *Kant's Ethical Thought*. Cambridge: Cambridge University Press.

Wood, Michael. 2005. *Literature and the Taste of Knowledge*. Cambridge: Cambridge University Press.

Woolf, Virginia. 1992. *To the Lighthouse*. New York: Penguin.

Index